Reinventing the Middle School

Reinventing the Middle School

THOMAS S. DICKINSON, EDITOR

RoutledgeFalmer
New York   London

Published in 2001 by
RoutledgeFalmer
29 West 35th Street
New York, NY 10001

Published in Great Britain by
RoutledgeFalmer
11 New Fetter Lane
London EC4P 4EE

RoutledgeFalmer is an imprint of the Taylor & Francis Group.

Copyright © 2001 by RoutledgeFalmer

Printed in the United States of America on acid-free paper.

Design and typography: Scott McCarney/VisualBooks

A CIP catalogue record for this book is available at the Library of Congress.

10 9 8 7 6 5 4 3 2 1

ISBN 0-415-92592-4 (hb)

ISBN 0-415-92593-2 (pbk)

To Joan S. Lipsitz and April Tibbles
Two women who showed me how to reinvent myself
TSD

CONTENTS

ACKNOWLEDGMENTS

Any book is a product of multiple individuals. So it is with this work.

The chapter authors in this work are some of the finest middle school educators in the entire movement. Even more importantly, they are some of the finest individuals anywhere. Working with each of them has been a profound and humbling experience and I owe each one a heavy debt for their work here and also for their courage and continuing dedication to the cause of young adolescent education.

I also want to single out and thank three individuals for their thoughts, comments, and shared good humor throughout the development of this book—James A. Beane, Thomas O. Erb, and C. Kenneth McEwin.

I was fortunate to have not one but three editors helping me steer a clear path—Jim Fraser, editor of the *Transforming Teaching* series of which this work is part, and Heidi Freund and Karita Dos Santos, my editors at Routledge. I am most grateful to them for their faith and guidance.

Finally, to Deborah, thanks for the dialogue and discussion from day one, the collegial support and editing, the peanut butter crackers, and the toleration of my piles of stuff.

PREFACE

In middle school after middle school, a syndrome of "arrested development" has set in. Schedules have been changed, but they are not flexibly adapted to changing student or instructional needs. In many cases the master schedule has become an unresponsive master. Teams have been organized, but either teachers do not meet during their team planning time or when they do they fail to plan instruction, focusing instead on a recurrent litany of student failure and inattention. Teachers, many of whom come to the school without any formal training involving young adolescents or the role and function of the middle school, waste their time and energy in trying to change their students' behavior or implement a curricular or instructional program based on other students. The list goes on and on. What is ironic at this point in the evolution of middle schools as an educational entity is that we know what needs to be done and we have the research to support those directions. What remains, however, despite this emerging evidence of what should be done, is a large number of middle schools mired in practices and programs that serve no one.

This book attempts to break this log jam, not by suggesting small reforms or technical fixes, but by suggesting that schools stuck in a stage of arrested development can cure their ills only by reinventing themselves. The approach is not one of narrow technical solutions or discussions of how-to-do-it, but instead an examination of what Maxine Green called "doing philosophy." These "stuck" schools must implement the ideals, philosophy, and beliefs of the middle school concept, not merely its surface structure.

Reform and Reinvention

JAMES A. BEANE

National-Louis University

The emergence of the American junior high school around 1910 is a fairly complicated story, involving a convergence of a number of powerful forces and voices. It is a story that is not always known by people who now work within and advocate for the middle level of education. At the turn of the century, K–8 elementary schools in metropolitan areas were becoming overcrowded with the large influx of immigrant children. This overcrowding was compounded by increasing numbers of students, also mostly immigrants, who were held back for academic failure. Faced with the prospects of an unfriendly school environment and a disengaging educational program meant for younger children, it was hardly surprising that many of those young people left school to join parents and relatives as laborers in the factories of the industrial revolution. So large was the exodus, that of those young people who completed the sixth grade, roughly two-thirds dropped out before completing the eighth grade. Thus, as part of the struggle to enact child labor laws, welfare advocates developed a keen interest in ideas that might keep children in school and out of the factories. That idea also fit well with concerns of social efficiency advocates who were interested in providing immigrant children with a mix of vocational preparation and "Americanization" character education so that they might better "fit" into society.

Meanwhile, for almost two decades G. Stanley Hall and other educators had argued that early adolescents were neither children nor fully mature adolescents and, therefore, should be educated separately to accommodate their uniqueness as well as to prevent that age group from being negatively influenced by older adolescents, and, in turn, negatively influencing younger children. Meanwhile, Charles Eliot and the rest of the National Education Association's Committee of Ten, as well as the elementary-focused Committee of Fifteen, had already concluded in the early 1890s that the average age of students entering college (18) ought to be lower, and that one way of expediting that "need" was to introduce college preparatory courses earlier than high school (National Education Association 1893, 1895).

An obvious way of simultaneously satisfying these multiple interests presented itself: remove grades seven and eight from the elementary school, thus relieving overcrowding and opening the door for reconsidering the kind of education provided in those two grades, with an eye to keeping immigrant children in school and providing college preparatory courses for their privileged peers who were destined for college. In retrospect, it is clear that the arguments of professional educators were not alone sufficient to warrant institutional change (Kliebard 1986; Toepfer and Marani 1980). In combination with the interests of child welfare and social efficiency advocates, however, they were part of a mix that would prove strong enough to accomplish a rarity in American education—the creation of a new institution.

What is instructive about this brief historical sketch is that it allows us to understand the emergence of the American junior high school in two interconnected ways. One is as an *educational reform* carved out of the ideas of professional educators like G. Stanley Hall, Charles Eliot, and John Dewey. This is, of course, the way in which many current advocates for the middle level would prefer to have their origins. The other way, and the one which is more accurate, is to understand the junior high school as *a social invention* whose beginnings had a great deal to do with assuaging what were seen as serious problems concerning the lives of immigrant families, the education of their children, the seedy side of the industrial revolution, and the interest of the dominant culture in maintaining social hierarchy in the face of large-scale immigration. In short, the creation of junior high schools was more a solution to a set of social conditions than an educational reform.

Thus understood, the long and persistent history of the junior high school as a combination of college preparation and social efficiency is no mystery. It was meant to be that way. The desire for an institution dedicated to the developmental interests of young adolescents was certainly a part of the mix, but it served more as a matter of rhetorical support to other, more expedient purposes. This explains why, even after the passage of laws abolishing child labor and extending the age of compulsory school attendance, the junior high school remained largely unchanged in succeeding decades. Such matters of child advocacy might be rectified, but those of classical education forms and social efficiency are part of the deeper, dominant structures of the American society and its schools. True, the progressive impulses of the 1930s and 1940s found their way into many junior high schools, largely in the form of problem-centered "core" programs that emphasized democratic education, personally and socially significant content, and the like, but the number of such cases was far from overwhelming (Wright 1958). Their fate, like that of other progressive adventures, was sealed by the right-wing fanaticism of the McCarthy era and the seemingly endless capacity of elite intellectuals to reassert their dominance over the school curriculum whenever it starts to get socially or culturally interesting.

This portrayal of the American junior high school may seem overly dismal. However, one cannot overestimate the depths to which that institution had sunk by mid-century. In 1972, Brenan reported that when adults he interviewed identified the most "humiliating" experiences of their lives, the majority of those named took place in junior high schools. Such information was not a professional secret either. After visiting schools across the country, journalist Charles Silberman (1970, p. 324) had this to say:

> Because adolescents are harder to 'control' than younger children, secondary schools tend to be even more authoritarian and repressive than elementary schools; the values they transmit are the values of docility, passivity, conformity, and lack of trust . . . mindlessness affects the high school curriculum every bit as much as the elementary curriculum. And the junior high school, by almost unanimous agreement, is the wasteland—one is tempted to say "cesspool" of American education.

Those values, of course, are just the kind that the dominant culture might have hoped for in the upstart immigrants, since they are preferred on the floor of the industrial factory. In this sense, not only had the junior high school remained largely unchanged pedagogically, it had persevered in its unseemly role as one of the gatekeepers of the social and cultural hierarchy. While the elementary schools might have seemed little better than the secondary schools to Silberman, it is surprising that progressive junior high school advocates had not by then begun to wish aloud that grades seven and eight had been left in the former rather than attached to the latter (after all, elementary schools have proven themselves to be much more amenable to humaneness than secondary schools), but by the 1970s, many of them had taken up a new cause that they hoped would lead to real reform while maintaining a distinct identity. That cause came in the form of a new incarnation of middle level education whose beginnings were only a little less complex than those of its predecessor.

By the late 1950s, the post-war "baby boom" generation had literally overrun elementary schools around the country. The most obvious way of dealing with the situations, building more elementary schools, would clearly be a formidable task as sprawling suburbs would necessitate so many of them. In the end, a more popular option offered itself: Add a wing on the high school, move grade nine to that wing, and bring the sixth grade out of the elementary school into a combination with grades seven and eight. Such an arrangement could be sold to the public not only as a cheaper option but, with the inclusion of a new gymnasium in the wing, one that could actually enhance the high school's place in the community. This same argument proved to be popular in districts that used the moment to build a new high school and renovate the old one for the 6–8 grade facility. In some cases, the fifth grade was moved out of the elementary school with the sixth, an arrangement that was especially useful in getting children out of segregated neighborhood elementary schools earlier than usual. While some of these new configurations were called intermediate schools, most were known by the name that would stick as the new moniker for schools meant to house young adolescents: "middle school."

What happened in the years following is a remarkable story too long to tell here in detail, but a sketch of it is necessary to understand how we come to the current situation in middle level education and the need for a book like this one. In my own case, I had the incredible good fortune in the early years of the middle school movement to be a student of Conrad Toepfer, one of its founders. He kindly took me along to many of the events which now mark the early history of "middle schools" and introduced me to the influential people and literature associated with middle level education. The historical sketch here is thus also a personal memoir.

As administrators began to look at new grade configurations and potential building renovations, long-time advocates for middle level reform argued that the time was right, in fact overdue, to look again at what happens inside those schools. That a journalist like Silberman would make the scathing analysis noted earlier meant that the reform sentiments of middle level educators might even play well with the public. That sense of the moment proved largely accurate. Certainly the administrative rationale created the impetus for rearranging the grade levels; even today, it is almost impossible to find a middle school that was formed primarily for educational reasons.

But just as certainly, several moves made by middle school reform advocates captured the interest of the professional and public communities. The kind of reform they advocated is the reason why the middle level schools in many communities across the nation are very different today from the educational "cesspools" that Silberman encountered three decades ago. From the large array of examples, three nicely illustrate how reform advocates used the moment.

As the young baby boomers created their administrative dilemma, new data surfaced in England documenting a decline in the average age for achieving puberty (Tanner 1962). By the 1950s, according to new data, "early adolescence" was centered in an age window of 10–14 rather than the 12–15 period to which it previously had been assigned. That being the case, the administrative desire for a new grade configuration could be bolstered, or even hidden, by an argument that grades five or six through eight were now the appropriate ones to include in a school for young adolescents. Having made that point, middle level advocates were able to open up a larger discussion about the physical, social, and cognitive aspects of young adolescent development. That discussion, in turn, formed the empirical basis for the claim that accomplished middle level educators knew about young adolescent development and used that knowledge to inform decisions about everything from school climate to classroom management and instructional methods.

In a second example, middle level reform advocates followed the line of reasoning that young adolescents were not yet "mature" adolescents in order to make claims about what the structure of middle schools ought to be. Perhaps the most popular of these had to do with the anonymity and isolation that grew out of the large, highly departmentalized secondary school model. A remedy better suited to "young" adolescents, they claimed, was a house or team organization where the school could be broken down into smaller, more knowable clusters of teachers and students. To blend that more elementary-like personal environment with the more secondary-like, discipline-centered curriculum most people expected at the middle level, they also recommended that the teams have common planning time in which to discuss the students they shared, coordinate structural arrangements, and make connections across the school subject areas.

Third, by combining the argument that young adolescents are not "mature" adolescents with the claim that they experience dramatic changes in social and physical development, advocates also called for the middle school educators to play a much more explicit role in offering affective guidance for the young people who populated their classrooms. Struggling themselves with the emerging adolescent attitudes and behaviors of their children, many parents not only agreed with this idea but hoped that it might help out at home as well. Structurally speaking, however, it was impossible to imagine that the few guidance counselors in any middle school could provide the kind of persistent mentoring that was needed. So, reform advocates turned to teachers whose daily contact with students would allow a closer watch over them. The problem though was what kind of form that mentoring would take. The curriculum was already stuffed with the collection of subjects that had been carried over from the junior high schools pretty much intact. An answer that soon surfaced, and which would eventually become one of the more controversial pieces of the new middle schools, was an updated version of an old idea. In the early days of junior high schools, many had homeroom periods in which teachers provided some guidance for students. By the 1960s, the overwhelming number of "homerooms" had been reduced to a few minutes at the beginning of the day to make announcements and take attendance. Now, to provide a venue for affective mentoring in the new middle schools, the old homeroom period would surface again, reinvented this time as the "advisor-advisee" or "teacher-advisor" program. In this arrangement, a single teacher would meet with a small group of students four or five times a week for affective guidance and otherwise serve as their advocate in school matters.

Clearly, advocates for middle level reform were able to take advantage of the historical moment that presented itself and, in that moment, offer a new agenda for that level. Their success was made by three strategies that, in retrospect, proved both timely and effective. First, as they made their run at reforming the middle level, they took the high ground in staking their claims. Not only did they speak to ideas more educationally compelling than the need to relieve overcrowded elementary schools, but they eschewed the classical humanism and social efficiency arguments of the early junior high school in favor of the idea of making the middle schools appropriate places for young adolescents. Second, they capitalized on mid-century public and professional dissatisfaction with dehumanizing institutions, one of which was the junior high school, by arguing for a kind of school that was more affectionate toward and sensitive to the young people who attended it.

Third, early advocates of the new middle schools understood that collaboration and organization would benefit their efforts. By the late 1960s, a small group of leaders in the new movement had formed the "Emergent Adolescent Learner Council" within the well-known and powerful Association for Supervision and Curriculum Development. The publication, conference, and professional development resources of that organization offered a visible venue for quickly popularizing middle level reform ideas. At the same time, several of the same leaders spread their ideas through publications and weekend conferences sponsored by a consulting agency based in the Northeast known as the Educational Leadership Institute. By the mid-1970s, members of the Midwest Middle School Association along with advocates from elsewhere around the country organized themselves into the National Middle School Association. This secured a more defined focus for their work as well as a "place" to consolidate reform ideas and the people who put them forward. The rapid growth of the association reflected that specialized focus and signaled the growing spread of the movement. It is more than a little important that the leading middle school reform advocates made themselves available to local school districts around the country and worked hard to forge relationships with the teachers and administrators who worked in them. In this sense, specific details of the reform agenda emerged from the schools themselves and those persons mainly responsible for promoting reforms were never far removed from the realities of the schools.

Substantial as the movement to reform the middle level school became, it would be a mistake to suggest that the professional community in and around schools fully embraced the reform agenda. As Dickinson points out in the opening chapter of this book, many within the middle level community itself failed to fully embrace the philosophical and pedagogical grounds of the middle school movement. For some, the move to the middle school meant little more than changing the name on the school stationery. For others, the move amounted to implementing one or a few structural innovations that improved school climate but accomplished little else. As recent research has suggested, it is those schools that pursue the middle school agenda over several years as an integrated set of reforms, that demonstrate significant academic and affective advantages (e.g., Felner, Jackson, Kasak, Mulhall, Brand, and Flowers 1997). Those that move little or no distance from the junior high school model demonstrate few, if any, such gains and simply discredit the legitimate movement.

In addition, even among the early advocates, few called for the kind of substantive curriculum change (e.g., Lounsbury and Vars 1978) that would actually move middle schools beyond the traditional academic fare of the junior high school. Without curriculum reform, the day-to-day lives of young adolescents in schools would be little different from what they had been before. Finally, as Dickinson notes, politics within the middle school movement and its national organization have gotten in the way of meaningful progress at crucial moments when the middle school concept could have been more widely spread and more fully implemented.

Ironically, the very ideas that brought the new middle schools into ascendance, also made them vulnerable to wider forces that were beginning to press on the American schools. No matter what the wishes of some educators are, schools are not immune to wider public influence. In the case of the middle school, the once-heralded argument for making a more humane and humanistic institution in the 1960s and 1970s was turned aside by the Conservative Restoration of the 1990s. Ironically, this would have meant that many parents, who themselves attended early middle schools, stood by as reform efforts they experienced were rolled back by the neo-Puritan critique favoring schools that were less joyful, more stressful, focused almost solely on academics, and less concerned about young adolescents as people. More than anything else, of course, that critique has mostly to do with the "manufactured school crisis" (Berliner and Biddle 1995) created by conservative business, political, and educational officials and eagerly foisted on a scared public by both the public and professional media. But in the standards and testing world that has followed, a responsive school planned from the ground up around generally progressive ideas would inevitably be in trouble.

As I have pointed out elsewhere (Beane 1999a, b), the middle school reform movement became especially vulnerable in the 1990s as some of its advocates began to push for more egalitarian arrangements in both the structures and curricula of the schools. If middle schools were to provide more access to more knowledge for more children in a positive and nurturing climate, efforts would have to be made to emphasize collaborative learning, get rid of tracking, create heterogeneous grouping, develop curriculum integration, involve students in curriculum planning, celebrate cultural diversity, respond to diverse learning styles, and connect schools to community life. Obviously, the push for such ideas put the middle school movement on a collision course with the standards and testing juggernaut. The progressive framework didn't have a prayer. As attacks on the middle school idea surfaced, it also became increasingly clear that many insiders, including some whose careers were made speaking *about* the middle school concept, had neither the courage nor the commitment to speak *for* it.

As we embark on the twenty-first century, the middle level school has come to what Dickinson calls "arrested development," brought on by the internal limitations of the movement he outlines, as well as the larger social forces I have described. Structurally speaking, it is true that many middle level schools have institutionalized arrangements like teacher teaming and block scheduling, but these are hardly enough to warrant claims that the deeper meanings of the middle school concept are progressing on a large scale as they seemed poised to do a decade ago. Instead, the middle school concept as it was really meant to be is found on a whole-school basis in relatively few places. To see it in action one doesn't visit schools per se; rather, one tries to find particular individuals or teams who are managing to keep the concept alive inside a school, often under attack from colleagues and public critics. The rhetoric of the movement may still be heard at national and state conferences, but its reality has simply not been brought to scale. Indeed, as the more progressive push of the 1990s is beaten back by the conservative critique, the version of middle school reform that involves only cosmetic structural changes has resurfaced.

In his autobiography, *The Long Haul,* long-time social activist Myles Horton (1998, p. 200) tells us that "there are times when you can't go ahead . . . the forces out there are such that you can't. That's the time to hole up and start thinking. You watch the wind, and wait for it to blow your way." Clearly, for those who have advocated for substantive and deeply meaningful change in schools for young adolescents, now is such a time. But as we "hole up and start thinking," there is the danger that the progressive intentions of the middle school movement will be forgotten. This is why a book like *Reinventing the Middle School* is particularly important. At the very moment when the most meaningful parts of the middle school concept seem most in danger of withering away, the various authors in this book come forward to remind us that even in such a desperate time, the gains that have been made must not be forgotten.

Collected here are a series of fine chapters by authors whose commitments to the middle school concept have been as well demonstrated over time as they are by the ideas expressed in this book. What they have to say is not about shocking new revelations or brand new ideas. Rather, it is about the kinds of really good ideas that were supposed to be present in good middle schools and which now ought to be emerging on a larger scale as the middle school movement matures: ideas that will enhance academic achievement for all young people, engage them in intellectually stimulating experiences, and provide a caring environment within the school.

It is possible that some middle level educators will be surprised by what is here. After all, if they have come to the movement in the years since "arrested development" set in, they may not know that it was meant to be more than simply cosmetic structural changes and a stage for consultants. To now learn otherwise would be good. Hopefully, those middle level educators who were around before the "arrested development" set in, will be reminded of what this work was supposed to be about. Perhaps they will feel inclined to get past the internal politics that have nearly brought the movement to a standstill. Perhaps they will get past their fear of the criticisms that inevitably come to those who stand for worthwhile ideas. Perhaps they will remember that the purpose of the movement was to overhaul the middle level, not just rearrange it. If that should happen, then perhaps we might get on with the important business of bringing a better education to young adolescents, even in these difficult times. Perhaps we might "reinvent" this idea that is still worth having.

References

Beane, J. (1999a). Middle schools under siege: Points of attack. *Middle School Journal, 30*(4), 3–9.

Beane, J. (1999b). Middle schools under siege: Responding to the attack. *Middle School Journal, 30*(5), 3–6.

Berliner, D., and Biddle, B. (1995). *The manufactured crisis: Myths, fraud, and the attack on America's public schools.* Reading, MA: Addison-Wesley.

Brenan, J. (1972). Negative human interaction. *Journal of Counseling Psychology, 19,* 81–82.

Felner, R.D., Jackson, A.W., Kasak, D., Mulhall, P., Brand, S., and Flowers, N. (1997). The impact of school reform for the middle years. *Phi Delta Kappan, 78*(7), 528–550.

Horton, M. (1998). *The long haul: An autobiography.* New York: Teachers College Press.

Kliebard, H. (1986). *The struggle for the American curriculum: 1893–1958.* Boston and London: Routledge and Kegan Paul.

Lounsbury, J., and Vars, G. (1978). *A curriculum for the middle school years.* New York: Harper & Row.

National Education Association. (1893). *Report of the committee on secondary school studies.* Washington, DC: U.S. Government Printing Office.

National Education Association. (1895). *Report of the committee of fifteen on elementary education, with the reports of the sub-committees: On the training of teachers; On the correlation of studies in elementary education; On the organization of city school systems.* New York: American Book.

Silberman, C. (1970). *Crisis in the classroom.* New York: Random House.

Tanner, J.M. (1962). *Growth at adolescence* (2nd ed.). Oxford: Blackwell Scientific Publications.

Toepfer, C.F., Jr, and Marani, J.V. (1980). School-based research. In M. Johnson (Ed.), *Toward adolescence: The middle school years,* Seventy-Ninth Yearbook of the National Society for the Study of Education, pp. 269–281. Chicago: The Association.

Wright, G. (1958). *Block time classes and the core program.* Washington, DC: U.S. Government Printing Office.

Theoretical Foundations

Reinventing the Middle School:
A Proposal to Counter Arrested Development

THOMAS S. DICKINSON
Indiana State University

There is nothing wrong with the middle school concept.

The concept—a school for young adolescents that was based on their developmental needs—is as valid today as it was in either of its previous iterations at the turn of the twentieth century or in the early 1960s. The concepts that the founders of the middle level school proposed, either the classical six functions of the junior high school (articulation, integration, exploration, differentiation, guidance, and socialization) that Gruhn and Douglass (1947) made famous in the early twentieth century or Alexander's classical definition of a middle school ("a school of some three to five years between the elementary and high school focused on the educational needs of students in these in-between years and designed to promote continuous educational progress for all concerned"; Alexander and George 1981, p. 3), are valid because they are based upon responding to the unique developmental needs of a child in transition.[1] The concept is not frozen in its adherence to any of a number of school-related patterns or even the most current fad of educational practice. It is a flexible, responsive, integrated concept with an aim of providing a safe, secure, and appropriate environment for a young adolescent to learn challenging content that will enable him or her to explore self, others, and the larger world (Ames and Miller 1994; Feldman and Eliott 1990; George and Alexander 1993; George, Lawrence, and Bushnell 1998; Manning 1993; Simmons and Blyth 1987; Stevenson 1998). The concept is, at its base, an idea for a democratic school in that the students that attend are as much a part of the school and its efforts to educate them as any other structural element or adult figure (Dewey 1990, pp. 17–18).

But if there is nothing wrong with the middle school concept, what is wrong with many contemporary middle schools? In middle schools across this nation the story is the same—schools with signs outside that say "middle school" but with almost no identifiable aspects of the concept at work inside; teachers organized into teams but who do not meet on a regular basis, even though they have allocated time in their schedules, or when they do meet they continually mire themselves in the rut of student difficulties and failures; a deep cleavage between core and exploratory teachers—in numbers of students, organizational structure, and curricular approaches; advisory programs that look like administrative homerooms, or "seats-and-sheets" holding patterns; competitive athletics for the few; lack of parent and community involvement; and a curriculum dominated by classical recitation, boring textbooks, and instructional blandness (McEwin, Dickinson, and Jenkins 1996).

In school after school the words "middle school concept" have become what Daniel Kain refers to as "the middle school mantra."[2] It is a phrase mindlessly uttered, but with no understanding of the real meaning or importance of the phrase. What has happened across this country at the middle level is the arrested development of the middle school concept. While there are many schools that have implemented the entire concept, these lighthouse schools constantly mentioned in the literature or referred to by word of mouth, are too few in number. The majority of middle schools are in some stage of arrested development—where the middle school concept has not been completely implemented, or where it was once implemented and has now grown static and unresponsive (McEwin, Dickinson, and Jenkins 1996). Arrested development then, is both a structural problem of the lack of implementation as well as a disposition problem of belief in and attention to the concept. Arrested development can be seen in the daily activities, or lack thereof, in a middle school and the dispositions and beliefs that middle level faculty and administration hold and act upon in a consistent manner.

Arrested development applies to schools along a continuum of implementation, from those schools that never really began the transition to middle school's to those that implemented almost all the elements. Despite a school's place on the continuum, one that may offer a school faculty and administration pride in what has been accomplished, the truth of the matter is that the concept has not been implemented fully, only in pieces, and often in unrelated fashion. Therefore, the promise of the concept, the whole concept, is not realized.

What misleads many middle level educators, seduces may be a better word, is the feeling that some is better than none. What they are not acknowledging, what the movement has not made a forceful argument over, is that the original concept is a totally integrated ecology of schooling, the likes of which we have never seen before. It is an organizational, curricular, instructional, and relational environment that cannot be parsed or broken (Felner, Jackson, Kasak, Mulhall, Brand, and Flowers 1997). Any attempt to do so, as in many well-intentioned schools, leads to the condition of arrested development.

Arrested development

James A. Beane, in his introduction to this volume, provides a historical narrative of the middle school movement and how we have arrived at this point in our educational history. His introduction provides the deep background for the rest of this chapter, which examines the elements of transition to middle schools as they have been played out over the last 40 years and that have come to create arrested development. The failure is widespread, both historically and across groups—middle school faculty and administrators, teacher educators, state licensure boards, policy makers, consultants, and even professional organizations. The message is that we did not arrive at this state of arrested development overnight and we will not get out of it without the help, dedication, and hard work of many individuals and groups.

The following discussion examines a number of elements that have contributed to arrested development in middle schools. While these are examined in a linear fashion, the reader should be aware that these elements operated in a synergistic fashion throughout the history of middle schools. No single element caused arrested development in its own right. The interplay of the elements, over time, cast against broad historical movements in American education, brought about the present condition of many middle schools (Hechinger 1993).

1. The incremental stage implementation model used by middle schools to implement the concept.

When the first middle schools began their transition from junior high schools in the early 1960s, the field was wide open for this process. While much of the concept had already been articulated by the founders of the movement—individuals such as Alexander, Lounsbury, and Vars—there was no set pattern for conversion. After the first wave of early transitions, which were close collaborative efforts between early advocates and school-based personnel, a pattern began to take root that would in itself contribute to arrested development: this was an incremental stage implementation model.

A particular junior high school would decide to make the transition to a middle school and, for example, would begin with teaming in the seventh grade (this often happened since the sixth grade was still in the elementary school). Teachers, with or without appropriate inservice and preparation, and most without any university training, would find themselves on teams, or even a pilot team, at a grade level. The next year the eighth grade would follow, and then the sixth. After this, the exploratory (elective) teachers would be grouped as a team, although nothing in their assignments, student loads, or other preparation would change. Five years into the transition an advisory program would be implemented along with a flexible schedule, but by then the original com-position of the first core teams would be different. None of these elements, all introduced in a linear fashion, would be integrated vertically—grade level teams with each other, core teams with exploratory teams, teams with advisory, or all these elements with the flexible schedule.

Somewhere along the line the school would stumble—a change in an ad-ministrator or administration commitment, disenchantment, and then overt resistance on the part of a small but vocal faculty group, or even more com-mon, a lack of understanding that the job wasn't finished—that the middle school concept was much more than mere structural changes. Most telling was that through all these incremental changes, the curriculum and its instructional delivery pattern were virtually untouched.

One of the biggest lies that the incremental stage implementation model carries with it is the belief that at some point the transition to a middle school will be finished. It carries this lie because the model is based on a structural un-derstanding of the concept, but not an ecological one. Rather than seeing all the parts related both horizontally *and* vertically, it only sees the horizontal di-mension. This preserves the lie that somewhere, just over the horizon, when the next phase of the concept is in place, the job will be finished.

2. The lack of teacher education programs and licensure that focus on the middle school level.

One of the primary failures of the junior high school, the original school in the middle, was its failure to establish teacher education programs to educate professionals for this new school. This failure, coupled with the failure to influ-ence licensure, contributed mightily to its demise. Without a supply of teachers prepared to specifically teach at this level, schools were forced to implement the new ideas of the junior high school with staff who were trained for teaching other students and who, as a consequence, were often unhappy about being as-signed to a junior high school (Dickinson and Butler 1994; Dickinson and McEwin 1998a; McEwin and Dickinson 1996).

Much of the middle school's history duplicates this historical trend (Gate-wood and Mills 1973; McEwin 1984; McEwin and Allen 1984; McEwin and Dickinson 1996). While noteworthy progress has been made in preparation programs (McEwin and Dickinson 1995), state licensure (Valentine and Moger 1992; McEwin and Dickinson 1997a), and even national standards for middle school teachers (National Middle School Association 1996), the sad fact re-mains that the majority of teachers throughout the history of the middle school movement's last 40 years have not been educated to teach at this level. That sit-uation is not yet changing (McEwin, Dickinson, and Jenkins 1996).

The result of the lack of middle school teacher preparation and middle school licensure is that professionals, even those who find that they enjoy teaching this age group, often find themselves woefully ignorant of middle school theory and philosophy, unschooled in appropriate curriculum and instruction for young adolescents, and ignorant of the place and purpose of middle school organizational practices and the complex role of the middle school teacher (Alexander and McEwin 1982; McEwin 1984; McEwin and Allen 1984; McEwin, Dickinson, Erb, and Scales 1995; Scales and McEwin 1994). Thus, many middle schools find themselves spending an inordinate amount of staff development time and money reeducating their faculty on essential skills and abilities while more often than not, the essential dispositions about working with young adolescents remain unexamined. Other schools, less serious about their purpose, totally neglect the reeducation of faculty (McEwin and Dickinson 1996).

In essence, many middle schools have been operating outside their original purpose as schools for young adolescents, adding an unenviable burden of undergraduate education to their agenda, often at the expense of developing the school and its understanding of the complex concept of a middle school. This form of arrested development is played out in middle schools across the country every time a school year begins and new teachers—educated with either elementary or secondary preparation, but not middle level—are introduced (McEwin and Dickinson 1996).

Because of this lack of appropriate preparation, middle schools often find that they are continuing to process unprepared teachers through a revolving door. As one middle school team teacher said to me recently, with a sharp edge of shrillness: "Just once I'd like to have the same language arts teacher for two years in a row!" In the last five years the team had been through five different language arts teachers—both elementary and secondary trained—who all chose to transfer to a school and a curriculum they were prepared for.

3. The lack of middle school principal preparation.

In line with the lack of appropriately prepared teaching personnel for the middle school, goes the lack of middle school preparation of principals. One would think that educational leadership programs at the university level would be cognizant of the organizational, curricular, and instructional differences that the middle school concept attempts to implement. One would also hope that the prime leader of a school, its principal, would have more knowledge and experience than his or her staff (Ames and Miller 1994, pp. 135–156). Hope, however, is not always realized.

At the middle school level, principal preparation—preparation to lead a school based on the tenets of the middle school concept—is even more rare than middle school teacher preparation programs. The same can be said for licensure of middle school principals.

Coupled with this lack of primary preparation is another current trend in principal preparation that adds to the condition of arrested development—the movement away from the role and preparation of an instructional leader to that of a generic building manager. The move at universities from "principal preparation" to "educational leadership" has meant that curriculum and instruction have taken a back seat to physical plant, personnel issues, and budgets (Indiana Professional Standards Board 1998).

As a result, in too many middle schools the chief educational leader has little or no formal middle school education as a teacher or as an administrator. In fact, it is possible to administer a middle school in many states without having taught at this level. Commitment to the concept and its involved ecology is therefore often lacking. The disestablishment of aspects of the concept that do not fit into conventional thinking—team planning times, intramural programs, integrated curriculum—are often abandoned by untrained administrators without thought to the consequent impact on the concept and the appropriate education of youth.

4. The inability to balance good places for young adolescents to learn with challenging and involving work in those good places.

One of the most devastating elements of arrested development is an image of middle schools that took hold in the 1960s. This image, like the lie of incremental stage implementation, has been difficult to eradicate. This is the inability to balance the middle school as a good place for young adolescents to learn and grow with challenging and involving academic work in those good places. If middle schools are to reinvent themselves, this is one element that must be attacked head on. For in no way did the founders and early advocates of this movement ever speak, write, or intend that the school should be less than a positive place to be *and* a challenging and involving intellectual environment. It is sad to think that some of the best curricular minds of this century—individuals like Alexander, Lounsbury, and Vars—would be associated with a school that lacked appropriate intellectual rigor.

School-based personnel, however, in their rush to make the former junior high school into a middle school with a safe and secure environment, disregarded challenging academic work as part of young adolescents' intellectual needs and a necessary component of middle schools. While this move went in the wrong direction, let me be clear that the then reigning junior high school curriculum, a watered-down version of the separate subject high school curriculum, was itself highly inappropriate for young adolescents.

Thus began a false dichotomy—if middle schools were to be good places for young adolescents, nurturing environments, then they were "soft" learning places that didn't overtax or overburden students. In part, this stance developed as a move away from a heavily specialized junior high/high school curriculum organized around a departmental structure, but no curricular substitute for the separate subjects was offered. This left the door open to subsequent charges from the public, and from those looking for a way to criticize a democratic-leaning school, that the middle school, like the previous junior high school, was, to use Silberman's term, "a wasteland."

What is so important about the current research about the total middle school concept, the ecological approach referred to previously, is that this research confirms that good middle schools create and balance appropriate learning environments with the stimulating learning of important and rigorous content.

5. The parade of self-serving consultants.

The middle school movement—the drive to create appropriate learning environments for young adolescents—has attracted the attention of an army of highly qualified and respected educators, policy makers, researchers, and advocates. From its founders to the present, middle level education can look to the likes of Alexander, Lounsbury, Vars, Toepfer, Eichhorn, Thornburg, Lipsitz, George, McEwin, Mac Iver, Wheelock, Eccles, Arnold, Beane, Erb, Wood, Irvin, Strahan, and Stevenson. These individuals and others began and continue the foundation for a responsive and responsible middle school.

Still the middle school movement has also drawn other, not so well-intentioned, individuals. From the outset of the movement there has been a circus-like parade of consultants hawking themselves more than ideas and contributing to schools' arrested development as a result.

Some of these individuals have been located in middle level schools, or in colleges and universities, while others have been private consultants. Regardless of their location, they have contributed to a less-than-complex understanding of the middle school concept, while taking hard-to-come-by staff development dollars and conference registration fees. Working more as entertainers than educators, these individuals minimized the difficulty of the concept, telling audience after audience stories that, while on the surface were entertaining, were, upon examination, of little help in furthering the work of the school community (Arnold 1993).

While laughs were planned and catchy phrases delivered on cue, no growth resulted afterward. Audiences did not have a deeper understanding of the complex dynamics of working with other teachers in teamed situations. They did not understand complex developmental research involving learning. Emotional growth, or the needed fit between learner and school, was not explained or grounded in research. The consultants did not convey the long, hard work involved in the implementation of a new educational idea. What they offered was what the Roman emperors offered the masses during the last days—circuses.

6. The absence of significant and qualified researchers from the dialogue about creating middle schools.

No educational reform movement can sustain its efforts without comprehensive and systematic research on the impact and effect of its reforms. To attempt to do so would invite appropriate criticism as well as remove a vital ingredient in the overall reform mix. But for much of the middle school movement the problem has not been the absence of research, but the absence of researchers from the mainstream dialogue. Significant research was being done and published, but for most of the movement this research did not receive appropriate focus and has not become part of the recognized knowledge base of the middle school concept (Feldman and Elliott 1990; Simmons and Blyth 1987).

One of the most evident examples of this situation is the work of Jacqueline Eccles and her highly cited study on stage/environment fit (Eccles and Midgley 1989). Eccles is not alone in this situation—it applies to the work of Lipsitz (1980, 1984), Wheelock (Wheelock and Dorman 1988; Wheelock 1992), and a whole host of others.

The end result is that for the majority of the current middle school movement there has been little impact of significant research—little penetration into the overall dialogue and discussion about middle schools and young adolescent learning—to the detriment of the implementation of the middle school concept. Thus, another aspect of arrested development has been sustained.

7. The lack of attention to curriculum and the hesitancy to implement integrated curriculum.

From the start of the current middle school movement advocates and practitioners concentrated their attention on the organizational structures of the middle school concept. While there were a number of recognized curriculum leaders among the founders—Alexander, Lounsbury, Vars, Eichhorn, and Toepfer, for example—little attention was given to their curriculum proposals. In middle school after middle school the curriculum that existed prior to transition remained untouched. While the focus on teams brought a consequent linkage to interdisciplinary curriculum, little was actually done to promote connections between subjects. Even when this was realized the separate subjects still remained virtually untouched. This situation—a school without a curriculum of its own—meant that the middle school concept existed as a shell in even the best middle school. While the movement to create good places for young adolescents to learn may have caused much organizational structure change, little of substantial meaning occurred in actual learning environments where a secondary school separate subject approach dominated. Where the separate subject was found, the presence of textbook domination was not far behind.

This lack of an appropriate curriculum for the middle school and for young adolescents was extremely debilitating in its effect on the democratic elements of the middle school because it disenfranchised young adolescents with a highly circumscribed, highly specialized curriculum dominated by the perspectives of experts. Young adolescents are not content experts and do not frame their questions and inquiries as experts but as generalists. Their questions about self and others are broad, transcend subject matter boundaries, and represent their non-specialist views (Beane 1990).

The consequent impact of the absence of an appropriate curriculum on middle schools and its contribution to arrested development should be evident to the reader. In fact, this absence of an appropriate curriculum contributed to one of the fundamental dichotomies in the movement—the either/or situation of good places for youth vs. challenging and involving work. The message of the separate subject curriculum was not lost on young adolescents; they were not a part of the school, no matter what environmental structures existed. For those teachers who found themselves in the middle school, without training in the middle school concept or young adolescent developmental needs, the separate subject curriculum with its textbook domination was a "safe haven" in a sea of little understood middle school change.

When James A. Beane's work on integrated curriculum burst on the middle school scene in the 1990s, the middle school concept had at last its own distinctive curriculum. The clarion call of Beane's work brought forth an outpouring of related efforts by other curriculum theorists as well as practitioners who had been practicing this approach, often for years, in disconnected enclaves around the country (Arnold 1993; Dickinson 1993; Pate, Homestead, and McGinnis 1997; Stevenson and Carr 1993). This outpouring of theory, application, and stories of practitioners engaged in integrated curriculum work made the early 1990s seem, to many of us, a golden age of curriculum. Now the movement had a curriculum focus that pulled together tenets of the concept with existing organizational patterns and appropriate instructional practices.

But these heady days were quickly followed by other, different forecasts. While isolated individuals "came out of the cold" with their stories and examples, the movement (particularly certain elements of it) was slow to embrace it, if at all. After all, who was trained to do this kind of work? It was definitely more work, albeit with appropriate results for students. And what about the place of particular subjects, especially mathematics? And where was the research base? And what about test scores?

Time and again questions were raised, some legitimately, but more often than not as stumbling blocks in the path of significant change. This window of change, as a significant curriculum component of the middle school concept, may in fact be gone with our headlong rush into standardized testing and the consequent impoverishment of the middle school curriculum. This lack of adoption of integrated curriculum and the blind adherence to a secondary separate subject approach may forever seal the fate of middle schools in arrested development.

8. The failure of national content organizations to focus on the middle school level.

To a large extent it is understandable why the national content organizations should look at the middle school level as nothing more than an extension of the secondary school. This was their basic position on the junior high school throughout its history. Wasn't the middle school just the junior high school, updated somewhat?

Curricular-wise the content disciplines are invested in a separate subject approach. That should be self-evident from their very organization and separation from each other. This organization and separation are reflected in both national textbook patterns and standardized testing approaches.

Only recently have the separate subject disciplines begun to recognize the middle school level through their publications, conferences, and activities. This late entry, while laudable, still preserves the separation of subjects and does little to further dialogue about their integration at the middle school level.

9. The failure of the National Middle School Association to fully realize leadership for the middle school level.

If the separate subject organizations have failed to address and embrace the middle school movement, their omissions are somewhat understandable. Less so are the actions of the professional association founded to address the education of young adolescents—the National Middle School Association (NMSA). Throughout its brief history, this professional association has broadcast itself as an association that stood for the appropriate education of young adolescents and welcomed all who would join and participate in it. While the Association has done much that is positive and laudable, especially through its rich and extensive publications program, for much of its brief history the Association has been insular and inward-looking.

A principal function of a professional association is that of education of its members. Yet, as was alluded to earlier, the research agenda of middle schools and young adolescent learning have not been placed in the mainstream of the middle school dialogue. Prominent researchers and their work have not been featured at conferences or as major authors within the Association; while a strand of research has been continually ongoing, promoted by a stalwart few in the mainstream of the Association, even they and their work have not been given a rightful place and focus (Irvin 1997). Research, as an agenda within the Association, has been, at best, a minor concern.

Another function of professional associations is that of advocacy. The National Middle School Association, with respect to integrated curriculum, has not adopted a position advocating this curriculum for middle schools and the implementation of the middle school concept. In the early 1990s while the

Association advocated conference sessions and supported a variety of publications trumpeting this approach, NMSA and its board focused its attention on governance and restructuring with more concern for the role and status of state affiliates than the curriculum that young adolescents received. This governance effort, with its overstated focus on state affiliates rather than broad, national representation, is another reason why the Association has failed to attract, after the work of its early founders, nationally prominent board members and officers from the ranks of policy makers, researchers, and other advocates. The National Middle School Association has, throughout its history, been hesitant to aggressively advocate, through stated official policy or official position papers, much of any official position other than that promoted in its main philosophy document *This We Believe* (National Middle School Association 1995). As a result the Association, rather than lead, has followed the movement.

This "following behind" stance is most recently visible in relation to two major initiatives outside the Association—the Carnegie Council on Adolescent Development's *Turning Points* (1989) and the research spawned by the Association of Illinois Middle Level Schools (Felner, Jackson, Kasak, Mulhall, Brand, and Flowers 1997). *Turning Points* has a long and well documented history, but in relation to it, NMSA has followed along in Carnegie's shadow, urging its members to adhere to the dictates of Carnegie, but not even challenging this position when it was at cross purposes with stated middle school practice. An example is *Turning Points'* advocacy of endorsements for middle school teachers rather than a focus on distinct middle school teacher preparation (Alexander and McEwin 1982, 1988; McEwin 1984; McEwin and Allen 1984). This lack of advocacy or challenge by the Association sent mixed messages to members, state licensure boards, other policy makers, and the field as a whole.

The most important research in the history of the middle school movement was not conceived, directed, or supported by the National Middle School Association, but by a state affiliate in Illinois. Growing out of its summer institutes for teams and schools, the Association of Illinois Middle-level Schools (AIMS) grew a grass-roots network of reformed schools. Turning to a U.S. Department of Education grant in the late 1980s, the Association, in concert with the University of Illinois, began research on reformed middle schools in its network—those taking an ecological approach to middle school change. This research, reported by Felner, Jackson, Kasak, Mulhall, Brand, and Flowers (1997), has had profound impact on the movement, but not because of aggressive publication and advocacy through overt and focused NMSA activities as a whole, but through the efforts of a small minority both within and outside the national association (Erb and Stevenson 1999a, 1999b, 1999c). Any professional association exists to lead. The absence of overt and aggressive leadership on the part of this Association has contributed to the arrested development of middle schools across the nation.

10. The absence of research, until recently, to sustain the middle school concept.

For the majority of the middle school movement, the research that was conducted was done on particular elements or aspects of the middle school concept, substructures, if you will. While this form of research is necessary, little work was done on the entire middle school concept, on its total ecology and its impact on young adolescents and learning. This type of research is complicated, time-consuming, and costly. It takes significant support beyond that of most individual researchers, support more akin to that available to national associations, private foundations, or governmental agencies. Because of this lack of holistic research, much of the middle school movement and the implementation of the middle school concept was built on faith. Advocates "knew" in their hearts and minds that this was the way to go (Van Zandt and Totten 1995).

Nonadvocates, however, were not so easily persuaded, especially when they looked for a research base that would support the implementation of the concept. This absence of significant holistic research contributed to the arrested development of many middle schools, especially those using an incremental stage implementation model. Jumping ship, as it were, became a relatively easy task anywhere along the implementation process when a school faculty, principal, or school board became tired of it. They just pointed to the lack of research to sustain their efforts and the implementation came to a halt.

Now that significant research is available, it sustains the position of middle school advocates and is a sign of hope for the future, if schools caught in a state of arrested development will but reinvent themselves (Felner, Jackson, Kasak, Mulhall, Brand, and Flowers 1997). But, as is the case with integrated curriculum, time may have passed the movement by.

11. Our overall misunderstanding of the original concept as a total ecology of schooling.

As I have alluded to throughout this chapter, one of the significant elements of arrested development has been the use of an incremental stage implementation model. The use of this model, which atomizes aspects of the middle school concept to be developed and implemented, is unfortunate since it does not apply to a concept that is a total ecology of schooling rather than a package of parts. The middle school concept, as a total ecology, is made up of both horizontal and vertical aspects, all interrelated. The use of teams, for example, does not confine itself to different grade levels in isolation. Articulation issues exist as strongly between grade levels as they do between schooling structures (elementary to middle; middle to high school) and teams do not exist only as ways of organizing students and teachers—they also impact the organization of time and curriculum. Flexible block schedules and integrated curriculum are as much a part of teams as team meetings so that teams and their curriculum impact other teams and their curriculum, especially exploratory teams, advisory programs, and whole school climate. This interrelatedness plays out throughout all aspects of the entire concept (Ames and Miller 1994; Arnold and Stevenson 1998; Dickinson 1997, 2000; Dickinson and Erb 1997; Erb and Dickinson 1997; Erb and Doda 1989; George 1991).

The middle school concept, then, is like a Persian rug. Different threads are woven together into complicated patterns and colors until finally it is not discernible where a particular thread goes or where a particular color begins. It is the rug as a whole at which we look and admire. It is the overall integrated effort that *is* the rug as well as the behind the scenes process of weaving all the threads together.

Yet in middle school after middle school our rug has been hacked to pieces; torn asunder; mutilated. Different pieces have been hauled into the school, incomplete and unraveling, and thrown down upon the floor. Carving up the middle school concept has wounded it in many places and killed it in others because an ecology cannot exist without all its elements in place. While organizational issues are necessary to implement, so is an appropriate curriculum. While affective programs are necessary, so too are reciprocal relations among all parties to the school—students, parents, faculty, and administration.

If we are to reinvent the middle school, if we are to return to the original middle school concept, then we must begin by acknowledging the complexity of the original concept as a totally integrated organizational/curricular/instructional/relational/developmental concept, the likes of which we have not seen. We must continually work to establish and develop those individual aspects of the concept with an eye to the total integration of our efforts into a seamless whole. We must become weavers of the whole rug rather than isolated specialists. We must become responsible for the whole school, rather than just its parts.

Reinventing the middle school

If we are to create good middle level schools along the lines of the middle school concept that was articulated in the early 1960s, we must embark on a process of reinvention. Middle schools must reinvent themselves as they were intended to be.

The process may be daunting, but it is not impossible. We are not without our lighthouse schools, schools that have taken a total ecological approach to the process of implementation and that have continually revisited and adapted their work to the changing nature of their students (Lipsitz 1984; Powell, Zehm, and Garcia 1996). As well, we have a significant body of research to guide and sustain our efforts and this research supports the implementation of the total concept (Felner, Jackson, Kasak, Mulhall, Brand, and Flowers 1997; Irvin 1997; Lipsitz, Jackson, and Austin 1997; Mac Iver and Epstein 1991).

We have significant work on organizational structures over the history of the movement that can positively inform our reinvention (Arnold and Stevenson 1998; Clark and Clark 1994; Dickinson and McEwin 1998b; Erb and Dickinson 1997; George 1991; George and Alexander 1993; George, Lawrence, and Bushnell 1998; McEwin and Dickinson, 1997b). Finally, we have a curriculum model—integrated curriculum—that places the student at the fore (Arnold 1993; Beane 1993; Butler and Manning 1998; Dickinson 1993, 1994; Pate, Homestead, and McGinnis 1997; Stevenson and Carr 1993).

To reinvent middle schools mired in a state of arrested development, we must first acknowledge where we are—as painful as that may be. Then, we must examine both our attitudes and practices and begin to rework our schools along the lines proposed by the authors of the following chapters. Blame for how we got here is unimportant at this stage; getting schools out of a state of arrested development is important.

In 1991 at the beginning of the integrated curriculum movement, I wrote an editorial column in the *Middle School Journal* (Dickinson 1991, p. 43) where I asked three questions about the implementation of integrated curriculum.[3] These questions can, I believe, be recast to fit our present moment:

1. Do we believe that we are capable of making thoughtful, intelligent choices about important issues facing middle schools?
2. Do we trust ourselves to make these decisions?
3. Do we trust ourselves to allow these decisions to be made?

The process of reinvention is important for the middle school, but mostly for those young adolescents who are its students. This movement was founded on their appropriate schooling. The original concept that embodied it is still valid. We need to reinvent middle schools in that image once again.

References

Alexander, W.M., and George P.S. (1981). *The exemplary middle school.* New York: Holt, Rinehart & Winston.

Alexander, W.M., and McEwin, C.K. (1982). Toward middle level teacher education. *Middle School Journal, 14* (1), 3–5, 15.

Alexander, W.M., and McEwin, C.K. (1988). *Preparing to teach at the middle level.* Columbus, OH: National Middle School Association.

Ames, N.L., and Miller, E. (1994). *Changing middle schools: How to make schools work for young adolescents.* San Francisco: Jossey-Bass.

Arnold, J. (1993). A curriculum to empower young adolescents. *Midpoints, 4* (1), 1–11.

Arnold, J., and Stevenson, C. (1998). *Teachers' teaming handbook: A middle level planning guide*. New York: Harcourt Brace.

Beane, J.A. (1990). *Affect in the curriculum: Toward democracy, dignity, and diversity*. New York: Teachers College Press.

Beane, J.A. (1993). *A middle school curriculum: From rhetoric to reality* (2nd ed.). Columbus, OH: National Middle School Association.

Butler, D.A., and Manning, M.L. (1998). *Addressing gender differences in young adolescents*. Olney, MD: Association of Childhood Education International.

Carnegie Council on Adolescent Development. (1989). *Turning points: Preparing American youth for the 21st century*. New York: Carnegie Corporation.

Clark, S.N., and Clark, D.C. (1994). *Restructuring the middle level school: Implications for school leaders*. New York: State University of New York Press.

Dewey, J. (1990). *The school and society*. Chicago: University of Chicago Press.

Dickinson, T.S. (1991). Of revolutions, relations and riches. *Middle School Journal, 23* (2), 43.

Dickinson, T. (Ed.). (1993). *Readings in middle school curriculum: A continuing conversation*. Columbus, OH: National Middle School Association.

Dickinson, T.S. (1994). Common threads in an emerging tapestry: The jagged edge of excellence. *Middle School Journal, 26* (2), 3–4.

Dickinson, T.S. (1997). Pushing Humpty off the wall: Stories for a new age of teaming. In T.S. Dickinson and T.O. Erb (Eds.), *We gain more than we give: Teaming in middle schools* (pp. 3–18). Columbus, OH: National Middle School Association.

Dickinson, T.S. (2000). The middle school learner: Contexts, concepts, and the teaching connection. In *Mathematics education in the middle grades: Teaching to meet the needs of middle grades learners and to maintain high expectations: Proceedings of a national convocation and action conferences* (pp. 32–37). Washington, DC: Center for Science, Mathematics and Engineering Education, National Research Council, National Academy Press.

Dickinson, T.S., and Butler, D.A. (1994). The journey to the other side of the desk: The education of middle school teachers. In F.M. Smith and C.O. Hausafus (Eds.), *The education of early adolescents: Home economics in the middle school*, Yearbook 14 of the American Home Economics Association (pp. 183–191). Peoria, IL: Macmillan/McGraw-Hill.

Dickinson, T.S., and Erb, T.O. (1997). *We gain more than we give: Teaming in middle schools*. Columbus, OH: National Middle School Association.

Dickinson, T.S., and McEwin, C.K. (1998a). The origins and meaning of the middle school concept. In W.G. Wraga and P.S. Hlebowitsh (Eds.), *Annual review of research for school leaders* (pp. 13–38). New York: Scholastic and Reston, VA: National Association of Secondary School Principals.

Dickinson, T.S., and McEwin, C.K. (1998b). Lessons learned from successful middle level advisory programs. *Focus on Middle School, 10* (4), 1–6.

Eccles, J.S., and Midgley, C. (1989). Stage environment fit: Developmentally appropriate classrooms for young adolescents. In C. Ames and R. Ames (Eds.), *Research on motivation in education* (pp. 139–186). New York: Academic Press.

Erb, T.O., and Dickinson, T.S. (1997). The future of teaming. In T.S. Dickinson and T.O. Erb (Eds.), *We gain more than we give: Teaming in middle schools* (pp. 525–540). Columbus, OH: National Middle School Association.

Erb, T.O., and Doda, N.M. (1989*). Team organization: Promise—practices and possibilities.* Washington, DC: National Education Association.

Erb, T.O., and Stevenson, C. (1999a). What difference does teaming make? *Middle School Journal, 30* (3), 47–50.

Erb, T.O., and Stevenson, C. (1999b). Fostering growth inducing environments for student success. *Middle School Journal, 30* (4), 63–67.

Erb, T.O., and Stevenson, C. (1999c). Middle school reforms throw a "J-curve": Don't strike out. *Middle School Journal, 30* (5), 45–47.

Feldman, S.S., and Eliott, G.R. (Eds.). (1990). *At the threshold: The developing adolescent.* Cambridge, MA: Harvard University Press.

Felner, R.D., Jackson, A.W., Kasak, D., Mulhall, P., Brand, S., and Flowers, N. (1997). The impact of school reform for the middle years, *Phi Delta Kappan, 78* (7), 528–532, 541–550.

Gatewood, T. E., and Mills, R. C. (1973). *Preparing teachers for the middle school, junior high: A survey and model.* Mt. Pleasant, MI: Central Michigan University.

George, P.S. (1991). Student development and middle level school organization: A prolegomenon. *Midpoints, 1* (1), 1–11.

George, P.S., and Alexander, W.M. (1993). *The exemplary middle school* (2nd ed.). New York: Harcourt Brace.

George, P.S., Lawrence, G., and Bushnell, D. (1998). *Handbook for middle school teaching* (2nd ed.). New York: Longman.

Gruhn, W.T., and Douglas, H.R. (1947). *The modern junior high school.* New York: Ronald Press.

Hechinger, F.M. (1993). Schools for teenagers: A historic dilemma. In R. Takanishi (Ed.), *Adolescence in the 1990s: Risk and opportunity.* New York: Teachers College Press.

Indiana Professional Standards Board. (1998). *Standards for building level administrators.* Indianapolis, IN: Author.

Irvin, J.L. (Ed.). (1997). *What current research says to the middle level practitioner.* Columbus, OH: National Middle School Association.

Lipsitz, J. (1980). *Growing up forgotten: A review of research and programs concerning early adolescence.* New Brunswick, NJ: Transaction Books.

Lipsitz, J. (1984). *Successful schools for young adolescents.* New Brunswick, NJ: Transaction Books.

Lipsitz, J., Jackson, A.W., and Austin, L.M. (1997). What works in middle-grades school reform. *Phi Delta Kappan, 78* (7), 517–519.

Mac Iver, D., and Epstein, J. (1991). Responsive practices in the middle grades: Teacher teams, advisory groups, remedial instruction, and school transition programs. *American Journal of Education, 99*, 587–622.

Manning, M.L. (1993). *Developmentally appropriate middle level schools*. Wheaton, MD: Association for Childhood Education International.

McEwin, C. K. (1984). Preparing teachers for the middle school. In J. H. Lounsbury (Ed.), *Perspectives: Middle school education 1964–1984* (pp. 109–120). Columbus, OH: National Middle School Association.

McEwin, C. K., and Allen, M. G. (1984). Moving toward middle level teacher certification, *Middle School Journal, 16*(4), 18–20.

McEwin, C.K., and Dickinson, T.S. (1995). *The professional preparation of middle level teachers: Profiles of successful programs*. Columbus, OH: National Middle School Association.

McEwin, C.K., and Dickinson, T.S. (1996). *Forgotten youth, forgotten teachers: Transformation of the professional preparation of teachers of young adolescents*. Background paper prepared for the Middle Grade School State Policy Initiative (MGSSPI), Carnegie Corporation of New York.

McEwin, C.K., and Dickinson, T.S. (1997a). Middle level teacher preparation and licensure. In J.L. Irvin (Ed.), *What research says to the middle level practitioner* (pp. 223–229). Columbus, OH: National Middle School Association.

McEwin, C.K., and Dickinson, T.S. (1997b). A twenty-first century middle school. In W.J. Bailey (Ed.), *Educational leadership for the 21st century—Organizing schools* (pp. 133–155). Lancaster, PA: Technomics.

McEwin, C.K., Dickinson, T.S., Erb, T.O., and Scales, P.C. (1995). *A vision of excellence: Organizing principles for middle grades teacher preparation*. Chapel Hill, NC: Center for Early Adolescence and Columbus, OH: National Middle School Association.

McEwin, C.K., Dickinson, T.S., and Jenkins, D.M. (1996). *America's middle schools: Practices and progress—A 25 year perspective*. Columbus, OH: National Middle School Association.

National Middle School Association. (1995). *This we believe: Developmentally responsive middle level schools*. Columbus, OH: National Middle School Association.

National Middle School Association. (1996). *NMSA/NCATE-approved curriculum guidelines*. Columbus, OH: Author.

Pate, P.E., Homestead, E.R., and McGinnis, K.L. (1997). *Making integrated curriculum work: Teachers, students, and the quest for coherent curriculum*. New York: Teachers College Press.

Powell, R.R., Zehm, S., and Garcia, J. (1996). *Field experiences: Strategies for exploring diversity in schools*. Englewood Cliffs, NJ: Merrill.

Scales, P.C., and McEwin, C.K. (1994). *Growing pains: The making of America's middle school teachers*. Columbus, OH: National Middle School Association.

Simmons, R.G., and Blyth, D.A. (1987). *Moving into adolescence: The impact of pubertal change and school context*. New York: Aldine de Gruyter.

Stevenson, C. (1998). *Teaching ten to fourteen year olds* (2nd ed.). White Plains, NY: Longman.

Stevenson, C., and Carr, J.F. (Eds.) (1993). *Integrated studies in the middle grades: "Dancing through walls"*. New York: Teachers College Press.

Valentine, J. W., and Mogar. D. C. (1992). Middle level certification—An encouraging evolution. *Middle School Journal, 24*(2), 36–43.

Van Zandt, L.M., and Totten, S. (1995). The current status of middle level education research: A critical review. *Research in Middle Level Education, 18* (3), 1–25.

Wheelock, A. (1992). *Crossing the tracks: How 'untracking' can save America's schools.* New York: New Press.

Wheelock, A., and Dorman, G. (1988). *Before it's too late: Dropout prevention in the middle grades.* Boston: Massachusetts Advocacy Center and Chapel Hill, NC: Center for Early Adolescence.

Notes

1. Alexander, known as the father of the modern middle school, articulated what he called "essential characteristics of exemplary middle schools," a list of twelve elements that included philosophy and school goals based on knowledge of the educational needs of young adolescents; a system for school planning and evaluation; curriculum that provides for their continuous progress, basic learning skills, use of organized knowledge, personal development activities, and other curriculum goals; a program of guidance; an interdisciplinary teacher organization and appropriate interdisciplinary units; the flexible use of methods of student grouping for instruction; block scheduling and other time arrangements to facilitate flexible and efficient use of time; and instruction which utilizes a balanced variety of effective strategies and techniques to achieve continuous progress of each learner (Alexander and George 1981, pp. 18–19). These concepts, merged with other knowledge about young adolescents, became the template for what has come to be known as the middle school concept.

2. D. Kain, personal communication, October 5, 1998.

3. The original three questions were:
    1. Do we believe that our students are capable of making thoughtful, intelligent choices about important issues in their lives, both in school and out?
    2. Do we trust our students to make these decisions?
    3. Do we trust ourselves to allow these decisions to be made?

The School and the Child and the Child in the School

DEBRA ECKERMAN PITTON
Gustavus Adolphus College

Sitting in a meeting with a group of teachers who were discussing plans for the conversion of their district's junior high into a new middle school, I overheard one eighth grade teacher say, " I don't know about expecting all of this interdisciplinary teaching stuff and flexible scheduling to really make a difference. It was so much easier back a few years ago . . . the kids listened to you and did what you asked. Now it seems that the kids don't care, they don't do the work, or they just aren't as capable. There is so much need for discipline and . . . "

One of the administrators cut her off. "The kids who come in our doors are the kids we need to teach. The parents aren't keeping all the good ones at home. We have to find ways to meet students' needs, whatever they are, not pine for the good old days. Yes—students are different today, our society has changed. With technology and the impact of the media, very little is the way it was ten or fifteen years ago, so why would you expect the students to remain the same?"

Unconvinced, the teacher just shook her head. I listened to the rest of the discussion, but thought for a long time about those comments. I was aware of the challenges involved in the process of moving a junior high toward a middle school philosophy, yet I wondered why this was so. I wondered if the difficulty of embracing a middle school approach was related to this perception that kids today are somehow not as capable and bright as their predecessors.

What do we want in a middle school?

Many individuals have looked at the impact of middle schools on the learning of young people and much has been said in favor of the principles and strategies proposed by the middle level concept. A longitudinal study by Felner, Jackson, Kasak, Mulhall, Brand, and Flowers (1997), that looked at the levels of implementation of educational reforms suggests that increased achievement, fewer behavior problems, and easier student adjustment to school are associated with higher levels of implementation of middle level concepts.

Lee and Smith (1993) reviewed data which identified that students in restructured middle schools (schools that were using team teaching, interdisciplinary curriculum, and other middle school concepts) scored significantly higher in the areas of achievement and engagement than students attending traditional schools.

Studies by Feldlaufer, Midgley, and Eccles (1987) and Midgley, Feldlaufer, and Eccles (1989) identified that self-contained classrooms (similar to the structure provided by teaming and flexible or block schedules prescribed for middle schools) provided more correlation of learning and learning opportunities than departmentalization. Proponents of student-centered curriculum identify that a movement away from departmentalization and the use of integrated curriculum make learning more meaningful. Research by Vars (1996) that looked at studies from the last 60 years concluded that students involved with a combined curriculum of any form do as well as, and often better than, students in a traditional program.

According to Brazee's work summarizing research on middle school curriculum, "The underlying features of middle school philosophy; physical, social, emotional and intellectual development and the contexts in which they occur are frequently acknowledged in the literature, but less often applied in schools" (Brazee 1995, p. 7). Brazee (1997) and others agree that there is a disconnection between developmental issues and middle level curriculum, and that this is a major factor inhibiting the advancement of middle level education (Eccles and Midgley 1989; Hillman, Wood, Becker, and Altier 1990; Jackson and Hornbeck 1989). So it seems that even though educators are aware of the issues that face young adolescents, middle school curriculum is often ambiguous (Beane 1997) and does not address the needs of middle school students.

Almost any organization that has reviewed the issues facing young adolescents comes to similar conclusions: that the developmental needs of middle school students must be addressed across all aspects of the school community (NMSA 1995; Carnegie Council on Adolescent Development 1989). However, Brazee (1997) states that while middle schools have initially worked hard to incorporate organizational and climate changes into the structure of schools for this age group, the application of what we know about adolescent development has been superficial in many cases.

Perceptions of young adolescents

Despite the positive reviews regarding various aspects of middle level learning, something still keeps many teachers, administrators, and parents from embracing the philosophy wholeheartedly. If we know that students of this age need teaching and classroom interactions that provide them with meaning and address their developmental issues, why do many middle school classrooms still reflect a teacher-focused, content-directed, autocratic approach?

Perhaps it is because we, as educators, have not been willing to give any real credence to the insights provided by developmental theory. As adults, we know that we work harder on things we enjoy, we learn more when we choose to do something and are involved in the decision making, and we strive to do our work well when it means something to us. Yet when we face a classroom full of young adolescents, it is easy to pull rank and dictate what WE think is important, what WE think is relevant and meaningful. Why is it so easy to tell young people what to do rather than asking them?

As adults, most of us would never think of forcing another individual to follow our directives. We ask for input, we work in committees, we gather multiple perspectives, and we build consensus. Even without reviewing the research on group dynamics (Johnson and Johnson 1991), adults are aware that a higher quality work product is produced when individuals have a say in what is completed and how it is accomplished. At least here in the United States, it is a commonly held belief that if someone has a voice in a decision they are more likely to support it. Our democratic society demands active participation in making decisions that affect us as individuals. As research into group interaction and the effects of group participation identify, being a part of a group, as opposed to being dictated to, results in a more productive worker (or learner) and product (Johnson 1990; Johnson and Johnson 1991). Well intentioned adults strive to positively interact and give everyone a voice in our communities, in the work place, and in government. So why doesn't this occur in our classrooms, where our purpose is to develop future citizens?

Perhaps it is that teachers find a classroom of hormonally charged young people innately threatening, so keeping control becomes paramount. We know that all of the changes young people are going through at this time create anxiety and often confusion and hostility, and it is scary to think about unleashing all of that emotional energy in a classroom. It feels more comfortable to keep things under control, to manage all aspects of the classroom. Middle school philosophy asks the teacher to give up much of that control and to begin to work with their students as they would another adult. This is asking for change that is just too much for many of us to handle. We are moving out of our comfort zones if we let go of our control of the curriculum and ask students what they would like to learn. We let go of our control if we ask other teachers with differing perspectives to share in the development of curriculum. We let go of our control if we have to teach in areas that stretch us beyond our current level of knowledge and preparation, and we let go of our control if we give the students opportunities to express themselves freely.

Behind all of the concepts espoused by middle level philosophy lies the premise that we need a different structure for children of this age because they are developmentally different than elementary and high school students. If teachers do not recognize the impact of these developmental differences, then they will not be able to respond accordingly. Research by Eccles, Lord, Roeser, Barber, and Josefowicz (1996) states that middle school students require different types of educational environments in order to meet each individual's developmental needs at that particular time, as well as to help them continue to develop. Students at this transitional period, between grade school and high school, need schools and classrooms that help them move through this adjustment.

The influence of classroom climate

While structural changes such as teaming, flexible schedules, exploratory options, interdisciplinary curriculum, and advisory groups are central to creating this supportive environment, teachers must also adjust their view of the student. Several studies (Eccles and Midgley 1989; Eccles, Midgely, Buchanan, Wigfield, Reuman, and Mac Iver 1993) identify that despite awareness of the physical, social, emotional, and cognitive changes occurring in young people, classrooms for students between the ages 10 and 14 often reflect strong teacher-centered control and emphasis on discipline along with limited input from students in the way the class is run. Decisions about curriculum and learning opportunities are most often left to the teachers. Eccles and Wigfield (1997) refer to Mac Iver and Reuman's (1988) work which says that this mismatch between the emerging adolescent's need for self-management and the opportunities provided for them in the classroom may result in the student's lack of motivation and interest in school. These studies point out that for many young adolescents, there seems to be no purpose to being in school, no feeling that they are being allowed to develop and have a voice, and so they choose to act out.

Robert Sylwester's (1995) work, synthesizing brain research, identifies the influence of classroom atmosphere on student learning. Sylwester clarifies the link between the brain's ability to function on higher levels with the need to respond with caution in a fearful and threatening situation. If middle school classrooms feel uncomfortable and scary to young people, they focus on survival and the brain shifts its support to those systems that can provide "fight or flight" reactions. Focus on higher level thinking is limited under such circumstances. Therefore, it seems obvious that classrooms need to provide safe, supportive environments so children in the schools can indeed learn more complex knowledge and processes. If students are afraid that they will be ridiculed by other students or be threatened (verbally or physically) by a classroom bully, little learning will take place as the students will be mentally "on guard" and not connected with the lesson.

How do we create safe, nonthreatening environments in our classrooms? The teacher sets the tone by his or her own interactions with the students. If the teacher believes that the students are rowdy unruly children who need to be kept under control, the atmosphere will not be as welcoming and comfortable as if the teacher sees his or her students as young adults in search of meaning and support for their development. In addition, the teacher needs to facilitate classroom interactions between students that protects every child—emotionally and physically. Students need to have the opportunity to learn how to interact in positive ways.

Goleman (1995), in his work on emotional intelligence, says that students need to have opportunities to develop their ability to read emotions in others and respond empathetically. This is certainly not a traditional component of school curriculum, yet Goleman states that emotional IQ is what enables individuals to manage their emotions, to interact with others, to exhibit empathy, and to persevere despite other emotional distractions. When we think about the emotional rollercoaster that middle school students are on as they work through relationship issues, it seems logical that students should be focusing on developing their emotional intelligence. In this way, the classroom can become a safe place, and high level learning can happen. Advisory programs are the perfect match for integrating activities to develop students' emotional intelligence.

Another issue to consider is that middle school students are at the crossroads in their educational development, and for many, the sense that there is no purpose to their schooling creates a feeling of apathy and disinterest. This can result in failure or dropping out of school altogether. Teachers must recognize that adolescent changes cannot be downplayed, rather, that the incorporation of student choice and active support for the young adolescents' myriad of physical, emotional, and social stresses and concerns must be included in every classroom. While many educators can recite a litany of young adolescent needs, their own reaction to the adolescent's push for independence and self-determination is often to try to squash the emerging sense of self with control and directives. Teachers may ignore the interactions within the classroom that create an atmosphere of fear if they focus solely on academics and their agenda for learning. It is easier to try and control the tensions and emotional ups and downs among students than to try and help them learn to deal with such issues. However, as Sylwester states, the brain will not respond to requests for higher level learning if there are concerns about personal and emotional safety. It often feels more comfortable for teachers to keep a tight hold on the reigns in their classrooms, yet it is only through the sharing of decision making that students will feel invited into the learning process. Extending an invitation to students to join in the educational process says that the teacher values them as individuals. Being a part of such a supportive, safe environment enables young adolescents to more fully develop their potential. Who better to assist students with the issues of adolescent social and emotional change than teachers who can offer opportunities to discuss, plan, reflect, and review options for appropriate responses to these developmental concerns?

Just as we know middle school students are going through an adjustment period and that they need support to accomplish a successful transition to adulthood, so too do teachers moving into a middle school concept need support as they transition into a new dimension of teaching. Teacher preparation programs must provide more emphasis on the links between adolescent development and best practice in the classroom. However, McEwin and Dickinson (1995) report that many issues, such as lack of program availability, interest, teacher resistance, and a dearth of advocates for the middle level concept have prevented widespread implementation of specialized middle school teacher preparation. Thus, there are too few teachers who have studied to any extent the needs of young adolescents or the appropriate educational responses to those needs.

Changing perceptions

It is hard to view students as individuals who deserve respect when we have been used to being effective and efficient teachers by "working with the whole and keeping control." I found myself in just such a position a few years earlier—one where I preferred keeping control and focusing my teaching on the group, not on the individual students. I was teaching a basic speech class and had several students who were hearing impaired. The first two hearing impaired students who were mainstreamed into my classroom wore hearing aides and specifically told me that they wanted to improve their speaking ability. I treated them no differently than my other students, although I gave particular attention to their articulation and offered suggestions and exercises for them to work on at home to improve in these areas. In addition to tests over content areas, these students were expected to deliver numerous speeches and were evaluated with the same criteria as everyone else in the class. I was quite pleased that they seemed to improve, if not as much in articulation, certainly in their confidence level. However, the following semester a student came to class with an interpreter. The interpreter told me that she would be signing for this particular hearing impaired student. I replied that she should tell the student, Andrea, to let me know when she was comfortable enough to begin speaking in class.

The next day, I received a notice from our special education department that Andrea's language was sign language and that she would be using an interpreter throughout the class, and that I was violating her rights if I required her to speak. I was a bit flabbergasted. After all, this was a SPEECH class. I replied that my other hearing impaired students had done quite well, but was again informed that this student had a legal right to use sign language. This seemed ridiculous and impossible. After all, I evaluated students on their inflection, the appropriateness of their tone, volume, and their ability to convey meaning through their words. How in the world would I ever be able to evaluate someone who signed everything they presented in class? I would be evaluating the interpreter, not Andrea!

I began the next day by trying to convince Andrea to take a drama class as an elective, instead of speech, saying that she would be able to develop expressive skills that didn't require words more effectively in an acting class. This was not what she wanted. She informed me, through her interpreter, that she intended to develop her ability to communicate because she wanted to be an advocate for the deaf, so she needed to be able to speak persuasively and eloquently.

When I went with frustration to the special education teacher to complain that I just didn't see how I was going to provide Andrea with any new learning, the teacher suggested that I look into deaf education, and gave me the names of some specialists to call. She also said that perhaps if I identified the specific criteria that COULD be met without speaking in the assignments I gave in my class, it might help. Without much enthusiasm, I called a professor of hearing disabilities education and a professor of speech communication at the local college. Among the suggestions were two that seemed somewhat manageable; to ask for a written text of each speech and evaluate it for the persuasive or informative structures and to identify the nonverbal skills and presentation style that would best serve to enhance the sign language presentation. After several phone calls for clarification and examples, these individuals' comments began to chip away at my rationalizations and help me develop criteria to use with Andrea.

In retrospect, it seemed curious that I was so reluctant to try something that would benefit my student, when I had prided myself on being a "caring teacher." It was a matter of holding on to what I saw as a rigorous academic experience. I thought the process we had devised was inappropriate for a "real" speech class. While I had been told about the research on the use of sign language and educational efforts for individuals who were totally deaf, I was still convinced that this was not really going to work—that I would be, in effect, grading the sign language interpreter. It was extremely difficult to move out of my comfort area, but with the threat of legal action, I reluctantly began to try and see how I could help Andrea improve.

It was the rest of my class who clued me in to Andrea's development in her "speeches." This was in contrast to what I expected to happen. I thought Andrea's speeches would be difficult for the other students to watch. While the students initially observed the interpreter, they soon began to watch Andrea closely during her speeches. Andrea's expressive face and her elegant signing did indeed communicate her words. As I worked with her to strengthen her written text and make her signs a bit bigger and more visible to her audience, it was obvious that she was getting better at communicating the meaning and message of her speeches. She was indeed meeting one of my main objectives for the class, even though it was communicated in a different way. Her final presentation, an oral interpretation of a story of a girl coming to terms with a deaf sister, moved some of the students, along with me, almost to tears.

When I think back on this incident, I realize it was a critical shift in my development as a teacher. I was forced to let go of my control and to help a student meet her own learning goals, not mine. It was extremely uncomfortable to acknowledge that my expertise was insufficient in meeting this girl's needs. I had been the expert speech teacher. I had made the decisions about what was learned, when, and where. To have someone outside of my classroom imply that I needed to do more was unsettling. However, by being forced into this situation, I began my movement toward student-centered teaching and learning.

Nancie Atwell, noted middle school writing teacher, describes a similar epiphany she experienced after working with a student who didn't follow her prescribed writing program. Atwell wrestled with ideas from experts who suggested that she needed to let go of her extensive writing curriculum. At first she resisted, but after observing her students at work, she stated " I saw that my creation (the curriculum) manipulated kids. . . . Students either found ways to make sense of, or peace with, the language arts curriculum, or they failed the course" (Atwell 1998, p. 4). Here was a teacher who had created a very thoughtful, detailed curriculum, and who struggled to identify what would make her teaching better. "I rationalized . . . what I needed were even more creative, more open topics (for writing). . . . I needed better students—kids who consistently made my assignments their own, . . . who came to me prepared by their teachers to write well. I needed better colleagues" (Atwell 1998, p. 11).

A new definition of teacher

I find it interesting that Nancie Atwell also complained about the students, hoped for better ones, and felt that if only somehow the kids were different and their prior classrooms were more effective, she would be successful. The fact was that she herself needed to change, just as I needed to change how I taught speech, and as many teachers have to change before they can truly help middle school students learn. Atwell goes on to say, "I didn't know how to share responsibility with my students and I wasn't too sure I wanted too. I liked the vantage of my big desk. I liked being creative, setting topic and pace . . . taking charge. Wasn't that my job? If responsibility for their writing shifted to my students, what would I do?" (Atwell 1998, p. 13).

Atwell articulates the unspoken fear that many educators hold—"What will my role be if I no longer dictate every move in the classroom?" We know what the research says about development and the needs of students. As teachers, we have to change ourselves to be able to create classrooms and schools where students can learn. We need to let go of the image of what teachers used to do and what we thought kids were like. Kids haven't changed that much, but society has, and those kids who, as Atwell said, "didn't make peace with the curriculum," who used to leave school or fail, can no longer be ignored or pushed out. Society is demanding that all students be given the opportunity to learn. Standards are being set, and the expectation is that teachers can and must help students learn. Yet it is not easy to let go of these tightly held beliefs about teaching that shape educators' perceptions about their role and responsibilities in a classroom.

Joel Barker (1989) describes what happens when individuals remain rigidly faithful to an image or perspective or way of doing things and refuse to even look at or consider the possibilities of a new paradigm. In his work, he cites examples of major opportunities that were missed when people kept on the blinders of old paradigms. Educators cannot close their eyes to what we now know about how students learn. We cannot afford to miss any opportunities to provide appropriate educational experiences to our youth. Something has to change in our classrooms so that all students are able to learn what they need to be happy, productive members of society. We need to see our students for what they are—not children, but emerging adults who need opportunities to learn how to make decisions and who need to have their concerns taken seriously. A new paradigm that moves control in a classroom from the teacher alone to the teacher and students together must be embraced. If we see our students differently—as developing adults, and if we see our role as assisting their transition into adulthood, then it becomes obvious that we cannot hold on to total teacher control. The concept of student-centered classrooms, which lies at the heart of effective middle schools, is a critical component of this new educational paradigm.

Reading about Atwell's evolution, as well as reflecting on my own experience made me realize how difficult it is to make a paradigm shift toward student-centered teaching. This is a huge obstacle for teachers to overcome. However, I have come to believe that if we, as teachers, do not let go of some of our control and begin to ask the students what it is they need, we will fail to provide many of our young people with an education that is meaningful or useful. As middle school teachers, we must work to meet the students' learning needs, not just our own personal, prescribed idea of what is a valuable learning experience. We need to overcome our fear and resistance to giving students a voice in their own learning if we want to fully actualize the middle school concept in our schools.

Becoming responsive to young adolescents' needs

Specifically, what can teachers do to move out from behind the desk and work with students to develop appropriate educational experiences? The answer has always been out there—in the concepts proposed by the middle school model. What concepts can middle school educators embrace to make the child in the school the focus, not the teacher? Two primary areas to start with are the advisory program and the curriculum.

In their twenty-five year perspective on middle schools, McEwin, Dickinson, and Jenkins (1996) describe research on the implementation of the middle school concept which indicated that teacher-based guidance type programs had declined slightly from 1988 to 1993. For advisory programs that were in place, there seemed to be an increase of time allotted to them, although there was some question as to what was occurring during those advisory times. Again, lip service to the concepts of supporting young adolescent needs and creating strong connections between caring adults and adolescents seems to be the common experience. Advisory is a foreign experience for many teachers, and McEwin, Dickinson, and Jenkins' work identifies that teachers are often opposed to this role. Lack of preparation heightens teachers' feelings of inadequacy when leading advisory type activities, discussions, and lessons. If schools are set up to meet teacher needs, then of course, it becomes easy to acquiesce to teachers who do not want to participate in advisory sessions. If schools are created to meet the needs of students, it becomes paramount that teachers be involved in opportunities that develop their skills and heighten their comfort level so they can support and lead advisory programs. It is not an option to simply use advisory time for a study hall or revert to a homeroom model. Students at this age need opportunities to discuss issues about which they are concerned, they need to feel a sense of belonging, and they need to connect with an adult who cares. If teachers view their students as emerging adults and acknowledge the needs and concerns of the young adolescent, then it makes sense that the teacher's role must also include facilitating opportunities for student discussion and skill building in the social and emotional areas. All of these things happen in a well-developed and carefully facilitated advisory program.

In many middle schools, advisory programs have been times set aside in which students work with an adult from the school in a small group setting. Some of these adults have been administrators and counselors as well as teachers. The small numbers are helpful, but more important is the fact that the adult is comfortable with their role as advisor. However, it might create more opportunities for supporting young adolescent development if advisory concepts were addressed throughout the curriculum, rather than just during the advisory time. Teaching teams ought to provide this integrated advisory process for students, because facilitating students' learning about emotional development and social concerns should not be relegated to one particular time, but should be woven into the curriculum in a seamless fashion. In this way, students would get support from many adults, and would not have to wait for an advisory period.

Integrating advisory programs across the curriculum would also enable teachers to support each other as they develop their skills in working to address the emotional and social needs of their students. This can't happen when one teacher leads an advisory group. Teachers moving into new areas of their own development need collegial support, and perhaps the isolation created by small groups of students working with one teacher is not the best model to use when implementing an advisory program in a school.

Regardless of the structure of an advisory program, the bottom line is, if a teacher can dismiss the concerns of young people and ignore their needs, they ought not work in a middle school. Teaching is not static. It should be ever changing as educators work to address new ideas, knowledge, and competencies that students need to develop into adulthood. Any job that makes you stretch and move into areas that are uncomfortable has the potential to make you a better person as you rise to meet the new challenges. So, too, with teachers who work to develop the skills and competencies that enable them to create effective advisory groups. It may not initially be within their comfort zone, but like Nancie Atwell says, it is the students who must have their needs met, not the teacher.

Once middle school teachers have embraced the effective use of advisory programs to support their students, the other area where educators need to let go of their preconceived images of middle school students is in the area of curriculum. There are two important shifts that need to occur: Content has to connect to the lives of the students in order to be meaningful, and students need to have some voice in the decisions about what they will learn.

Inviting students to share in curriculum decision making is another difficult step for teachers. Atwell, describing what she has learned about curriculum for young adolescents, states, "Learning is more likely to happen when students like what they are doing. Learning is also more likely when students can be involved and active and when they can learn from and with other students" (1998, p. 69).

I am one of those middle school teachers who started out in a high school and who, like Atwell, initially used a very detailed English curriculum that I had spent years developing. Due to job changes that took us to different parts of the country, I found myself being interviewed for a job at a Texas middle school after teaching high school for many years. The principal asked me if I was really interested in children of this age, if I was prepared to make commitment to middle school education or if I was "just passing through" on my way to high school. Because I needed a job, I asserted (although not with complete honesty) that I was looking forward to the change and to working with middle school students.

I proceeded to find that the eager, interested, enthusiastic, and energetic middle school students were quite a bit different from the sometimes jaded high school students. These middle school students told me what they liked or didn't like in my classes and often asked "why are we doing this?" My high school students might have thought this same question, but at that point in their educational career, they no longer asked it out loud very often. My middle school students questioned everything and always wanted to know "Why?" They were like large two year olds—searching for independence from adults, needing the support of adults, wanting answers immediately. (Those of you who have not raised a two year old need only watch one for a while to see the resemblance between the learning processes exhibited by both groups.) The resistance I got when I assigned topics at the start of our work on a formal research paper led me to ask in frustration one day, "OK—so what **do** you want to find out about?" The students shouted out their ideas. I was stunned. I had assumed that they needed me to tell them what to research because they were inexperienced. I had also felt that my ideas would be more appropriate topics that would facilitate their learning. Of course, they wouldn't learn *anything* if they didn't do the research or if they rushed through readings on an uninteresting subject to just "get it done."

After some discussion, during which students described their dreams of visiting far off places, we settled on researching their ultimate vacation. Students generated questions, gathered research from texts and travel agents, figured out costs, and wrote up a report that identified their knowledge of the place where they wanted to travel. While this might not have been a highly sophisticated piece of research, I was impressed with what the students accomplished. Some students did need more support and encouragement, but all of the students completed the project, something that hadn't happened before. The positive energy and enthusiasm that permeated the room when they were working on something they cared about was captivating. The end result: I began to let the students make some choices about what they learned. I found that the students were able to make good decisions about their learning, and that they worked harder when they had a voice in the curriculum. I also found that teaching was more enjoyable when the students and I worked as a team. I chose to stay at the middle school.

Making connections

Giving the students a voice in deciding what they learn is only part of the curriculum shift that must happen in middle school classrooms. Interdisciplinary or integrated curriculum is another way to make the learning meaningful, but it is another middle school concept that teachers often resist. Brazee states that "While there are numerous arguments for an integrated curriculum, perhaps the most compelling one is that an integrated curriculum best addresses the unique needs of young adolescents, yet it is the least developed in practice" (1995, p. 16). Another curriculum expert, James Beane, adds that "Curriculum integration begins with real-life problems as themes, proceeds according to the organic integration of knowledge and serves the purpose of enhancing self and world meaning" (1995, p. 28). George, Stevenson, Thomason, and Beane (1992) suggest that middle school curriculum needs to begin by seeking out answers to young adolescents' concerns about their world, and that teachers must discuss this with their students as a part of curriculum planning. This is very different from the traditional curriculum developed and implemented by most teachers, and while it may "hook" students and excite them about learning, it is a scary step for teachers.

Many of us are fearful of going somewhere we haven't been. Descriptions of appropriate middle school curriculum suggest major shifts in the way teachers have developed their lessons in the past. "The definition of who is learning in the school should be expanded to include teachers and other adults. . . . adults cannot simply provide answers to powerful questions, but must seek them along with young people" (George, Stevenson, Thomason, and Beane, 1992, p. 97). This echoes what Nancie Atwell proposed: we must be involved with our students in their learning. If a teacher does not have everything all lined up and ready to go in the classroom because she wants to ask students for their input, then there are many opportunities for the teacher to "lose control." This is the heart of many teachers' fears: that the students will overwhelm them with their voices and energy and the teacher will lose control of the classroom.

Teaming is the answer—holding hands and going together makes the process more comfortable. Teachers who are developing new curricula and seeking connections to provide adolescents with relevant learning experiences cannot make this change overnight. Working together they can structure class discussions on curriculum development to allow for student voice and yet maintain a focus. School systems should provide scheduling that supports teaming and does not undermine efforts to link content and help students make sense of the curriculum. However, McEwin, Dickinson, and Jenkins (1996) state that decisions to share faculty with high school or elementary programs often creates further roadblocks to the implementation of a curriculum that addresses young adolescent needs through interdisciplinary and team approaches.

We cannot point fingers at teachers who struggle to let go of the control they traditionally have held over the curriculum and shift their view of young adolescent learners without identifying the teachers' need for support. This support must come from school districts in the form of money and time. McEwin, Dickinson, and Jenkins state that the "lack of money to support two prep times for development of team teacher project(s) and no common planning time for teachers" (1996, p. 107) are major obstacles to the implementation of middle school concepts. Teachers need to discuss and reflect with their colleagues about their fears and frustrations as they work to move their classroom interactions in a new direction. Two prep times give teachers time to plan for their classes and also provide valuable interaction time for colleagues during the team planning time. Common planning time underpins the concept of teaming and provides the opportunity for personal interactions that must be provided to the teachers before they can model it for their students. Interdisciplinary curriculum cannot be generated and coordinated if the teachers involved never have a chance to talk. Districts that provide the financial means to support two prep times for faculty teams are doing their part to help teachers implement middle level concepts.

Support for change

With all that we know about young adolescents, why is it that, despite 25 years of discussion and study on the positive effects of middle schools, some districts still refuse to provide the resources that will enable students' needs to be met? If a doctor discovered a new way to help a patient, no one would say, "It is too expensive." or "It takes too much time for us to use with most people." Efforts would be made to have that process made available to everyone who needed it as quickly as possible.

A longitudinal study of middle schools involved in comprehensive school transformation identified that there was higher achievement by students in schools with high levels of implementation of the middle school concept (Felner et al. 1997). More than 15,000 students were involved in this study which showed increased levels of achievement in reading, mathematics, and language arts scores. The implication from this study is clear: young people in schools that implemented middle school concepts at a high level "achieve at a higher level academically than those in nonimplemented schools and substantially better than those in partially implemented schools" (Felner et al. 1997, p. 544).

Research such as this cannot be ignored. We need to disseminate what we know about middle school teaching and learning so parents, teachers, and administrators are as aware of the best practices for middle schools as they are with medical research. As Felner's study indicates, the more comprehensive the implementation of middle school concepts, such as those in *Turning Points* (1989), the better the results for students. Indeed, "the presence or absence of a particular element of the program may affect the levels of implementation of other components" (Felner et al. 1997, p. 543). Middle schools and middle school teachers cannot pick and choose which of the middle level components they want to use. All of the elements need to be present, especially those difficult for teachers to embrace—advisory and student-centered curriculum. Time and money for teacher development and interaction are crucial to the effective implementation of all of the middle level concepts. Parents need to be informed that schools cannot simply consider what is efficient, but must find the resources to implement what is good for young people. Referendums that provide money to fund the operation of middle schools must be supported. In addition, those responsible for educational funding in our state governments need to be informed about the components of effective middle schools and their positive impact on young adolescents' educational experiences. Working with a team creating interdisciplinary curriculum demands that teachers have the time and financial resources to collaborate. More importantly, however, is the need for teachers to have support as they "let go" of some of the control of the curriculum taught in their classroom.

The interpersonal interactions that are a part of advisory groups and the connections generated in student-centered classrooms are key components for bringing the child into the school and engaging students with their education. Teachers need an advisory group (or class) of their own to help meet their needs as they move toward true student-centered teaching. They need opportunities to increase their comfort level with the ideas provided by brain research and the concepts behind the development of emotional intelligence along with all the other processes and discussions that they will be incorporating in advisory sessions. Without time to meet with colleagues and support to assist their development, teachers cannot comfortably move in new directions.

Besides time with their team, teachers need opportunities to work with other teachers who are successfully implementing middle school concepts so they can gain new knowledge. Even if middle school teachers have come from a program at their college that provided coursework in middle school philosophy and methods, it is easy to revert to "what school was like for me" when facing all the expectations placed on them as a new teacher. Therefore, both experienced teachers and novice educators need to be given the time and money to attend ongoing interactions that focus on middle level concepts. Facilitating advisory groups is a new dimension for many teachers. A one shot workshop or lecture will not provide sufficient support. Teachers moving out of their comfort zone need ongoing opportunities to discuss and argue and share what they've tried in a safe, collegial environment. The use of a mentor teacher, participation in a course on middle school, or the use of school-wide study groups are some options that districts may want to provide for teachers working to develop the skills necessary to implement advisory opportunities and interdisciplinary curriculum. When Nancie Atwell describes what influenced her move to a student-centered teaching style, she credits a graduate program where her rationalizations were challenged (Atwell 1998). All teachers need the opportunity to talk through their concerns and fears with colleagues before they can begin to incorporate developmentally appropriate practice into their classrooms and feel confident facilitating advisory sessions.

Making a difference

For students to be supported in their middle school years, for them to be a part of the school, teachers need to be supported by district funding so they have the time, money, and other resources to develop their understandings of teaming, curriculum, and student-centered learning. However, in describing barriers that can impede the movement toward implementation of middle school concepts, Lipsitz, Mizell, Jackson, and Austin (1997) state that "A lack of individual will to persevere despite formidable obstacles has been the most persistent, albeit understandable, barrier to school reform" (1997, p. 539). Ultimately, teachers must let go of their old perceptions of young adolescents, learn to enjoy and appreciate their students as young adults, and allow themselves to learn how to work in teams to implement concepts such as advisory and student-centered curriculum.

Middle school students are still open to new ideas, still searching for answers, and undecided about who they are and what they will ultimately be. This creates a wonderful opportunity to be a part of their journey into adulthood, but as with all adults, we cannot force the learning process; we must invite the students to join us on the journey. The children who are in our middle schools today are the best we have. There are none of those "perfect children" hidden away somewhere waiting for teachers to fill their heads with knowledge. Students today are a part of a world that is active, mobile, and ever-changing. We need to change our perception of them and help them deal with issues of violence, sex, justice, honesty, environment, and all of the problems that they will have to face as adults. Think about the changes we have witnessed in our lifetime. Who knew that cloning would be a reality? What other ethical decisions will our young people have to make regarding genetics and human life? How will they determine appropriate uses for future inventions and discoveries in technology and medicine? We need to bring these issues into the classroom, to weave our curriculum and our standards around current issues and the developmental needs of middle school students, so that we can provide them with the processes and knowledge they need to continue to learn and grow into competent, caring adults.

This will happen only when we bring the child into our school, into our classroom, and make the school a place that supports his and her world. Middle schools will never reach their potential until the human element, the teachers, stretch themselves and learn to focus on the students. Franklin D. Roosevelt once said "we have nothing to fear but fear itself"—a great quote for a middle school teacher. We cannot fear going forward, changing our world view, and inviting the young adolescent learner into the classroom as a partner. Through teacher commitment in the areas of advisory and student-centered curriculum, middle level classrooms can provide a meaningful learning experience for every child in the school.

References

Atwell, N. (1998). *In the middle: New understandings about writing, reading and learning* (2nd ed.). Portsmouth, NH: Heinemann.

Barker, J. (1989). *Discovering the future: The business of paradigms.* St. Paul, MN: ILI Press.

Beane, J.A. (1995). Myths, politics and meaning in curriculum integration. In Y. Siu-Runyan and V. Faircloth (Eds.), *Beyond separate subjects: Integrative learning at the middle level* (pp. 25–38). Norwood, MA: Christopher-Gordon Publishers.

Beane, J.A. (1997). Curriculum for what? In J.L. Irvin (Ed.), *What current research says to the middle level practitioner* (pp. 203–207). Columbus, OH: National Middle School Association.

Brazee, E. (1995). An integrated curriculum supports young adolescent development. In Y. Siu-Runyan and V. Faircloth (Eds.), *Beyond separate subjects: Integrative learning at the middle level* (pp. 5–24). Norwood, MA: Christopher-Gordon Publishers.

Brazee, E. (1997). Curriculum for whom? In J. Irvin (Ed.), *What current research says to the middle level practitioner* (pp. 187–201). Columbus, OH: National Middle School Association.

Carnegie Council on Adolescent Development. (1989). *Turning points: Preparing American youth for the 21st century.* Washington, DC: Carnegie Council on Adolescent Development.

Eccles, J.S., Midgely, C., Buchanan, C.M., Wigfield, A., Reuman, D., and Mac Iver, D. (1993). Development during adolescence: The impact of stage/environment fit. *American Psychologist, 48* (2), 90–101.

Eccles, J.S., Lord, S.E., Roeser, R.W., Barber, B.L., and Josefowicz, D.M.H. (1996). The association of school transitions in early adolescence with developmental trajectories through high school. In J. Schulenberg, J. Maggs, and K. Hurrelmann (Eds.), *Health risks and developmental transitions during adolescence* (pp. 283–320). New York: Cambridge University Press.

Eccles, J.S., and Midgley, C. (1989). Stage environment fit: Developmentally appropriate classrooms for young adolescents. In C. Ames and R. Ames (Eds.), *Research on motivation in education* (pp. 139–186). New York: Academic Press.

Eccles, J.S., and Wigfield, A. (1997). Young adolescent development. In J.L. Irvin, (Ed.), *What current research says to the middle level practitioner* (pp. 15–29). Columbus, OH: National Middle School Association.

Feldlaufer, H., Midgley, C., and Eccles, J. (1987). *Student, teacher, and observer percep-*

tions of the classroom environment before and after the transition to junior high school. Ann Arbor, MI: University of Michigan.

Felner, R.D., Jackson, A.W., Kasak, D., Mulhall, P., Brand, S., and Flowers, N. (1997). The impact of school reform for the middle years. In Research on Middle Grades Special Insert. *Phi Delta Kappan, 78* (7), 528–549.

George, P.S., Stevenson, C., Thomason, J., and Beane, J. (1992). *The middle school— and beyond.* Alexandria, VA: Association for Supervision and Curriculum Development.

Goleman, D. (1995). *Emotional intelligence.* New York: Bantam Books.

Hillman, S.B., Wood, P.C., Becker, M.J., and Altier, D.T. (1990). Young adolescent risk-taking behavior: Theory, research and implications for middle schools. In J.L. Irvin (Ed.), *Research in middle level education: Selected studies* (pp. 39–50). Columbus, OH: National Middle School Association.

Jackson, A.W., and Hornbeck, D.W. (1989). Educating young adolescents: Why we must restructure middle grade schools. *American Psychologist, 44* (5), 180–187.

Johnson, D.W. (1990). *Reaching out: Interpersonal effectiveness and self-actualization* (4th ed.). Englewood Cliffs, NJ: Prentice-Hall.

Johnson, D.W., and Johnson, F. P. (1991). *Joining together* (4th ed.). Englewood Cliffs, NJ: Prentice-Hall.

Lee, V., and Smith, J. (1993). Effects of school restructuring on the achievement and engagement of middle-grades students. *Sociology of Education, 64* (3), 190–208.

Lipsitz, J., Mizell, M.H., Jackson, A.W., and Austin, L.M. (1997). Speaking with one voice: A manifesto for middle-grades reform. In Research on Middle Grades Special Insert. *Phi Delta Kappan, 78* (7), 533–540.

McEwin, C.K., and Dickinson, T.S. (1995). *The professional preparation of middle level teachers: Profiles of successful programs.* Columbus, OH: National Middle School Association.

McEwin, C.K., Dickinson, T.S., and Jenkins, D.M. (1996). *American middle schools: Practices and progress—A 25 year perspective.* Columbus, OH: National Middle School Association.

Mac Iver, D., and Reuman, D. (1988, April). *Decision making in the classroom and early adolescents' valuing of mathematics.* Paper presented at the annual meeting of the American Educational Research Association, New Orleans.

Midgley, C.M., Feldlaufer, H., and Eccles, J.S. (1989). Changes in teacher efficacy and student self- and task-related beliefs during the transition to junior high school. *Journal of Educational Psychology, 81* (2), 247–258.

National Middle School Association. (1995). *This we believe: Developmentally responsive middle level schools.* Columbus, OH: National Middle School Association.

Sylwester, R. (1995). *A celebration of neurons: An educator's guide to the human brain.* Alexandria, VA: Association for Supervision and Curriculum Development.

Vars, G. (1996). Effects of interdisciplinary curriculum and instruction. In P.S. Hlebowitsh and W.G. Wraga (Eds.), *Annual review of research for school leaders* (pp. 147–164). Reston, VA: National Association of Secondary School Principals and Scholastic Publishing Company.

3

Hope for Sandy: Transformation Points: A Reinvention Paradigm

MARY M. GALLAGHER-POLITE

Southern Illinois University Edwardsville

Sandy has been a middle grades teacher for twenty-five years now, and has spent most of her time in the same classroom, in the same building, in the same community. Sandy doesn't complain; she doesn't rock the boat; and, sadly, she also doesn't contribute much anymore. She is on time for school each day to meet her classes and consistently turns in the required forms and paperwork on time. She has an endowed chair in the lounge that new teachers are warned about early in the year so they don't accidentally invade her turf before school or during lunch. Sandy's planbook isn't laminated, yet, but each year she adds fewer new lessons or units and relies more heavily on what has worked in the past. Sandy attends the required professional development sessions sponsored by her district and school, but she uses the time to get some of her unending paperwork done. She's heard it all before anyway.

Sandy didn't start out that way when she began some twenty-five years ago. She entered the profession like most new graduates; eager, excited, and filled with a desire to work with children and to make a difference in their lives. Sandy had the latest knowledge and research on effective teaching in her toolkit and wanted to be part of something meaningful and real. Twelve years ago she even took a leadership role in the school when the decision was made to transition from a traditional junior high to a middle school. But now, she is disillusioned by kids and their parents, by administration, the school board, and community and feels there is little she can do to make any kind of difference anymore. Sandy is not retired, but many in the school are counting the years until that happens.

What happened to Sandy during the course of her career that led her down the path of mediocrity isn't unusual. Unfortunately, there are "Sandys" teaching in middle schools all across America. Perhaps you have a Sandy teaching down the hall from you; or you try to supervise Sandy and motivate her to do more. Perhaps your child was in Sandy's classroom, and though you're certain no harm was done, you'd hoped for so much more for your child. If you are Sandy yourself, you know better than the rest that you are both a witness and a participant in a crime that resulted in the loss of your professionalism; and you know as well that you are capable of so much more.

"Anyone who spends time in public schools can feel the growing and deepening malaise among educators . . . " (Fullan 1997, p. 288), and middle schools are no exception. A growing number of Sandys find themselves in daily battle with fatigue, depression, and apathy. Over the long haul of their professional careers, they have witnessed restructuring, reorganizing, realigning, and reforming, through linear, logical, strategic, systemic, centralized, decentralized, and collaborative approaches. They have been exposed to information that describes, analyzes, and reports on historic and current middle school trends, best practices, exemplary programs, and model schools, yet, they know that middle schools are not living up to their promise because they are in one every day that doesn't. They watch young adolescents who learn to fail by failing to learn; who come to school with problems and deficiencies sometimes so overwhelming that the village that is supposed to help raise this child doesn't feel like quite enough help; who face daily pressure which "has taken the joy out of teaching for large numbers of the teaching profession" (Fullan 1997, p. 289).

If middle schools are to be good schools for students, they must also be good schools for adults. In essence, a middle school organization must model the middle school concept for all its various constituents and treat all adults the way they are expected to treat their students. Schools feel duplicitous to adults in them when a needs responsive mission for young adolescents is espoused and no consideration is given to the needs of the teachers, administrators, staff, and parents who are required to implement that mission. Bringing middle school philosophy and effective practices into alignment for adults as well as students may not only help the Sandys in the school, but everyone else as well, reach the higher levels of engagement and learning that are possible when middle school works at its best.

Turning Points: A reform paradigm

Since the 1989 publication of *Turning Points: Preparing American Youth for the 21st Century*, middle schools have used the Carnegie Council recommendations as a framework for school restructuring (Carnegie Council on Adolescent Development 1989). The Council urged schools to:

- Develop small communities for learning.
- Provide a core academic program for all learners.

- Ensure success for all students.
- Empower teachers and administrators in decision-making.
- Hire teachers who are expert at teaching young adolescents.
- Improve academic performance through health and fitness.
- Reengage families in the education of young adolescents.
- Reconnect with their communities (pp. 27–29).

With these recommendations, middle level educators were armed with the recognition and support that gave middle level school improvement a national agenda. Early adolescence was recognized as a unique and distinct phase in the developmental process, and as thousands of educators across the country set out to find ways to respond to these needs, core programs, policies, and practices emerged. In good faith, and with tenacity and courage, school boards, central office staff, building administrators, teachers, parents, and community members made the transition from traditional junior high schools to middle schools with energy and enthusiasm. Long- and short-range plans were developed to implement block scheduling, interdisciplinary teaming, integrated curriculum, advisory, and exploratory programs. School revenues were allocated for professional development workshops, institutes and retreats that provided teachers the knowledge and skills they needed to bring about necessary changes in classroom instruction. Different materials were purchased; additional teachers were hired; parents were invited to participate in new ways on school councils; collaboratives were formed with business and industry partners; and over time, some schools demonstrated that their efforts had a positive impact on student outcomes (Felner, Jackson, Kasak, Mulhull, Brand, and Flowers 1997).

Yet even in the most successful schools, institutionalization has made innovation routine. Maintaining momentum and surviving a mid-life crisis of change is taxing; energies wane, disappointments occur, and new hires are expected to take up the banner of continued reform because their veteran colleagues are simply worn out. The *Turning Points* recommendations initiated a successful reform paradigm, but perhaps more than reformation is required.

Beyond reformation

Many middle schools seemed to have reached a reform plateau; a leveling off of energy and innovation following years of progress and improvement. More than a reform paradigm will be needed in order to maintain and sustain the progress that has already been made and to forestall a backslide to less effective, traditional practices. A transformation paradigm that can elevate middle schools to the next level will require new perspectives of the complex dimensions of schools. Marcie (1997) developed a model of five dimensions of work, all of which are needed to maximize organizational effectiveness. She contended that "a healthy organization would have a balance of material and physical development, intellectual growth, and a deep concern for human issues" (p. 28).

Five Dimensions of Work

Physical: concerned with physical life issues, work design and working conditions.

Intellectual: includes the collective intelligence of staff, the continuing drive for learning, as well as abilities to create challenging work or helping people see jobs or responsibilities differently.

Emotional: involves the interpersonal work environment, how well people get along and how effectively they can team.

Volitional: the desire or will to change for the better.

Spiritual: concerned with moral issues, such as justice, respect, and empathy; understanding each individual to be a unique human being, a sacred soul, with dignity (adapted from Marcie 1997, pp. 28–29).

The middle grades reform agenda has focused primarily on the physical, intellectual, and volitional dimensions of schools. Though these efforts alone are not sufficient, they should not be abandoned in light of the strides that middle schools have made to design and implement effective programs for students.

Table 1: Dimensions of Middle Grades Reformation

Physical Dimensions	• Space allocation and reorganization • Block scheduling • Teaming designs • Program modifications • Curricular innovations • Fiscal accountability
Intellectual Dimensions	• Shared quality indicators • Professional development and life-long learning • New challenges, roles, and opportunities • Recognition of risk-taking, innovation, and creativity
Volitional Dimensions	• Transition from traditional junior high design • Shared sacrifice during change process • Acknowledgment of resistors and supporters

Yet, if the momentum for improvement in middle level schools is to be maintained over the long haul, we cannot simply continue to repeat the old and not suffer. Working harder is not smarter and every once in a while we must swallow hard, take the leap, and build our wings on the way down (Yamada 1999). This leap may require an infusion of Marcie's (1997) emotional and spiritual dimensions that are "absolutely essential yet largely overlooked in management thinking" (p. 29), and arguably, not part of a typical reform agenda in middle schools either.

From turning points to transformation points: A reinvention model

In addition to the *Turning Points* recommendations, which forged a reform agenda for the physical, intellectual, and volitional dimensions of schools, *transformation points* will be needed to address the emotional and spiritual dimensions in schools. Transformation points recommendations are intended to elevate the school's thinking by infusing an understanding of the often-overlooked aspects of school improvement: personal growth, spiritual development, and holistic thinking. By fully including all five dimensions of work, middle schools may become the engaging, nurturing learning enterprises that fulfill the promise of their potential.

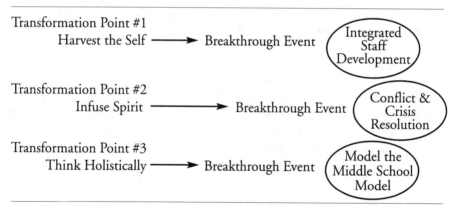

Figure 1: Transformation points recommendations: A reinvention paradigm.

Transformation Point #1: Harvest the Self

Harvest the Self: Personal growth cannot be separated from professional growth. Teachers, principals, staff, and parents alike carry with them the sum total of their life experiences when they enter the schoolhouse door just as students do. Recognition is needed for the interplay of personal and professional growth issues and the various ways individuals respond to career and life demands.

Adults in schools live in a pressure cooker. Everyone watches; everyone has expectations; and absolutely everyone thinks they know how schools should be because they have been in one. Educators not only expect themselves, but are expected by others, to go the extra mile because that's what professionals who care about students do, and in the short run, people can sustain incredibly demanding schedules. In the long run, however, it is the individual who deals with the emotional fallout of an unbalanced life. Trying to reconcile a personal conception of what it means to be good at my job with other life choices and responsibilities for being a good spouse, or good parent, or good friend, or a good caregiver to an aging parent often takes a toll that is ignored in the school. In addition, other major, personal, and sometimes life-changing events happen to people all the time. Yet in schools, we only give lip service to the impact personal issues have on professional effectiveness.

Educators know well enough by now that children come to school as whole beings who cannot ignore the out-of-school and personal experiences that sometimes interfere with learning. To expect adults to act as if they have no emotional or personal needs once they step into the school building is like expecting a young adolescent to ignore the social and emotional turmoil that characterizes that age group. They can't do it and neither can adults.

Acknowledging the whole life experiences for educators does not excuse unprofessional behavior. There are certainly times when all of us have to shelve our personal agenda in order to carry out our job responsibilities, but to deny that personal issues exist at all is sending a mixed message to teachers who daily have to honor and recognize these issues for their students.

Schools can't mandate personal growth nor can the most creative program identify the key that each person holds to personal change and development. Personal growth and self-change are life-long endeavors that require enduring commitment from the individual and the school. Each person will need to understand the adage "you don't have be sick to get better" to know that personal growth is about wellness not illness. When personal growth is taken seriously in schools, the people in them will be better able to transform the school into a more caring, vibrant environment for all who come there to learn.

Transformation Point #2: Infuse Spirit

Infuse Spirit: Adults are complex beings with personal growth needs that transcend the concrete, visible, tangible aspects of life. Recognition is needed for ways that spirituality, dignity, integrity, truth, honor, joy, and love can be infused in schools and how spiritual resources can enhance individual development, school culture, and outcomes.

"The very idea of focusing on spiritual resources in organizations is startling and confusing to many" (Marcie 1997, p. 30). Conversations about spirituality, dignity, integrity, truth, honor, joy, and love are carried on only secretly in isolated corners of schools, if at all. While organizations have grown comfortable developing shared beliefs and mission statements (see, for example, Schurr, Thomason, and Thompson 1995; Shockley 1992), common principles (Covey 1989), or organizational virtues (Marcie 1997), it is less common to embrace what it means to honor and value the spiritual development that can lead to organizational soul. "We are an educational community of organized bits and pieces, sound bytes, rules, regulations, deadlines, and rat races; a maze of bureaucratic objectives and outcomes. Instead, we must seek to be a community of spirit and truth" (Magnusen 1998, p. 14).

Spirituality is more than religion and dogma, which may have confused us about our spirituality. Spirituality is the calming center of peace that helps bring meaning, direction, and purpose to our lives (Hawley 1993). Religious dogma can certainly be one source for better understanding spirit and soul, but "hope, service, potential, vision, and faithfulness" (De Pree 1997) are nondenominational.

Virtues of spirit identified by Marcie (1997) have been discussed in "ancient as well as modern writings, so they are not new concepts" (p. 45). This "package of behaviors, attitudes, decisions, and policies that reflect the organization's spiritual essence" (p. 45) includes "trustworthiness, unity, respect and dignity, justice, service and humility" (p. 46).

Similarly, De Pree (1997) identified truth, access, discipline, accountability, nourishment for persons, authenticity, justice, respect, hope, workable unity, tolerance, simplicity, beauty and taste, and fidelity to a mission (pp. 100–112) as attributes of vital organizations that acknowledge and nurture individual and collective spirit.

Vital, imaginative school communities are needed that address the spiritual pain and disconnection educators feel (Palmer 1993). Just as personal change cannot be mandated, a school cannot coerce spiritual resources into being, nor do attributes such as integrity, trustworthiness, dignity, and respect simply appear because they are desirable. Each person must search their own soul to identify the ways in which their beliefs and behaviors honor spirit and hold one another accountable for behaving in ways that cause harm.

Transformation Point #3: Think Holistically

Think Holistically: Core middle grades practices have been implemented in a fairly compartmentalized fashion. While implementation of each component separately allows for careful study and refinement, it does not take into account the interactions and influences of the practices in total. Recognition is needed for a more holistic analysis of middle grades reform by people in the school who have new insights into self and spirit.

Core practices have emerged that characterize an effective middle school (McEwin, Dickinson, and Jenkins 1996; Kellough and Kellough 1996; Schurr, et al. 1995; Ames and Miller 1994; Clark and Clark 1994; George and Alexander 1993; Lounsbury 1992). These core practices include:

- A shared commitment to a *needs-responsive philosophy* that drives program and practice.
- Various *organizational structures* that promote the flexible use of time, space, and resources.
- Various *collaborative supports* that organize students, school personnel, parents, and community members on teams, councils, and partnerships.
- An *integrated curriculum* that makes connections within and between core (language arts, reading, math, science, social studies) and encore (fine arts, applied arts, health, physical education) subjects.
- A broad-based *exploratory program* that provides encore courses, minicourses, and cocurricular programs.
- An emphasis on *student advocacy* that addresses the affective needs of young adolescents.
- Use of *effective classroom practices* that engage and involve young adolescent learners.
- Authentic and varied *assessments* that monitor student and school progress.

In good faith, teachers and administrators have implemented new programs; purchased additional instructional materials; worked to get supportive policies in place at the district and building levels; informed parents and community about the changes underway in the school; and have then been called to task when less than expected results in school improvement were realized. Scratching their heads, middle grades advocates have gone back to the drawing board often to fine tune and tinker with the ways and means of bringing about the promise of middle school reform.

Unfortunately, as with sand castles, in too many school districts the creation of middle schools has eventually yielded to the educational equivalents of wind, pounding waves, and marauding teenagers, and too little attention to maintenance after the excitement of creation passes. . . . The outcome is that, while there may be nearly 15,000 schools that carry the designation of "middle school" by the end of the century, far fewer are likely to exhibit the core traits that make them effective learning environments for young adolescents. (George, Weast, Jones, Priddy, and Alfred 2000, p. 3)

Obviously, something is not working. We need to think differently about how core practices might be implemented, yet it is impossible to predict the possibilities from our current vantage point because we're looking through lenses limited by our past accomplishments and failures. Successes in the past need to be duplicated, yes; however, if that is all we strive to achieve, our past will become our future. Failures are learning opportunities indeed; yet overcoming mistakes alone will limit and narrow a potential for exceeding prior expectations.

Most schools implemented core practices initially by introducing parts of the model each year, building on the level of implementation over time. Once all components are in place, schools can begin to look at these practices more holistically. Thinking whole is different than parts thinking because the interaction and influence of practices, as well as the combined impact all practices have in total can be analyzed. Looking at the model in its entirety will require honesty, rather than defensiveness, so that the extraneous dead wood can be cut away to make room for new growth. If harvesting self and infusing spirit have been undertaken, the people in the schools making these analyses will be coming at it from a very different perspective.

Getting to transformation through breakthrough events

Individual paradigm shifts, a notion first introduced by Kuhn (1962), "what we might call the 'Aha' experience when someone finally 'sees' the composite picture in another way" (Covey 1989, p. 29) may be triggered by a breakthrough event. Planned carefully, a breakthrough event could provide paradigm shifting experiences that will "move us from one way of seeing the world to another. And those shifts create powerful change" (Covey 1989, p. 30).

Finding breakthrough events to operationalize the transformation points recommendations will require the same experimentation, innovation, and trial and error strategies that were needed to implement *Turning Points* recommendations. Simple solutions cannot be used to solve complex problems, and no single event will likely engage schools in the systemic, introspective, personal investigations that will result in truly reinvented middle schools. The following breakthrough events are therefore provided only as a starting point for the kinds of activities that might be developed as schools engage more deeply in the process of transformation.

Harvest the self through integrated staff development

Typically, staff development is thought of as an activity, a program, an event, or at best, a process that is external to the inner world of the teacher. It happens to teachers, who sometimes pick up kernels of new knowledge or skills, but often do not recognize that real growth is a choice, and are more likely prompted by events which occur outside the school. If middle schools are going to be truly reinvented, then staff development will need to be redesigned in ways that help teachers grow personally and will need to link the out-of-school lives and experiences of teachers to instructional improvement. Rethinking staff development should value the various routes that individual journeys might take and explore ways to explicate the sometimes random, often haphazard ways, that personal growth, or the lack of it, finds it way into classrooms.

Differentiated staff development is not a novel idea (Oliva and Pawlas 1997). Since we know that adults, like students, have varying learning needs and styles, it makes sense to allow individuals to make plans that address their unique needs. Even at best, however, individual plans most often focus solely on professional growth areas, and are not integrated so that teachers can better see the connections between their personal growth and teaching effectiveness.

Journaling, action research, team development, team advisory, and portfolios, are also not new techniques for staff development (Oliva and Pawlas 1997). These strategies have focused solely on instructional issues, however, which disconnect the teacher from other areas of growth. By embedding a personal growth component, each could be a more integrated method for life-long learning and renewal.

Table 2: Redesigned Integrated Staff Development Options

Activities	Group/Team Strategies	Individual/Personal Strategies	Making Connections
Journaling	Daily/weekly log of instructional decisions and outcomes	Daily/weekly log of personal decisions and outcomes	Readings Reflection
Action Research	Team/classroom inquiry on learning issues	Personal inquiry on problem	Readings Reflection
Team Development	Team designs and carries out improvement plan to increase team effectiveness	Identification of interpersonal dynamics related to teaming issue	Readings Reflection
Team Advisory	Conversation during team planning on team goal for affective development	Individual makes connection of topic to personal life	Readings Reflection
Portfolios	Individual or team documentation of class/unit/project	Documentation of personal life event	Readings Reflection

Reading and reflection help make the connections and clarify the interplay between personal and professional growth and instructional effectiveness. A broad range of materials could be used for these activities to encourage staff to engage in both professional and personal learning. Traditional references on middle school curriculum, instruction, and assessment could be read by individuals or teams. Likewise, more nontraditional references might help teachers understand the personal issues that sometimes inhibit professional engagement.

During team planning, building inservice, or district professional development, teachers could be provided opportunities to reflect on their experiences individually, in teams, or in larger group sessions where appropriate. The point is that time should be provided for the conversations teachers need to have that will support both their professional learning and personal growth. Just as the connections across subject areas often need to be made explicitly for students, the connections between teacher's role expectations in the classroom and life experiences they have outside of the classroom need to be uncovered.

Infuse spirit through conflict and crisis resolution

Conflict is a two-sided coin. Depending on your view, it can be a catalyst for change or a barrier to improvement. The conflict itself, however complex or simple, is less the problem than the strategies used for resolution. While some minor conflicts can be avoided, putting our heads in the sand and ignoring the underlying professional and personal conflicts to protect the school's public face does nothing more than cause the conflict to go underground. People in schools know conflict exists between teachers, between teachers and administrators, between school personnel and parents, and between adults and students. Denying these conflicts lacks honesty and creates a culture of subterfuge and sabotage; it is an unhealthy climate where students are expected to resolve their conflicts, although they see adults in the school behave differently. Unresolved conflicts create internal turmoil, and depending on the severity, source, and type of conflict, can drain energy, impede an individual's effectiveness, and seriously harm the sense of integrity in the school.

Breakthrough events will not always be positive. Some of our most significant shifts in the way we see schools result from an individual or collective crisis. Though we hope these are rare, accidents happen, violence occurs, and bad things happen to good people. Schools have gotten better at responding to crises, sadly because more and more of them occur. We know that counseling support is needed, that interventions are required for some students and adults, and that follow-up is necessary in some situations to mend the wounds incurred.

Both conflict and crisis provide opportunities for school personnel, parents, and community to undergo individual and collective paradigm shifts. As breakthrough events, these occurrences can help us see one another and our-selves differently so we can work together in more collaborative ways. By deal-ing with our differences with honesty, integrity, and respect, we build a sense of community that values the uniqueness of each human being. How a school deals with conflict and crisis is an indicator of the spirit, health, and vitality in the school. With purpose and insight, adults need to explore the ways in which school-related conflicts and crises intersect with their out of school life experi-ences, and how both may interfere with or support their effectiveness in the ed-ucational process of students.

Think holistically by modeling the model

The core practices that have emerged to meet the developmental needs of young adolescents, though not a recipe, form the basis of how an effective mid-dle school is defined. Good middle schools create nurturing environments that acknowledge and accept a wide range of students. Adults are not always treated with the same respect. Hawley (1993) contends that employees universally give an organization what they feel they are getting from it, so if we are not seeing what we think should happen in classrooms and schools, perhaps we need to look at the way we treat people. An eagle sees new vistas by soaring high above the clouds. So too, we must rise high above the school to know whether every-one in the building is modeling the exposed middle school philosophy and practices for themselves and one another.

• If the school's mission is "success for all students," how do we also provide "success for all adults?" Do we work hard at finding ways to utilize the strengths and talents of all staff, or do we rely instead on the same few to be on all of the committees, do all of the "extra" work, take on the leadership roles, and then wonder when they burn out what's wrong with them?

• If the school's philosophy is to "meet the social, emotional, physical, and intellectual needs of young adolescents," do we do the same for staff? Are the developmental needs of beginning, mid-career, and late-career teachers given due consideration in team organization, staff development, assignments, and supports?

• If the school is organized into "interdisciplinary teams" to create small communities of learning and support for students, do we promote teaming across the school? Do building administrators team or does the principal carry out a building-level instructional leadership role leaving all of the student disci-pline to the assistant principal? Are counselors, social workers, school nurses, and clerical and custodial staff on teams? Do we truly include parents on leader-ship or grade level teams, or is their involvement marginalized and peripheral?

• If the school provides an "integrated curriculum" to help students make connections between and across subject areas, is the same approach taken in staff development? Are teachers required to sit through a series of one-shot workshops on single topics, which may or may not apply to their particular growth needs, or are thematic plans developed to make connections across topics? Are parent sessions designed to help them better understand the interrelatedness of school activities, school policies, and programs, or do we dish out single topic presentations?

• If the school provides a "broad-based exploratory program" to allow students opportunity and choice, are adults allowed to make choices from a wide variety of options, or are all decisions made for them?

• If the school provides "student advocacy" through an advisory program and student personnel services, do we promote teacher advocacy, parent advocacy, or administrator advocacy as well? Are supports in place that help teachers, parents, and other educators navigate through the sometimes perilous politics of the school bureaucracy? Do all groups have the commitment to advocate for the important role that each plays in the education of students, or do we instead continue to promote the "us-them" mentality?

• If the school monitors student and school progress through "various authentic and performance-based assessments," are teachers, staff, and administrators evaluated the same way?

• If people in the school modeled the middle school model in their daily interactions, they would bestow on their students, themselves, and one another the gifts of integrity, respect, truth, access, honor, and trust through the fidelity of a shared philosophy, the unity of teaming, the authenticity of integrated curriculum, opportunity through exploration, the dignity of advocacy, and the accountability of authentic assessment.

Middle schools have used the term "transition" for several decades as a way to both describe the needed articulation between elementary, middle, and high school programs, as well as to describe the process of changing a traditional junior high school into a middle school (Clark and Clark 1994; Raebeck 1992; Spear 1992), but transition, according to De Pree (1997) really means much more than that.

> Transition is a matter and a process of becoming. Transition is a great deal more than change. It's a growing and maturing and an understanding and wisdom-gaining process. Transition gives us the opportunity to rise above polarization. Transition is a marvelous polishing of our intellectual and spiritual and emotional faculties. (p. 35)

Identifying and implementing practices that responded to the unique and ever-changing needs of young adolescents helped schools successfully transition

Table 3: Middle School Core Practices for Students and Adults

Core Practices	Implications for Students	Implications for Adults	Attributes and Outcomes for Spirituality
Philosophy	Decision making to meet the social, emotional, and intellectual needs of young adolescents.	Decision making to meet learning needs for early, mid, and late career professionals.	FIDELITY ↓ Integrity
Teaming	Small community of learning that connects students and adults.	Inclusive teaming for all adults in the school.	UNITY ↓ Respect
Integrated Curriculum	Instructional planning and delivery that links subject matter and learners.	Professional and personal development that links various topics.	AUTHENTICITY ↓ Truth
Exploratory	Instructional planning and delivery that provides choice and opportunity.	Personal and professional development that provides choice and opportunity.	OPPORTUNITY ↓ Access
Advisory	Student advocacy and support services.	Adult advocacy and support services.	DIGNITY ↓ Honor
Assessment	Authentic and performance-based assessments to monitor student and school progress.	Authentic and performance-based assessments to monitor teacher, staff, and administrator progress.	ACCOUNTABILITY ↓ Trust

to safer, more effective places of learning for students. Looking more holistically at this process gives us the opportunity to use the wisdom of maturity in order to not only meet, but to transcend earlier expectations of what middle schools might become.

Reinvention revisited

Blazing new paths is not foreign to middle level educators, who have made the progress they have because they have been nontraditional thinkers. The formation of the National Middle School Association broke the mold for membership in a professional association by encouraging teachers, administrators, university faculty, students, and parents to join together to promote the agenda for young adolescents. Similarly, middle grades educators began teaming long before it was vogue; understood the importance of relevant, integrated curriculum under pressure to focus on single subject mastery; and remained firm in the face of opponents who thought the middle school was too soft, too easy, and all fluff. Once again, it is time for middle level pioneers to break new ground in thinking about school reinvention.

Just as the *Turning Points* recommendations have had to undergo thoughtful consideration and various attempts at implementation, so too will transformation points recommendations need to be analyzed and digested for the possible ways they can be used to enhance school improvement. Breakthrough events that lead to paradigm shifts will enable adults to behave differently when they see things differently, and until they do, middle schools will not transform into their potential. What a crime that would be.

Hope for Sandy

I have often heard the public lament that what happens to children in some schools borders on being criminal. Sadly, in some cases this may be true and public outcry for these injustices should not cease until all problems are solved. All children deserve modern facilities, the latest technology, effective instruction, dedicated school personnel, supportive parents, and a caring community. So do the teachers, administrators, parents, and other adults who also come to school each day to learn and to grow. I don't hear much complaining about what happens to the Sandys in the school, and that, I believe, is criminal as well.

If there is any hope for Sandy, then her colleagues, her principal, her superintendent, her school board members, her parents, and ultimately Sandy herself will need to accept responsibility to reinvent middle schools by first reinventing themselves. Middle schools cannot cultivate, encourage, and support personal growth until the people in them, including Sandy, make harvesting the self a priority. Middle schools will not become sacred havens of dignity and integrity unless the people in them, including Sandy, infuse spirit into their daily lives. If middle schools really want to maximize the potential that the philosophy and practices have for students, then they need to see the model holistically and internalize it to reshape the school. Then, there is indeed hope for Sandy and for the promise of middle school to finally come true.

References

Ames, N., and Miller, E. (1994). *Changing middle schools: How to make schools work for young adolescents.* San Francisco, CA: Jossey-Bass.

Carnegie Council on Adolescent Development. (1989). *Turning points: Preparing American youth for the 21st century.* New York: Carnegie Corporation.

Clark, S., and Clark, D. (1994). *Restructuring the middle level school: Implications for school leaders.* Albany, NY: State University of New York Press.

Covey, S. (1989). *The seven habits of highly effective people: Restoring the character ethic.* New York, NY: Fireside.

De Pree, M. (1997). *Leading without power.* San Francisco, CA: Jossey-Bass.

Felner, R., Jackson, A., Kasak, D., Mulhull, P., Brand, S., and Flowers, N. (1997). The impact of school reform for the middle years. *Phi Delta Kappan, 78* (7), 528–532, 541–550.

Fullan, M. (1997). Emotion and hope: Constructive concepts for complex times. In M. Fullan (Ed.), *The challenge of school change: A collection of articles* (pp. 287–304). Arlington Heights, IL: Skylight.

George, P. S., and Alexander, W.M. (1993). *The exemplary middle school* (2nd ed.). New York, NY: Harcourt, Brace Jovanovich.

George, P., Weast, J., Joncs, L., Priddy, M., and Alfred, L. (2000). Revitalizing middle schools: The Guilford County process. *Middle School Journal , 31* (3), 3–11.

Hawley, J. (1993*). Re-awakening the spirit in work.* San Francisco, CA: Berrett-Loehler Publishers.

Kellough, R., and Kellough, N. (1996). *Middle school teaching: A guide to methods and resources* (2nd ed.). Columbus, OH: Prentice-Hall.

Kuhn, T. (1962). *The structure of scientific revolutions.* Chicago, IL: University of Chicago Press.

Lounsbury, J. (1992). Perspectives on the middle school movement. In J. Irvin (Ed.), *Transforming middle level education: Perspectives and possibilities* (pp. 3–15). Boston: Allyn & Bacon.

Marcie, D. (1997). *Managing with the wisdom of love: Uncovering virtue in people and organizations.* San Francisco, CA: Jossey-Bass.

McEwin, C. K., Dickinson, T.S., and Jenkins, D.M. (1996). *America's middle schools: Practices and progress—A 25 year persepctive.* Columbus, OH: National Middle School Association.

Magnusen, C. (1998). *Spirituality and leadership.* Unpublished manuscript. St. Louis University.

Oliva, P., and Pawlas, G. (1997). *Supervision for today's schools* (5th ed.). New York, NY: Longman.

Palmer, P. (1993). *To know as we are known: Education as a spiritual journey.* San Francisco, CA: Harper & Row.

Raebeck, B. (1992). *Transforming middle schools: A guide to whole-school change*. Lancaster, PA: Technomic Publications.

Shockley, R. (1992). Developing a sense of mission in middle schools. In J. Irvin (Ed.), *Transforming middle level education: Perspectives and possibilities* (pp. 93–101). Boston: Allyn & Bacon.

Schurr, S., Thomason, J., and Thompson, M. (1995). *Teaching at the middle level: A professional's handbook*. Lexington, MA: D.C. Heath & Co.

Spear, R. (1992). The process of change: Developing effective middle school programs. In J. Irvin (Ed.), *Transforming middle level education: Perspectives and possibilities* (pp. 102–138). Boston: Allyn & Bacon.

Yamanda, K. (1999). Quotation from motivational product created for Compendium Incorporated, Edmonds, WA.

4

The Arc of Equity in Reinvented Middle Schools

JANET E. McDANIEL, JUAN NECOCHEA,
FRANCISCO A. RÍOS, LAURA P. STOWELL,
CHARLOTTE KRITZER

California State University San Marcos

"The arc of a moral universe is long but it bends toward justice."
—Martin Luther King Jr.

Education for social justice is both a goal and a process. To realize the ideals of a just middle school that creates ethical, caring, involved citizens, we need to think of our work like that of architects, masons, engineers, geologists, and carpenters. We are building toward something not necessarily achievable in our lifetime, and we are also building a *process*—a process directed toward social justice. Social justice includes a vision of society in which the distribution of life chances is genuinely equitable and all members are physically and psychologically safe and secure—a society in which individuals are both self-determining (able to develop their full capacities) and interdependent (committed to interacting democratically with others). Social justice involves social actors who have a sense of their own agency as well as their social responsibility toward others and society as a whole (Adams, Bell, and Griffin 1997).

In his book *The Cathedral Within*, Shore (1999) discusses cathedral builders. Like Martin Luther King Jr., those who built cathedrals had a vision of what could be rather than what was, a vision many thought (and today still may think) impossible. Cathedral builders and advocates of social justice, middle level educators among these, work back from that vision, from their inner desire to be part of something larger than themselves and to make a difference in this world. They are devoted to a task that spans an entire career and still might well not be completed. They toil for something not bound by time, propelled by the collaborative energies through the ages of a multitude of participants. Diverse resources, materials, and talents are needed to build arcs, cathedrals, pyramids, and space stations. Likewise, building visionary and socially conscious middle schools requires the work of many—students, teachers, parents, social workers, policy makers, business owners, community leaders, textbook publishers, education advocates, and other professionals—who are intrinsically driven by their vision for the possible: the creation of a just and caring educational system for diverse students. In essence, everyone with the vision for social justice can contribute to the building of socially responsive middle schools, just as everyone can participate in the building of a morally just society for all our children.

No two arcs, cathedrals, or middle schools are identical. There is no pat formula or road map for success in achieving social justice and equity. But there are important lessons to be learned, stories to be shared, and essential principles to help guide us from those who have made significant progress on their journey toward a just and caring middle school. What are these lessons? We learn that one should not be afraid to risk failure; this task is a lifetime commitment; and many must work as one. "The most successful efforts to create social change are more rather than less inclusive, drawing on the shared strength of not just the experts, but the entire community" (Shore 1999, p. 265). Working toward social justice is not a task for loners or the faint-hearted.

Any structure must have a foundation in place before it can reach toward the sky. Just as an arc or a cathedral must be grounded and structurally sound, so too must some critical, systemic components be in place if we are to move toward social justice. What are the critical elements that allow us to move forward? The arc of justice must be grounded in both principle and practice. It must be visionary and functional. Builders cannot focus on one element to the exclusion of others. All must be embedded in a larger system and considered as interlocking and interacting parts.

Schorr and Wilson (1998) noted the folly of looking for quick fixes and easy answers to the challenges facing educators:

> The time has come to give up searching for a single intervention that will be the one-time fix—the lifetime inoculation—that will protect against the effects of growing up in neighborhoods of despair, violence and unemployment, in neighborhoods without decent schools, safe streets, stable families, or a sense of community. Forget about selecting among economic development, public safety, physical rehabilitation, community building, education reform, or service reform in an effort to find the single most promising way to intervene. . . . Take a broader view. (quoted in Shore 1999, p. 266)

When Schorr and Wilson (1998) examined thousands of models of excellent schools, effective job training, youth development, and antipoverty programs, they concluded, "we have learned to create the small exceptions that can change the lives of hundreds. But we have not learned how to make the exceptions to the rule to change the lives of millions" (p. 2). The arc, like the cathedral and the socially just middle school, is no longer about proving *whether* or not an idea works, but proving that those ideas that we *know* work can be taken to a larger scale.

Collins and Porras (1994) describe the characteristics of visionary companies that have endured, despite changing times and economic conditions. Visionary companies distinguish their core values and purpose (which should never change) from their operating practices (which should change constantly in response to a changing world). Visionary companies also commit to the daunting challenges of "big hairy audacious goals" (BHAGs). Like visionary companies, educators know what works for young adolescents. We know the work that needs to be done. The middle school reform reports of the 1980s and 1990s clearly laid out our BHAGs. They are deceptively simple: adolescents must have sustained, caring relationships with adults; receive guidance in facing serious challenges; become valued members of a constructive peer group; feel a sense of worth as a person. But for adolescents and those who work with them, these are in fact audacious goals.

This chapter seeks to describe the "big hairy audacious goals" that we believe will support the arc that bends toward justice in middle level schools. We set the stage by examining the developmental readiness of early adolescents to engage in the hard work of seeking social justice. We then look at some appropriate practices that are readily available to teachers in middle schools. We continue with a careful rendering of the key elements of what we believe to be a morally directed middle school movement: diversity and equity. We conclude with a program of professional development that would support the quest for social justice in the schooling of early adolescents.

Early adolescence: The developmentally opportune moment

Early adolescents are *developmentally capable*, given the opportunity and support, to engage in the complex issues associated with pursuing social justice. While early adolescence is a time of great change overall, educators' reactions to those changes shape the ways in which those changes influence middle level students (Berk 1996). For example, while middle level students are keen to question the contradictions they see between what adults say they value and how they actually behave, our response to their "identification" of these contradictions can either foster greater critical thinking or suppress it.

While acknowledging important individual variation, developmental psychology plays a significant role in informing us about general changes taking place for early adolescents and what we typically can and cannot expect from them. This work looks at changes in early adolescents' physical, psychological, cognitive, social, and moral growth. A key to these is the recognition that these changes are interrelated such that changes in physical growth, for example, impact how the middle level student feels about herself (psychological) and how she sees others (social) (Berk 1996).

The Swiss psychologist Jean Piaget's work is widely known in the education profession with respect to cognitive development. Piaget (as described by Wadsworth 1996) noted that early adolescents are moving from concrete operations—that is, "reasoning about and understanding" the concrete world—to formal operations—that is, "reasoning about and understanding" the abstract world of abstract ideas, principles, and laws. Young adolescents are also becoming more aware of their own thinking (meta-cognitive); they also begin to see knowledge not as absolute but rather as constructed by people and thus relative—that is, valued only to the degree that it is correct and helpful in specific situations (Perry 1970). In short, young adolescents are cognitively capable of reasoning about the reality and ideal of social justice, of thinking about why/how they come to that reasoning, and whether that reasoning is helpful/accurate for a specific situation.

Not only are early adolescents more reflective about their thinking, they are more reflective about themselves (personality development). While this might give the appearance of egocentrism, the reality is that middle level students are coming to think of themselves vis-à-vis others, especially their peers. Thus, early adolescents are keenly concerned about their own identity (the major developmental crisis, according to Erickson 1968) in relation to and in response from others. Gilligan (1992) argues that females in particular tend to develop their personal identity in the context of intimate and significant relationships with others.

One aspect of identity of particular salience to early adolescents is their own understanding of themselves as members of an ethnic group. This has two dimensions. The first is how students think about themselves in relation to ethnicity. For Euro-American middle level students, this means coming to recognize their "whiteness" as a concrete feature but also to recognize the privileges associated with their ethnicity. It also means dealing with negative feelings (guilt) associated with contemporary and historical instances of discriminatory behavior by whites against members of ethnic minority communities (Tatum 1992). Fortunately, middle level students want to work to overcome racism once they recognize that it exists (Quintana 1998) and that it conflicts with the ideals of our nation's democratic heritage.

For ethnic minority middle level students, experiences (both overt and subtle) of prejudice make them painfully aware of their differences from the mainstream (Quintana 1998). They must face decisions about whether they wish to (1) distance themselves from their ethnic roots and identify with the white mainstream (assimilate); (2) distance themselves from the mainstream and only associate with others from their ethnic group (separate); (3) distance themselves from both groups (become "raceless") (Fordham 1991); or (4) identify with both groups (integrate) (Phinney, Chavira, and Williamson 1992). Obviously, the choices they make depend upon the context and their development at the moment. These choices are made even more problematic for middle level students when academic achievement is associated with "acting white."

A second aspect of identity is how middle level students come to think about others based on ethnicity. Quintana (1998) points out that middle level students are operating on a level where they develop a social perspective of ethnicity. For middle level students, this means an understanding of subtle aspects of ethnicity—beyond food, fashion, and folklore to deeper aspects of differences in values, world-view, and especially socioeconomic connections to ethnicity, etc. Perhaps more importantly, it means an awareness that ethnicity is a key factor in social relations (e.g., ethnic differences in friendship patterns, especially having friends of one's own ethnic group) and an awareness of ethnic-based discrimination and prejudice.

As suggested earlier, connected with a greater awareness of the self is greater awareness of the social world (social development). According to Selman (1980), early adolescence is a time when middle level students are equally aware of their own perspective about phenomena and the perspectives of others (and that these might differ!). Importantly, the perspective of others includes those who the middle level student knows but also some "generic others" like themselves (e.g., teenagers generally) as well as "generic others" unlike themselves (e.g., people from a different cultural or socioeconomic background). This social perspective taking is critical to the development of empathy, care, respect, and kindness for others (central to the tenets of social justice) in middle level youth (MacQuiddy, Maise, and Hamilton 1987).

With respect to moral development, early adolescents are moving between moral decision making that bases what is "right" on what will be rewarded or what pleases others to decisions based on following the rules to preserve the social order (Kohlberg 1981). It is also a time when early adolescents are idealistic, are developing a strong sense of "fairness," and are interested in finding just, positive alternatives to prejudice and discrimination, especially when they have the opportunity to develop close friendships with those who differ from themselves (McEady-Gilliad 1994).

Collectively, middle level students seem "ripe" for school contexts that support a communal vision as well as instructional and curricular experiences directed at social justice. They are cognitively capable of (1) thinking about the ideals of social justice; (2) recognizing that identity and ethnicity, in the least, are salient aspects of living in this country and impact one's life chances; (3) taking the perspective of a variety of others to see whether the ideal of social justice is true for all; and (4) morally concentrating on issues of "fairness" central to any social justice framework.

It's also true that we need to support students in their movement along this path. We can do so by allowing students to work in concert with others, including adults. For their part, adults need to find ways to scaffold and support the learner in these new emerging ways of experiencing the self and the world within the context of pursuing a vision of social justice. In this way, Lev Vygotsky's (1962) work is instructive of how we can lead students toward the social justice arc: "What the child can do in cooperation today he can do alone tomorrow. Therefore the only good kind of instruction is that which marches ahead of development and leads it; it must be aimed not so much at the *ripe* as the *ripening* function" (p. 104). As the adults with a vision for a better society, we must be ahead of the youths in our care—helping them not only to dream that future but also to take steps that will bring us and them farther along the path.

Practices in support of the arc

When exploring what builds or hinders democratic practice in middle schools, we should turn to the central role of the teachers. As Thomas (1990) noted, "Our schools depend ultimately on the moral agency of the individual teacher" (p. 290). Teachers hold the key to making democratic practice in the middle school a success or failure. O'Loughlin (1995) observed that 95% of the time, students participate in "passive learning" environments where "mimetic" teaching occurs. Mimetic teaching is the transmission of information from the teacher to the student. Consequently, students' voices were absent. He found that when students are in democratic environments, this cycle of "mimetic" teaching ends and students benefit positively. Unfortunately, both new and experienced teachers can become socialized to taking power away from students. Herbert Kohl (1994) attributes this socialization to "modes of thinking and functioning . . . learned in teacher education schools, from colleagues, and supervisors" (p. 77). For example, novice teachers learn to fear being "out of control" and therefore they often adopt an "authoritarian" program that brings a more secure feeling.

Creating democratic schools is a long and sometimes arduous process. Kohl (1994) noted that "just as we as a nation are still struggling to achieve a democratic society, we as educators are still struggling to understand what education in a democracy should look like" (p. 125). Therefore, a middle school working toward social justice has a formidable yet not impossible endeavor. One of the problems hindering teachers is a lack of access to specific democratic curriculum, unlike what other disciplines offer. Wade (1995) argued that teachers are in the business of teaching what democracy means, but are they practicing it? She defined a democratic classroom as one in which students make choices and decisions that affect their daily lives in school. The student would say "our classroom" as opposed to the "teacher's classroom." Wade observed that one of our most meaningful teaching strategies is "hands on experience," yet many teachers are not practicing these strategies. Wade makes the Deweyan argument that students do not need isolated civic lessons; they need opportunities to practice civic behavior. There must be a platform in the classroom for this to occur.

Various definitions of democratic schooling have brought about different interpretations and implementation from school to school. Apple and Beane (1995) discuss and define what a democratic school looks like and argue that although "the idea of democratic schools has fallen in hard times, . . . we must keep the long tradition of democratic schools reform that has played a valuable role in making many schools lively and powerful places for those who go to them" (p. 3).

Apple and Beane (1995) characterize a democratic classroom as exhibiting:

- The open flow of ideas.
- Faith in the individual and collective capacity of people to create possibilities for resolving problems.
- The use of critical reflection and analysis to evaluate ideas, problems, and policies.
- Concern for the welfare of others and the common good.
- Concern for the dignity and rights of individuals and minorities.
- An understanding that democracy is not so much an ideal to be pursued as an idealized set of values that we must live and that must guide our life as a people.
- The organization of social institutions to promote and extend the democratic way of life.

These guidelines provide a foundation upon which educators can bring democracy to life. They suggest this can be done with a two-fold plan. One is by creating democratic "structures and processes," the other by creating a "democratic curriculum" (Apple and Beane 1995). An example of creating democratic structures and processes in middle schools is in the establishment of class meetings. Class meetings not only help create community in the classroom, but reinforce social skills and academic skills, such as listening, taking turns, hearing different points of view, negotiating meaning, and taking responsibility for one's own behavior (Bien and Stern 1994).

Academic lesson plans should also integrate democratic curriculum. Atwell (1987) defined a kind of reading program that offers teachers and students a democratic curriculum. Reading workshop is a reading program based entirely on student self-selected reading material. Students can read whatever they prefer, which is empowering to early adolescents.

Service learning is yet another instructional practice that supports social justice goals in middle schooling. Through service in support of the academic curriculum, early adolescents connect to the community and learn valuable citizenship skills that will serve them well as young adults. When middle school students become "resources, problem solvers, and producers of goods and services rather than passive, consuming members of the community," they help to repair the "rift" that too often characterizes the "school" versus "real" lives of youth (Fertman, White, and White 1996, p. 3).

While instructional practices such as these have long been available to individual teachers and schools, they have not been powerful enough to transform middle schooling in the way we envision. Many educators have simply given up on democracy as an ideal for structures and processes or curriculum, especially in the current political climate of academic standards, high-stakes testing, and accountability. Isolated practices have proven insufficient in light of these conditions. Comprehensive, explicit, and collaborative (whole-school) plans of action are required. The challenge of making a dent in an inequitable and uncaring system of schooling is enormous. Upon examination, we can see these challenges clearly; and we can see as well how we might envision a way through and beyond them.

Diversity and equity in middle schooling

The inequitable impact of middle level schooling on diverse students is well documented in the literature. The chronic school failure of students from diverse backgrounds—poor, minority, English language learners—has at times been considered a "normal" phenomenon of schooling, for these students are often viewed as unprepared to deal with the rigorous academic requirements of middle level education. To justify this school failure, educators often "blame the victims" for their inability to achieve in a school system that is essentially "rigged" against poor and minority students by incorporating a monochromatic pedagogical orientation that provides undeniable advantages or privileges to the dominant group (Euro-American, middle class, English speaking).

As a rule, therefore, students from the privileged group do well in middle schools, while those who vary from this modal group tend to experience school failure consistent with their degree of differentiation. The reasons are obvious: most structures, instructional practices, and other middle school systems are designed with little regard for poor, minority, and non-English-speaking students. To this formula of neglect, we can add the powerful but little understood social forces associated with the elusive organizational norms, expectations, and belief systems that tend to have compounded and disastrous consequences on students from diverse backgrounds because of the school "attitude" that relegates them to the lowest stratum of social and academic life. To achieve in middle school, therefore, diverse students have to fight multiple uphill battles, both structural as well as social, that render their chance of success almost nil, allowing only those with extreme self-determination and resiliency a slim chance to get out of the social pyramid's lower levels.

Rarely do middle school educators examine the structures, instructional practices, and attitudes that tend to produce these inequitable school outcomes. To increase equity in middle level schools, therefore, there must be recognition from policy makers and educators that school structures, instructional practices, and social attitudes often serve as insurmountable—albeit artificial—barriers to social justice. The basis for school reform must be an unequivocal and concerted movement toward the implementation of just and humane pedagogies that are aggressively created to meet the social and academic needs of diverse students. Rather than blaming students and their families, middle schools must drastically reform their organizational structures, instructional practices, and attitudes through "deep reflective-action" as they consider their essential role in achieving educational equity for all students. Indeed, equity must be viewed as an essential outcome of schooling, a mission to give diverse students their due, and a powerful calling for middle school educators to create learning communities that follow basic principles of justice and fairness in an increasingly diverse society.

Although there has been some recent progress in the journey toward educational equity, particularly at the awareness and rhetorical levels, our democratic goal of "equity for all" in middle level education is still a distant and elusive dream that is often compromised by the flurry and pendulum-swing of school reforms. The recent "back to basics" movement—including high stakes testing, teacher accountability, standards, traditional transmission pedagogy, sage-on-the-stage, no social promotion, phonemic awareness—is of particular concern for those in search of just, caring, and humane learning environments at the middle level for diverse students. In spite of the rhetoric of holding schools accountable for student performance, the results of these back to basic reforms are predictable: invariably those who find themselves on the short end of the stick of school change will be poor, minority, and non-English speaking.

Indeed, recent back to basics reform efforts, especially high-stakes testing and the standards movement, may become effective mechanisms to sort and classify students according to their degree of variation from the privileged group, committing poor and minority students to the lower echelons of the school's academic strata. The perceived threat to classroom teachers and principals of holding them accountable if test scores do not improve will not result in educational equity for diverse students. Rather, the response will focus on quick fixes as more and more instructional time is dedicated to "teaching to the test." The current frenzy to improve test scores will likely result in a reduction of curricular offerings in poorly achieving diverse communities as "frivolous" (e.g., art and music) content is removed from the curriculum as schools move toward a test-driven instructional program. This test frenzy exacerbates an already existing reduction of opportunities for inner city students to access college-prep, honors classes. These classes remain abundant and readily available to students in high SES settings, guaranteeing privileged access to upper echelon universities. The potential for student success in society is a reflection of the structural inequities found in their schools. Opportunity and privilege trump potential and motivation every time on this uneven playing field.

For many, public education appears to function as an effective mechanism that duplicates the social strata in society, with the resulting tendency toward the maintenance of the status quo and the tenacity of traditions that fail in the schooling of students from diverse backgrounds. With this custodial orientation, what schools value highly are conformity, assimilation, and traditional instructional practices, often under the guise of educational reform. Indeed, school reform for many poor and minority students is more like a "rearrangement of the furniture" rather than a fundamental change in the essence of teaching.

Equity requires a drastic departure from tinkering with reform, toward bold new pedagogical paradigms that will result in the creation of just and humane learning communities in middle schools. The search for equity in middle schools may be viewed as a justice journey that began during the birth of this nation. This beginning is best illustrated by Thomas Jefferson, when he established the rights which were to become the often quoted foundation of a democratic, free society: the rights to life, liberty, and the pursuit of happiness. Although these rights were initially intended only for white wealthy males, they nevertheless set the nation in motion with a firm philosophical foundation of social justice that formed the democratic ideals of American society. Certainly, if "life, liberty, and the pursuit of happiness" was a good principle that applied to wealthy white males, then it must also be good for poor white males, women, and minorities. Therefore, in many ways, the fight for social justice could be viewed as an extension of these "rights" to other groups within the U.S. population. Although the final destination may never be reached, the social justice arc that comprises the American ideal for educational equity at the middle level must continue to incorporate effective pedagogy for poor, minority, and English language learners current in our schools.

Envisioning the arc in middle schooling

Using Jeffersonian logic as a point of departure for democratic education, middle schools in a multicultural society should guarantee four basic individual rights for students from diverse backgrounds: the right to learn, the right to hope, the right to dream, and the right to self-determine (Necochea & Cline 1999). If middle school pedagogy were designed with these rights at the center of reform, then a very different paradigm than the "back to basics," high-stakes testing, and elevated standards would be at the forefront of the change process. A middle school curriculum that is "rights driven" would place the students, their culture, and their language at the forefront of the change process, with the explicit directive to address the diverse linguistic, social, and academic needs of an increasingly diverse student population. Rather than playing a social replication function, schools would design pedagogy that utilizes the strength of diverse students for the explicit purpose of allowing them to reach their maximum potential, without restrictions associated with their language background, ethnicity, and social economic status. Unhampered by the current structures and systems that favor the dominant group, students from diverse backgrounds would be able to chart their own journey as they fulfill their destiny as productive members of society. Thus, rather than playing the insidious replication role, middle schools could see their primary function as that of creating pedagogy that unleashes the potential inherent within every child. This would allow diverse students to become the "person they wish to become" and begin to more genuinely approach the democratic ideals that Americans hold dear.

To alter the replication role that schools currently play necessitates a fundamental change in reform efforts toward the implementation of contextualized learning environments (CLEs). Rather than a "quick fix" or "one best system" approach to reform, a contextualized learning environment is guided by the meticulous and careful alignment of student profiles, school structures, and social press. Transforming middle schools so that they become more just and humane institutions will require that reform focus on meeting the social and academic needs of the growing diversity of students. "Best practice" for a particular middle school, then, would be determined on a case-by-case basis as the diversity of students is used as the fundamental mechanism to determine the reform journey. Let us examine each of the components needed for the creation of CLEs at the middle level.

Student profile is defined as the rich personal histories that students bring to schools, including their language and culture, socioeconomic background, family stories, learning styles, strengths and weaknesses, as well as the school experiences that young adolescents have had as a result of their personal characteristics. Generally speaking, middle schools are currently suited to serve a delimited student profile—usually middle class, white, English-speaking students with linguistic and mathematical strengths, two-parent home, and an ability to "sit still" for six hours a day (Gay 1994; Legters and McDill 1994; Necochea and Cline 1993). Students who are consistent with this profile are generally successful within the school system, for middle school curriculum was generally developed with this success profile in mind. Similarly, deviation from this success profile is likely to result in school failure due to incompatibilities between teaching practices and the needs of diverse students. While this school failure may not manifest itself immediately, sadly it becomes too obvious during the high school years.

School structure refers to the instructional strategies, curriculum, standards, assessment procedures, grading systems, age-level groupings, scheduling of classes, discipline approaches, staff development, and other organizational routines that define "how business gets done here." These school structures are usually designed for efficiency, resulting in a tendency to continue the "factory model" (Gay 1994) as the premier educational paradigm into the twenty-first century, with rational, hierarchical, bureaucratic school organizations that are cost-effective at mass-producing graduates. Indeed, from a more cursory analysis, middle school faculties are divided into "specialties," with every teacher responsible for a particular component (content area) of the educational assembly line, supervised by administrators, and organized into various units. Although current reform rhetoric gives the appearance of deep transformations in the schooling process, a critical analysis reveals that, for the most part, middle schooling has not been transformed into a radically different structure.

Social press refers to a complex, interactive, and integrative process that pertains to elusive although powerful social-psychological school factors, such as norms, values, and expectations, which assign a "social status" to students, from those who are "most desirable" to those who are the "least." Social press is related to group dynamics that are rather difficult to quantify, define, or even understand, but appear to have a profound influence on student success. The social forces at play within the school community produce a "social preference" for high status students (usually compliant, middle class, English speaking). This preference usually determines the treatment that students receive in ways that profoundly impact their cultural identity, self-esteem, motivation, academic success, and social acceptance.

The current reform agenda for most schools, epitomized by high-stakes testing, the standards movement, and accountability, is not likely to result in the creation of contextualized learning environments for diverse students or fundamental change in school structures. On the contrary, the pressures for middle schools to go "back to the future" create systems which will inevitably lean towards "sorting and classifying" students as a natural outcome of the reform initiatives. Poor and minority students are usually sorted and classified into the lowest rungs of the social and academic ladder of middle schools. "The more things change, the more they remain the same" is an appropriate cliché that may explain the inherent inequities in the current high stakes school reform agenda.

Middle school reform, therefore, must deemphasize the current high stakes commotion by addressing the developmental, social, and academic needs of early adolescent students through a concerted effort to create contextualized learning environments for all children. We advocate the implementation of a contextualized learning environment through the application of systems thinking (Wheatley 1994; Keefe and Howard 1997) to a comprehensive professional development program.

Professional development toward a more just middle school

As we have suggested, individual activities and small groups of committed, socially responsible educators will never create the change we know to be powerful for the widest circle of learners. We need to consider the whole system of schooling. Systems thinking, in the world of professional development, allows for an analytical process that will provide a deeper understanding of the critical interdependent and interconnected relationships of the key components that will lead to fundamental change (Keefe and Howard 1997; Tyack and Cuban 1995; Wheatley 1994). Indeed, the creation of just and humane middle schools that address the social and academic needs of diverse students necessitates the design of new professional development paradigms that are all encompassing. The arc will bend toward social justice only when professional development activities have as their essential purpose the transformation of middle schools, rather than ancillary and transitory goals driven by reform frenzies that come and go at the same rate as our "education politicians," creating havoc for middle school educators. Oftentimes staff developers look to one aspect of the whole, such as professional growth activities, while neglecting to see how this will impact or be interconnected to other parts of the system, such as principal support for the innovations sought (Keefe and Howard 1997). Without consideration for other essential components, therefore, institutionalization of reform is unlikely because other key system parts will not support the fundamental changes needed.

Professional development is, by definition, an essential element of reform initiatives in middle level schools attempting to create just and caring educational environments. Therefore, policy makers and practitioners engaged in middle level reform must understand the different components that will increase the probability of institutionalizing the changes sought by implementing effective staff development programs. Otherwise, as Tyack and Cuban (1995) noted, the resiliency of school organizations to fundamental change invariably leads to the perpetuation of the status quo, particularly after the original reformers disappear from the scene, even as claims to reform are being made.

To increase the effectiveness of a professional development program using Wheatley's (1994) lens on system thinking, the interactive and interconnected nature of the key components must be uncovered to be able to focus on the "deeper, embedded processes" that will result in improved learning for middle level schools. Addressing systems thinking, Wheatley said:

We need to learn more about this "interweaving of processes" that leads to structure. In ways we have never noticed, the whole of a system manages itself as a *total* system through natural processes that maintain its integrity. It is critical that we see these processes. It will shift our attention away from the parts, those rusting holdovers from an earlier age of organization, and focus us on the deeper, embedded processes that create whole organizations. (p. 118)

Here we will present the essential "interweaving of processes" that are needed for an effective professional development program toward a socially just middle school. Although these components are presented individually, their separation is rather artificial because of the difficulties of isolating complex conceptual categories when applying system theory to social phenomenon. The obvious overlaps of the components will be implicit in the individual descriptions, where comments related to one component can at times be attributed to the other. The separation noted, therefore, is analytical, rather than practical; thus it is to be viewed as a conceptual explanation of a complex social phenomenon associated with the implementation of effective staff development programs for middle schools. What follows is a brief discussion of the critical components of staff development for middle level schools.

All-inclusive. In systems thinking, the professional development program is designed to be all-inclusive, implying that all members of the school participate. The reasoning for this is simple: the program should address the essential structures and instructional practices of schooling, particularly those that most influence the creation of a just and caring learning environment. It is critical that all voices and perspectives are heard, especially those who have traditionally been disenfranchised or excluded (e.g., secretaries, custodians, and paraprofessionals). Parents and community members also must have an opportunity to understand their roles and contributions to the transformation of the school. When professional development programs become all-inclusive, teachers, classified employees, administrators, parents, and community supporters have a unique opportunity to interact with each other, building bonds across levels and thus increasing cohesiveness in the middle level program.

Preservice professional preparation. An effective starting point for a comprehensive professional development program is the preparation of teachers before they are hired into middle schools. The lack of teachers who achieve their licensure through middle level teacher education programs is well-documented (McEwin and Dickinson 1997). The vast majority of early adolescents pass through middle school never having been taught by a teacher who intended to teach middle school and/or secured preservice preparation and licensure in middle grades education. Regardless of the type of preservice program, more than half of middle grades teachers rated their preparation to respond to students' cultural and language diversity "poor" or "inadequate" (Scales and McEwin 1996). Clearly, there is a need to start the professional development of middle school teachers in a more rational manner than "sink or swim" or "on-the-job training." A comprehensive program of middle school teacher education can make a difference in the preparation of teachers to work toward social justice (Ríos, McDaniel, Stowell, and Christopher 1995). Until specific middle school teacher preparation programs and licensure become the norm, however, professional development programs will need to continue to carry the weight of both initial and continuing education for many teachers of early adolescents.

Principal leadership. An appropriate axiom guides this key component: principals should not require teachers to participate in professional growth activities that they are not willing to engage in themselves. The symbolic messages that reverberate throughout the organization, especially in terms of the expected norms for life-long learning, become a powerful driving force that tends to augment the importance of staff development when the principal is actively engaged in the activities. Only when issues of social justice and equity become visibly important to the principal are they likely to become a fundamental part of staff development.

Also, it is critical that principals play an active supportive role, particularly for teachers who are ready to implement the innovations sought, as well as to include defending those who fail from possible organizational sanctions. The principal's support must be made public and notorious so that others know the organizational expectations with regard to implementation.

In the matter of teacher evaluation, principals should incorporate commentaries on the "transfer of skills" or changes in teacher behaviors that support just and caring classrooms. If the creation of a socially just middle school is important to the organization, then it should become part of the evaluation process.

Materials and resources. Perhaps nothing is more frustrating to a teacher who attends a great staff development program than being unable to obtain the materials and resources needed for implementation of suggested instructional practices. Providing the materials and resources (e.g., time) requested by classroom teachers to design lessons in accordance with the suggested instructional strategies facilitates the fundamental changes required to meet the needs of diverse students.

On-going and long-term. The literature has well documented the ineffectiveness of one-shot professional development in terms of the transfer of skills into the classroom. Indeed, creating contextualized learning environments will necessitate on-going, long-term staff development that focuses on what teachers need to do to transform schooling at the middle level. In addition, on-going long-term professional development more closely approximates the idea of life-long learning, a necessary condition for any learning organization. This commitment to long-term professional development must be guided by the vision of social justice, thus providing participants with a framework to anchor the program.

Celebrating diversity. The creation of contextualized learning environments requires a professional development program that views diversity as an asset, and that becomes part of the daily experiences of students as it is cultivated and incorporated into all school programs. Similarly, the language and culture of diverse students must be viewed as important tools that will become part of the school program. In this manner, the staff development program will also target the preparation of school personnel toward meeting the academic and social needs of diverse students, always working through their strengths and particularities. The success of students, therefore, especially poor and minority, is regarded as an artifact of who they are rather than "in spite of" who they are. In this regard, the difficult task of middle level teachers is to "reveal" the students as they help them become the persons they want to become. Rather than blaming the victims for their failures, there is a concerted effort to acquire practices that are effective for diverse students. Such staff development must also be explicitly and robustly antiracist. The arc of the moral universe that bends toward social justice is saturated with the values and voices inherent in the diverse community.

Collegial observation and feedback. The importance of teachers observing others and receiving feedback from colleagues about the transformation of practice is extremely important. Teaching has often been described as the "lone-ranger" profession, whereby events occur largely in isolation and full autonomy from colleagues. Due to this isolation and autonomy norm, rarely do teachers actively collaborate with others for the purpose of improving instructional practices. Therefore, as part of becoming reflective practitioners who participate in meta-analytical processes, middle level teachers engaged in transforming schooling must have the opportunity to observe other professionals, give and receive feedback, and actively collaborate with others in creating contextualized learning environments for diverse students. Establishing the norm of professional collegiality within the school serves as a model for building the community critical to the pursuit of social justice.

Support from the greater organization. Large-scale transformations in middle schools will not occur in the absence of support from the greater organization. It is not uncommon, for example, for progressive teachers to clash with the traditional or custodial orientation of middle schools, thus making it extremely difficult for the systemic implementation of contextualized learning environments in diverse settings. Systemic implementation of new structures is doomed without active support from the greater organization of personnel such as other teachers, administrators, and school board members.

Bottom-up professional development. Unquestionably, professional development must have a school-centered orientation, driven by the specific social and academic needs of students in particular settings, and focused on providing teachers the strategies and skills required to implement contextualized learning environments for diverse students. It is not surprising that schools respond begrudgingly to professional development mandates emerging from external agencies that fail to honor the voices of those who are closest to students in classrooms. Consequently, the school-level resistance—even sabotage—of the mandated changes is a "natural" response, particularly when school personnel view the "required" changes as meddlesome, ineffective, or counterproductive. If middle school teachers are to be agents of change, par excellence, for social justice, then their voices must be the raison d'être for the professional development program at the local site.

Conclusion

Implementing contextualized learning environments for diverse students that will lead to social justice and equity and, thus, protect the natural rights to learn, to hope, to dream, and to self-determine requires that middle schools reinvent current structures and practices by designing and implementing comprehensive, site-specific professional development programs. To achieve this, the critical components for systemic implementation must be distilled for the purpose of understanding their interactive and overlapping nature as they determine the eventual success or institutionalization of socially just structures and systems. We proposed several components that could lead to more effective professional development activities for middle schools with diverse student populations. In systems thinking, the intensity or degree of presence of critical components will largely determine whether or not an innovation will be fully institutionalized. Therefore, those interested in designing successful programs that lead to more just and humane learning environments for all students must understand the interactive nature or "systemic influence" of key components to be able to create conditions that will result in changes to the essence of schooling. Leaving a key component "inactivated" may result in partial implementation, or worse, abandonment of the desired transformations. In this scenario, the more middle schools change the more they remain the same. Equity will require a change in every aspect of the school. To say it differently, we cannot continue to do the same things and expect to get different results. The journey of middle school reform must continue toward the destination of social justice and equity.

We return to our thinking about cathedral builders and the lessons they provide to middle school educators. Most middle school educators want to build educational cathedrals. Most middle school educators see the beacon for socially just middle schools at a distance. So, what is getting in the way? They need leadership in discovering their path. They need to reconnect with the teaching souls that compelled them to become middle school educators. They need to become participants in something bigger than themselves. They need to be part of a grandiose plan that catapults them toward the creation of just and caring middle schools for diverse students. They need to see themselves participating in a marathon, not a sprint—as providing light, not lightning—as participants in the struggle for the long haul. They need to see the arc of the moral universe bend toward justice as a result of their collective passion and commitment to make a difference with middle school students. For this, we owe them the tools to make their difficult journey possible.

As visionary Deborah Meier says, "The question is not, Is it possible to educate all children well?" but rather, "Do we want to do it badly enough?" (Meier 1995, p. 4). We have the tools to build our arc toward morally just middle schools. We know the tasks as well. The question remains, "Do we have the will?"

References

Adams, M., Bell, L., and Griffin, P. (1997). *Teaching for diversity and social justice: A sourcebook*. New York: Routledge.

Apple, M.W., and Beane, J. A. (Eds). (1995). *Democratic schools*. Alexandria, VA: Association for Supervision and Curriculum Development.

Atwell, N. (1987). *In the middle: Writing, reading, and learning with adolescents*. Portsmouth, NH: Heinemann.

Berk, L.E. (1996). *Infants, children, and adolescents*. Needham Heights, MA: Allyn & Bacon.

Bien, E.C., and Stern, S.S. (1994, March). *Democracy as discipline*. Paper presented at the annual meeting of the National Association of School Psychologists.

Collins, J., and Porras, J. (1994). *Built to last: Successful habits of visionary companies*. New York: Harper.

Erickson, E. (1968). *Identity: Youth and crisis*. New York: Horton.

Fertman, C.I., White, G.P., and White, L.J. (1996). *Service learning in the middle school: Building a culture of service*. Columbus, OH: National Middle School Association.

Fordham, S. (1991). Peer-proofing academic competition among black adolescents. In C.E. Sleeter (Ed.), *Empowerment through multicultural education*, (pp. 69–93). Albany, NY: SUNY Press.

Gay, G. (1994). *At the essence of learning: Multicultural education*. West Lafayette, IN: Kappa Delta Pi.

Gilligan, C.F. (1992). *In a different voice*. Cambridge, MA: Harvard University Press.

Keefe, J.W., and Howard, E. R. (1997). *Redesigning schools for the new century: A systems approach*. Reston, VA: National Association of Secondary School Principals.

Kohl, H. (1994). *I won't learn from you*. New York: New Press.

Kohlberg, L. (1981). *The philosophy of moral development: Moral stages and the idea of justice*. San Francisco: Harper & Row.

Legters, N., and McDill, E. L. (1994). Rising to the challenge: Emerging strategies for educating youth at risk. In R. J. Rossi (Ed.), *Schools and students at risk: Context and framework for positive change* (pp. 23–50). New York: Teachers College Press.

MacQuiddy, S.L., Maise, S.J., and Hamilton, S. (1987). Empathy and affective perspective taking in parent identified conduct disordered boys. *Journal of Clinical and Child Psychology, 16*, 260–268.

McEady-Gilliad, B. (1994). Preface. In M.L. Manning (Ed.), *Celebrating diversity: Mulituicultural education in middle level schools*. Columbus, OH: National Middle School Association.

McEwin, C.K., and Dickinson, T.S. (1997). Middle level teacher preparation and licensure. In Irvin, J.L. (Ed.), *What current research says to the middle level practitioner* (pp. 223–229). Columbus, OH: National Middle School Association.

Meier, D. (1995). *The power of their ideas: Lessons for America from a small suburban school in Harlem*. Boston: Beacon Press.

Necochea, J., and Cline, Z. (1993). Building capacity in the education of language minority students. *The Educational Forum, 5* (4), 402–412.

Necochea, J., and Cline, Z. (1999). The role of education in the pursuit of equity and social justice in diverse settings. In Z. Cline, J. Necochea, and J. Brown (Eds.), *Advances in confluent education: Multicultural dynamics of educational change* (pp. 3–15). Stamford, CT: JAI Press.

O'Loughlin, M. (1995). Daring the imagination: Unlocking voices of dissent and possibility in teaching. *Theory into Practice 34* (2), 107–115.

Perry, W.G., Jr. (1970). *Forms of intellectual and ethical development in the college years*. San Diego: Academic Press.

Phinney, J.S., Chavira, V., and Williamson, L. (1992). The acculturation attitudes and self-esteem among high school and college students. *Youth and Society, 23*, 299–312.

Quintana, S.M. (1998). Children's developmental understanding of ethnicity and race. *Applied and Preventive Psychology, 7*, 27–45.

Ríos, F.A., McDaniel, J.E., Stowell, L.P., and Christopher, P.A. (1995). Sharing the responsibility: A study of a comprehensive approach to teacher preparation for cultural and linguistic diversity in urban middle level schools. *Research in Middle Level Education, 18* (2), 89–103.

Scales, P.C., and McEwin, C.K. (1996). The effects of comprehensive middle level teacher preparation programs. *Research in Middle Level Education Quarterly, 19*(2), 1–21.

Schorr, L., and Wilson, W.J. (1998). *Common purpose: Strengthening families and neighborhoods to rebuild America*. New York: Doubleday.

Selman, R.L. (1980). *The growth of interpersonal understanding: Developmental and clinical analyses*. San Diego: Academic Press.

Shore, B. (1999). *The cathedral within*. New York: Random House.

Tatum, B.D. (1992). Talking about race, learning about racism. *Harvard Educational Review, 62*(1), 1–24.

Thomas, B.R. (1990). The school as a moral learning community. In J.I. Goodlad, R. Soder, and K.A. Sirotnik (Eds.), *The moral dimensions of schooling* (pp. 266–295). San Francisco: Jossey-Bass.

Tyack, D., and Cuban, L. (1995). *Tinkering towards Utopia: A century of public school reform*. Cambridge, MA: Harvard University Press.

Vygotsky, L.V. (1962). *Thought and language*. Cambridge, MA: MIT Press.

Wade, R. (1995). Civic ideal into practice: Democracy in the elementary school. *Social Studies and the Young Learner, 8*, 16–18.

Wadsworth, B.J. (1996). *Piaget's theory of cognitive and affective development*. White Plains, NY: Longman.

Wheatley, M.J. (1994). *Leadership and the new science: Learning about organizations from an orderly universe*. San Francisco: Berrett-Koehler.

Curriculum Issues

5

Standards, Students, and Exploration: Creating a Curriculum Intersection of Excellence

P. ELIZABETH PATE
The University of Georgia

Newspapers, journals, legislatures, and the media across the United States are publishing articles and voicing opinions about educational standards and their impact on schools and students. At the 1996 National Education Summit, 44 governors and 50 corporate CEOs joined together with a commitment to the following set of priorities fundamental to achieving excellence in the nation's system of K–12 education (Achieve 1998):

- High academic standards and expectations for all students.
- Tests that are more rigorous and more challenging, to measure whether students are meeting those standards.
- Accountability systems that provide incentives and rewards for educators, students, and parents to work together to help students reach these standards.

So, what are standards and whose standards are they? Gordon Vars, a key leader of middle level education for decades, says standards are "society's expectations" (Vars 1999), expectations of what students should know and be able to do. Standards remind me of the movie *Gremlins*, a movie about little multiplying creatures. One minute there is one and when you turn around there are four and then eight. Standards are like gremlins . . . multiplying at the whim of whomever. According to O'Hair, McLaughlin, and Reitzug (2000), the whomevers include private foundations, nonprofit lobbying groups, professional associations, textbook publishers, makers of standardized tests, media companies, state governments, professional organizations, business and industries, and local, state, and national policy makers and educators. In a recent search of Library-In-The-Sky (Northwest Regional Educational Laboratory 2000) I came across links for standards for civics, the arts (e.g., dance, music, theater, visual arts), core subject areas (e.g., language arts, mathematics, science, history, geography), work skills, economics, foreign language, health, vocational, physical education, assessment, technology, behavioral studies, and life skills. I also found association standards (e.g., National Council of Teachers of Mathematics, International Reading Association, National Science Teachers Association). As well, I found state standards (e.g., Georgia Quality Core Curriculum [QCC], Texas Essential Knowledge and Skills [TEKS], Maine Learning Results, Washington Essential Academic Learning Requirements).

Increasingly, standards are driving test scores and test scores are driving the curriculum. What does this mean to the middle school movement? Recently, John Lounsbury, a key leader of middle level education for several decades, remarked, "*We are in danger of winning the battle of test scores but losing the battle of education.*" When Dr. Lounsbury made this statement to a class of preservice middle school teachers at The University of Georgia, it gave me goose bumps. Goose bumps because I knew his prediction may come true.

In the midst of a standards-based and testing reform era, is it appropriate to ask: Can standards be implemented in a true middle school? Can the school that claims to be an "exploratory school" and a "responsive school" create learning environments that also promote excellence? Can we do anything about changing the climate to be one of winning the battle of education and raising test scores at the same time? Can integrated curriculum fit with these and other demands? Standards, students, and the need for exploration *can* be woven into complimentary and supportive relationships within a model of curriculum integration.

According to *This We Believe* (National Middle School Association 1995), developmentally responsive middle level schools should provide curriculum that is challenging, integrative, and exploratory. Curriculum in middle schools should address the needs of students. Young adolescents display a wide range of intellectual ability. They prefer active learning experiences, especially in combination with peer interactions. Young adolescents also respond positively to learning in the context of real life situations and may not show much interest in studying formal academic subjects in school (National Middle School Association 1995). Curriculum that addresses the needs of students should be relevant, engaging, and rigorous (Beane 1998). Curriculum should encourage responsibility and accountability (Haberman 1991; Higgs and Tarsi 1997). Curriculum should utilize appropriate and available resources (Pate, Homestead, and McGinnis 1997). Curriculum should be democratic in nature (Apple and Beane 1995; Dayton and Glickman 1994). Curriculum should provide meaningful involvement in the school and larger community (Baker 1996; Bernard 1993).

Curriculum integration is challenging, exploratory, and addresses the needs of middle school students. It involves the collaboration with students and teachers on what is to be learned, why it is to be learned, how it is to be learned, and how it is to be assessed. James Beane (1997) defines curriculum integration as

> . . . a curriculum design that is concerned with enhancing the possibilities for personal and social integration through the organization of curriculum around significant problems and issues, collaboratively identified by educators and young people, without regard for subject-area boundaries. (pp. x–xi)

In curriculum integration, themes of study are developed around student interests and concerns with mandated content and skills addressed within the themes. Themes might revolve around environmental problems (e.g., Learning and Living Together: Saving the Etowah Watershed), racial issues (e.g., If I Were in Your Shoes?), societal needs (e.g., Pulling Together to Prevent Domestic Violence), and personal concerns (e.g., School Cafeteria Food: What Can We Do About It?). The role of the teacher in curriculum integration shifts to that of facilitator and instigator of learning. The teacher is no longer viewed as the "keeper and dispenser of knowledge" but rather the "seeker and co-learner of knowledge." The role of the student in curriculum integration also shifts. Students become active rather than passive participants in their own learning. In a curriculum integration classroom, context revolves around the dynamics of teaching and learning.

In *Curriculum Integration: Designing the Core of Democratic Education* (Beane 1997), Beane maintains there can be an intersection of excellence between standards, students, and exploration. He states:

> It is true that the curriculum almost everywhere is shaped by widely held expectations regarding basic skills, by goals and mandates that are remarkably similar across states and local districts, by nationally administered standardized tests, and by widely distributed resources such as textbooks and taped television documentaries. But it is also true that the curriculum is shaped by the local politics of textbook selection, the demands of special-interest groups, the desires of various parents, the aspirations of particular students, and, of course, the beliefs of teachers who finally decide about the curriculum when they close their classroom doors. (pp. 90–91)

This statement gets to the heart of curriculum integration: democracy. Schools in general should be a place where democracy is lived and learned. They should be a place where decisions are made by students and teachers through consensus rather than majority rule. Every person in the classroom should have a voice. Each person should have the right to be taken seriously and be involved in decision making.

Curriculum integration takes place in a democratic classroom community and does not ignore standards, rather, it embraces them (Nesin and Lounsbury 1999). It should be implemented in middle schools not only to improve student learning and increase student achievement but to provide opportunities for collaborations to occur which foster trust, risk-taking, empathy, and exploration.

So how does a teacher make sense of standards and address them in a curriculum that is responsive, relevant, and engaging? The best way to provide an answer to this question is through telling stories: stories of middle school teachers who are addressing standards, students, and the need for exploration within a model of curriculum integration; stories from real students and teachers engaged in making decisions about the curriculum; and stories from schools where work is shared and honored with classroom doors open. Emphasis in the following stories will be placed on what and how standards were met.

Kids in P.C. (partial control)

Sixth grade students in Julie Payne's language arts class at Clarke Middle School spent weeks working on an Internet project. Julie, along with Nancy Lewis and Shannon Flynn (undergraduate preservice teachers), started by introducing a rough idea for an Internet project to her students. Julie also told the students there were important things she must still teach them related to language arts during the project. As a group, Julie and her students decided what their goals would be and how they would be met. After much discussion, the group decided to do a project that would help all sixth grade teachers in the school in their knowledge of Internet sites useful for their required curriculum. According to the students, these sites would make the curriculum more interesting and in many cases update the information from the textbooks. Students thought their teachers would have more success with the topics they were teaching if they used computers to "spice up" their classes.

To begin the project, students individually searched through their current sixth grade textbooks for curriculum topics that might need web sites. They came together in groups of four and using building consensus strategies combined their lists to create one list for the group for each subject. Finally, one master list per subject was created by the students. Each student then privately ranked each of the four subject areas (language arts, mathematics, science, and social studies) in order of importance to them. The group used this information to create four working groups, one for each subject area.

Julie then taught the "friendly letter format" so the students could write to the sixth grade teachers about their project.

1235 Baxter Street
Athens, Ga, 30606
March 23, 1999

Dear 6th grade Science teachers,

Why do you think computers are important? Mrs. Payne's first period
Language Arts class is doing a project to find
which topics you would like to have an annotated bibliography of science
sites for. From the list below, please rate the topics from one to five.
Please feel free to add any additional topics you think are important.
-Scientific Method
-Energy
-Magnetism
-Elements
-Biomes (Tundra, Desert, Rain Forest, Deciduous Forest, Ocean animals,
         Plants & Photosynthesis)
-Senses
-Atoms
-Water cycle
-Lunar cycle
-Solar System
-Insect cycle
-decomposition cycle
-Nutrition/exercise
-Simple Machines
Please return this to Mrs. Payne by tomorrow afternoon. Thank you for
taking the time to do this.

Sincerely,

Upon reply, needs were tallied and the results determined the list of subject topics students were to research.

The next step was for Julie to teach basic Internet skills. For example, she taught her students how to access the World Wide Web, how to use search engines, and how to use the tool bars on the web sites. Following the Internet instruction, the four groups of students started searching the web for appropriate web sites for their subject topics. It was at that point the students started questioning the accuracy and reliability of web sites.

These student questions and concerns became the impetus for the next phase of the project . . . the development of a rubric for evaluating the validity of a web site. The rubric eventually included space for a site summary and student evaluative comments. Each of the four groups surfed the web for appropriate Internet sites (of course Julie was also mindful of inappropriate web hits). Throughout the project, Julie had students complete a self-evaluation form. Students utilized the rubric effectively with the exception of their summaries. Julie gave the summaries back to the students and retaught summary writing.

According to Julie, the academic connections to standards that were made during the project included such things as

- summarizing, taking notes, using key words in research
- learning a friendly letter format
- averaging numbers (survey results)
- creating a rubric for determining validity of a web page
- learning Internet surfing skills
- recognizing themes of study for language arts, mathematics, science, and social studies
- evaluating web page content for validity
- composing an annotated bibliography of web sites grouped according to topic
- identifying purpose when searching for sites
- writing a persuasive paper
- recognizing propaganda and false information
- using effective communication skills
- writing a How-To-Paper on making an effective web site
- evaluating grammar

Working kids at play

Eighth grade students at Sweetwater Middle School, along with their teachers Cathlene Criss and J. R. Mitchell, researched, drafted, and designed a recreational playground facility aimed at meeting the needs of residents at a local homeless shelter catering to families. Although the project took place within a math class, students learned about their community, assessed specific needs, used basic knowledge not only in math, but in language arts, social studies, health, and physical education as well. Initially, students wrote a brief rationale and purpose statement based on interviews conducted with personnel and residents of the homeless shelter to determine a needs assessment for the recreational facility. While designing the recreational facility, students addressed such issues as working within a projected budget, utilizing existing space and equipment, revising and editing plans, meeting deadlines, and recording data.

Students learned mathematics through the construction and understanding of making blueprints for the playground. Students learned ratio scales so their blueprints could be accurate and proportional. They learned area through taking dimensions of the equipment from magazines and using them to see if they would be able to fit in the playground area. Students learned budgeting through keeping track of how much each piece of equipment cost and the total cost of the playground.

Journal
Explain how math is   4/13/
incorporated in the making Mat
of blueprints. Give specific
examples.

     Math is incorporated in
the making of blueprints in
many ways. In blueprints
you have to use rulers to
get straight lines and
exact measurements. You
also use scale drawings,
ratios, and equivalent
fractions in the making
of blueprints to get exact
measurements. You also
use area to determine the
scale factor. Math is
incorporated in many more
ways than I can think
of or name.

In language arts students improved their writing skills through writing a project proposal and a persuasive needs statement. They also used creative writing skills in their journals. They worked on an oral persuasive speech to justify and support their ideas on why they should or should not keep certain equipment in their plans.

> **3-28-99**
> **period 3**
>
> **Journal:**
> **Elementary**
>
>   I think it is important for children ages (7-10) to have certain kinds of equipment available for their use. They include: a slide, pole-to slide down, tunnels-to crawl through, monkey bars to climb on, tearther balls, jungle gym-to climb on and afeild and benches which would come in handy for all ages. The reason I chose these things is because it was not that long ago when I used to enjoy playing on all of this equipment and also most of this equipment can be used for other age groups as well.
>
>   If there is any equipment the playground can do without it would a pole. The reason is because the monkey bars can serve the same purpose.

Students learned health and physical education related standards as they researched which equipment served which health and physical needs. In addition, students learned to work cooperatively with others in their groups, shared ideas, and offered constructive criticism. According to Cathlene and J.R., their students' subjective responses greatly improved when evaluating their groups' blueprints and debating ideas in the classroom.

Students helping students:
Curriculum for the recording for the blind and dyslexic

Language Arts
April 26, 1999   2nd period
Reflection Paper

This has been an interesting, unique, and different project. Other projects are traditionally based and aren't much fun. RFB&D has been difficult at times having to think of assignments and activities that were fun yet equally enriching. With other projects or papers, you go to the library, do some research, take notes, write a paper and get graded. With the RFB&D assignment, we have had to think more creatively and at the same time, continue to listen and learn. With this project not only do you have to perform cognative and associative tasks and research skills, but also you have to think with a good attitude.

In an eighth grade classroom at Snellville Middle School, eighty-four students and their teacher, Elaine Homestead, spent one-half the school year on a project in collaboration with the Georgia Recording for the Blind and Dyslexic (RFB&D). The RFB&D is a nonprofit, volunteer organization providing educational materials recorded in computerized formats, at every academic level, for people who cannot effectively read standard print. Currently there is no written curriculum to accompany the recorded books. To meet this need, the students researched dyslexia and blindness to determine appropriate teaching strategies. Following the research, Elaine showed the students how to create curriculum. Students then wrote novel-study curriculum for books they chose using consensus, including *Nothing But the Truth* (Avi 1991), *Brian's Winter* (Paulsen 1996), *The Incredible Journey* (Burnford 1960), and *Across Five Aprils* (Hunt 1964).

The curriculum students developed included "Talking Points," vocabulary and comprehension questions, study guides, contracts, and traditional and alternative assessments appropriate for blind and dyslexic students.

> 4-26-99
>
> My learning experience with this project has been excellent. I think writing material that will be nationally published is a great way for us to learn very creatively, and also help other people in the process. Learning while helping others is great in my opinion, and I have never done an activity like it before. I think the field trip we took to Athens was very educational and also gave us an idea of what a college campus is like. Last year, the most creative activity we did was models of characters. Now, I am helping to create curriculum that will be published nationally! Overall, I think this project was and is a success. As I read over the contract and edited it, I finally realized that pretty soon some real-world students and teachers will be reading it for an activity or a grade! That in itself is a very big accomplishment and I think Snellville middle should keep a record of this activity and any others that follow in it's path.

While engaged in this project, students learned and applied language arts skills and content (e.g., research, grammar, punctuation, writing, reading, speaking, listening, problem solving). They also developed needs assessments, researched the context surrounding blind and dyslexic disabilities, wrote goal statements, developed action plans, created rubrics and tests, piloted their work, engaged in public relations, created curriculum, assessed their knowledge, and reflected on their experiences. Through emphasis on real-life problems and contextual application of knowledge, students deepened their content expertise, gained a greater sense of confidence through meaningful and valued work, and viewed themselves as actively involved citizens making a difference.

Multiple intelligence in the science classroom

At Jefferson Middle School, Kathy Rogers and seventy-seven seventh grade students learned about Howard Gardner's Theory of Multiple Intelligence (MI). In this project, students first identified their own strengths and needs using a teacher-made checklist. The checklist was created using various resources that defined MI and their characteristics (Zephyrpress 1999). After students completed the checklists they discussed the characteristics of each intelligence and how knowledge of their strengths and needs could help them in and out of school. Following the discussion the students brainstormed ways to use MI in their science classroom.

> I learned that I was interpersonal and bodily. I've begun studying with my friends and found that it helps me remember things much better. When I get the chance to, I do things physically which helps me understand things more. It has helped me in studying, and in working on my weaknesses. I was able to see that my mathmatical points were low, so I needed to work on that. My grades have improved since I learned my strengths.

Students then got into strengths groups and designed posters for each intelligence (e.g., verbal-linguistic, musical, bodily-kinesthetic, interpersonal, intrapersonal). Students also designed science projects based on their intelligence strengths.

"Once we examined the theory of MI, we began to do MI projects. Being the practical person I am, I wanted to keep the objectives and national standards in mind at all times. At first, I didn't share the objectives with the students but as we got off into tangents, I realized they couldn't choose ideas unless they knew what was required. After we discussed the QCC [Georgia Quality Core Curriculum] it was easier because we had a focus to keep us straight."

"First period just finished their MI presentations. I had anticipated that it would be difficult for them to present various organisms using their strengths, but they were so creative. One student created a Venus fly trap from cardboard and felt. She discussed its eating habits and demonstrated with a paper fly. Another student, a young man that is NOT known for his effort and high achievements, made a giant spider with pipe cleaners and black masking tape. He used a false voice and put on a puppet show for the class. All the kids clapped and laughed at the end. I could tell by his facial expressions that he was enjoying the attention. (This was more valuable to me than his new found knowledge of Black Widows.) This is a student who rarely shines or participates in class. I honestly feel that if he were given more opportunities to be funny in a productive manner he would be a much happier person and possibly strive a little more in school."

"One of the suggestions from the National Middle School Association is to give students an opportunity for success in the classroom. Another important point is that the teachers should be sensitive to the needs of adolescents. I feel that activities like today's can accomplish both. We very much felt like a community as we shared our knowledge and information."

"As we began to do the MI activities I learned a lot about my students as individuals. For instance, Robert, a special education student, has a wonderful talent of working with his hands. He and Nathan created a model of a bone using a cardboard tube, a Dixie cup and red yarn. They explained it to the class and I used it several times later on for demonstration."

"When I began this project I was very excited about the possibilities. I often try to vary my instructional techniques to include hands-on activities, but often find it hard to work those activities into my everyday curriculum. This project allowed me to cover curriculum AND do the hands-on, minds-on activities that I feel middle schoolers really need. I will no longer feel the need to justify my activities if they are QCC related. This project will help me analyze my activities and see what is crucial enough to spend extra time (and resources) on and what can be skimmed."

"So far I am pleased with this project's growth and development. My ideas have changed somewhat throughout the project. What I initially set out to accomplish is no longer my biggest goal. I now have focused more on the students developing the activities and my being a facilitator rather than a leader of the whole process.

Listed below are some connections between academics and this project:

- Seventh grade Life Science = All QCC were met through various activities and presentations.
- Other content areas that were impacted were language arts, mathematics, art, and drama.
- The National Science Standards for Life Science were taught or demonstrated through MI activities for this project."

S.P.E.E.D.: Stopping poverty from ending everyone's dreams

In S.P.E.E.D.: Stopping Poverty from Ending Everyone's Dreams, seventh grade students and Victor Devine of Coile Middle School decided to focus on poverty and homelessness as a topic of concern for the year. During the school year students developed and organized events including can drives, coat drives, rummage sales, and paper drives. The goal of these events was to address the problem of poverty and homelessness locally and globally. Toward the end of the school year the students felt there was a need to get their message out to others. They decided on hosting a county wide "See for Yourself Day" at their school. Students spent two weeks developing a public service announcement for this culminating event. First they brainstormed ideas as to how to develop a public service announcement. Several ideas were tossed around until the students came to a consensus on a plan. The plan was to use a wall in the school's rotunda to build a public service announcement. This included a mural, Hyperstudio presentation, collage, and pamphlets designed to inform the public about the problems of homelessness and what was being done to help.

The next step was to gather their research of the problem of poverty and homelessness in the local area, the United States, and the world. From this information they picked the most compelling facts as "sound bites" for their public service announcement (e.g., 40.15 percent of all homeless people are children). They interviewed people who participated in their year-long charitable events as well as guest speakers who had previously spoken to their class.

After this information was gathered, students began the actual design of the public service announcement. Students volunteered for different jobs and worked on their assigned duties. Different groups of students worked on wall construction and assembly, collage, pamphlets, the mural, interviews and word processing, the Hyperstudio presentation, artwork, and the sign. Each working group selected a project leader. The public service announcement wall ended up being an impressive 10 feet by 12 feet.

The academic connections included research skills, social studies, mathematics, art, critical thinking skills, language arts, and technology.

"The S.P.E.E.D. public service announcement would have been impossible to justify without the facts that the children researched. The students learned how to use the Internet, 'ABC News Current Events' CD, and the infotrac database of periodicals. The students also used traditional media such as newspapers, magazines, and books that focused on homelessness and poverty."

"A year long focus in social studies has been current events. While working on the S.P.E.E.D. public service announcement, the students were able to employ the skills that they have developed in social studies regarding the selection, citation, and interpretation of current events."

"Math skills were also needed in the development of the S.P.E.E.D. public service announcement. The students had to be able to interpret the data, that was often in different forms, and use it to understand and convey the significance of the problems associated to homelessness and poverty."

"The research, statistics, and cold facts regarding homelessness and poverty was given life by the ingenuity and creativity of the voyagers [students]. The students had to be able to engineer, arrange, and decorate the S.P.E.E.D. service announcement."

"The voyagers had to be able to use their critical thinking skills in order to distinguish between relevant and irrelevant information regarding the state of homelessness and poverty in our world. The students also had to compare and contrast different facts in order to decide which facts would make more effective 'sound bites.'"

"In order to bring the public announcement to life quickly and effectively, the students had to be proficient in several different forms of technology. The Internet, 'ABC News Current Events' CD, and the infotrac database of periodicals were mentioned as means by which the students found information essential for research. Also, Hyperstudio and Print Shop Deluxe were used to bring those facts across to the public in a multimedia rich approach."

"Of course language arts is essential in the creation of any written project. The S.P.E.E.D. public service announcement is certainly no exception with grammar, composition, and bibliographic citations as a cornerstone of the process."

Conclusion

What do all of these stories have in common? The teachers in each story had confidence: confidence in their understanding of standards, confidence in their content knowledge, confidence in their knowledge of young adolescents, confidence in co-creating curriculum, and confidence in their ability to understand the dynamics of teaching. They had confidence in their ability to understand, build upon, and improve content knowledge while meeting the needs the young adolescents. They also had confidence in the intellect and dedication of their students to real issues. And they had confidence in democratic classrooms.

In each story documentation strategies were used to keep track of learning. Some of the teachers copied required standards and students kept track of their own learning along with the teacher. Some of the teachers kept running lists of covered standards. Other teachers reflected on their project and noted standards covered after the project was over. According to Nesin and Lounsbury (1999) teachers can also

> . . . post specific curriculum objectives and leave them up all year as a constant reminder of school and state expectations. As students help plan units and activities, they refer to the charts to determine if appropriate skills and knowledge are being included. In curriculum integration, not all students learn the same information at the same time or to the same degree. Teachers must find a way to keep track of students' individual progress in the given curriculum. Students and teachers can keep track together of standards touched upon or met. (p. 13)

Standards in each classroom were measured and taught by a variety of instructional strategies which actively engaged and met the needs of all students (Schrenko 1998). Assessments, both traditional and alternative, were designed to measure whether students were meeting standards.

In each story, the curriculum was challenging, integrative, and exploratory. Middle school students and teachers moved beyond "covering material." They opened their classroom doors. Students engaged in activities that helped them understand themselves and the world around them. In each case learning was rigorous. Yes, the classrooms were structured around the traditional subject areas of language arts, mathematics, science, and social science because of preset organizational structures within the school. Yet connections were made between ideas and fields of knowledge, extending beyond course requirements and subject areas.

Content and skills were applied in each classroom in context rather than in isolation. Students constructed knowledge rather than just consuming it. In each classroom, curriculum was exploratory. Students were able to discover their particular abilities, talents, interests, values, and preferences. Each classroom allowed young adolescents to make contributions to society. Each classroom helped students explore opportunities not found in a more traditional curriculum. And in each classroom, the organization of curriculum was around problems and issues collaboratively identified by students and teachers, without regard for subject-area boundaries. The curriculum in each was responsive, relevant, and engaging for students and teachers.

Integrated curriculum and democratic education can fit into middle schools. Not only can curriculum integration fit, but if the middle school is to reinvent itself—if it is to ultimately be the place that Lounsbury and other founders dreamed it could be—then we must weave this together. When I think about his prediction, I still get nervous; but when I visit classrooms such as the ones described in this chapter, I know the battle of education is being won. Teachers can make sense of standards and address them in a curriculum that is responsive, relevant, and engaging. Middle school students and teachers CAN create a curriculum intersection of excellence.

References

Achieve. (1998). *Aiming higher: 1998 annual report.* [On-line]. Available: *http://www.achieve.org.*

Apple, M.W., and Beane, J.A. (1995). *Democratic schools.* Alexandria, VA: Association for Supervision and Curriculum Development.

Avi. (1991). *Nothing but the truth.* New York: Avon Books.

Baker, A. (1996). Major disciplinary violations in a junior high school: An explanatory study. *Research in Middle Level Education Quarterly, 19*(3), 1–20.

Beane, J.A. (1997). *Curriculum integration: Designing the core of democratic education.* New York: Teachers College Press.

Beane, J.A. (1998). Reclaiming a democratic purpose for education. *Educational Leadership, 56*(2), 8–11.

Bernard, B. (1993). Fostering resiliency in kids. *Educational Leadership, 51*(3), 44–48.

Burnford, S. (1960). *The incredible journey.* New York: Bantam Doubleday Dell Books for Young Readers.

Dayton, J., and Glickman, C.D. (1994). Curriculum change and implementation: Democratic imperatives. *Peabody Journal of Education, 9*(4), 62–86.

Haberman, M. (1991). The pedagogy of poverty versus good teaching. *Phi Delta Kappan, 73*(4), 290–294.

Higgs, G.E., and Tarsi, N.L. (1997). New learning and agency in the at-promise student. In R. F. Kronick (Ed.), *At-risk youth: Theory, practice and reform* (pp. 78–92). New York: Garland Publishing.

Hunt, I. (1964). *Across five Aprils.* New York: Berkley Books.

National Middle School Association. (1995). *This we believe: Developmentally responsive middle level schools*. Columbus, OH: Author.

Nesin, G., and Lounsbury J. (1999). *Curriculum integration: Twenty questions—with answers*. Atlanta, GA: Georgia Middle School Association.

Northwest Regional Educational Laboratory. (2000). *Library-in-the-sky*. [On-line]. Available: *http://www.nwrel.org/sky2/*

O'Hair, M.J., McLaughlin, H.J., and Reitzug, U. C. (2000). *Foundations of democratic education*. Orlando, FL: Harcourt College Publishers.

Pate, P.E., Homestead, E.R., and McGinnis, K.L. (1997). *Making integrated curriculum work: Teachers, students, and the quest for coherent curriculum*. New York: Teachers College Press.

Paulsen, G. (1996). *Brian's winter*. New York: Bantam Doubleday Dell Books for Young Readers.

Schrenko, L.C. (1998). *Georgia's quality core curriculum: Raising expectations*. Atlanta, GA: Georgia Department of Education.

Vars, G.F. (1999) State testing threatens curriculum integration (and all genuine learning!) *The Core Teacher, 49*(4), 1–8.

Zephyrpress. (1999). *The eight intelligences*. [On-line]. Available: *http://zephyrpress.com/eight.htm*

6

Connecting Caring and Action:
Teachers Who Create Learning Communities in Their Classrooms

DAVID STRAHAN
University of North Carolina at Greensboro

TRACY W. SMITH
Appalachian State University

MIKE McELRATH
Coordinator of Guidance, Jamestown (NY) City Schools

CECILIA M. TOOLE
University of North Carolina at Greensboro

A number of recent studies suggest that teacher expertise is one of the most important factors in determining student achievement, followed by the smaller but consistently positive influences of small schools and small class sizes. That is, teachers who know a lot about teaching and learning and who work in environments that allow them to know students well are the critical elements of successful learning. (Darling-Hammond 1998, p. 6)

Smaller schools and smaller classes have been the centerpiece of almost every recent call for reform. The first recommendation of *Turning Points: Preparing American Youth for the 21st Century* (Carnegie Council on Adolescent Development 1989), for example, was to "create small communities for learning where stable, close, mutually respectful relationships with adults and peers are considered fundamental for intellectual development and personal growth" (p. 9). This recommendation reaffirmed one of the fundamental principles of the middle school concept, that young adolescents learn best in smaller settings. From the outset, middle school advocates emphasized the "smallness" of middle schools in contrast to "larger" junior high schools. If middle schools had to be big, it was important to make them feel smaller to students by creating teams or houses or pods, organizational structures designed to make big schools feel smaller.

Researchers soon learned that organizational changes, in and of themselves, had little effect on students' learning. In a comprehensive review of studies of organizational factors, Calhoun (1983) concluded that there was little difference in academic achievement between middle and junior high school pupils and that the quality of the program was more important than its grade organization. In the years that followed, researchers found that the same was true for team organization. Interdisciplinary team organization, in and of itself, had little effect on achievement; what mattered was the quality of teaming (Arhar, Johnston, and Markle 1989).

These studies and many others like them encouraged researchers to focus on the quality of classroom interactions. Over the past decade, researchers have become more aware of the ways that academic learning occurs best in the context of a "learning community." This term, learning community, captures the essence of what we have learned about the dynamics of school success: students and teachers "learn" best as members of "communities."

A growing commitment to community

In recent investigations, researchers have learned a great deal about the nature of successful learning communities. Based on their comparisons of schools in the Child Development Project with matched nonproject schools, Lewis, Schaps, and Watson (1996) identified five principles of practice that create what they call "the caring classroom's academic edge":

- Warm, supportive, stable relationships,
- Constructive learning,
- Important, challenging curricula,
- Intrinsic motivation, and
- Attention to social and ethical dimensions of learning.

Their data highlighted the "synergy of academic and social goals" and illustrated specific ways that "caring" classrooms can also be highly academic classrooms. They concluded that it is impossible to separate affective and academic dimensions of learning.

Finally, we need to recognize that community and learning are interdependent and must be pursued in context. This means that it is not enough to ask whether a new science curriculum increases students' mastery of important scientific concepts; we must also ask whether or not it fosters their capacity to work with fellow students, their intrinsic interest in science, and their recognition that science depends upon both collaboration and honesty. (p. 21)

Summarizing a number of studies of school culture and leadership, Peterson and Deal (1998) identified five recurring characteristics that describe schools that have become learning communities:

- Staff have a shared sense of purpose; they pour their hearts into teaching;
- Norms of collegiality, improvement, and hard work underlie relationships;
- Rituals and traditions celebrate student accomplishments, teacher innovation, and parental commitment;
- Informal network of storytellers, heroes, and heroines provide a social web of information, support, and history; and
- Success, joy, and humor abound. (p. 29)

While these research reports provide convincing evidence that community enhances learning, they offer less insight into the ways that teachers go about creating learning communities on a day-to-day basis. In the rest of this chapter, we describe how some of the teachers we have studied have created learning communities. Over the past year, the four of us have had opportunities to spend time in the classrooms of more than forty middle-level teachers. Working on three separate research projects, we have observed over one hundred lessons and conducted over two hundred interviews with teachers and their students. One of our research projects focused on the identification of expertise in teaching (Smith 1999); another on the analysis of successful teaming (McElrath 2000); and the third on students' responses to learning strategy instruction (Strahan and Toole, in progress). We found that in all three studies the essential dynamic was the creation of learning communities.

In this chapter, we present three cases that have taught us a great deal about ways teachers create communities for learning. Each of these cases takes place in a very different setting. Betty Roberts teaches in a small K–8 school setting in the mountains of North Carolina. Jay Burns teaches in a prosperous suburban community in North Carolina. Darlene Wilson and Ashley Cooper teach in a large, urban middle school in North Carolina. Each of these teachers responds to the needs of students in a unique way and uses carefully crafted procedures to create a sense of community.

Betty Roberts creates community in a rural setting

Betty Roberts teaches in a small school in the southwestern region of North Carolina. Her school serves students in pre-kindergarten through eighth grade. During the 1998–99 school year, approximately 220 students were enrolled in the school. Although the school is situated in a small town, Betty describes the school setting as rural. Betty suggests that most of her students come from "poor" families. More specifically, she says that approximately five percent of the students come from well-to-do families with few if any financial problems. About ninety percent of the students come from families who can afford the basic necessities of food, clothing, and shelter, and the remaining five percent of the students in her class come from families who cannot even afford the basic necessities of food, clothing, and shelter.

During the 1998–99 school year, Betty had thirty students in her class. She taught all academic subjects to her students, including social studies, science, reading, writing, spelling, and health. At the time these data were collected, Betty was at the end of her fourteenth year of teaching.

A visit to Betty Roberts' classroom

Thirty students, two goldfish, one worm snake, one ringneck snake, five toads, one frog, a five-lined skink, a salamander, a preying mantis, thirty quail eggs, a teacher assistant, and Betty Roberts were the inhabitants of the classroom on the day we arrived to observe. At the time of her observation, Betty's students were working on an assignment they had started the previous day. At the beginning of the lesson, Betty spent less than seven minutes reviewing the purpose of the assignment with the class before they moved to work in groups at clusters of desks and spaces on the floor. Each group of students worked to write ballads about one of four different pirates. This assignment was a follow-up to the beach trip the class had taken. Betty explained the assignment:

> What we started yesterday was to begin to get a ballad together about the pirates you were assigned to study during the trip. Now what I'd like to do when we get back together today is to ask that you refine your ballad to begin with, okay? I want you to look at the text that you have in your booklets or that you have on your paper. . . . And make sure that in your pirate ballad you are retelling the story of your pirate. . . . We didn't get to perform at the coast and finish up what we were doing because of the wind. We're going to do it now. . . . I'm going to give you some time to work on the writing and completing of the actual ballad and then I'm going to ask you to figure out how you're going to present that with some sort of actions that go along with it so that [they] help[s] us visualize your pirate. (Smith 1999, p. 79)

After Betty provided these directions, students went to work in their groups for about twenty-seven minutes. Each group included six to eight students. Betty and her teacher assistant circulated from group to group, monitoring students' progress and answering questions. Betty reviewed the characteristics of a ballad with one group. She crouched on the floor to work with a second group, reading aloud to them and providing additional directions and encouragement. At one point, she stood and patted her knees to demonstrate rhythm for a ballad. Betty moved quickly from group to group leaning into each group to read their drafts and make comments. She used her hand and body movement to demonstrate rhythm to one group. During the group work, students were chatty but seemed productive. Each group seemed to have a "leader" although leaders were not assigned. All students seemed to be involved in the group's activities.

At one point, a student from one of the groups approached Betty. The student seemed upset about something that was happening in his group. Betty moved to his group, crouched down on the floor at students' eye level and eventually got on her knees and leaned over to work on the floor with the students. While she was working with this group, the teacher assistant separated another student from his group. Betty went to talk with him and assigned him to complete an eight-line ballad on his own. When Betty flashed the lights, students instantly raised their hands. Betty gave additional directions for the remainder of the activity. She gave a two-minute countdown before the students needed to wrap up their work. After this, students went in groups to the front of the room to "perform" their ballads. The student who was isolated from his group "performed" the ballad he had written while the teacher assistant read it aloud. The teacher led the class in applause after each performance. Betty did a brief assessment of the group work by having students raise their hands if they thought working with the group was fun or easy, or if they learned something new. At the end of the lesson, Betty summarized the information about the pirates, asking students questions to review.

Betty reflects on her teaching

Betty speaks with personal conviction about her classroom community. She articulates without hesitation one of her primary goals: "My goal is social interaction as much as anything else and especially with all the stuff we're hearing is happening, children killing children. We're taking a real serious look at how children react with one another and interact" (Smith 1999, p. 84). She understands that her students must feel "safe and free to take risks" (Smith 1999, p. 79).

While many accomplished teachers pursue administrative or university positions, Betty has decided to stay in the classroom, working directly with students. Betty knows each of them well and takes a personal interest in them. She describes their lives, situations, needs, and backgrounds and is able to articulate the actions she has taken in response to these details. She speaks passionately about the importance of reaching one young man, John. John has had a history of breaking classroom and school rules. His infractions have often led to administrative disciplinary actions, including suspension. Betty has made efforts to understand John's situation. She has evidence that he has been abused at home, and she wants him to know there are adults who "love and don't hit." She asserts, "If we can't find a way to reach him, we're going to lose him" (Smith 1999, p. 85).

Later, she uses John to represent her philosophy of service to the community: "My basic philosophy is if I can save one John, good enough for me. I'd love to be able to save several Johns. I'd like to be able to save six or seven a year. . . . That's why I'm here" (Smith 1999, p. 85). Betty has seen some progress in John's behavior, attitude, and academic effort. She already has plans to meet with John's teacher for next year to help him or her understand the progress John has made and the strategies that have been effective with him.

Betty's description of Colin's performance provides another illustration of how she understands individual differences and approaches to learning:

Colin is generally eager to do anything that we want him to do and he is sort of an average performer. So there are times when he gets a little frustrated and he wants some help. He's tentative a lot of times about what he's doing. So he wants to have some feedback that makes him feel like he's on the right track. He does not like to write although he's not a poor writer. But he doesn't like to do a written response generally. And he will get upset because he's not sure he's responding the way people want him to respond. I have a feeling there were expectations set somewhere along the line that he feels he's not meeting so he's always concerned, "Am I going to meet the expectations?" There are days when he is distracted. And I don't know why. I've never been able to quite figure it out. (Smith 1999, pp. 116–117)

Betty's approach to reaching her students is to spend time with them one-on-one. She prefers to talk quietly with individuals or small groups rather than to address the entire class at once. She sometimes tries "to figure out why they're discouraged. Is something going on in their lives?" She is interested in their struggles and wants to "let them know we can work things through" (Smith 1999, p. 86). Betty also uses nonverbal cues to communicate effectively. During lessons, she moves from group to group. An observer might notice that as she moves among students, she smiles, nods, pats individuals on the back, touches them on the shoulder, even claps. She is careful to make eye contact with groups and individuals. As she circulates, she gets close to her students in a literal sense (Smith 1999, p. 86).

To build a successful community, Betty has established a number of class-room procedures. One of the most important is her emphasis on teamwork. Betty believes that people are more likely to stay involved in community work if they have opportunities to collaborate with each other. She explains, "Unless they are actively grouped and working together, most of them are not engaged. This engages more [people] when they work in teams. So I try to do more teamwork, any kind of interactive planning together" (Smith 1999, p. 87). Betty likes to roll up her own sleeves and work with her students: "I'm not a stand up and lecture kind of a person because I don't know it all and I'd rather discover with them and set up the learning situations that we sort of discover along together" (Smith 1999, p. 87).

Betty speaks passionately about her students. She believes that the key to building a strong community, comprised of strong individuals, is to help each person find a niche in the community, a role he or she can play. Her personal goal is to convince her students "that they are valued and that they have a gift within them that is valuable and that they need to find it, find out what it is and they need to make the most of it . . . And I try to let them see what their beauty is and they are good folks and there is something to be joyful in every day" (Smith 1999, p. 87). She clearly views her classroom as an interdependent community of learners. She emphasizes teamwork, collaboration, and responsibility, values that Jay Burns encourages in different ways in a very different setting.

Jay Burns creates community in a suburban school

Jay Burns teaches in an affluent middle school in the central region of North Carolina. His school serves students in grades six, seven, and eight. During the 1998–99 school year, approximately 750 students were enrolled in the school. Jay suggests that most of the parents of his students are educated and interested in their children's education. Jay estimates that eighty percent of the students in his classes come from well-to-do families with few, if any, financial problems, fifteen percent come from families who can afford the basic necessities of food, clothing, and shelter, and five percent come from families who cannot afford the basic necessities of food, clothing, and shelter. During the 1998–99 school year, Jay taught language arts to ninety-eight different students during the school day.

At the time that these data were collected, Jay was at the end of his twenty-eighth year of teaching. Previously, he has taught language arts and social studies to students in grades seven, eight, and nine. He has also taught English to students in grades eight through twelve. He has been teaching eighth grade language arts for the past seventeen years. Jay explains why he chose teaching as his profession:

I chose it for a number of reasons, I think. There were some teachers I admired. [The teachers] were models, and I thought highly of them. I was away from my family during the last couple of years of high school and college. And during that time some of the teachers provided me with models. I also wanted a profession where I could do a variety of things, you know summers off, vacations, time to do summer camp work and others things like that was attractive. I also just liked ideas and literature and especially doing English provided that. . . . I like the lifestyle it [teaching] allows. I also, I've always kind of generally liked people and kids. I like to talk to kids. I like to hang out with people. (brackets added; Smith 1999, p. 72)

A visit to Jay Burn's classroom

Jay Burns' third period students sauntered into class, loaded down with Eastbay bookbags on their shoulders, Tommy Hilfiger sweatshirts on their backs, and Nike tennis shoes on their feet. Twenty-eight of their growing bodies barely fit into this eighth grade classroom. Jay was writing on the board as they entered. A nod of his head was direction for one student to distribute a set of heavily-illustrated file folders to her classmates. Without further direction, students began to copy the problematic sentences into their notebooks:

in northern minnesota I did a number of things writed letters laying in the sun and read.

Yes dan the phone ringed at three oclock in the morning it were a wrong number.

When they had finished copying and correcting, Jay began a discussion of the daily oral language activity. Jay asked questions about which changes were made and then commented on those changes with such questions and observations as the following: "And why was that? So you made a new sentence? You could do that. If it were a specific place, yes." During the discussion, there was some confusion about the conjugation of the verb "to lie," meaning "to recline." Jay indicated that he would look up the conjugation and explain it to the class later. Jay provided encouragement to students with comments such as "There you go. Pat yourself on the back. Good. Okay, you can, that would work. You are right! How did you know?" (Smith 1999, p. 76).

Following the daily oral language exercise, Jay reviewed the objectives for the day's class session. Next, he took the "status of the class" by calling the names of the students and recording what they said they would be working on during the class time. After the status of the class was taken, some students moved to the computer stations to word process and a few moved to designated areas to do peer conferences. The rest of the students worked at their desks.

Jay moved around the room with a set of papers returning them to students who were seated at their desks. As he discussed papers with students, he leaned over or crouched to their seated height. He answered student questions and used hand gestures to communicate. Jay made comments to students regarding issues such as theme, tone, and realism, and he praised students with comments such as "This is good. Very supportive, very thorough. Good" (Smith 1999, p. 76).

Just before the class session ended, Jay reminded students of their homework—to complete their portfolios. He suggested that some students may need to come by later in the day to pick up edited papers from him.

Jay reflects on his teaching

Data collected for Jay Burns' case revealed that Jay's curriculum and instruction are responsive to the needs of individuals and groups in his classroom. Jay's priority is developmental appropriateness, and he considers students' social, physical, intellectual, and cognitive development as he plans and implements instruction. Jay began his career as a high school teacher. Then he "found that middle school was not just bratty little kids, . . . there was a challenge, there was something to do" (Smith 1999, p. 91).

The writing workshop structure Jay uses in his classroom allows him to monitor the progress of each writer individually. He describes his students as "a sociable group." He explains that "they laugh and fool around while they're working . . . they just have fun with it" (Smith 1999, p. 92). Jay tries to strike a balance between a directive leadership style and student input: "There are procedures and expectations that I have, but also they have a lot of input" (Smith 1999, p. 92). He understands that students will produce better quality work if they believe they have ownership in the product. His classroom is often noisy with the sound of keyboards, computer printers, and voices. Writers are busy moving about, getting the tools and information they need to complete their assignments. Jay is also busy and moving. He spends most of his day talking to students, providing feedback on drafts they have submitted to him. Rather than just impose his idea of correctness on the pieces, Jay wants to discuss student works, using them as opportunities to help the individual writers grow.

Although Jay enjoys collaborative work with his colleagues, it is the one-on-one work with students that he enjoys most. Jay works personally and individually with each writer. On early assignments, Jay often encourages students to write personal pieces about subjects that they know. Eventually, they work toward more expository pieces balancing them with personal response. Jay spends more time with some writers than others, depending on the development of the writer and the content of the particular assignment. Jay suggests that one of the most important concepts he tries to communicate is that writers must have an understanding of their audiences and that each piece they write must be directed to their specific audience. Also, writers must have evidence to support what they write. They cannot make claims or statements without sources and support.

Based on developmental considerations, Jay has developed what he calls a sequence overview for the types of writing students will do during their eighth grade year. He suggests that "students start with autobiography, go to biography kinds of narrative, then nonnarrative things. Going from first person to third person, dealing with other realities and other people and so forth. So we started very egocentrically writing kind of about ourselves and that sort of thing. And that has been kind of a trajectory I've tried to maintain" (Smith 1999, p. 93).

Working with individuals is not always easy. Middle school students tend to be very sensitive about their work because, in a sense, the writing they produce is their original creation. Jay must be confident and tactful when dealing with temperamental talent. His goal is to help writers refine their skills without discouraging them. The following excerpt from Jay's interview illustrates the breadth of his knowledge about the students in his class:

> INTERVIEWER: Tell me about the individual differences in your third period class.
>
> JAY: Okay, one little boy that was sitting next to you, Sahid, wrote a two or three page dissertation on the appropriate measures for NATO to take in dealing with the eastern block degradation and Russia and what their position was and so forth. I'm sure he got stuff off the Internet. I'm sure he interacted with his parents at home, but they didn't write anything of it. He just talked around, and it was very difficult to reconcile these things, and he didn't just take one simplistic point of view. I mean the kid's out the top. And at the same time there are kids that are still not formal thinkers. There's one kid over here, very sharp kid, Jeremy over there, but he kind of misses the abstract stuff. One of my sharpest girls who kept trying to participate and participated a lot in the back, doesn't always balance specifics and generalities, although she is extremely sharp. But she'll make just a lot of general statements, and so she doesn't always make connections. And the danger with her is that she's a good kid, and so she's memorized all the right stuff, and so she tells you all the right stuff. And so to push her back and say, "Okay, well what does this have to do with the text or what does this have to do with anything else?" (Smith 1999, p. 115)

Jay's response indicates a deep level of knowledge about individual students in his classroom. On the spot, Jay remembers Sahid's topic, addresses his process for writing, alludes to his family situation, elaborately describes his written product, and speculates on his cognitive process. He understands his students' mental processes at such a level that he not only can describe them, but also compare them, as he compares Sahid's more complex cognitive ability to Jeremy's less abstract approach. He is able to diagnose a female student's deficiency because he has clearly and carefully observed her responses. Because he knows her tendencies well, he knows that his approach must be to help her balance generalities and specifics.

Jay's daily routine includes a mini-lesson and status of the class. Jay's mini-lessons are based on common patterns or problems Jay observes as he conferences with students on their writing. Following the mini-lesson, Jay takes the status of the class. At this time, he calls each student's name. Students respond to their names by providing their plan for the day. They state the type of writing (mode) they will be doing and their stage of the writing process for that particular piece. Jay may ask clarifying questions concerning students' responses. The status of the class procedure allows students to work toward independence with the guidance of the teacher.

Jay Burns has a few suggestions for other teachers who wish to have effective relationships with their students:

1. Combine a high sense of structure and guidance with a high sense of choice and control.
2. Separate content from correction.
3. Model early, withhold judgment during the process; correct thoroughly when they are done and let them correct/revise what you have pointed out.
4. Focus on process. (Smith 1999, p. 95)

Jay's advice captures some of the ways he has learned to create learning communities in his classroom. His students demonstrate a sense of connection with their classmates, with the tasks of writing, and with their teacher. Students on the STAR team at Washington Middle school also show a sense of connectedness. Their teachers, Darlene and Ashley, encourage a sense of community in a different fashion.

The STAR Team creates community in an urban school

Washington Middle School is located on the eastern side of Hanford, the largest city in Goings County. There are 675 students and sixty staff members at Washington. The student population is sixty percent African American, twenty percent Caucasian, and twenty percent Asian/Hispanic descent. The section of the city surrounding Washington Middle is dotted with small bungalows built in the 1940s and 50s. While the immediate neighborhoods help to define the roots of this working class community, the extended community is more impoverished, with striking resemblance to an inner city urban district (McElrath 2000).

Washington Middle is not immune to the problems facing other inner-city schools across the nation. Transient populations and higher than average teacher turnover rates make it difficult to establish and maintain a positive school culture. Over the past five years, a number of the working class families in this attendance zone have moved to more suburban settings, causing a shift in the school and community population. Despite these challenges, Washington Middle maintains a core group of dedicated and caring teachers.

The STAR (Strive To Attain Respect) team is a two-teacher team at Washington Middle School. Darlene Wilson teaches math and science while Ashley Cooper teaches language arts and social studies. They are the only two-teacher team in the seventh grade at Washington. Darlene Wilson is the team leader. A veteran of nine years in teaching, she has a unique awareness of the needs of her students gained through her experiences as both teacher and parent. She is admittedly the mothering type, the one students feel they can go to with problems and concerns without disregarding her authority. She is a kind and giving person who cares equally about the welfare of her students and the mentoring role she assumes with Ashley.

Ashley Cooper is a second-year teacher with an undergraduate degree in middle grades education from the local university. With this middle grades background, she has become a positive addition to the Washington Middle staff and contributing member of the STAR team. Ashley feels fortunate to be teamed with Darlene, who not only understands the setting, but also is willing to learn from and not squelch Ashley's progressive ideas about teaching middle school children. Ashley has a solid command of her subject areas as evidenced by the improved reading and writing scores of her students. She has also aligned herself with Darlene in taking a leadership role on the school improvement team, a worthy effort for such a young teacher.

A visit with the STAR team

On the day of this observation, all forty-six students gathered in one classroom. The activity was an auction, and the front tables in the room were filled with well over a hundred different prizes. This was the Big Bucks Auction and Ms. Wilson served as the auctioneer. Students on this team had received Big Bucks as incentive for good behavior throughout the semester. Today's activity is the culminating event. Students could choose to bid on items of interest such as volleyballs, hair gel, WWF t-shirts, or chocolate bars. Ashley and Darlene had been orchestrating this event for months, seeking donations from a number of local stores and a wide variety of community sources to fund this activity, carefully selecting an odd montage of items that young adolescents crave. Observers watched as the students slowly entered the room and quietly took their places, anxiously anticipating their opening bid on the item they hoped no one else would want.

The students were cooperative, sharing prizes with one another, lending money to those in need, and cheering with excitement as the bidding wars escalated. Observers noted that there were almost fifty students in this room, and these two teachers had the control and attention of every one of them. After class, Ashley shared her thoughts on having so many students in the room at once:

> Last year we started bringing them all together second semester once we had picked up the kids from the other class, so we had up to seventy students in here at once. I didn't feel quite as comfortable with everyone being in here then, but now I really don't have any problem. I don't feel worried about it like I did last year, and I think its partly because they know what we expect from them and they do, for the most part, what we ask of them. (McElrath 2000, p. 127)

Putting their beliefs in practice, the team has initiated a number of community service projects allowing students to demonstrate citizenship and build character. Some of these projects were undertaken during school hours while others occurred after school through the SAVE (Students Against Violence) club activities sponsored by Darlene and assisted by Ashley. Interestingly enough, even after long and often tiresome days, these teachers' rooms were almost always open after school for tutorial sessions, small group discussions, or club meetings; a true indication of their commitment to the students. Darlene explained:

> We try to get the kids involved in different projects. You know, some kids are not so good at schoolwork. Maybe they can't draw, maybe they can't do some of these other things, but they can bring in some canned goods and they can go with us to deliver the stuff or they can go out here and weed the flowers around the school. (McElrath 2000, p. 129)

Through their own energy and example, Darlene and Ashley often showed students how to put caring into motion. As one illustration, Darlene reported her reactions to their visit to a nearby nursing home.

> It was a lot of fun watching the kids progress through our nursing home visit. When we first went in, I was the protector, all the kids were standing behind me, as a matter of fact Ms. Cooper was standing back there as well. It was hard, I mean there were people with no legs, who couldn't talk and didn't know us. I'd jump in and just start conversations with people

who were not even talking back and I would have them laughing or smiling. All the while, the kids were watching. About a third of the way through I was stepping back and the kids were going in and Ms. Cooper was going in. The kids were getting involved and they loved it, they would read the name on the door and go in and greet the person say "Hey, Louise, how are you?" By the last half of the tour I wasn't even going in the rooms. The kids really responded and that was a very good feeling for us. We just want them to be good people. (McElrath 2000, p. 129)

Darlene and Ashley reflect on their teaching

When asked to talk about those aspects that have allowed them to become a more successful team, Ashley began with the following:

The one thing I think about is this—I look at Darlene and me and how we are like friends, best of friends, so this school thing just kind of fits into what we do. We know each other well enough to know how the other is going to react in certain situations. We can play off that and read off that. The kids also see that we work together and there is nothing one of us does without the other one knowing about it. They see this and don't try to pull anything over on us. I really think that is the one thing that helps our team behave and respond, for the most part, to what we do. (McElrath 2000, p. 125)

Darlene agreed.

There is also very open communication in front of the kids. We'll say 'Ms. Cooper what do you think? Ms. Wilson what do you think? Let's sit down, let's talk about this.' And we do this openly with the kids as a whole group or one-on-one. It's never me with a kid playing against her or the two of us teaming up against a student. It's all of us sitting down and talking about it. (McElrath 2000, p. 126)

Ashley added a comment about their efforts across the year.

We have been consistently demanding and our expectations have not changed since the beginning of the year. Since day one, we made it known that we wanted them to do the best they could do, and we were not going to accept less. We are going to continuously demand that they do more, even those who get good grades can do more. (McElrath 2000, p. 126)

Both teachers emphasize consistency and high expectations as the keys to being successful with their students. In this particular setting, control is an issue that must be addressed early on in order for team teachers to provide the kind of activities and experiences that allow students to excel. In essence, a hierarchy of authority and established set of procedures must be practiced and understood prior to engaging in more independent pursuits such as group work or outside activities. The intimacy of a two-teacher team, guided by some unique strategies, allows this to occur more naturally. These teachers know their best chance for control is within the confines of the team. They have worked to establish and maintain this kind of community, aware of the other distractions that may reveal themselves.

> We have worked hard to establish control. I mean, when they are with us and without distractions around they are under our control, totally, and they will pretty much do whatever we ask of them. But when we let them out to the world outside our door, they become influenced in a heartbeat, which is sad. But at least we know that they know what is right and wrong within the confines of the team. (McElrath 2000, p. 126)

Darlene and Ashley know that they need to rely on parents as much as possible in order to develop the sense of community and common cause that will allow their students to excel both academically and socially. Darlene reminds us of just how difficult a challenge this can be at times:

> With the diverse population in our community, we have to deal with a lot of problems, everything from racial feelings of injustice to an inability to communicate because of language barriers. Sometimes we have to go through liaisons, and sometimes the children are the only liaison we have. That can be hard. We have a few kids this year whose parents have not been involved because there is no liaison and this seventh grade child is the only one who speaks English in the family. That can make things difficult. (McElrath 2000, p. 129)

In spite of these, and other obstacles, the team continues to make a conscious effort to invite parents to participate in team activities. They have worked to create more positive feelings between school and home by intentionally promoting a more open and communicative atmosphere.

> We try to let the parents know that we can talk things out, that it is okay to come in and see us. We know that the parents can get scared and intimidated when they have to come into school. We wanted to establish

this policy from the beginning of the year. We called the parents and the kids before school started and told them how glad we were to have them on our team, then we followed up with a letter inviting them to our open house. At the open house we had helium balloons, snacks, and punch. We tried to make it really festive and very welcoming from the very first day they walked in. After Christmas we made the effort to call again. Not just bad phone calls but good phone calls to thank the parents. As a parent, it's such a rewarding sound to hear that you have done a good job with your child or that its obvious your child has been taught how to act. Parents don't usually get told those things. I know that from being a parent. It's funny, you start talking with them and before you know it they have brought up a situation that is troubling the family or the child. They seem to appreciate having someone to share with. (McElrath 2000, p. 130)

Darlene and Ashley believe that involving parents and communicating on a regular basis can solve a great deal of problems. Initial phone calls, positive messages, and informal social gatherings invite parents to participate in their child's education and model team beliefs to parents and students alike. The STAR team teachers have found that these efforts can help diffuse traditional barriers associated with home and school relationships while enhancing community views of team and school.

The parents we have had contact with this year have thanked us for what we have done for their children, and I know that what they were referring to was not just the bookwork, it was being there for their kids. A good example was with one of our students who, prior to this year, had no interest in school. Now he enjoys coming to school, he wants to come to school. His mother was going to pick him up at 2:45 yesterday (before the end of the day) and he didn't want that, he wanted to stay. That's something she had never seen with him before. (McElrath 2000, p. 130)

As evidenced by the data presented in this section, the STAR team teachers work closely to forge positive relationships and to develop a supportive, caring environment for their students. They accomplish this by having open discussions between and among adults and students, high behavioral and academic expectations for all students, modeling consistent and continual messages about right and wrong, and establishing a teaching and learning atmosphere that emphasizes group work, creativity, and humanistic values. In the process, the STAR team teachers balance friendship with professional growth by examining differences of opinion, sharing individual roles and responsibilities, and maintaining constant communication and support for one another.

Conclusions

Educational researchers and policy makers have agreed that one of the most powerful factors in promoting accomplishment is the extent to which the classroom is a learning community. The authors of *Turning Points* (Carnegie Council on Adolescent Development 1989) articulated the essence of the concept of learning community as "a place where close, trusting relationships with adults and peers create a climate for personal growth and intellectual development" (p. 37). Recent studies have documented ways that constructivist learning, challenging curricula, and intrinsic motivation contribute to the success of learning communities (Carnegie Council on Adolescent Development 1989). Most importantly, these studies have identified caring relationships as the heart of these communities. The four teachers profiled in this chapter have illustrated some of the ways that individual teachers work with their particular students to bring to life the concept of community. While their situations are unique, their cases have offered us four powerful insights into the dynamics of learning communities.

First, the classroom communities that teachers create grow from their own personal commitment to their students. While the concept of community seems to indicate the importance of group, the participants in this study were equally, if not more focused on the individuals in their classrooms. In fact, so much evidence supported the importance of the teacher/student relationship that this proposition may in some ways capture the essence of their expertise. In a follow-up e-mail, teachers in one of our studies were asked, "What is the most important thing that beginning teachers need to know?" In their replies, all of the participants emphasized the importance of building relationships with students. While these veterans maintained that new teachers must show confidence and understand their new positions of authority, each one also indicated that relationships with students are the key to effectiveness.

The participants in this study demonstrated their interest in the student/teacher relationship in a number of ways. They showed a vast knowledge of individual students. They spoke to the emotional, physical, cognitive, intellectual, and family needs and circumstances of students in their classes. These teachers learned a great deal about their students by working side by side with them. As Betty moved from group to group, she got down on her knees to work directly with students. During his lessons, Jay was moving about the room, conferencing with students. He worked closely with them, kneeling, bending, leaning, or crouching to their seated height. When they visited the nursing home, Darlene and Ashley showed their students how to interact with the patients by taking the lead and demonstrating ways to initiate conversation. Learning with their students, side by side, elbow to elbow, face to face, may have been the most powerful way that these teachers demonstrated their own personal commitment.

Second, they put their commitment to students in motion through procedures that fuse academic and social accomplishment. Students in their classes experienced very little tension between "what we learn" and "how we learn" or between "my success" and "our success." Their students achieved a great deal. They also learned to collaborate. These four teachers have developed working procedures that foster connectedness.

One procedure they share is the development of assignments that link inquiry and collaboration. During Betty's lesson, while children were working in groups, Betty got the students' attention several times to have them assess their group dynamic. She also debriefed with the students at the end of the lesson to monitor the effectiveness of the group work and to have the students consider their contributions to their groups. Betty also took time to assess the effectiveness of the group activity:

> Some positive things I saw happening were some leadership things happening among the groups with new leaders emerging. Because when you do this kind of work, there are certain children who emerge because they have a knowledge about this or an interest in this that maybe they don't have a textbook knowledge of or they bring something to the group that the others don't have. And sometimes they're unexpected ones that do this. (Smith 1999, pp. 112–113)

Jay incorporated collaboration into his writing workshop structure. Students provided oral and written responses to each other's writing, always working toward improving writing produced in the workshop. Darlene and Ashley linked academic and social learning in a flexible fashion.

> We do like to mix up the way they learn, allowing some leeway in the activities that we do. Sometimes we'll do a one-period activity, sometimes a two-period activity. We do group work, we go outside, and we even bring them all into one room together. That has worked really well for us. We are not totally controlling all the time, we certainly like to do things they enjoy and we try to seek their input into what works for them, but they have to know the difference between playtime and serious time. (McElrath 2000, pp. 126–127)

Third, they involve students in classroom decisions on a continuous basis. In response to the question "What do you think makes you a successful writing teacher?" Jay wrote, "Kids largely have control over topics and content, while aiming at a rubric or criterion for the end result" (Smith 1999, p. 110). Jay seemed not only to indicate that he is willing to share control of the curriculum with his students but also that his success is derived from sharing ownership and control. His advice to writing teachers is to "combine a high sense of *structure* and *guidance* with a high sense of *choice* and control by *students*" (Smith 1999, p. 110). The STAR Team also encouraged active participation. Ashley notes:

> We really try to talk to the kids and this is something we do from the first week on. We tell them that we're not just here to teach math, science, reading and social studies, we're here to try to make them a better person. We let them know that it (decision-making) is a constant battle. All of us have to make choices all the time about which way to go, about the right and the wrong decisions. Sometimes we will explore these issues in a round table discussion, sometimes just in my class, and sometimes just in Darlene's class, but we are constantly making the effort to discuss them. (McElrath 2000, p. 128)

Related to student ownership is **student responsibility**. In Betty Roberts' classroom students are given daily responsibilities to keep the classroom functioning. One of the most important responsibilities is care of the classroom animals. Students are assigned different animals that must be fed and watered and whose cages, aquariums, and terrariums must be cleaned. Betty explains that on family nights, students are eager to "lead their parents by the hand to show them the classroom animals and explain their daily responsibilities for their animal" (Smith 1999, p. 111). She says that students are proud to be a part of this class family. Providing care for living things in the classroom requires shared responsibility between the teacher and students and among the students themselves. Such shared responsibility contributes to a sense of community in Betty's classroom.

Finally, each of these teachers extends the community beyond the walls of the classroom. Betty Roberts believes that the most effective way to involve parents is a teacher-by-teacher approach. Although she supports school-wide open house meetings, she believes she has to take additional steps to involve parents. For several years, she has been hosting after-hours gatherings. She sees these activities as ways to break down the barriers between the school and parents who have had negative experiences at school or who feel uncomfortable in the traditional open house structure. Some of her after-hours events have included Night Walks, a Star Party, a Weekend Stream Walk, a Computer Night, and a Christmas Candlelight. Many of these activities are outside or off-campus. As a single mother, she sees herself as "a peer and partner with parents."

Jay Burns suggests that communication with parents is vital to a student's success in his classroom. He prepares a letter and syllabus describing the year's activities and expectations and sends it home for parents to review with their students. The letter is to be signed by students and their parents and returned to school. In addition, Jay makes frequent calls to parents, mostly when students are doing well. He suggests that parents are more supportive and students more attentive and motivated as a result of these calls. In the past couple of years, Jay has added student-led parent writing portfolio conferences to his efforts to involve parents. He explains that one of the greatest benefits of the conference is it "allows parents to encourage and to connect with their son or daughter. In middle school students often stop talking to their parents as much as they did when they were younger. Yet, at this age they need the stability and the nurture and the guidance as much as ever. . . . This sort of interaction with the portfolio provides one more piece of common ground for parents and children" (Smith 1999, p.120). With the student-led parent conference, Jay is not only facilitating the school-home relationship but also the parent-child relationship. The STAR team encourages continuous communication with parents but also emphasizes service to the school community. Whether by bringing in canned goods, working on the school grounds, or visiting nursing homes, students learn to link their work in school with their membership in community.

As we think back to our experiences in these classrooms, we realize that these teachers have affirmed what we have long known about classroom communities. If we want all of our students to experience this level of learning, there is little mystery about what we must do: recruit teachers who care passionately about their students and their work, support these teachers in developing hands on/minds on lessons, and assist them in reaching out to parents and community. When we walked away from the classrooms of Betty, Jay, and Darlene and Ashley, we realized that we had witnessed something powerful: teachers who transformed their classrooms from the ordinary to the engaging, students who accomplished challenging tasks in ways that seemed natural to them, learning that inspired us as outsiders. Our best evidence is that their students are also inspired. When asked to comment on his teachers, one of the seventh graders on the STAR team replied:

She has been a mother to all of us. When something happens to us it happens to her. Ms. Wilson will sit down and talk to you, like she is your mother or your friend. You know, sometimes you don't want to share with your friends, you need someone older, who you feel comfortable with, to share what's going on. If she sees you crying she takes you out in the hallway and talks with you and asks you questions. Her teaching ways are very unique. She is very involved. She wants everyone being together and being involved. She doesn't want anyone to feel left out. When she sees someone left out or something she'll go over there and she'll talk to them and just make them feel good. (Seventh grade student, STAR Team, Washington Middle School, Spring 1999; McElrath 2000, p. 117)

References

Arhar, J.M., Johnston, J.H., and Markle, G.C. (1989). The effects of teaming on students. *Middle School Journal, 20* (3), 24–27.

Calhoun, F.D. (1983). *Organization of the middle grades; A summary of research.* Arlington, VA: Educational Research Services, Inc.

Carnegie Council on Adolescent Development. (1989) *Turning points: Preparing American youth for the 21st century.* New York: Author.

Darling-Hammond, L. (1998). Teachers and teaching: Testing policy hypotheses from a national commission report. *Educational Researcher, 27* (1), 5–15.

Lewis, C., Schaps, E., and Watson, M. (1996). The caring classroom's academic edge. *Educational Leadership, 54* (3), 16–21.

McElrath, M. (2000). *Cause and affect: Examining the dynamics of high functioning middle school teams and the perceived impact of these teams on the well being of students.* Unpublished doctoral dissertation, The University of North Carolina at Greensboro.

Peterson, K.D., and Deal, T.E. (1998). How leaders influence the culture of schools. *Educational Leadership, 56* (3), 58–60.

Smith, T.W. (1999). *Toward a prototype of expertise in teaching: A descriptive case study.* Unpublished doctoral dissertation, The University of North Carolina at Greensboro.

Strahan, D., and Toole, C. (2000, in progress). *Data and dialogue: Collaborative evaluation of middle schools.* Unpublished manuscript, The University of North Carolina at Greensboro.

7

On Headpieces of Straw: How Middle Level Students View Their Schooling

RICHARD R. POWELL

University of Colorado at Denver

We are the hollow men
We are the stuffed men
Leaning together
Headpiece filled with straw. Alas!
Our dried voices, when
We whisper together
Are quiet and meaningless
As wind in dry grass
　　　　—T.S. Eliot, 1930, p. 77,
　　　　　　from the poem *The Hollow Men*

This life in the fire, I love it,
I want it,
This life.
　　　　—L. Hogan, 1993, p. 11,
　　　　　　from the poem *The History of Red*

Introduction: A memoir

Schools tailored to the needs of eleven to fourteen year olds are filled with personal experiences that are often exploratory in nature. A hoped for outcome for middle level education is for these personal experiences to be positive and growth producing. However, some school experiences, because of varying circumstances, cause our students to feel quiet and meaningless, as if they had, as Eliot notes in the quote above, a headpiece filled with straw. What could be more tragic, in my judgment, than causing any student to feel this way: This is particularly true when students in early adolescence are, at the same time, filled utterly with a desire to be needed and filled utterly with the fire and passions of life.

Except for extreme circumstances, early adolescents want life so much, and middle schools, when they work according to such long held ideologies as child-centered schooling, hold potential for helping students realize this life. These kinds of schools help students build what Hogan (1993) would call productive fires from which to learn and then from which to love to learn. Part of these productive fires is helping middle school students be heard, although some students might need encouragement to express themselves, and others might need guidance for how best to bring their voices to the collective conversation (Powell 1997).

Students neither want nor need to whisper together in silence as they make their way through their middle school years; on the contrary, the early adolescent years, as argued in this chapter, and throughout this volume, are when their voices need to be lit with a fire and a passion for learning that continues beyond middle school. However, as a student in traditional junior high school many years ago, my youthful voice was silenced by the practice of tracking, and my life in school became more part of the margins than the mainstream, as I relate below.

I grew up in a town in southwestern Kansas. The mid-sized rural town where I lived was mostly segregated. My family, one filled with total unpredictability and pervasive alcoholism, lived in a small mobile home on the fringe of a lower socioeconomic (SES)[1] Black community. Consequently, I attended a lower SES ethnically diverse elementary school. I spent much of my out-of-school time playing back lot sports with friends who represented many varied ethnic groups, all lower SES. I remember really liking my elementary teachers, especially Ms. Mitchell who in fifth grade taught me long division after much effort. I was made to feel proud of the work I did in elementary school, thanks to the goodness and kindness of so many dedicated teachers.

My hometown had two highly traditional junior high schools (JHS). These schools were, in a rather uncreative way, called West JHS and South JHS because of their location in the town. Due to zoning, I was required to attend West JHS, the school that contained, in addition to me and my lower SES associates, middle and upper middle class students. At West JHS I was put in the lowest academic track. I remember, as if the day were yesterday, how badly I felt during the very first day of junior high school. After all students were assembled in the auditorium first thing in the morning, the principal began calling out groups of names. The first group of students was the highest academic track in the school; they were known as the bright students. In junior high we called them *the brains*. Each group of students whose names were called would leave the auditorium together. With growing anxiety and much disappointment, I remained sitting, waiting for my name to be called, only to watch group after group leave the auditorium. Finally, there were only a small number of students remaining to be called, and I was one of them. Over half of the students remaining attended my elementary school. We were the last to leave the auditorium; we comprised the lowest academic track at the junior high school. This was my first real experience with social class and academic discrimination at school. I began losing confidence in myself as a learner. According to the academic organization of the school, I clearly was not one of *the brains* in school. I began viewing myself as less than capable in learning school subjects. This tracking lingered on with me throughout high school. The lower level education I received in junior high school qualified me only for the lower level classes in high school. Being in the lower academic track throughout junior high, and then high school, when coupled with a very challenging and dysfunctional home life, ultimately led me to graduate in the lower one-fourth of my large high school class. The counseling I received in high school was that I should attend only trade school, and that I probably would not succeed in college. Yet I attended college because that was my mother's dream for me.

I have not returned to West JHS to see if the school, and the school district, has made changes in how they group students for learning. I hope changes have been made. Otherwise, I know students like me will be constructing personal meaning about themselves from living the experience of being labeled low achieving early adolescents, those who are viewed as being capable of learning only minimal content using highly structured instructional designs. After being placed in the lowest track, and then left there for the whole junior high experience, I felt that all I could do was whisper in the margins, not speak out in the mainstream, and I felt meaningless in the greater conversation of the school. Many years would pass until, later in college, I developed a fire and passion for learning; had it been instilled at West JHS, I might have felt better about myself and had more confidence as a learner throughout the years that followed.

I want to believe that in the three and one-half decades since I attended West JHS at least some progress has been made in lifting self-esteem and confidence of early adolescents. Yet practices such as tracking remain firmly embedded even in schools that carry the name *middle school*. This point is further supported by Bigelow's (1995) notion of victim blaming. Bigelow notes,

> Today, students who prove unresponsive to . . . memory games are often labeled "slow learners"—or worse—and find themselves dumped in a low-track class, called "basic" or "skills," understood by all as "the dumb class." This is classic victim blaming, penalizing kids for their . . . failure to recall disconnected factoids. (p. 155)

In junior high school I was clearly viewed as being in "the dumb class," where I remained for six years of my life. Today, many years after viewing myself as a member of this dumb class, I still struggle with affirming my academic and personal accomplishments. The latent effect of my school experiences along with family dysfunctioning had a profound influence on how I viewed myself for many years, perhaps my whole lifetime.

What this chapter is about

I need to clarify here that this chapter is not about academic tracking per se. Tracking was an important part of my memoir to demonstrate how traditional, subject-centered schooling with firm ability grouping can and did influence how I viewed myself, and how I still view myself today. Perhaps more importantly, being the last to be called in the auditorium at West JHS in part silenced my young and yearning voice. After being placed in the lower academic track, I was shuffled from one low-expectation class to another low-expectation class for many years. No one ever asked me what I needed, perhaps wanted, or what I hoped for in the future. However, what is clear is that traditional subject-centered schools, those with practices such as tracking, are not in a general way about student voice; they are about student obedience, about students whispering together in a somewhat quiet and meaningless tone, and for some students about eventually seeing self as academically hollow. About traditional subject-centered schools Dewey writes:

> Since the subject matter as well as standards of proper conduct is handed down from the past, the attitude of pupils must, upon the whole, be one of docility, receptivity, and obedience. (1938, p. 18)

When we find reinvented schools that affirm student voice, especially *some* schools that have overcome arrested development and indeed manifest themselves as middle schools in both policy and practice, then we find students who have voices that talk openly together, that are vocal and meaningful, and that are negotiating their education in part with their teachers and administrators (Boomer, Lester, Onore, and Cook 1992; Powell 1997, 1999; Powell and Skoog 1995). Another name for these kinds of schools is democratic. Such schools happen when students and teachers alike have common and shared interests, freedom of interaction, beneficial and equitable participation, and mutual social relationships. These same schools are where students and teachers demonstrate a democratic ideal called *solidarity*, a term described by Rorty (1995) that suggests a sharing of common goals, values, and intentions. Although some democratic ideals have been criticized more recently as eroding the scholarly approach to education, Apple and Beane (1995), in a claim that promotes democratic ideals, write:

> We admit to having what Dewey and others have called the "democratic faith," the fundamental belief that democracy has a powerful meaning, that it can work, and that it is necessary if we are to maintain freedom and human dignity in our social affairs. (p. 6)

Because of my former experiences in a traditional junior high school—one that was replete with subject-centered curriculum, academic tracking, non-negotiable relations between teachers and students, and limited if any academic freedom, the notions of progressive and democratic schooling were unavailable to me. Consequently, I have been driven these past years to explore students' lives in middle schools, the kind of schools that attempts to be more student-centered, that are progressively interdisciplinary and integrative, and that engage students more democratically in decisions about their own learning. To explore students' lives in these schools, I have turned to methods that ask students their *viewpoints,* that cause me to listen to *what they say,* and to *watch what they do* at school. Specifically, I have been striving to understand how middle level students live out the experience of being a student, and to understand what meaning they make from their school-based experiences when they are—and when they are not—given opportunities to express themselves in authentic and meaningful ways, what in postmodern discourse is called given opportunity to have *voice* in school contexts (Gergen 1991; Soohoo 1993). Consequently, the purpose of this chapter, and the research I did at Mountain Middle School (MMS)[2] to attain this purpose, is to build an understanding of the meaning that selected students derived from their middle school experience as they lived out their lives as students.

Searching for "meaning making" and "lived experience"

In my memoir above I sought to illuminate some of my experiences as a junior high school student in western Kansas through personal narrative.[3] Following the writing suggestions of Van Manen (1990) and following the exemplar offered by Ellwood (1997), I used my own experiences in junior high school as a starting point for this chapter, a chapter that proposes to heighten awareness of the meaning that one middle school had in the personal and academic lives of early adolescents.

Using an introductory memoir as process, I attempted to establish a context for which to explore the experiences of selected middle school students who are presently in school. That is, through the memoir I first offered a glimpse at the reflective *lived experiences* (Van Manen 1990) of my middle school years as I recalled the experiences many years later. Following the opening memoir and following teachers' views of their middle school context, I then consider the reflexive lived experiences of the students in this chapter, as students were presently embedded in these experiences, and as they expressed the views of the place these experiences had in their lives. Dilthey (1985) describes lived experience the following way:

> A lived experience does not confront me as something perceived or represented; it is not given to me, but the reality of lived experience is therefor-me because I have a reflexive awareness of it, because I possess it immediately as belonging to me in some sense. Only in thought does it become objective. (p. 223)

Van Manen (1990) interprets Dilthey's (1985) writing to mean that "lived experience is to the soul what breath is to the body" (p. 36). Striving to explore middle school students' lived experiences, I thus strove to understand the connection, if any, between one middle school's experiences and the soulful meaning students made from these experiences.[4] Such meaning, I assumed, would provide a view of the educational reality of the students, and provide a fuller understanding of how students internalize the processes that emanate from one school's interpretation and implementation of middle level ideology.[5]

A passageway

MMS was clearly different from West JHS that I attended. For example, where MMS was core-centered, West JHS was department-centered; where MMS was interdisciplinary, West JHS was subject-centered. MMS also fostered collaboration among students with their after-school program, West JHS fostered competition in both academics and sports. West JHS represents, as Lounsbury (1992) has argued, "the very practices that most middle level schools are seeking to move away from" (p. 3). MMS has been restructured to emulate contemporary versions of schooling for early adolescents, and has moved away from the model of schooling represented by West JHS.

MMS was my passageway to understanding how selected early adolescents perceived their school experience. Out of convenience I selected MMS. This was convenient because the school is a partner school with the university where I am currently working. Although a school of convenience for me, the school is in an interesting social situation. With approximately 930 students, the school has 70% mobility and 48% free and reduced lunches. The school is situated in the center of the largest mobile home community in the nation. Driving into the community that surrounds the school was clearly an eye-opening experience for me. Nothing but a series of mobile home communities surrounds the school for miles in any direction.

MMS is well maintained, clean, and somewhat manicured. The tennis courts on the south side of the school are very well kept. When I entered the school for the first time I noticed posters on the walls: "An open mind accepts what a closed mind rejects." "Diversity creates dimension in our world." "Give respect, get respect." Other similar posters were on the walls. I don't recall posters like these at West JHS. MMS consists of sixth, seventh, and eighth grades. Special education and ESL programs are in all grades. The school endorses interdisciplinary core teaching. In sixth grade there are two-teacher cores, which involve mathematics and science. In seventh and eighth grade there are four-teacher cores, which involve mathematics, science, English, and social studies. MMS has 22 clubs and organizations that students can participate in after school, including for example art club, barbell club, chess club, drama club, MathCounts, spelling bee, student council, and so on. In addition to the clubs and organizations at MMS, athletics is available for both young women and men, including softball, wrestling, volleyball, and other predominant sports.

Holding conversations

To explore students' views of their schooling, I talked with selected eighth grade students and their core teachers. I talked to teachers and students separately. For these conversational interviews, I followed the suggestions offered by Oakley (1981). By following these suggestions, the same suggestions I used in an earlier study (Powell 1997), I assumed the role of participant and co-discussant rather than detached interviewer.

Prior to talking to students I had a lengthy conversation with teachers during one of their team planning sessions. All four of the core teachers came together for the purpose of having a conversation with me about the school, about being middle level teachers, and about teaching early adolescents. The core teachers had been a team for eight years. As I interacted with teachers in their classrooms, and then as I sat with them to have a conversation, I became aware that I was in the presence of four highly professional teachers who functioned exceptionally well together, almost in total harmony. The classrooms of Dave (mathematics), Sue (English literature), and Mary (social studies) were adjacent to each other. Sharon's science classroom, however, was in the science wing of MMS, which was away from the other three classrooms. I was excited to talk with these teachers, to learn from them about their core teaching situation. I was also awed and certainly humbled when I sat in the midst of their obvious professionalism, their self-respect, their strong solidarity, and their collective consciousness as a team of like-minded teachers. They were taking time from their busy daily schedule to talk with me, and they approached my questions with patience, concern, reverence, and interest. I taped and transcribed our conversation.

At another time I also had a conversation with Kathy, a former teacher not part of the core team of teachers, who at the time of my visit to MMS was a site coordinator. MMS was a partner school with a local university, and Kathy was MMS site coordinator for the university. The conversations I had with all teachers were mostly informal, yet highly focused.

My time talking with students was more limited. Teachers were rightfully concerned about taking students out of class to have interviews with me. Consequently, I talked to the students after school, as time permitted, and taped and transcribed all interviews. Most of my conversations with students were approximately 30 minutes, and were semistructured.[6] Although brief, these conversations were highly informative and pertinent for exploring their lived experiences at MMS, and consequently their views of their school.

Teachers' perspectives

Although the central purpose of this chapter is to explore MMS students' views of their school, as the middle school ideology is implemented by the administration and by faculty, teachers' perspectives of their school context must first be examined. Students' voices must be heard within the context of the school, and within the context of their core (Oldfather and McLaughlin 1993; Powell 1993; Soohoo 1993). At MMS the teachers' and the school's formative nature provide the culture in which the students understand schooling on that campus, just as West JHS provided the culture in which I understood and interpreted my junior high school experience. Moreover, listening to teachers talk about their school and their teaching team provides needed insight into the pedagogical atmosphere in which teachers and students cocreate and coexist. Bollnow (1989a) describes pedagogical atmosphere as "all those fundamental emotional conditions and sentient human qualities that exist between the educator and the child and which form the basis for every pedagogical relationship" (p. 5). Following the writing of Bollnow, I assumed that the team of teachers, and the core culture they supported within the school, provided students with crucial emotional conditions that instantiated students' feelings of well being, or on the other hand their possible feelings of marginalization. I also assumed that emotional conditions, especially for early adolescent students, can and often do transcend academic conditions. Emotional well being, especially feelings of being cared for and personally valued, is as much a part of life for middle schoolers as is making good grades. Indeed, being cared for and personally valued ultimately influence what and how students learn. Kramer (1992) notes, "Students think about school; their interpretations of school life and the meanings they confer on teachers' actions, classroom processes, and school events have real consequences for how much they learn" (p. 28).

What I sought to obtain from the teachers was an idea of how the team

worked together on a daily basis. This, I hoped, would characterize the pedagogical atmosphere of the core team, and of the school in which the team existed. Because the core was such a significant structure in the school, I asked
teachers to describe it to me. Sue explained how the core works relative to an
interdisciplinary focus. Sue noted:

> English and Social Studies do interdisciplinary things the whole year
> long. Mary and I work back and forth. And English is set up in eighth
> grade to support interdisciplinary things. So that goes on all year. And
> then in seventh grade we did what we call a 4-person core interdiscipli-
> nary unit. That was a wetlands unit. We do anywhere from a 2 to 6 week
> unit on wetlands and the environment. And then we do a unit on world
> hunger around Thanksgiving. That is a four-person unit. We take our
> discipline and study hunger in each area.

I understood Sue to mean that the core has a few well defined interdisciplinary units, but most of the interdisciplinary effort was an ongoing, amor-
phous process. Dave confirmed my understanding of this process. He
explained:

> In math our focus has been to increase the writing and communication
> that occurs in math. Sue and I worked together on this. We said to our-
> selves, "This is the math component we want to achieve, so what would
> the writing component look like to achieve the math component?" So we
> put together an outline form for the kids to lead them through a five
> paragraph essay. That is now going to help them answer their mathemat-
> ical problems through a writing process.

What I concluded from teachers' descriptions of their unified academic work
was an ongoing blending of at least some agreed-upon interdisciplinary goals.
While some of these goals are explicit and reflect an interdisciplinary ideology
(e.g., wetland unit), others are less well defined and reflect a volitional collegiality that results in valuable cross-disciplinary collaboration (e.g., writing in math
class). Emerging from these explicit and implicit processes is a cohesive instructional subculture, what MMS calls a core, within the school.

In addition to the core structure, another important dimension of middle
schools—especially those schools that have clearly implemented a middle
school ideology—is purportedly bringing students into some kind of decision
making about their life at school. I sought to understand how these four teachers at MMS involved students in such decision making. I asked them how
much negotiation they did with students about the curriculum. Sharon quickly
commented:

I think our hands are more tied behind our backs here as far as having the time to allow kids to make some choices in their curriculum. This is because the amount of testing we do yearly now takes so much of our time that fitting student choices into my science curriculum in a year is just nearly impossible. So I feel quite limited in what I can allow kids to do.

Sue added a comment, "We don't have the luxury of that kind of time [that is needed to plan with students]." Mary then noted:

The kids bring up some good ideas and you don't want to discourage them, but at the same time you just can't spend a whole period on it. So it is very frustrating because of all our constraints. And it is getting worse! The fixed curriculum. The assessments we all have to do. It didn't seem to be that way ten years ago, but now they are really forcing all this on us.

Given the fixed curriculum, standardized testing, and instructional timelines, teachers felt they were unable to bring students into even minimal levels of decision making about either the social or academic curricula. Forces beyond the apparent control of the teachers, then, are interfering with the decision making ideology of the middle school structure at MMS.

Surfacing in my conversation with the core teachers and with Kathy was the metaphor of *family*. I first discovered the metaphor when I asked Kathy what the core means to teachers and students. Kathy replied:

The core means that you have the same kids, see the same teachers on a daily basis. The purpose is so you can be more consistent with kids. If teachers see something that is happening for a student in one classroom and the same thing happening in another core classroom, then they can help meet the needs of kids more appropriately. So I think the kids feel more like a family. They know what four teachers they go to, and those four teachers have the same rules and the same expectations. The kids know that there is a small group, a cohesive group, they can go to. The four teachers are like leaders of the family.

Although Dave didn't use the word "family," his comments clearly align with the family sentiment of Kathy. Dave noted,

I think there is more collaboration with us because we are more of a core of teachers working together. We have a lot more opportunity to be consistent and meet student needs. We all see a particular student and we can all have a common plan for that student. I think the success of the student is a lot higher in that setting. This way the student is getting the same basic classroom rules, procedures, policies, and expectations. Everything is concrete for the student.

Mary also spoke directly about the family dimension of the core. She noted, "If one of us says we are going to do something then we know it is going to get done. And that is just a family comfort feeling." Sue said, "Now we are at the point where we finish each other's sentences."

The teachers' core, as a family structure and as reflected by teachers' comments, has certain qualities that provide for a specific pedagogical atmosphere. I understood their core as offering a sense of communion between and among the teachers and their students, as providing a subcultural sense of identity (within the overall culture of the school), as offering a collective sense of unity and shared purpose, and as providing a place to go within the larger school context. The family dimension of the core reminded me of Carollyne Sinclaire's use of the *home* metaphor in her study of a school classroom. Sinclaire (1994) wrote:

> For me, "home" is a place which provides us with a sense of communion with others that helps the individual self emerge. Home helps us become conscious of the world around ourselves and establish an identity with others. Home calls to each of us a search for the familiar, the intimate, the safe, the place where one can take risks, fall and be accepted back in. (p. xix)

An experience I had while visiting the teachers' classrooms also reflects, in my judgment, the family effect that the core had on the students. After my interview with the teachers, I spent the remainder of the day moving among their classrooms. As I moved from class to class in the core, I expectedly moved with many of the same students. Later in the day one student asked me what I was doing since she had also seen me in two of her other classes. One way to interpret the student's curiosity is with the family metaphor. Had I been only in one of her classes perhaps she would not have asked me anything. But since I was attending the core family classes, she was curious about my intentions, and asked about my purposes. She wanted to be sure she knew why I was visiting her family.

As an educational family, the teachers had a felt moral obligation to guide their students into specific kinds of behaviors and actions; most of these behaviors and actions seemed to be nonnegotiable for students. The core had its rules and expectations, and students were simply expected to comply with these things. I asked Kathy what students must be willing to do in order to function successfully in such a situation. Kathy noted:

I think students must do the basics. Like if they are respecting other people. And if they are living up to the expectations of the core. Well, I wouldn't say living up to the expectations of the core, but I think doing what is expected of them in the core. I don't think anyone is unreasonable in their expectations.

Aside from the notion of reasonableness mentioned by Kathy, to function successfully, the students must align themselves in a wholesale manner with what is expected of them academically and behaviorally, although these expectations appeared to be constructed with little negotiatory input from students. Yet the actions of the teachers (e.g., to develop a certain set of expectations that not only is consistent with the culture of the core but also consistent with the broader culture of the school) suggest a felt need of teachers to care for the members of their family, especially since the core teachers have the same students for both seventh and eighth grades. During these two years the teachers have considerable responsibility to and high levels of accountability for developing a core-specific pedagogical atmosphere that influences students a certain way, hopefully a positive way. This means that the teachers have to continuously discern what is good or appropriate, or not good or inappropriate, for a group of students. Van Manen (1991) notes:

> Pedagogical action and reflection consist in constantly distinguishing between what is good or appropriate and what is not good or less appropriate for a particular child or group of children. In other words, pedagogical life is the ongoing practice of interpretive thinking and acting on the part of adults, but also and especially on the part of the children who continually interpret their own lives and who constantly form their own understandings of what it means to grow up in this world. This does not imply, of course, that every single thing we say and do with children places us in a situation of moral choice. But it does mean that our living with children is oriented in certain directions and that, as adults, we are accountable with regard to the reasonableness or goodness of our influencing of children. (p. 60)

This kind of accountability, I believe, when accompanied with an ongoing teacher attitude of concern and caringness, has brought about a certain value system shared by the core teachers. This value system, when transformed into school life, has put the core teachers in particular instructional roles. These roles are not necessarily *guide* or *facilitator*, although the teachers might occasionally assume such roles. Rather, the roles of teachers in the core, as I interpreted these roles, were *instructional leader* and *parent*, thus offering students a clear albeit challenging pathway. Consequently, the core as it functions within the broader culture of the school has established an atmosphere that has roots in traditional educational contexts, where negotiation between teachers and students is minimized, and where this same kind of negotiation between teachers and the larger administration is likewise minimized. In this situation negotiation and decision making, as democratic processes, are illusionary at best.

Despite limited decision making by students, a notable dimension of traditional school contexts, what certainly was a dimension for the core discussed in this chapter is a high level of predictability regarding academic and behavioral expectations, and regarding teacher personality and congeniality. This provides students with a basis for experiencing solidarity. This further provides them with a basis for developing feelings of safety, if the predictability indeed brings students into the collective conversation of the core and gives them a sense of meaningfulness and personal worth.

A function of having greater predictability relative to core expectations and established guidelines is providing students, as noted above, with lesser decision-making power and lesser freedom to express self. That students at MMS were not engaged in democratic forms of decision making was clear in the following comment made by Dave, who noted:

> I don't think there is a whole lot of decision making by the kids. And I would say the kids will say that too. Our district has a safe schools policy which means the kids cannot wear any professional sports teams' shirts and logos at all. That is definitely an issue with the kids because they like their sport logo clothing and can't wear it. Some years the kids say, "Why can't we have more dances or more socials? How come we don't have a Halloween party?"

That decisions are made *for* students, and not necessarily *with* them, is a feature of MMS, and thus a feature of the core. Although the school has a student council that is intended to bring issues to the forefront of the student body and to the school faculty, that this council makes significant strides to alter existing student expectations and freedoms is not clear.

Sue also pinpointed why she believes that students have less opportunities to make decisions beyond the curriculum, and consequently to have less freedom. Sue noted:

> The freedom outside the curriculum that we can allow kids to have has tightened up within maybe the last ten years because of safety and gang issues. A lot of things have been changed at the school. We are told what we can allow kids to do. As teachers we are told what the structure has to be.

Sue also felt that having a definite school structure has made the school a much safer place today, and that this structure is good for the students and good for instruction.

Interacting with these four teachers during our conversation and then interacting with them in their classrooms during and between classes led me to conclude that they have an obvious team focus on their instruction. They have this same focus on the social dynamics that occur for them and the students within the core. The teachers had worked together for eight years, which had given them time to develop a core consciousness. In other words, they thought together as a team and they worked with a high level of collegiality to address daily challenges. The teachers in some ways depended upon each other for assistance in their teaching, and consequently they produced notable interdisciplinary units. The notability of the units is evidenced by the district's publication and circulation of them for use in other schools. The interdisciplinary practice of the core, the same practice that other teams in the school also demonstrated, is consistent with instructional trends in middle schools elsewhere. McEwin, Dickinson, and Jenkins (1996) report that "interdisciplinary teams at the three grade levels in 6–8 middle schools [are] growing toward the predominant instructional plan for core area instruction" (p. 26). Despite the interdisciplinary nature of the core, the teachers lack sufficient time, as Sharon noted, to move beyond curricular constraints to be more innovative with curriculum and instruction.

Although the four teachers work together on some instructional units, they also maintain independence in their content areas. The pedagogical atmosphere of the core, an atmosphere that is commensurate with the family metaphor, is one filled with consistent, clear, and predictable expectations for students. Concomitant with these expectations is a high level of teacher commitment to student success. The teachers, as I heard them talk about student productivity, want their *family* of students to be prepared for future learning. The core teachers viewed a certain degree of rigor as necessary. Students are expected to work diligently. As an example, when I visited the core's classrooms I was struck by the on-task behavior in all classes, that both students and teachers were focused on learning while at the same time mutual respect was clearly evident.

What is not clear to me after being with the core is the dimension of democratic schooling. Students, as Dave noted, do not really have much decision-making power. Sue indicated that freedoms beyond the taught curriculum are very limited for students. This was the pedagogical atmosphere, as I understood it, that the students associated with during seventh and eighth grades. When I talked to the students they had completed two months of their eighth grade year, and they had experienced the core's pedagogical atmosphere for over one school year. Talking to eighth graders, I assumed, would provide a valid indication of how some students viewed their schooling experiences not just within the subculture of the core, but also within the broader culture of the MMS.

Students' voices

An important construct that is providing a means to explore lived experiences of students is *student voice*. The notion of voice has two purposes, both of which will be addressed in the remainder of this chapter. One purpose is to explore the reality of students' lives at school, as they offer verbal reports about these lives in conversations and interviews (Powell and Skoog 1995). Achieving this purpose can result in empirical reports that offer readers insight into how school impacts the daily lives of students. Moreover, the empirical nature of student voices draws our attention to students' experiences, and makes their lives central to our understanding the efficacy of middle school contexts. A second purpose is to use the construct of student voice as a political phenomenon. With this second purpose the idea of voice becomes a powerful metaphor for examining the extent that students, as individuals, are brought into the collective educational conversation of the school; that is, the extent they are involved as decision makers, and the extent they are provided with freedoms that they deem necessary for increasing the value of the school experience.

Regardless of which of the aforementioned purposes are sought, the construct of student voice is complex. Perhaps one of the biggest challenges when working with voice, certainly a challenge I faced in this chapter, is to report students' voices validly and authentically. As I listened to the students who talked to me, and later as I transcribed the interview tapes, I sought as much as possible to organize their expressions into valid categories that best depict their views of their schooling experience. These categories are below.

Best case school: "It has less students in the class . . . and they have like more time to talk to you"

One goal of the middle school structure, namely the school-within-a-school structure (i.e., core), is to offer students a sense of belonging to a smaller part of the school. Belonging to a smaller part of the school leads to knowing certain teachers better, perhaps communicating with them on more personal levels. However, when class size remains excessive, students still feel they get less time from core teachers, and they want their teachers to talk to them more often in class. While larger class size does not totally minimize the effects of the core structure, it does support longstanding instructional classroom practices of factory-like schooling, where large numbers of students are managed with century-old approaches to education, approaches that were in place well before the middle school movement. Such factory-like approaches can cause students to feel less connected to teachers and their classes (Beane 1997; Lounsbury 1992), as students' comments suggested. For example, I asked Joan to characterize a middle school that would be named after her. She thought for a few moments, then replied: "Because it has more talking to students, and it has less students in the class, so teachers aren't swamped with work and they have like more time to talk to you so you understand it better. That is the kind of school that would be named after me." Similar findings were reported by Poole (1984) in her study of adolescents' expressed needs for school.

Despite students' concerns over excessive class size and consequently over having less classroom time with teachers, students still felt more familiar with their core teachers than other teachers in the school. Moreover, students knew more clearly what was expected of them from core teachers than non-core teachers, and they felt like they were part of the core family, although none of the students used *family* as a metaphor to describe the core or the teachers. I talked to Jane and Mike about their experiences in the core.

RICHARD: What has it been like being in a core for two years?
JANE: I do like the core idea.
MIKE: I like the core idea too. Its pretty cool to have the same teachers cause you know how they teach. You expect what you are going to get for homework. And you expect how you are going to keep up your grades and stuff too.
JANE: You get to know the teachers really well.
MIKE: You really know them.

As I listened to the students talk about their core experience, the family metaphor became more valid, certainly more real. Joan's perspective is a valid depiction of the core structure at MMS. Joan noted:

RICHARD: What is a core?
JOAN: A core is like you have four teachers and they are all teaching different things but they all get the same kids. And the teachers may be in different classes but they are teaching the same kids.
RICHARD: What is that like for you?
JOAN: I really don't know anything else but core so I couldn't really tell you. But I think it is pretty nice. Like in high school you go to this one teacher, and then to a different teacher someplace else. But our core does like stuff together. Like we just went outside and we watched a movie today for all these tests we have to take.
RICHARD: Did all the students watch the movie as a core?
JOAN: Yeah. And we do field trips together and stuff like that. And I like that.
RICHARD: What does that mean for you?

JOAN: It's pretty nice because you get to know the people in your core. I mean you know people out of your core, but you get to know the people in your core better cause you are always getting together and stuff. And this gives you more confidence for having friends and stuff. And having like best friends. So I like it.

One function of teachers being in a core is so that students can see teachers working together on units thus giving some kind of instructional coherence to the taught curriculum. This is a central feature to the cross-disciplinary ideology of the middle school movement. Teachers who work closely together, who actually strive to achieve the cross-disciplinary ideology, provide students with various opportunities to see the collegiality that predominates the pedagogical atmosphere of the core. I talked to Jane and Mike about this collegiality.

JANE: Some of our classes are linked together. For American History we are doing, well, American History. But in English we have to do a book report each trimester on fiction or nonfiction related to American History. And you know that area down by the creek, that is actually a wetlands. And last year we all did a unit on that. We did some stuff on science and math and everything.

MIKE: In math we measured the length of the creek, how far it is. In science we learned about creatures in the creek. If we found one we would catch one, examine it, then let it go.

JANE: And we cleaned the creek up. There were like tires, a baby stroller, stuff down there, all sorts of junk. This is because we only do this once a year.

RICHARD: Sounds like in various classes you went to the wetlands.

JANE: Yeah, just in our core. Only in the core.

Not all of the students I talked to were complacent with the core structure. Ann and Christy, for example, had other perspectives.

RICHARD: What is it like being in a core for two years.

ANN: It gets boring after two years.

RICHARD: Why is that?

ANN: You have different friends in another core, and you should get a chance to be with friends in other cores and have different teachers and a little variety. But you have to be in the same classes with the same teachers.

CHRISTY: I don't like it because you don't get to have different teachers, but we stay with the same teachers so I already know how they are.

RICHARD: What are advantages and disadvantages of that?

CHRISTY: I think an advantage is that you know how the teachers act and all that. This is a hard question. I don't know, I can't really explain.

ANN: Well, I kind of like it but then I don't like it. Because like [Christy] said, we don't get to be with our other friends.

RICHARD: Do you know when the core teachers are doing something together.

ANN: Only when they are having an assembly for the core, like on Mondays. You can tell they plan things together, because they always talk about what the other teachers are doing.

The students I interviewed had clear conceptions of the core structure. Some liked it, and others felt socially constrained by it. Importantly, none of the students reported that they felt academically constrained by the core structure. Indeed, that academic expectations were made more clear by being in the core is notable.

Whether constrained or not, what is important to note is that the students definitely felt like they were part of the core, what several of the teachers have described as an educational family. Certain features of the core, as implied by students' comments, surface as crucial to the development of the students. The structure and expectations of the core are "clear, orderly, and predictable" (Bollnow 1989b). This structure and corresponding expectations, to follow Bollnow (1989b), are central to the development of the students. Bollnow (1989b) writes: "Despite the fact that intrusions by threatening events will occur, it remains true that the child can properly develop only in an environment which is relatively clear, orderly, and predictable" (p. 17). That the teachers have striven to develop such an environment is clear from both teacher and student interviews. A middle school environment that is clear, orderly, and predictable, I assume, is also an environment that offers a feeling of security and safety. Importantly, this provides a space in the school, if needed, where students can withdraw and feel secure, even feel sheltered and trusted. The central task for the core teachers, as derived from Bollnow (1989b),

> . . . is to create a space for such trust, which will form the ground of a sense of security in spite of all calamities and all threats. The child must be able to perceive the possibility of a sound world because without this basis no human existence can stand. And where this trust is omitted one may expect the occurrence of inner and outer disintegration. (p. 16)

My conversation with Christy and Ann suggested that not all students value the core structure. Although this valuing is based on social not academic values, I got the impression that Christy and Ann felt secure in the core, that the core did not present them with any kind of personal threat academically or socially. I also got the impression that neither Christy nor Ann felt their personal lives were being threatened on any level by being in a core. Bollnow (1989b) writes: "That is why we must cultivate this feeling of security in a trusted realm, even if children at certain stages of development do not seem to value it" (p. 18). The teachers I interviewed were clearly striving to develop this trusted realm, to give students a refuge and a safe place to be themselves.

What was evident in the conversations I had with Joan and Ann was that students trusted their core teachers. I was surprised by their responses to specific questions in the following dialogue:

> RICHARD: If you met me the first time I came into this school, [Mountain Middle School], and you were going to show me the most important thing in this school, would that be?
> ANN: A classroom. I would want to show you how well children can learn in a good environment.

Ann could not have said "classroom" in the aforementioned dialogue unless she trusted her teachers, unless she felt that the classroom was indeed a refuge for her personhood. When I asked Joan a similar question, her response reflected her primary interests in school.

> RICHARD: If I came into this school for the first time and you met me at the door, what is the first thing you would show me at [MMS]?
> JOAN: Probably the gym. Cause I feel proud that our school works on sports. Most middle schools work on their academics mostly and don't work on their sports and stuff. But our school works on sports. It works on sports and academics. And I think that is a good thing. But I would also show you the library because I really like to read.

In many respects the core of teachers and students I explored may be already *best case* given external curriculum constraints, and given the values that teachers have for the personal lives of students. Students clearly have pride in the kind of instruction they are receiving from their core teachers, otherwise they would not want to take me to classrooms, gymnasiums, and libraries as key features of their school. They trust their teachers, and they see various parts of the school as a refuge (e.g., classroom, gymnasium, library). While students would prefer to have fewer students per class, and while they would like to have more individual attention from teachers, they also feel like they are an integral part of an educational family, what MMS calls a core. In the next section I consider more closely why some students want to move away from the core structure in middle school and move into high school.

On family discontent: "I can't wait to get to high school."

The discontent I recorded from Ann and Christy about the core may very well be a function of their developmental readiness to move away from the boundaries of the family, and into the wider freedoms of high school structures. This is not, in my judgment, a student criticism of the core, but rather a felt need these students had to move into a culture that aligned more with their needs as developing eighth grade female students, as the following conversation suggests:

> ANN: In elementary you get a bunch of attention because they are younger children, and have more fun. And high school you have more fun too, like dances and everything. You get more opportunity and privileges. Like in middle school you are too young to do some things, and too old to do other things that elementary students do.
>
> RICHARD: When you say more privileges at the high school, [Ann], and not as much here at the middle school, what do you really mean?
>
> ANN: High school has more activities and because you are older you can go somewhere else. You could also go off campus for lunch and everything. So things are kind of unfair here at the middle school.
>
> RICHARD: [Christy], what about you?
>
> CHRISTY: I don't like it here. I think they are too tough on us here. Too many rules, like that one where we can't hug another person. We can't even hug like a girl or they get all mad at us. I want to get to high school. I can't wait to get to high school. Cause we get like homecoming and prom. And they are more lenient about hugging and all that.
>
> RICHARD: What is the hardest thing about being here at MMS.
>
> ANN: The rules.
>
> RICHARD: What about you, [Christy]?
>
> CHRISTY: The work and the rules.

The rules of MMS, when combined with the rigor, structure, and expectations of the core, and when combined with minimal decision-making opportunities in school, caused Ann and Christy to feel discontent with their middle school experience. As I noted above, I also attribute part of this discontent to the developmental maturation of the girls. This maturation brought about new personal needs that the middle school context, as it was constructed and maintained, could not necessarily meet. Unlike educators at other levels, middle school educators are thus in a very challenging position to accommodate the developmental maturation of students. The physical and emotional changes that early adolescent students experience can cause them to develop considerable discontent with middle school life, as Ann and Christy demonstrated in the aforementioned conversation. Kathy, the non-core teacher with whom I talked, noted the challenges that middle level educators have with early adolescent students:

> I think that is something you have to keep in mind about middle school students, that their hormones are really changing. And one day they will be happy and the next day or even later that day they will be crying. So all the physical changes that go on with kids I think are difficult and I think teachers really need to be aware of that. I think the other thing too is middle school kids are trying to break away from their parents and be independent. But they still need structure and they still need somewhat of a mentor or someone there. Although many of them are trying to get away from that, deep down they need it and they want it. I think that structure is important too, and being able to have a school that would give structure but also the freedom to do other things.

In the foregoing comment Kathy makes several assumptions that when transformed in school practice leads to a structured environment where teachers become adult mentors. Of importance in Kathy's comment is that middle schoolers "are trying to break away from parents and be independent." Returning momentarily to the family metaphor for the core gives insight into the comments made by Ann and Christy. Both girls want to be in high school, they are tired of middle school rules and boundaries. Yet both girls had developed into young women, they were physically mature and emotionally ready for commensurate relationships with peers: they listed attending dances, attending proms, leaving campus for lunch, and hugging friends as reasons they wanted to be in high school. Viewing the core as an educational family and core teachers as surrogate parents, then, offers metaphorical reason that explains why the girls are discontent with middle school: as persons who are developing emotionally and physically into more mature beings, they are trying to break away from their educational family and be independent.

Having both structure and freedom for early adolescents, as Kathy notes above, is a challenge for any middle school culture. The question surfaces: What kind of structure allows students enough freedom so they can indeed realize their developmental nature? Kathy argues that a middle school should have structure but also freedom within the structure. In the next section I examine students' perspectives of freedom at MMS. To examine freedom I draw explicitly upon the construct of *student voice*.

On the boundary line: "I can't think of any freedoms we have here."

The construct of *voice* when applied to students and their teachers has now become idealized. Several phrases related to voice have become trendy in educational circles, and are often bantered about loosely without much thought as to the complexity of this construct. These phrases include, "Give students more *voice* in the classroom." "Give teachers more *voice* in school decision making." One way of understanding these aforementioned phrases is to stretch the established boundaries so teachers and students can be included in more decision making. Another way of understanding the phrases is to bring a democratic ideology into schools and classrooms, thus giving teachers and students more freedom in what they do. Central to stretching boundaries and bringing a democratic ideology into school is creating a collective conversation, where students are permitted to be more openly expressive about how school life might best unfold. This is explained by Gertrude Noar (1961):

> Classroom administration, control, and teaching techniques are all affected when schools change from authoritarianism to democracy. Teachers seek ways of allowing the students to have their rights respected. They admit them to the process of planning for the work to be done, and give them many opportunities to make decisions that are of importance to them. Students take part in setting up their goals and in evaluating the outcome of their activities in terms of their objectives. In these experiences, children clarify their thoughts, identify their problems, and learn to take action. Practice in doing adult things of this nature contributes to maturity. (p. 45)

Importantly, there exist many freedoms in Noar's description of a democratic classroom, including students setting up their goals, evaluating the outcome of their activities, and making decisions that are of importance to them. When I asked Kathy (teacher) about how democracy plays a part in the lives of students at MMS, she replied that school democracy has not been a concern or a focus of hers. She said that she and the other teachers "just do what is right for kids" regardless of whether or not this rightness aligns with the writing of Noar, for example, or others who endorse democratic schooling (Apple and Beane 1995; Beane 1997; Stevenson and Carr 1993). What appears right for most kids at MMS are clear and definite boundaries, straightforward expectations, and highly predictable behaviors, what Noar (1961) would call authoritarianism and what Dewey (1938) would call traditional education, despite the family orientation that surfaces from MMS's core design.

The authoritarian and mostly traditional infrastructure of MMS, an infrastructure that is misaligned with some progressive middle school models today (Powell 1999), delimits student voice, and thus delimits student freedoms like those mentioned above by Noar. I asked Christy and Ann about any freedoms they might have at MMS. They replied:

CHRISTY: I can't think of any freedoms we have here?

ANN: The only thing I can think about is after lunch they let you go outside if the weather is nice.

CHRISTY: We did that in elementary school though.

ANN: This is not exactly like a prison but they still have to keep you inside. It kind of gets boring after a while.

RICHARD: Can you think of anything at all where you have freedom at school?

CHRISTY and Ann: (shake heads no)

CHRISTY: In Miss [Sue's] class when we have reading time she will let us go outside if that's any freedom.

As I continued talking to students about freedom thus trying to explore the nature of their voice in the core and in school, I realized that what students viewed as freedoms were mostly unlike what adult educators viewed as freedoms. This became clear in my conversations with Mike and Jane.

RICHARD: Talk to me about what freedom means to you.

JANE: Well, it is like, you don't have to do stuff that people want you to do. And I would like it if they would make gym class an elective because that is not exactly my favorite class.

MIKE: Freedom to me in middle school would be picking your own classes, getting more time for lunch, a lot more things.

JANE: What I really like freedom wise is like they treat you sort of like an adult, at least more than in elementary school. They actually treat you like a human, or more so anyway.

RICHARD: When you say being treated like a human, what do you mean?

JANE: Well they treat you like an adult, like you are more mature and they know you can have intelligent conversation and stuff.

Interestingly, Jane equated freedom with being treated like an adult. I also related her comment about having intelligent conversation to having a respected voice in school. As I listened to Jane I was reminded of Gergen's (1991) perspective of the treatment—certainly democratic treatment—that today's students should receive in school. Gergen noted, "Teachers would invite students into modes of dialogue as participants rather than pawns, as collaborative interlocutors instead of slates to be filled" (p. 250).

Although Jane believed she was treated more like an adult and thus she owned some kind of freedom, the other students felt constrained by school rules and expectations. For students to have more voice at school is a question, as Greene (1993) writes, of *releasing* them from existing boundaries. Greene (1993) writes:

> It is not a matter of determining the frames into which learners must fit, not a matter of having predefined stages in mind. Rather, it would be a question of releasing potential learners to give them voice. (p. 219)

What MMS appears to be faced with is the question asked by James Beane (1993): "If we truly mean to have a school that is responsive to young adolescents, then we must ask, 'Where are their voices in this effort'" (p. 195)? Of course there necessarily exists varying interpretations for how a school can be responsive. Each interpretation is circumscribed by certain values; democratic educational values are not part of every interpretation. Because MMS has elected to follow a more authoritarian model, their potential for bringing student voice into the collective conversation about how classroom and school life should unfold is minimized. Consequently, students view themselves as having less freedom at school. However, should a school like MMS desire to provide students with an education that causes them to be more suitably prepared to function well in a democratic society and causes them to become more mature thinkers and decision makers in social contexts, then *student voice* as a political construct must be brought more explicitly into the collective conversation of the school. Gordon (1988) writes:

> The possibility of things that are worthy in themselves emerging in human society is contingent on the existence of what Arendt believed to be the *sine qua non* of freedom, namely, the existence of a public space in which a person can influence and be influenced by one's peers, through act and deed, through conversation and debate. So we seem to have reached a dilemma whereby thinking is necessary for education for democracy, while for that thinking to emerge one must have political freedom to begin with. (p. 55)

One way to interpret political freedom in Gordon's comment is to understand political freedom as student voice, since student voice is a political construct in school discourse. That students do not have such a political voice at MMS is clear. However, the kind of authoritarian model that MMS and its core teachers have implemented on a daily basis has clearly provided students with yet two other valued dimensions—namely trust and confidence. From talking to teachers I believe they have confidence in their students, and students have confidence and trust in their core teachers. About confidence Bollnow (1989c) writes: "Confidence is of high educational importance because it enhances the achievements and improves the development. True educational responsibility is demonstrated by the well-balanced amount of confidence we have in children" (p. 38).

From talking to students I also believe that they trusted their core teachers. Some students might not have been content with the core structure, others of them might be ready to move on to a more mature setting, and almost all of them believed they had no freedom, and hence no voice, in school. But they trusted their teachers. Bollnow (1989c) explains: "Trust demands a response. There is no trust without faith which we have toward a person who has trust in us" (p. 38). Although students felt they had no freedom in school, they yet trusted their teachers, and they had faith that teachers were doing what was needed for them. This is evident in student comments earlier in this paper that revealed students would take a visitor first to the classroom. Without trust and faith in their teachers, students would clearly choose other places in the school to first take a visitor.

MMS provides a view of a school that is certainly not unlike other middle schools. MMS is supporting certain dimensions of the middle school ideology (e.g., core structure, interdisciplinary curriculum), but maintains a curriculum infrastructure that is authoritarian, not negotiable or democratic. The originators of the middle school movement, particularly those that were more progressive in their educational beliefs, suggested that middle schools explicitly reflect democratic values and move toward constructing a culture that reflects a democratic ideology (David 1998; Noar 1961; Van Til, Vars, and Lounsbury 1961; Van Til 1971; Vars 1969). Two middle schools I have studied elsewhere, Brown Barge Middle School (BBMS) in Pensacola, Florida, and Carver Academy in Waco, Texas, have incorporated a democratic ideology almost to a profound level (Powell 1999). Students in these schools take a proactive part in determining how teaching and learning might best occur. Students especially at BBMS reportedly have a strong sense of ownership in the curriculum and in their own learning (Powell and Skoog 1995).

The core teachers I talked to at MMS did not seem to be concerned about the nondemocratic nature of MMS or about the theory of democracy as it might be implemented and as it might provide students with personal benefits, including more voice in decision making and more ownership of the curriculum. The teachers, however, were clearly concerned about the academic well being of their students and about how effectively the students were being prepared for high school. The teachers were also concerned about the safety of their students; that no harm would come to them while they were in school.[7]

Although students could think of no freedoms they had in school, and although they viewed themselves as existing within a set of rules and expectations that constrained their voices as political beings, they had an important level of trust and confidence in their teachers. The family orientation of the core caused the students I interviewed to feel cared for. I interpreted the middle school climate of MMS and of the core, then, to retain remnants of authoritarian schooling while subscribing to the structural dimensions of middle school ideology, namely core-centered interdisciplinary teaching. MMS had restructured itself relative to subject matter organization, yet elected to forego some of the political elements of middle schools that could have brought students more fully into instructional decision making. However, there was some decision making reported by the students, as described in the next section.

Looking inwardly: "Yeah. We have some decision-making power."

Middle school students are often faced with very simple decisions, such as choosing a specific candy bar at the local convenience store. Other decisions they make might not be so simple, like deciding which parent to visit on the weekend, deciding on whether to stay in school or drop out, or deciding whether to try cocaine with friends after school. Early adolescents are faced with many challenging decisions, and are forced to grow up very early in their life. As early adolescents are faced with challenging decisions, so are the middle schools they attend. Such school-wide decisions, which MMS faces every day, are not always about what content to teach, but about how to reach students in order to bring them to the content in meaningful ways.

As I talked to MMS students and as I considered the communities where they live, I began to wonder about the kinds of decisions they make at school. I began to wonder even more about what kind of student decision making that MMS promoted. If the students view themselves as having no freedom, how do they view themselves relative to decision making? Are the students asked to "reflectively step back, analyze [a] *situation*, deliberate about possible alternatives, decide on the best course of action, and act on this decision" (Van Manen 1991, p. 108)? Is the *situation* about an issue which can help students become responsible citizens? Is the *decision* they make based on critical thought, thus bringing about critical and responsible action and thus bringing about an outwardly perspective? On the other hand, given the personal challenges that so many students face, are school decisions minimized and focused on school-related issues, thus bringing about instructional obedience, forced gratitude, and an inwardly perspective?

Ideally, the middle school movement has consistently promoted the kind of decision making in students that can provide them with an outwardly perspective, and that can help them build self-confidence as thoughtful decision makers. I asked both MMS teachers and students about student decision making. When I asked Mary (teacher) about student decision making, she noted:

I think truly the only decisions they get to make are when they register for their classes each year. They get to pick electives. Band. Foreign language. They pick two or three classes, however many electives they have, and that is pretty much it. We tell them in high school they will get to choose more and more. But I am sure they probably go home and their parents tell them which electives to take. And so their choices probably even dwindle more.

These aforementioned comments of Mary were supported by Joan (student):

RICHARD: Joan, have you been involved in any kind of decision making at the school?
JOAN: Not really. The only decision I had to make was to go to Algebra.
RICHARD: No other decisions at all that you can think of?
JOAN: No. Not really.

When I talked to Ann and Christy I learned that they participated in some decision making, but this also was mostly about which classes to pursue.

RICHARD: What about decision making at MMS? Do you have any of that?
ANN: Yeah, we have some. Like at the end of the year they have a questionnaire they give out that lets you choose what classes you want to be in and what after school activity you want to be in. And you can say what activities might be good to add.
CHRISTY: Well, we have student council. And they can make decisions for different kinds of stuff. Like they get to plan spirit days and all that. But really there isn't much decision making here.

Another form of decision making for students was noted by Sue (teacher), although this decision making is also linked directly to instruction. I asked the MMS teachers to brainstorm the kinds of decisions that students are encouraged to make in school. Sue's comment I believe needs highlighting. She noted:

I don't know if kids could see the decisions [they make]. Like my students are working in groups right now and they had to come up with ten things they needed to do for this project. They could do it however they wanted and with whomever they wanted. I mean this is freedom and choice but I don't know if kids could see that. Because actually they have to do the lesson, but within the lesson they have choices.

Sue believes, as she reports, that students have at least some freedom and some decision making within her structured lesson. This kind of decision making and freedom are valuable in that students do have some autonomy, although this autonomy is limited to instructional decision making. That this limited autonomy actually builds students' self-confidence in making informed and reflective decisions in an outwardly manner is not clear. Moreover, an important aspect of Sue's lesson is that students were unable to negotiate those parts of the lesson where decision making actually occurred. Hence, the entire lesson and its perceived levels of freedom and decision making are in the control of Sue, not necessarily a function of negotiation between Sue and her students (Boomer et al. 1992). That Sue's lesson actually provides an outwardly form of decision making, where students can fundamentally reach toward self-actualization through negotiated decision making and negotiated lessons, is also unclear.

What surfaces at this point in my discussion is the question: What do we really want early adolescents to make decisions about? Within traditional middle school culture, like the culture of MMS, students are notably limited to decisions about school. Mostly, they are limited to decisions about a few classes to take, and about a few extracurricular activities in which to participate. Both students and teachers at MMS were clear that there is essentially no student freedom in this kind of decision making structure.

Interestingly, the middle school culture assumes a certain level of maturity in students. While the hormonal argument for maturity of early adolescents is indeed valid, it is also shallow and shortsighted. Society, in a general way, has instantiated an immature perspective for early adolescents, thus limiting what freedom they have in and out of school, and limiting what decisions they might make if allowed to have such an opportunity. As an example, I will draw from an important comment made by Sharon (teacher). During my conversation with the teachers, Sharon noted:

> I think the students are emotionally driven. All of their things are just emotional and if they could change things (in school) they would make their lunch periods longer and get to wear whatever they want and stuff like that.

Comments from students validated Sharon's claim. When I asked students what they would change about the school, they reported having longer passing periods between classes, wearing clothes they wanted, having open lunch times, and so on. After hearing Sharon and after confirming Sharon's comments with students' comments, I began to wonder about having more mature expectations for early adolescent students, about having students participate in activities both in and out of class that would cause them to move beyond the immaturity we have imposed upon these young people. Decision making that gives students an investment in the on goings of the school might cause adult educators to see early adolescents as more than hormone-raging beings that must look inwardly in their decision making, not outwardly toward the larger society and how they fit into this society with their ability to make decisions that are socially significant. A comment made by Ann (student) clarified, if not crystallized, the need to move beyond a perspective of early adolescents as immature hormonal beings in a holding pattern until they reach high school.

> RICHARD: If there is one thing you want me to share with the bigger world about who you are as a student, what would that be?
> ANN: That is a tough question. (pause) I would want you to share this: Don't ever over- or underestimate a middle school student. Some people think that middle school people are immature and some people, like younger kids, think we are bullies walking around or something. And high school kids think we are immature. But we are important people too. We can think. And we have important feelings. We are not little kids waiting to grow up.

Impressions and memories

I returned to MMS several times after gathering information for this chapter. During these later visits I usually arrived toward the end of the school day. Each time I pulled up to the school there were so many parents waiting to pick up their children that I could rarely find a parking space. By the time I made these final visits to the school I felt like I was finally developing an insider's view of MMS, if only a minimal insider's view, since I was not a teacher there. Over a period of weeks I had talked in a focused way with eighth grade students and their core teachers, talked extensively to a non-core teacher who was in the role of a site coordinator, eaten in the cafeteria with kids, interacted informally with the principal, visited with teachers in the faculty lounge, visited core classrooms during instruction, and interacted with some of my university students who were working at the school to become teachers. Most importantly, I transcribed all tapes made from conversations and interviews, and I examined the transcripts closely for themes that appeared to be the most telling about students' lived experiences in school. I realize that the themes I organized are limited by how I understood students' and teachers' responses to my questions. Other areas about MMS and the core that might have been discussed could have broadened and strengthened my impressions of students' lived experiences.

Listening to what students said about their schooling experiences provided me with an opportunity to compare my experiences at West JHS (WJHS) years ago with their experiences today at MMS. I used this comparison to see what strides MMS had made in transforming its earlier educational context into one called middle school. In some ways my earlier experiences were similar to the MMS students I interviewed. In other, important ways, they were dissimilar.

Like students at MMS, at WJHS I had no broader freedoms, very little decision making (about which few optional courses to take), and no student voice. Also like MMS, WJHS was not democratized on any level. Both MMS and WJHS were tracked. The tracking at MMS seemed to be more subtle until I talked to Joan (student), who explained more clearly how the tracking works at MMS. When I compared the two schools, I began to understand why MMS students told me that they had no freedom and only limited decision making.

On the other hand, MMS had moved beyond WJHS in important ways. The core structure of MMS provided a family effect for teachers and students that was totally lacking at WJHS. Listening to MMS students convinced me that they felt mostly comfortable with the core, and they trusted their core teachers more than other teachers in the school. I also sensed that teachers were deeply committed to helping students maximize their learning experiences. Students saw teachers working together collegially and collaboratively. I never saw or experienced any of this at WJHS. MMS had, in many ways, become a contemporary middle school. Yet I could not help but wonder how much further it might consider going to bring student voice more into the collective conversation about teaching and learning.

Although I had friends in junior high school, and although I had some memorable experiences at WJHS (e.g., I still have the cutting board I made in wood shop), instructionally I felt hollow. When I wrote my memoir about being at WJHS, no positive feelings came forth. Of course, this was a challenging time for my family at home, and that could have played a part in reactions to my early adolescent years in school. I am sure that there were students at WJHS who had a much better experience in school than I. Yet being in the lowest academic track day after day, I felt that my tracked peers and I, as a group perceived by teachers to be less capable of learning, had—as Eliot wrote—"dried voices [that were] quiet and meaningless as wind in dry grass."

I clearly talked to a limited number of students at MMS. Yet those I talked to, as they came to me from within a core family structure, gave me the impression that they wanted their school life, that they did not feel quiet and meaningless. There may have been students at MMS—those to whom I did not talk—who would have rather been anywhere else but school, but the school tried in so many ways to connect kids to MMS. The myriad of afterschool clubs and organizations provided something for every student, and the core structure enabled teachers to help meet the personal and academic needs of all students in a very real way. WJHS and its students would have certainly benefited from this arrangement.

That MMS has made strides to implement some aspects of the middle school movement is clear; that it might move farther along the continuum is a worthy consideration. I make this claim based not merely on the broader middle school philosophy, but also on the writings of Van Manen (1991), who notes:

A new pedagogy of the theory and practice of living with children must now stand in a relationship of thoughtfulness and openness to children and young people rather than being governed by traditional beliefs, discarded values, old rules, and fixed impositions. The pedagogy of living with children is an ongoing project of renewal in a world that is constantly changing around us and that is continually being changed by us. (p. 3)

In retrospect WJHS was replete with traditional beliefs, old rules, and fixed impositions. Many of the values that existed while I was there have now been discarded by contemporary middle school practitioners and theoreticians. However, there remain many middle schools that hold to traditional beliefs and that impose fixed expectations, curriculum, and rules on students. The time has now arrived, if schools like MMS are willing, to reinvent themselves and to redefine their goals in the midst of contemporary society.

With its existing goals and practices, I wonder about the kind of memoirs that MMS students might write about their school experiences in twenty or more years. Would they write about the core? Would they mention the watershed activity? Could they recall the interdisciplinary unit on hunger that the core of teachers taught students around Thanksgiving? Might they describe their afterschool activities? Would the notions of power and freedom become part of their memoirs? Would they really remember that they were able to make few decisions about their life at that time, and would this matter to them at a much later point?

Perhaps the real test for middle school instruction is not how well students perform in high school, but how well they perform in life. If there is some truth in this claim, then there must also be truth and validity in causing students to indeed write later in their life about the freedom they had in middle school, about how decision making was such a valuable part of middle school life that stayed with them for many years, and about how being in a smaller family in school helped them perform better in their classes.

Students want to have voice in school. They want to be heard and respected. For example, during my time at MMS I asked Ann (student) what she thought about talking to me. Her response was at once simple yet profound. Ann noted: "I think it is pretty nifty. Somebody can actually know the real truth about middle school and about us." I was disquieted by Ann's honesty and insight. How many of us have tried to write about middle schools without listening to students' perspectives? Extending this question, I began to wonder how many of the forepersons of the middle school movement and how many contemporary workers in middle level theory and practice actually listened to students' talk about their needs before they assumed what kind of schooling would be best for them, offering students another imposition of predetermined expectations and rules. The aforementioned comment by Ann suggests that the real truth about middle school can be learned by talking to students. Ann, who wants to do well in school, also wants to be heard and understood.

References

Apple, M., and Beane, J. (1995). *Democratic schools.* Alexandria, VA: Association for Supervision and Curriculum Development.

Beane, J. (1997). *Curriculum integration: Designing the core of democratic education.* New York: Teachers College Press.

Beane, J. (1993). *A middle school curriculum: From rhetoric to reality* (rev. ed.). Columbus, OH: National Middle School Association.

Bigelow, B. (1995). Getting off the track: Stories from an untracked classroom. In D. Levine, R. Lowe, B. Peterson, and R. Tenorio (Eds.), *Rethinking schools: An agenda for change* (pp. 155–168). New York: The New Press.

Bollnow, O. (1989a). The pedagogical atmosphere. *Phenomenology + Pedagogy, 7,* 5–11.

Bollnow, O. (1989b). The pedagogical atmosphere: The perspective of the child. *Phenomenology + Pedagogy, 7,* 12–36.

Bollnow, O. (1989c). The pedagogical atmosphere: The perspective of the educator. *Phenomenology + Pedagogy, 7,* 37–63.

Bollnow, O. (1961). Lived-space. *Philosophy Today, 5,* 31–39.

Boomer, G., Lester, N., Onore, C., and Cook, J. (1992). *Negotiating the curriculum: Educating for the 21st century.* Bristol, PA: The Falmer Press.

David, R. (Ed.). (1998). *Moving forward from the past: Early writings and current reflections of middle school founders.* Columbus, OH: National Middle School Association and Pittsburgh, PA: Pennsylvania Middle School Association.

Dewey, J. (1938). *Experience and education.* New York: Touchstone.

Dilthey, W. (1985). *Poetry and experience. Selected works* (Vol. V). Princeton, NJ: Princeton University Press.

Eliot, T.S. (1930). *Selected poems.* New York: Harcourt Brace & Company.

Ellwood, S. (1997). The power of possibilities. In A. L. Goodwin (Ed.), *Assessment for equity and inclusion: Embracing all our children* (pp. 77–99). New York: Routledge.

Gergen, K. (1991). *The saturated self: Dilemmas of identify in contemporary life.* New York: Basic Books.

Gordon, H. (1988). Learning to think: Arendt on education for democracy. *The Education Forum, 53*(1), 49–62.

Greene, M. (1993). Diversity and inclusion: Toward a curriculum for human beings. *Teachers College Record, 95*(2), 211–221.

Hogan, L. (1993). *The book of medicines.* Minneapolis, MN: The Coffee House Press.

Kramer, L. (1992). Young adolescents' perceptions of school. In J. Irvin (Ed.), *Transforming middle level education* (pp. 28–45). Boston: Allyn & Bacon.

Lounsbury, J. (1992). Perspectives on the middle school movement. In J. Irvin (Ed.), *Transforming middle level education* (pp. 3–15). Boston: Allyn & Bacon.

McEwin, C.K., Dickinson, T.S., and Jenkins, D.M. (1996). *America's middle schools: Practices and progress: A 25 year perspective.* Columbus, OH: National Middle School Association.

Nickles, T. (1981). What is a problem that we may solve it? *Synthese, 47,* 85–118.

Noar, G. (1961). *The junior high school today and tomorrow: A modern philosophy and proven guide for teachers and administrators of the junior high school* (2nd ed.). Englewood Cliffs, NJ: Prentice-Hall.

Oakley, A. (1981). Interviewing women: A contradiction in terms. In H. Roberts (Ed.), *Doing feminist research* (pp. 30–61). London: Routledge.

Oldfather, P., and McLaughlin, J. (1993). Gaining and losing voice: A longitudinal study of students' continuing impulse to learn across elementary and middle level contexts. *Research in Middle Level Education, 17*(1), 1–25.

Peshkin, A. (1997). *Places of memory: Whiteman's schools and Native American communities.* Mahway, NJ: Lawrence Erlbaum Associates.

Poole, M. (1984). The schools adolescents would like. *Adolescence, 19*(74), 447–459.

Powell, R. (1999). Reflections on integrative curriculum: A conversation with Camille Barr and Molly Maloy. *Middle School Journal, 31*(2), 25–34.

Powell, R. (1997). Teams and the affirmation of middle level students' voices: The case of Jimmie. In T. S. Dickinson and T. O. Erb (Eds.), *We gain more than we give: Teaming in middle schools* (pp. 271–298). Columbus, OH: National Middle School Association.

Powell, R. (1993). Seventh graders perspectives of their interdisciplinary team. *Middle School Journal, 24*(3), 49–57.

Powell, R., and Skoog, J. (1995). Students' perspectives of integrative curricula: The case of Brown Barge Middle School. *Research in Middle Level Education, 19*(1), 85–115.

Powell, R., Zehm, S., and Kottler, J. (1995). *Classrooms under the influence: Addicted families, addicted students.* Newbury Park, CA: Corwin Press.

Rorty, R. (1995). *Objectivity, relativism, and truth: Philosophical papers* (Vol. 1). New York: Cambridge University Press.

Sinclaire, C. (1994). *Looking for home: A phenomenological study of home in the classroom.* Albany, NY: State University of New York Press.

Soohoo, S. (1993). Students as partners in research and restructuring schools. *Educational Forum, 57*(4), 386–393.

Stevenson, C., and Carr, J. (Eds.). (1993). *Integrated studies in the middle grades: "Dancing through walls."* New York: Teachers College Press.

Van Manen, M. (1991). *The tact of teaching: The meaning of pedagogical thoughtfulness.* Albany, NY: State University of New York Press.

Van Manen, M. (1990). *Researching lived experience: Human science for an action sensitive pedagogy.* London, Ontario, Canada: University of Western Ontario.

Van Til, W. (Ed.). (1971). *Curriculum: Quest for relevance.* New York: Houghton Mifflin.

Van Til, W., Vars, G., and Lounsbury, J. (1961). *Modern education for the junior high school years.* New York: Bobbs-Merrill.

Vars, G. (1969). *Common learnings: Core and interdisciplinary team approaches.* Scranton, PA: International Textbook Company.

Wolcott, H. (1994). *Transforming qualitative data: Description, analysis, and interpretation.* Thousand Oaks, CA: Sage Publications.

Zeichner, K. (1989). Preparing teachers for democratic schools. *Action in Teacher Education, 11*(1), 5–10.

Notes

1. See a further discussion of my family and life situation in Powell, Zehm, and Kottler (1995).

2. Real names for persons and places have not been used.

3. While I am aware, as a phenomenologist, that beginning with self is a logical starting point of any writing that focuses on *lived experience,* I am also aware that I must avoid, to the extent possible, troubling readers with purely private, autobiographial facts of my life. Such facts and the experiences from which they are derived, both explicitly and implicitly, are woven into the tapestry of a researchers' perceptions and must therefore be made clear, as Peshkin continuously argues (e.g., Peshkin 1997), and as Ellwood (1997) so eloquently demonstrated. Importantly, too, some of my former school experiences, I am aware, are in some way also the possible school experiences of others, and are thus useful for creating solidarity between what I write and what others experience now and have experienced before.

4. A relevant discussion of lived experience is also offered by Bollnow (1961).

5. As I struggled to understand the lived experiences of the students I employed four orienting strategies suggested by Wolcott (1994, pp. 160–164) for making observations and for holding corresponding conversations, what many call informal interviews, that strive to explore such phenomenon as soulful meaning. First, to understand the school context in which selected students lived out their experiences and in which they derived personal meaning from school, I tried to observe and record everything I could, and everything that my own perceptual filters and mental maps would allow me to record given the purpose of this chapter. That is, I tried to get acquainted with the school context by observing daily life at the school, and by talking to teachers, students, and administrators casually as this daily life unfolded.

Second, realizing that my work in numerous middle schools in various locations could limit my ability to see important particularities in the context of MMS, and realizing my limitations in understanding variations in school contexts, I strove to observe and record events, processes, activities, and conversations that appeared to have salience over other events, processes, activities, and conversations that I reported in other school locations.

For a third orienting strategy, Wolcott (1994) suggests to look for and explore contradictions and paradoxes. Following this strategy, I looked for possible paradoxes in how the school understood and implemented middle school ideology, and what earlier writers of this ideology intended. I also sought to explore contradictions in what students believed democratic schooling and voice meant in the school, and what faculty and administrators at the school believed these phenomena meant. As I continued looking deeper into the school's context, I explored other contradictions and paradoxes as they arose.

Fourth, and perhaps one of the most crucial orienting strategies for this chapter, was to identify key problems facing the selected students with whom I had focused conversations and with whom I had casual conversations. I sought to look for *the* problem, or at least *a* problem that faced the students knowing well that another university educator or school teacher exploring the school may find alternative problems (Nickles 1981). Finding alternative problems is not necessarily a limitation of my work here, but rather points to the limited perspective I bring to the chapter. I also realized that by seeking to explore problems related to middle school ideology, I was transposing a certain theoretical framework on the problem(s) I discover, thus creating a somewhat politicized situation. Yet I also realized that the middle school issue, an issue that has been an inherent part of early adolescent education for many years (Dewey 1938), is *something* rather than *everything*. Middle school ideology is not—and in my judgment should not be—about everything, but it is about *something*. Finally, following Nickles (1981), I realize that there will remain in the context of MMS important problems that I am unable to discover in the brief time I am at the school, and that these problems could be illuminated in future studies.

6. In various other studies I developed specific protocols in an effort to get middle school students to talk to me mostly in focused ways. I try in every way to develop protocols that get students to open up, to usually give me thirty minutes of dialogue. Sometimes the protocols work, sometimes they do not work. Students are indeed students; they are who they are, and the protocol is what it is. Rarely do they meet successfully. There have been times in my best efforts that I got 5–10 minutes of dialogue from early adolescents, not because they don't want to respond or do not necessarily trust me, but because this is who they are. Other times I can get 50 minutes when I estimate a 30 minute dialogue. In every study I have tried to explore what happens when students of all expressive capabilities interact with the school context and convey this to me, however brief my time might be. Middle school students, I have found, are alarmingly honest and strikingly clear about what they mean. I do not have to ask the same question twice in a different way, because I will get the same response twice to questions stated similarly. The students are transparent in their naiveté, honesty, and clarity.

Long interviews are unnecessary with early adolescents. What is needed, however, are poignant questions, those that ask directly and pertinently. If the students do not know what you mean, they tend not to answer something to appear knowledgeable. They will just simply say, "I do not know what you mean." Or they will hesitate to the point that it is obvious they are unclear. This kind of interview situation that I have described here—to the point and matter of fact—is pleasant. I have found this kind of situation only with middle school learners, not with elementary or high school students, and not with teachers.

7. A point of practicality needs to be made here. Although the middle school movement has, over the past four decades, supported a democratic infrastructure for early adolescent schooling, democratization of middle schools is clearly not a panacea for bringing students more fully into the educational power structure. While traditional school models tend to disenfranchise some students, especially those in lower socioeconomic brackets and those in selected minority groups, and while the process of democratization intends to override such disenfranchisement thus bringing about more equitable conditions in the school, giving the majority of students more voice in school and thus more freedom about their own schooling will not be remedied by democratization alone (Zeichner 1989). While some schools and some individual classrooms have been successful in transforming democratic theory into school practice (Apple and Beane 1995), my experience as a researcher of middle school practice suggests to me that most middle schools align with the practice demonstrated by MMS. This practice occurs when a school implements some structural features of middle school ideology but puts aside those other features such as democratization that have potential for empowering students.

Issues of Practice

8

High-Quality Learning Opportunities in High Poverty Middle Schools: Moving from Rhetoric to Reality

DOUGLAS J. MAC IVER,
ESTELLE YOUNG, ROBERT BALFANZ,
ALTA SHAW, MARIA GARRIOTT
Johns Hopkins University

AMY COHEN
Philadelphia Education Fund

Introduction

Despite its rhetoric about equality, the United States tolerates disparities in students' opportunities to learn that are many times greater than the disparities found in other industrialized nations (Darling-Hammond 1997; Schmidt, McKnight, and Raizen 1997). The Maryland Middle Learning Task Force (2000) found the following:

> . . . some middle grades students attend schools with little or no modern science labs, equipment, or technology, while others have sophisticated science labs and four or five internet-accessible computers in every classroom. Some students sit in classes of nearly forty, while others have classes of twenty or less. Some students have few books to use in the classroom and none to take home, while others have an abundance of high quality resources with which they can produce sophisticated work. (p. 33)

Darling-Hammond (1997) echoes this finding:

> Although the United States came sooner than many others to the task of educating a wide range of students in public school, it has yet to meet the

challenge of providing equal access to quality education. What students have the opportunity to learn is typically a function of where they live, what their parents earn, and the color of their skin. (p. 264)

The plain truth is that urban middle schools that enroll large numbers of low-income students and poor rural middle schools that have little tax base are often weak learning institutions staffed by inexperienced and underprepared people who have had inadequate opportunities to learn about teaching, young adolescents, or the content area(s) that they are assigned to teach. Moreover, these schools often lack basic materials, are sometimes shockingly unsafe or chaotic, and experience high levels of student, teacher, and principal transience. Is it possible to "reinvent" these schools, to remake or redo them completely, so that they become strong learning institutions that effectively develop the talent of their students and staff? Or is this an impossible or impractical dream? Can these schools move beyond the rhetoric that "all children can learn" and actually provide all students with the instruction and support they need to meet high standards?

The Talent Development Middle School (TDMS) program at Johns Hopkins University has been working to develop research-based reforms of curriculum and instruction, school organization, partnerships, professional development, and technical assistance that show promise for helping nonselective high poverty middle schools to create a sustainable and replicable high-standards learning environment where all students are successful (Mac Iver, Mac Iver, Balfanz, Plank, and Ruby 2000; Balfanz and Mac Iver 2000). This chapter (a) describes the TDMS program's theory of action, (b) discusses how this theory of action is being fleshed out in ten urban middle schools, (c) details some of the daunting challenges that the TDMS program must meet in helping these schools establish standards-based instruction and supportive learning environments, and (d) reports evidence regarding the successes and failures of key components of the TD model in increasing teacher effectiveness and student learning.

The theory of action

Figure 1 summarizes Talent Development's three-pronged theory of action for transforming a school into a high performance learning community by providing all students with sustained, high-quality, standards-based learning opportunities, by providing all students with supportive learning environments, and by providing teachers with the training, support, and materials they need to deliver a world-class education. According to the theory, just like a stool is supported by three legs, the students and teachers in any middle school will develop into higher performers if they are provided with these three pillars of support. Conversely, if a middle school pays insufficient attention to one or more of these three pillars, the stool will not stand: the school will make little progress toward becoming a high performance learning community.

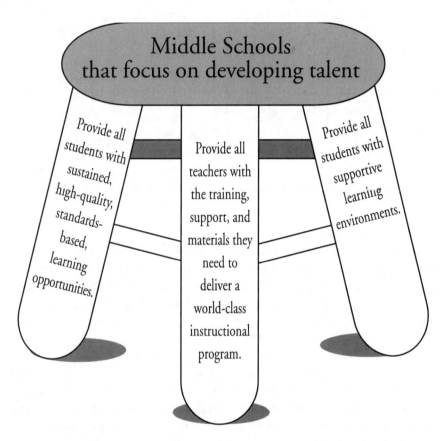

Figure 1: Talent Development's theory of action.

The first leg: Sustained, high-quality, standards-based learning opportunities

Achievement flourishes when students are provided a coherent, consistent, and increasingly complex standards-based curriculum in each major subject area which builds year upon year in a systematic and thoughtful manner (Balfanz, Mac Iver, and Ryan 1999). Figure 2 summarizes the Talent Development Middle School's curricular offerings. All students take the same curriculum.

Mathematics. The math program is designed to prepare all students to take algebra in eighth grade because research has shown that giving eighth graders algebra leads them to take more demanding courses once they enter high school and to do better in them (U.S. Department of Education 1997; Pelavin

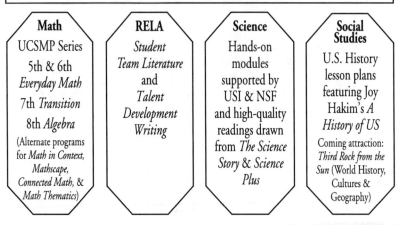

Figure 2: The first leg.

and Kane 1990). That is, even students who don't "test out" of high school algebra at the end of eighth grade, but repeat it in ninth grade, are put on a higher trajectory that leads to higher achievement in math and that increases the odds that they will attend college (U.S. Department of Education 1997). The TD math program is built around materials developed by the University of Chicago School Mathematics Project (UCSMP). Specifically, all students take *Everyday Mathematics* in fifth and sixth grade, and *Transition Mathematics* in seventh grade. This course sequence prepares all students to take and succeed in UCSMP's *Algebra* as eighth graders because students start hands-on manipulation using algebraic concepts even in fifth grade and then build upon this foundation with increasingly advanced and symbolic work as they progress through the middle grades.

In some cases, a school adopting the Talent Development Middle School comprehensive reform model is already implementing successfully an alternative standards-based instructional program in mathematics such as *Math in Context, Connected Math, Mathscape,* or *Math Thematics.* In these instances, the TD program assists the schools to strengthen and adapt these alternatives to TD's main program to make them more balanced, practical, and algebra-focused and does not require the school to implement the UCSMP curriculum. TD's goal is to ensure high-quality learning opportunities, not to enforce a bureaucratic consistency across all TD schools.

English. All Talent Development Middle Schools use *Student Team Literature,* a middle school language arts curriculum and instructional program that is designed to improve students' skills in reading vocabulary, literary analysis, and student collaboration by using outstanding literature, higher-level questioning, and working with other students. It includes (1) curricular materials (partner discussion guides) to assist students' study of high-quality fiction and nonfiction books, (2) recommended instructional practices, peer assistance processes, and assessments, and (3) staff development, mentoring, and advising for teachers to support the curricular and instructional reforms. The National Staff Development Council recently selected the Student Team Literature Program for inclusion in their *Consumer's Guide* of effective staff development programs that meet national standards in language arts (Killion 1999).

Each Student Team Literature partner discussion guide includes literature-related writing activities (e.g., "Write a newspaper article and headline about the bombing in Birmingham," "Write a poem about the Watson's trip to Alabama.") and a systematic study of the writer's craft as displayed in the book being studied (e.g., activities in which students interpret the impact of author's word choice, symbolism, and literary elements).

Talent Development Writing complements Student Team Literature and extends the explicit teaching and practice of writing, critical reading, and editing. It places especially heavy emphasis on several important steps in preparing students for the writing experience (e.g., a teacher thinking aloud and modeling his or her approach to writing, and "springboard activities" intended to spark the creative process). Talent Development Writing also emphasizes important activities situated between the steps of the writing process (e.g., teacher-student prewriting and editing conferences, and conferences with student partners).

Science. Talent Development Middle Schools implement effective new modules that meet national science standards and benchmarks. Talent Development Middle School science staff help teachers implement hands-on modules drawn from a number of recently developed curricula including *Science and Technology Concepts for Middle School, Full Option Science System, Science Education for Public Understanding Program, INSIGHTS, FACETS,* and others. This modular approach is integrated with high-quality science readings drawn from sources such as *Science Plus* and/or Joy Hakim's *The Science Story.* The readings and the hands-on activities help students better understand the concepts of science and the history of science so that they become equipped to make and answer inquiries into science topics systematically and so that the facts that they encounter make sense. The science instructional program stresses cross-disciplinary activities so that students realize the importance of reading, writing, and math to science and so that they can continue to build their literacy in these areas even while in science class.

History/Social Studies/Geography. The Talent Development Middle School's U.S. History curriculum is based on Joy Hakim's award-winning *The History of US,* a comprehensive set of books designed to engage students in investigating their national history. The goal of the curriculum is two-fold: to fascinate students with our national history, and to assist them in constructing their own individual scaffolds of basic information, knowledge, and concepts about the American experience.

How does the TDMS instructional program fascinate students with United States history? By getting them involved with intriguing questions. By listening to the voices and personal stories of the past. By peering into period paintings and photographs. By reading the actual words of the everyday people of the past. By unlocking historical puzzles. The TDMS curriculum emphasizes the personal stories, drama, and multicultural facets of history as it connects the past to today's world so that students see history as both vital and intrinsically interesting.

The central text, *A History of US*, is supplemented with primary sources, visual and audio materials, and active Student Team Learning lessons. Each lesson contains all necessary student materials and a Teacher's Guide, which include instructional information, strategies and techniques for the teacher, cooperative and individual activities, reflection and review activities, and assessment tools. The curriculum and materials are consistent with the *National Standards for United States History* developed by the National Center for History in the Schools and the *Curriculum Standards for Social Studies: Expectations of Excellence* developed by the National Council for Social Studies (National Center for History in the Schools 1996; Task Force of the National Council for the Social Studies 1994).

The second leg: Materials, training, and in-classroom support for teachers

Teachers' ability to teach is enhanced when they are provided with (1) a coherent curriculum that is coordinated and builds grade by grade; (2) the essential supplies and learning materials they need to teach; (3) on-going subject and grade-specific professional development which gives them the content knowledge, instructional strategies, classroom management advice, and hands-on experience they need to successfully implement standards-based instructional programs; (4) in-classroom implementation assistance from a respected peer who is there to support rather than to evaluate (Balfanz and Mac Iver 2000; Darling-Hammond 1998; Useem 1998b, 1999).

Figure 3 summarizes the materials, training, and in-classroom support offered to teachers in Talent Development Middle Schools. The materials created for TD middle schools differ from some of the materials developed by other reform initiatives because TD explicitly acknowledges that establishing benchmarks, providing examples, and identifying best practices or even studying student work are not strong enough interventions by themselves to transform a high poverty school. Initiatives that rely on these interventions frequently leave the hard work of creating a coherent, consistent, and increasingly complex set of standards-based activities to individual teachers working mostly in isolation or to study groups or work groups of teachers who have insufficient time or expertise to create a comprehensive, implementable, and scalable curriculum (Bol, Nunnery, Lowther, Dietrich, Pace, Anderson, Bassoppor-Moyo, and Phillipsen 1998; Glennan 1998; Newmann, Lopez, Gudelia, and Bryk 1998). Such initiatives can produce islands of excellence but do not typically lead to the consistent, day-to-day standards-based instruction in all grades and classrooms that students need to overcome poor prior preparations and perform at high levels (Balfanz 1997, 2000; Mac Iver and Balfanz 1999; Ruby 1999; Wilson and Corbett 1999).

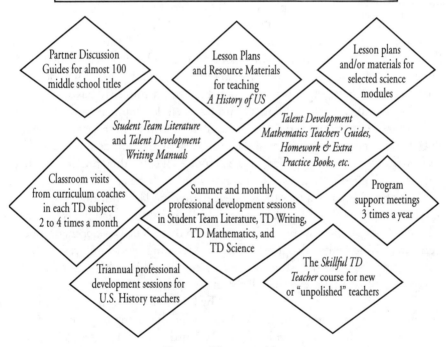

Figure 3: The second leg.

Each of TD's instructional programs comes with a coordinated and comprehensive set of student and teacher materials that provide students and teachers with the resources they need to engage in standard-based lessons every day. These materials include daily classroom activities, longer term projects, practice exercises, and assessments. The materials allow room for teacher choice (e.g., Student Team Literature materials are available for almost 100 different books with more partner discussion guides always being developed), innovation, and individuality but they provide a solid and comprehensive foundation which enables a baseline of good instruction to happen in every classroom and ensures a coherence across all grades in each major subject area.

In addition to describing some of the materials provided to teachers in Talent Development Middle Schools, Figure 3 indicates some of the multiple layers of sustained professional development, technical assistance, and implementation support that they are provided. Successful and sustained whole school reform in high poverty schools is labor intensive. It requires continual work and attention. Providing low performing, high poverty middle schools with a vision, a planning process, or even a blueprint accompanied by initial training and assessment tools is typically not enough. The "managed" chaos, day-to-day stress, and high faculty and administrator mobility rates that are characteristic of low performing middle schools continually sap the energy, divert the focus, and undermine the follow through needed to implement and sustain reforms.

To achieve systematic improvements in teaching and learning, we have learned that it is necessary to provide teachers with five layers of support. The first layer is on-going subject and grade-specific staff development that is explicitly linked to the curriculum they are enacting. This professional development needs to have three primary foci. First, on a monthly basis, in a very "hands on" and concrete fashion, TD professional development sessions model upcoming instructional activities for teachers. Second, these sessions provide both the content knowledge required by these activities and demonstrate effective instructional strategies tied to the activities. Third, they provide teachers with the opportunity to network and learn from each other.

The second layer of support is nonevaluatory in-classroom implementation assistance provided by a respected peer. This curriculum coach, who is often a school district teacher on special assignment to the Talent Development model, performs a wide range of support functions including modeling, troubleshooting, helping the teacher customize the curriculum to his or her classroom, and making sure that the teacher has all the materials he or she needs.

The third layer of support is provided by lead teachers in the school who receive intensive training in the instructional programs being implemented. The fourth layer of support is provided by TDMS instructional facilitators employed by Johns Hopkins University who work closely with both the curriculum coaches, lead teachers, and principals to design the on-going staff development, customize and localize the instructional programs, and keep the instructional intervention on track. The fifth and final layer of support is a methods course— The Skillful Talent Development Teacher—designed to provide new or "unpolished" teachers with classroom management skills and instructional strategies that have been proved effective for large and diverse classes of students. At one time or another, each of these layers of support has proven critical and together they have proven robust enough to enable substantial and systematic achievement gains in Talent Development's high poverty middle schools (Balfanz et al. 1999; Plank and Young 1999; Mac Iver et al. 2000).

The third leg: Supportive learning environments

Figure 4 lists six components of the Talent Development Middle School Model that ensure that all students experience supportive, culturally relevant learning environments where close student-teacher relationships and school-family-community partnerships can flourish and where students are offered a wide array of learning supports including extra help, enrichment, and exploration opportunities which increase their motivation to learn and enable them to succeed in high-level standards-based courses.

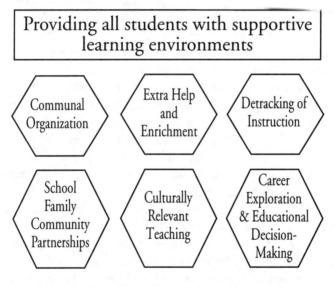

Figure 4: The third leg.

A Communally-Organized School. As students move from elementary to middle school, there is a dramatic decrease in the quality of teacher-student relationships (Eccles, Lord, and Midgley 1991). This deterioration of teacher-student relationships has a large negative impact on student motivation and teachers' instructional practices. According to TD's theory of action, if you wish to change urban middle schools, you must create a more communal organization of the school that personalizes adult-child relationships. Of course, many other middle level reformers have reached the same conclusion (e.g., "Changing middle schools begins with personalizing adult-child relationships," Ames and Miller 1994, p. 178).

The communal organization component of the model recognizes that student effort and teacher effectiveness can be greatly increased by implementing innovative approaches to school organization and staffing that allow teachers and students to establish enduring bonds and close caring relationships. Further, this component reflects the Talent Development Program's conviction that a strong bond between students and teachers and a shared sense of purpose are not frills but are necessary conditions to support teaching and learning for understanding. Deep learning will not occur unless students contribute effort and cooperation. Deep learning will not occur unless teachers know their students well enough to be able to take account of their prior knowledge and interests in planning instruction. Deep learning will not occur unless teachers feel safe to take risks in front of their students by using cooperative learning and active teaching strategies that prompt students to inquire, discover, and apply knowledge.

Many large urban middle schools have established interdisciplinary teams of teachers and small learning communities that break up these large schools into smaller schools within the school. Ideally, these small learning communities have their own part of the building, and their own students, faculty, and administration. Establishing interdisciplinary teams and small learning communities is an important first step toward strengthening relationships between teachers and students. However, the TD program works with the faculty and administration of TD middle schools to further strengthen student-teacher bonds by encouraging the judicious use of semi-departmentalization (with many teachers teaching more than one subject so that most teachers and students stay together for more than just one period a day) (Mac Iver and Plank 1997). We also encourage the judicious use of looping (assigning teachers to the same students for two or three years). Looping gives students and teachers the opportunity and incentive to establish strong bonds and a shared sense of purpose as they work together for two or three years. Mac Iver and Prioleau (1999) report evidence from one Talent Development Middle School and its district-selected comparison school suggesting that looping helps teachers to be caring, daring, and effective. They conclude that looping helps create atypically warm and productive student-teacher relationships, and helps teachers to increase their use of active and cooperative techniques aimed at deep learning.

Opportunities for Extra Help and Enrichment. Extra help and enrichment opportunities are essential if students are going to have the support they need to meet or exceed high standards. In TD schools, we encourage schools to offer extra help and enrichment in math and reading as part of their school's program of elective offerings. In math, our Computer and Team Assisted Mathematics Acceleration (CATAMA) Program has a proven track record of helping students accelerate their learning in mathematics (Mac Iver, Balfanz, and Plank

1998). CATAMA is a ten-week accelerated learning class that uses cooperative groups and computers to provide intensive learning experiences to students needing extra help or desiring enrichment opportunities in math.

The Talent Development Program is working with Amy Cohen of the Philadelphia Education Fund, the Boys Town Reading Center, and teachers in Philadelphia to develop a similarly effective extra help program in reading and language arts. So far, we have developed a full prototype of the CATARA (Computer and Team Assisted Reading Acceleration) program and have begun pilot testing some components of the program.

The emerging CATARA program is mutifaceted. It is designed to be delivered in an extra help lab at each school that will be set up with several learning stations among which small groups of students will rotate. One station is an *independent reading* station where students can choose from a variety of high interest, age-appropriate books and magazines for sustained silent reading. The books that we have selected for this station are written at levels which are manageable to the students being served to encourage reading in quantity. The books selected relate directly to information being covered in students' regular content classes and thus help students succeed in TDMS's demanding core curriculum in the major subject areas. Each book comes with "activity cards" that are directly related to the national standards in the content areas. These activities encourage students to write in response to the reading that they have done and engage their minds and imaginations while encouraging them to use information gleaned from the reading.

Another station is *books on tape*. This station allows students to listen to audiobook versions of the same great books that they are studying in their English Language Arts class as part of the Student Team Literature program. This station provides the extra scaffolding and advance exposure that weak readers need to fully participate and fully benefit from their regular English Language Arts class even though the literature being studied in that class is above their current reading level. Again, after listening to an audiotape, students are given the opportunity to do some writing directly related to the section of the book to which they have just listened.

Another station is the *explicit instruction* station. At this station, students receive instruction in reading skills based on the *Foundations* and *Adventures in Reading* courses developed at the Boy's Town Reading Center. *Foundations* is for students reading below the fourth grade level. The goal of this course is to teach the most common letter-sound correspondences (phonics) and to provide opportunities to apply this knowledge while reading books aloud. A list of words which follow a particular phonics rule is presented at the beginning of the week. Then each day, students spend about ten minutes playing a group game to reinforce learning of those words (Jeopardy, Password, etc.) followed by ten minutes in pairs on computers in the *computer lab* station using inexpensive spelling and word-attack software that is preprogrammed to reinforce the learning of the words and the rule. Next, students read aloud from a novel in groups of 4–5 with a teacher or a parent aide. There is also homework to reinforce the words/rules and a weekly test on the words. *Adventures in Reading* is for students needing extra help who are reading at or above the fourth grade level. The class format mirrors that of *Foundations*, but the emphasis is on achieving oral reading fluency.

We have great hopes for the CATARA program because it blends explicit instruction in phonics and other reading skills (which will be helpful in giving students a strong foundation of competencies and strategies) with other components (independent reading, audiobooks, and engaging follow-up activities tied to the TDMS curriculum) that will foster success across the curriculum and engender an enjoyment of reading and writing. Furthermore, the whole program is build upon straightforward, clear principles and relies on straightforward and clear methods, thus it will be easily understood and easily replicated. Also, the games and paired computer-use components lend themselves to creating a fun, supportive, and nonstigmatizing environment. Because the program is designed specifically for young adults and uses outstanding but readable books that appeal to young adults, it does not demean the students, even if they are reading well below grade level. A full year-long pilot test of the model in multiple schools is scheduled for the 2000–2001 academic year.

Detracking of Instruction. For too long, middle schools have sorted some students into receiving high-quality learning opportunities while relegating others to lower-quality educational opportunities. Talent Development Middle Schools seek to demonstrate that all young adults are capable of succeeding in demanding standards-based courses when given appropriate support. Because tracking causes gross inequalities in students' access to knowledge, instructional resources, and well-qualified teaching, the TD program assists all their schools to detrack the core academic instructional program. As a result, in most Talent Development Middle Schools students are either heterogeneously grouped for their core academic classes or (in other schools) participate in a "disappearing track" plan that moves all students who begin the middle grades in the "low track" (with the best teachers, best classrooms, and a reduced class size) into a heterogeneously grouped "high track for all" by seventh grade. Heterogeneous grouping for core academic classes helps Talent Development Middle Schools reach higher levels of academic performance by eliminating nightmare sections: those lower track sections that no one wants to teach and that typically feature a slow pace and dumbed-down content.

The extra-help programs described earlier help make detracking work well because the teachers of the regular classes feel little pressure to "dumb down" or "slow down" the curriculum: The teachers know that intensive extra help will be received by all students who need additional time and instruction in order to master the material. Furthermore, the professional development sessions, materials, and implementation support offered to teachers include many practical ideas for managing and instructing heterogeneous classes effectively.

School-Family-Community Partnerships. Talent Development schools participate in the National Network of Partnership schools. This network, established by researchers at Johns Hopkins University, brings together schools, districts, and states that are committed to developing and maintaining comprehensive programs of school-family-community partnerships. As part of the Network, Talent Development schools establish Action Teams that carry out school, parent, and community involvement activities in a focused and coherent way.

Cultural Relevance. Talent Development curricular materials and professional development emphasize culturally relevant materials and teaching practices. This component of the program recognizes that students will work harder and learn more if instruction is attentive to the student population's cultural patterns and norms, promotes cross-cultural understanding, and helps students connect to and interpret cultural traditions.

Career Exploration. The Career Exploration and Educational Decision-Making curriculum is designed to (a) provide students with weekly opportunities to find out about careers in which they are interested through a variety of activities, including reading, role-playing, interviewing, researching, and listening to career representatives in person and on video; (b) enable students to develop and view their own career aspirations in light of their interests and academic strengths; (c) give students facts about types of high schools and colleges, including entrance requirements and courses of study available to them; and (d) lead students to connect their current academic performance and the behaviors that help or hinder it, so they can set academic goals that will enable them to achieve their career aspirations.

Implementation

By the fall of the 2000–2001 school year, implementation of the Talent Development model will have been initiated in ten middle schools. Each shares the profile of a school that must meet myriad challenges prior to becoming a strong learning institution. These include high levels of staff and student transience, poorly prepared teachers and students, low faculty and student morale and expectations, and large size. Eight of these schools are located in Philadelphia, where the program was first implemented in Central East Middle School in the fall of 1996.

Prior to becoming a TD school, school staff have attended an "awareness session," presented by developers from Johns Hopkins, in which the model was presented in detail. Interested schools gathered additional information by visiting a Talent Development school, and/or attending follow-up subject-specific sessions with greater detail provided about the curricular content, support, and organizational structure of a Talent Development school. Finally, school faculty filled out a survey and held a vote to determine whether to adopt the model, with an 80% vote required prior to implementation to ensure sufficiently widespread faculty buy-in for the concept. The curricular components of the program are implemented in phases by grade and subject area, while the facilitated support and development of a supportive learning environment are emphasized from the beginning. Implementation support is most intense in the initial year of implementation of a curricular component, with weekly classroom visits and intensive professional development. The goal, however, is to develop the district's and school's capacity to sustain the Talent Development model after the implementation phase. The professional development and teacher on special assignment are important components in the development of internal capacity to maintain the model independently.

Each of the ten Talent Develoment schools shares certain core components of the model. Every school has adopted a standards based core curriculum. Each district has placed teachers on special assignment to serve as subject-specific curricular coaches. Every school has been reorganized to some extent in order to create supportive learning environments.

There are, however, important differences among schools in implementing the model. Some of these differences represent innovative adaptations of the model. For example, Central East uses the CATAMA lab as both an extra-help *and* an enrichment lab. The lab is available to students who, with some additional assistance, are in a position to apply for admission to one of the more selective public high schools in Philadelphia. Other differences reflect the in-built flexibility of the Talent Development model to meet a particular school's needs and build on its existing strengths. For example, while the model includes a standards-based curriculum for each of the four core subject areas, if a school is already using standards-based curricular material, the model will incorporate that curriculum rather than impose its own. In this way, faculty buy-in and ownership of the model are actively fostered through the model's flexible design.

Still other differences in implementation arise because of a range of problems and challenges toward which neither the schools nor the program developers have devoted sufficient time and effort to resolve. Some of these challenges represent natural growing pains of a developing model as new and unforeseen situations emerge and are subsequently studied and resolved. Others are more difficult and indicate potential limits of the model in creating high-quality learning institutions. Some of these challenges are outlined in more detail in the following section.

Challenges to implementation

A major challenge is the importance of interpersonal relationships to the successful and sustained implementation of reform. In essence, the model's theory of action, described in detail in the beginning of this chapter, is demonstratively effective. However, the soundest of programs is quickly and easily undermined if insufficient attention is paid to building and maintaining relationships with key personnel. In large, multilayered school districts, attention to this point is essential as a wide variety of administrative staff has the authority to interfere with implementation. The challenge of building and maintaining these relationships is extremely time consuming and would divert excessive attention from program implementation if model developers assume full responsibility. The developers of Talent Development have been extremely fortunate to have the assistance of the Philadelphia Education Fund. Fund representatives have served as a local ally, both willing and knowledgeable enough to speak on our behalf (Mac Iver and Balfanz 1999; Balfanz and Mac Iver 2000; Useem 1998b).

While the above-described challenge is critical, the principal constraint in implementing and ensuring the continued viability of this or any other whole school reform in high poverty schools is the degree of staff and student transience. The initial Talent Development school in Philadelphia has had five principals in as many years. The mobility between schools is compounded by the transfer of students and staff within a school. For example, it is not uncommon for a school's student roster of classroom assignments to change late into the fall. In another example, fully half of the science teachers in two Talent Development schools were reassigned between the 1997–98 and 1998–99 school years (Ruby 1999; Balfanz and Mac Iver 2000).

The sheer magnitude of this mobility poses a daunting challenge to the development of any internal capacity to sustain the model without outside intervention. The difficulties it poses are manifold. The professional development of a cadre of seasoned school level personnel is severely limited if teachers leave after receiving only one or two years of training and experience in the model. As these teachers leave, the school also loses internal mentors for incoming teachers and, more generally, institutional memory. Furthermore, new teachers and principals arrive at the school without having voted to adopt the model and may not support it.

To date, the developers at Johns Hopkins have responded to this challenge in several ways. First, significant attention is devoted to the development of strong relationships with the faculty to foster continued faculty support. The risk that a new principal will eschew the program is reduced if the incoming principal is greeted by a faculty which argues that the model be sustained. Second, the professional development and in-classroom implementation support

infrastructure is on-going rather than occurring only in the initial years of program implementation. In the long-run, however, the internal development of a
stable corps of teachers trained in the implementation of a standards-based curriculum is essential. The only way to achieve this is to stem the faculty hemor-
rhage by creating a better environment in which teachers feel a strong sense of
community and receive the support they need (Balfanz and Mac Iver 2000).
One of the main ways of creating a better environment and increasing the
teacher's commitment is to provide realistic hope that change can occur in the
teacher's school. The TD model does provide this hope by often facilitating immediate improvements in the supports provided for teachers and students and
in student achievement. Some of these improvements are summarized in the
next section.

Increasing teacher effectiveness and student learning: Successes and failures

Research results from the two initial implementers of the Talent Development
model, Central East and Cooke Middle Schools in Philadelphia, provide evidence that the model can realize substantial gains in student performance while
improving both student and staff morale, even during the first year of implementation. These findings are probably related and mutually reinforcing. Evidence that the program works in one's own school lends tremendous credence
in the program's efficacy to teachers, encouraging them to redouble their efforts
and raise their expectations. We believe that much of the credit for the speed of
improvement lies in the quality of the core curriculum and supporting material, training, and mentoring as well as the whole-hearted effort among faculty
and administration put forth toward the goal of establishing strong learning institutions.

During the first year of implementation of Student Team Literature at Central East and Cooke, the typical student at these Talent Development schools
significantly outperformed his or her counterparts in matched comparison
schools. In reading, Cooke students outgained comparison students by 5 scale
score points (Plank and Young 1999). At Central East, the difference was even
more substantial, at 12 points (Mac Iver, Plank, and Balfanz 1997). In math,
Cooke students outgained comparison students by over 3 NCEs in Total
Mathematics Achievement (Balfanz, Mac Iver, and Ryan 1999). Stating these
achievement differences another way, the effect size of being a student at a Talent Development school was between .24 and .51 standard deviations in reading, and .52 standard deviations in math (Mac Iver, Plank, and Balfanz 1997;
Plank and Young 1999; Balfanz, Mac Iver, and Ryan 1999). This indicates that
one-forth to one-half of the between classroom variance in classroom mean
achievement was comprised of the school effect. The magnitude of this effect is

sufficient enough to achieve substantial academic gains (Mosteller, Light, and Sachs 1996).

Both of these schools have continued to display outstanding and broad-based achievement gains in all subsequent years for which data are available. For example, in reading comprehension at Central East Middle School, the average annual effect size (measuring how much a typical Central East outgained a typical comparison student each year) across a three-year span was .29 standard deviations. At Cooke (which started a year after Central East), the average two-year gain was 14 NCEs in math and 14 NCEs in reading versus a 7 NCE gain in math and a 8 NCE gain in reading at Cooke's comparison school.

Findings from research involving focus groups with teachers in Talent Development Middle Schools indicate that they are generally quite favorable when asked to evaluate Talent Development's professional development sessions, curriculum materials, and instructional approaches. Teachers reported, with both surprise and immense pleasure, that they had received very useful training, consistent and helpful follow-up implementation support in the classroom, and materials on time and in sufficient quantity with which to teach (Useem 1998b, 1999).

Independent researchers have also found evidence of a notable positive impact of the Talent Development model on pedagogy, content, and learning environment. Wilson and Corbett (1999) included Central East Middle School in a larger study of reform efforts in high poverty middle schools. They compared Central East [School # 6] to five other schools not using the TDMS model and concluded that the model had produced "greater consistency in pedagogy, content, and environment . . . [and] a greater emphasis on mastering challenging content" (p. 92). Students at Central East were also more likely to report that their teachers adopted a firm but inspiring "no excuses" stance, maintaining high standards and expectations while helping each student until he or she achieved conceptual understanding (Wilson and Corbett 1999).

Although "Improvement Now!" is one of Talent Development's goals and slogans, three of our schools, unlike Central East and Cooke, did not significantly outperform their comparison schools during their first year of program implementation. Each of these schools obtained encouraging achievement gains and made significant progress toward implementing some of Talent Development's curricular and instructional components. However, the reading and math achievement gains they obtained in their first year of Talent Development-based reform were not significantly higher than those found in their comparison schools. We believe that this indicates that it takes some very troubled schools more than one year to turn around. Although each of these schools made progress in strengthening leg 1 (learning opportunities), they each need to pay more attention to providing consistently supportive learning environments for teachers (leg 2) and students (leg 3). As our theory of action indicates, a good curriculum is a necessary, but insufficient condition for school improvement. We also need to pay more attention to these schools and are now working with these schools to strengthen their weaker legs. Time will tell whether our optimism that these schools will become beacons of improvement by their third or fourth year of implementation is well-founded.

Discussion and conclusion

The Talent Development model's theory of action, described in detail in the beginning of this chapter, provides a coherent and integrated blueprint for reinventing troubled middle schools into strong learning institutions. The model's promise is underscored by the notable achievement gains across multiple years obtained in the nation's first two Talent Development Middle Schools as well as the positive shift in environment noticed by students and faculty alike. These improvements are real and have withstood careful evaluation. The accomplishments of these schools present a welcome departure from the often hopeless stance some pundits take toward the potential for rapid and real improvement in performance of high poverty middle schools. These results provide a source for cautious optimism.

However, the challenges inherent to sustaining and scaling-up such efforts are serious and ultimate success is far from certain. The first year results obtained in the three other Talent Development schools in our pilot evaluation were encouraging but not significantly different from those of their closely matched comparison schools. These schools were clearly less ready for reform than our two initial sites, Central East and Cooke. One of the three schools needed two faculty votes spread over several months to reach the required 80% level of consensus to adopt the Talent Development model. Even after achieving the required level of consensus, this school has been hesitant to implement some of the model's components. It has embraced Talent Development's math curriculum, but has generally eschewed Student Team Literature since the principal and other key actors believe the school needs help in math but does not need assistance in English and Language Arts (even though the school's performance versus national norms is no higher in Reading Comprehension than in Mathematics). Another school, a school of 1500 students, is understandably finding it much harder than Cooke and Central East (each having an enrollment around 1000) to create a communally organized school with learning communities that are small enough to build close and enduring teacher-student relationships. Meanwhile, the third school is slowly recovering from years of administrative chaos (at a level qualitatively different from the other Talent Development schools) and the constant teacher turnover, burnout, and cynicism about reform that such chaos engenders.

Making engaging standards-based instruction and supportive learning environments a reality for every student in every classroom every day is complicated (Wilson and Corbett 1999; Wheelock 1998). Such instruction is especially difficult to realize in most high poverty urban middle schools where low student achievement is actively manufactured. In these schools, insufficient attention is paid to providing high-quality learning opportunities and materials for students and teachers, and to creating supportive learning environments. The pervasive mobility of teachers, administrators, and students in these schools exacerbates this neglect, and continually threatens the sustainability and institutionalization of even proven reforms. The Talent Development Middle School Program offers a "map" (displaying the road to high achievement to be taken by high poverty schools), "sherpas" (skilled guides to assist the school in reaching new heights), and "outfitters" (curriculum writers who provide the standards-based activities and materials to teachers). Scaling the mountain of dramatically higher achievement with two schools gives us hope that the Talent Development Program (and other comprehensive school reform models that successfully put a similar theory of action into practice) may ultimately be able to help many high poverty middle schools transform themselves into strong learning institutions that consistently provide all students with the instruction and support they need to meet high standards. Only time will tell.

References

Ames, N., and Miller, E. (1994). *Changing middle schools: How to make schools work for young adolescents.* San Francisco: Jossey-Bass.

Balfanz, R. (1997, March). *Mathematics for all in two urban schools: A view from the trenches.* Paper presented at the annual meeting of the American Educational Research Association, Chicago, Illinois.

Balfanz, R. (2000). Why do so many urban public school students demonstrate so little academic achievement? The underappreciated importance of time and place. In M.G. Sanders (Ed.), *Schooling at risk: Research, policy, and practice in the education of poor and minority adolescents* (pp. 37–62). Mahwah, NJ: Erlbaum Associates.

Balfanz, R., and Mac Iver, D.J. (2000). Transforming high-poverty urban middle schools into strong learning institutions: Lessons from the first five years of the Talent Development Middle School. *Journal of Education for Students Placed at Risk,* 5(1&2), 137–158.

Balfanz, R., Mac Iver, D.J., and Ryan, D. (1999, April). *Achieving algebra for all with a facilitated instructional program: First year results of the Talent Development Middle School Mathematics Program.* Paper presented at the annual meeting of the American Educational Research Association, Montreal, Canada.

Bol, L., Nunnery, J.A., Lowther, D.L., Dietrich, A.P., Pace, J.B., Anderson, R.S., Bassoppor-Moyo, T.C., and Phillipsen, L.C. (1998). Inside-in and outside-in support for restructuring: The effects of internal and external support on change in the New American Schools. *Education and Urban Society, 30*(3), 358–384.

Darling-Hammond, L. (1997). *The right to learn.* San Francisco: Jossey-Bass.

Darling-Hammond, L. (1998). Teacher learning that supports student learning. *Educational Leadership, 55*(5), 6–11.

Eccles, J.S., Lord, S., and Midgley, C. (1991). What are we doing to early adolescents? The impact of educational contexts on early adolescents. *American Journal of Education, 90*(4), 521–539.

Glennan, T.K. (1998). *New American schools after six years.* Washington, DC: Rand.

Killion, J. (1999). *What works in the middle: Results-based staff development.* Oxford, OH: National Staff Development Council.

Mac Iver, D.J., and Balfanz, R. (1999, November). *Helping at-risk students meet standards: The school district's role in creating high performing schools.* Paper presented at the McRel Diversity Roundtable on At-Risk Student Populations, Aurora, CO.

Mac Iver, D.J., Balfanz, R., and Plank, S. (1998). An 'elective replacement' approach to providing extra help in math: The Talent Development Middle Schools' Computer- and Team-Assisted Mathematics Acceleration (CATAMA) Program. *Research in Middle Level Education Quarterly, 22*(2), 1–23.

Mac Iver, D.J., Mac Iver, M.A., Balfanz, R., Plank, S., and Ruby, A. (2000). Talent Development Middle Schools: Blueprint and results for a comprehensive whole school reform model. In M.G. Sanders (Ed.), *Schooling at risk: Research, policy, and practice in the education of poor and minority adolescents* (pp. 292–319). Mahwah, NJ: Erlbaum Associates.

Mac Iver, D.J., & Plank, S. (1997). Improving urban schools: Developing the talents of students placed at risk. In J.L. Irvin (Ed.), *What current research says to the middle level practioner* (pp. 243–256). Columbus, OH: National Middle School Association.

Mac Iver, D.J., Plank, S., and Balfanz, R. (1997). *Working together to become proficient readers: Early impact of the Talent Development Middle School's Student Team Literature Program.* (Report 15). Baltimore, MD and Washington, DC: Center for Research on the Education of Students Placed at Risk.

Mac Iver, D.J., & Prioleau, A.D. (1999, April). *Looping: Helping middle school teachers to be caring, daring, and effective.* Paper presented at the annual meeting of the American Educational Research Association, Montreal, Canada.

Maryland Middle Learning Years Task Force. (2000) *Middle grades matter: Meeting the challenge for systemic reform.* Baltimore: Maryland State Department of Education.

Mosteller, F.D., Light, R.J., and Sachs, J.A. (1996). Sustained inquiry in education: Lessons from skill grouping and class size. *Harvard Education Review, 6,* 797–842.

National Center for History in the Schools. (1996). *National standards for history.* Los Angeles: National Center for History in the Schools.

Newmann, F.M., Lopez, G.L., and Bryk, A.S. (1998). *The quality of intellectual work in*

Chicago schools: A baseline report. Chicago: Consortium of Chicago School Research.

Pelavin, S., and Kane, M. (1990). *Changing the odds: Factors increasing access to college.* New York: College Entrance Examination Board.

Plank, S., and Young, E. (1999, April). *In the long run: Longitudinal assessments of the Student Team Literature Program.* Paper presented at the annual meeting of the American Educational Research Association, Montreal, Canada.

Ruby, A. (1999, April). *An implementable curriculum approach to improving science instruction in urban middle schools.* Paper presented at the annual meeting of the American Educational Research Association, Montreal, Canada.

Schmidt, W.H., McKnight, C.C., and Raizen, S.A. (1997). *A splintered vision: An investigation of U.S. science and mathematics education.* Dordrecht, The Netherlands: Kluwer.

Task Force of the National Council for the Social Studies. (1994). *Expectations of excellence: Curriculum standards for social studies.* Waldorf, MD: National Council for the Social Studies.

U.S. Department of Education. (1997). *Mathematics equals opportunity.* White paper prepared for U.S. Secretary of Education Richard W. Riley. Washington, DC: Author.

Useem, E. L. (1998a). *Local education funds: What they do, how they do it, and the difference they make: A report on the Public Education Network.* Washington, DC: Public Education Network.

Useem, E.L. (1998b). *Teachers' appraisals of Talent Development Middle School training, materials, and student progress: Results from six focus groups at Central East Middle School and Cooke Middle School.* Baltimore, MD: Johns Hopkins University, Center for Research on the Education of Students Placed at Risk.

Useem, E.L. (1999). *Year two talent development at Cooke Middle School: A report from two focus groups.* Philadelphia: Philadelphia Education Fund.

Wheelock, A. (1998). *Safe to be smart: Building a culture for standards-based reform in the middle grades.* Columbus, OH: National Middle School Association.

Wilson, B.L. and Corbett, H.D. (1999). *"No excuses": The eighth grade year in six Philadelphia middle schools.* Philadelphia: Philadelphia Education Fund.

Preparation of this chapter was supported by grants from the Office of Educational Research and Improvement, U.S. Department of Education. The content and opinions express herein do not necessarily reflect the views of the Department of Education or any other agency of the U.S. Government.

9

Transforming Organizational Structures for Young Adolescents and Adult Learning

THOMAS O. ERB
University of Kansas

We did it because it seemed so right

It was the fall of 1967. Robert Kennedy and Martin Luther King were still alive and so was Hubert Humphrey, politically. Abby Hoffman and Jerry Rubin were not yet household names, let alone principals in the Chicago Eight drama. The country was still four months away from the beginning of that fateful year of 1968, and I was just beginning my teaching career—a 22-year-old neophyte.

I had graduated the previous spring from DePauw University with a B.A. in history—what heady times for a history major. America was in ferment, and I was enamored with the study of history. But what does a young B.A. holder in the idealistic 60s do with a history degree? Try teaching, but so were a copious number of other B.A. holders in the social sciences. The market for high school social studies teaching positions was very competitive. One high school principal counseled me, "Why don't you get a junior high teaching position, get some experience, and come back and see me in a couple of years?"

In seeking an internship position for my MAT program at Northwestern University, I interviewed for a couple of high school placements, to no avail. Finally, in the desperate spring months of 1967, I was successful in landing a teaching position—at Howard *Junior* High School in Wilmette, Illinois. So there I was the following fall, in charge of a three-hour block of time to teach social studies, English, and group guidance to twenty-eight eighth graders. I didn't even have a minor in English, although I had met the English requirements for college graduation. I had had no real experience in schools beyond my own twelve-year journey as a student in the public schools of Fort Wayne, Indiana. My understanding of young adolescents was limited to a cursory overview in an educational psychology course only partially devoted to developmental issues. But I was "in charge" of my junior high classroom while dreaming of landing a high school position at the end of the year.

An aspect of my personality that would not be clearly revealed even to me until I entered my doctoral program ten years later has some relevance to this story. My Myers-Briggs Type is INTJ and its most extreme score is on the "I" side of the "I-E" dimension. For those not conversant with the Myers-Briggs types, I do my best thinking running ideas through my head; dealing with ideas and decisions in group settings is problematic for me.

Given these background factors, the prognosis for a long and successful middle grades teaching career was not good. Yet over thirty years later, I am still in middle grades education—albeit now in teacher education at the University of Kansas and as editor of the *Middle School Journal*—and concerned with the organizational structures that give middle grades teachers the most support for what they do. What happened? Why didn't I flee teaching long ago, beaten down by young adolescents whose learning styles and developmental needs I was ill-equipped to deal with? People, situated in organizational structures that helped me grow while I was learning how to help youngsters grow, were the difference between another middle grades dropout and a third-of-a-century-long career in middle grades education.

Fortunately, I had the good luck to be assigned a room in Howard next to Yvonne Kuhlman. She had been both a high school and junior high English teacher for 25 years when I first encountered her. As luck would have it, she and I had a common planning time, occupied adjacent classrooms, and were assigned common teaching schedules. We did not share students as we were both designated to teach core curriculum (language arts, social studies, and group guidance) to our separate groups of students.

Without any theoretical basis for action nor any administrative mandate to do so, Yvonne and I started meeting together during our common planning time. We discussed a number of common concerns: student classroom behavior, motivating thirteen year olds, designing interesting lessons, relating to administrators and parents, and coordinating language arts and social studies topics. With all of the ingredients in place (common planning time, block schedule, and adjacent classrooms), by my second year of teaching we were exchanging students and had created our own two-person interdisciplinary team. In the third year the administration stepped in to expand the teaming experience in the school and added a third person and curricular area to the team: science.

I had been inducted into middle grades teaching in a very supportive, collaborative environment that had evolved for us through fortunate circumstances. It just made good sense to plan together, share perspectives on students taught in common, and counsel each other on our professional concerns. We discussed students, held joint parent conferences, planned together, integrated the curriculum, and grew professionally as teachers, both the neophyte and the veteran. It seemed so right. After three years I was so well established as a middle grades teacher that I gave up the quest for a high school teaching position. Teaching young adolescents was simply too satisfying to abandon. During my fourth year of teaching when Yvonne resigned to accompany her husband to a new job in California, I became the team leader and we carried on.

That was thirty-two years ago. In those thirty-two years, we, as a profession, have learned much about what we could not then generalize, that we *knew* only from personal experience: Teaming works to create a better work environment for teachers and a better learning environment for students. Imagine my chagrin two years ago—thirty years after having such a positive experience with teaming—when I became liaison to a Professional Development Junior High School (PDS) where half of the students are getting failing grades, the faculty are still laboring in isolated classrooms, and the administration runs around frantically trying to keep the lid on. Why have these intelligent educators— after thirty years of growth in our understanding of middle grades organizational structures that improve the capacity of teachers to do their jobs and the capacity of students to do the work of learning—not availed themselves of the professional tools that would make their work both more satisfying and more effective? This school is not alone in its failure to change. McEwin, Dickinson, and Jenkins (1996) found that only about half of middle schools in the country even claim to be teaming. Why is there such a gap between what we know can create better teaching and learning environments and the reality of so many seemingly dysfunctional middle grades schools?

Much of the answer lies in the degree to which team organization changes the nature of the schools where it is implemented. A school organized around teams is a fundamentally different place than a school organized around separate classrooms. In many situations, administrators and teachers fail to understand the transformative nature of team organization. Consequently, their vision of schooling, limited by their collective experience with older, departmentalized school organization, restricts their thinking about the promise and possibilities of teaming. To many educators, teaming is "just another program imposed by an administrator trying to make a name for himself." In fact, one of the professional reviewers that the National Education Association employed to review the prospectus for *Team Organization: Promise—Practices and Possibilities* (Erb and Doda 1989) panned the book on the grounds that it was advocating imposing new administrative oversight and constraints on teachers. What a gross misunderstanding of the concept of teaming in school organizations!

Beyond bureaucracy, transformative structures

To understand the extent to which interdisciplinary teams change school organizations one must understand the difference between bureaucracies and adhocracies. While the concept of bureaucracy needs very little introduction to modern-day readers, the concept of adhocracy is in the vocabulary of very few—that is a big part of the problem! The latter term first appeared in *Future Shock*: "We are, in fact, witnessing the arrival of a new organizational system that will increasingly challenge, and ultimately supplant bureaucracy. This is the organization of the future. I call it "Ad-hocracy"" (Toffler 1970, p. 125).

Work in schools is complex and uncertain

Nearly two decades after I began teaching and after studying special education in school settings, Skrtic (1991a, 1991b) provided us with an understanding of the differences between bureaucracies and adhocracies. Understanding these differences is critical to functioning in a transformative school structure. The differences between these two organizational structures can be grasped in terms of how work is organized in each type of organization. Both professional bureaucracies and adhocracies are designed to carry out complex work whose processes cannot always be clearly prescribed in advance. Teaching, which involves the interaction of a teacher and multiple learners who are engaging in idiosyncratic ways with a curriculum, is complex work that requires on-the-spot decision making to successfully accomplish.

Excellent teaching, though constrained by guidelines, curriculum plans, administrative procedures, high-stakes testing, parental expectations, and other parameters, is in many ways more of an art form than a scientific pursuit. Eisner (1994) has argued:

> Teaching is an art in that teachers, like painters, composers, actresses, and dancers, make judgments based largely on qualities that unfold during the course of action. . . . [In addition,] teaching is an art in that the teacher's activity is not dominated by prescriptions or routines but is influenced by qualities and contingencies that are unpredicted. (p. 155)

In teaching a group of students, an intelligent teacher selects, controls, and organizes such things as tempo, tone, climate, pace of discussion, and forward movement. The teacher must decide, while the classroom action is going on, whether to push ahead to keep the pace flowing or to increase wait-time to invite a new contribution from a pondering student. A teacher must decide in action whether to create a little tension by gently needling students to respond or to pull back to reduce the competitive tension in a classroom. Getting students engaged with the subject matter demands that teachers assess a complex set of factors and decide on appropriate action, sometimes doing things that are contradictory to what was done yesterday, last period, or even ten minutes ago.

Is there any teacher among us, armed with the best lesson plans, who has not been surprised by a student's unexpected comment or been disappointed by students' lack of enthusiasm for an activity that has never before failed? Eisner (1994) pointed to a contradiction that characterizes teaching as an art form in this sense. Though routines and prescriptions do not dominate teaching, a good teacher cannot function without them. The teacher must have readily available a repertoire of skills on which to draw. Having this repertoire allows the teacher to devote energy and attention to what is emerging in the class and allows the teacher to deal inventively with that emerging situation. "It is precisely the tension between automaticity and inventiveness that makes teaching . . . so complex an undertaking" (p. 155).

The work of schools is coordinated by the mutual adaptation of team members

Beyond these similarities, where professional bureaucracies and adhocracies both assume that the work carried out in schools is complex, they begin to diverge. Work in a professional bureaucracy is coordinated through what Skrtic calls the "standardization of skills." That is, through professional training and socialization, different types of professionals acquire expert knowledge peculiar to their separate specializations. Consequently, from an organizational perspective all social studies teachers are interchangeable as are all math teachers, physical education teachers, counselors, and so forth. Therefore, all professionals do what their specialized training has prepared them to do. Professionals each working in their own areas of specialization contribute to the total work of the organization—the complete education of the child. In an adhocracy, on the other hand, work (instruction of students in this case) is coordinated by the mutual adaptation of workers (teachers) operating as members of teams. In examining the dynamics on one team over the course of a year, Mills and Ohlhausen (1992) have described how mutual adaptation results from the negotiating that takes place among teachers who are working closely together. They described how classroom procedures ranging from management issues to enacting a common vision were negotiated. Second, how to assess the growth of both students and teachers was much discussed. Finally, seeking ways to foster both student and teacher empowerment emerged as a major theme in this interactive teaming environment. The expectations, procedures, and lessons created on this team were the result of the unique interaction of its members. Since the work of schools is too complex and uncertain to be left to professionals operating in isolation from each other, teams of teachers are required to work together to create solutions through mutual adaptations. Polite (1994) has documented how this process occurs:

> "Negotiation," "coaxing," "accommodating," and "simply requesting" were terms used to describe the decision-making processes used on the

teams. Teachers reported that at first they worked on things that were "tried and true," but as trust and rapport developed among team members and they gained familiarity with their students, they addressed issues which required shared decision making. (p. 71)

The work of teachers is interdependent, reciprocal, collaborative, and discursive

These two types of organization also differ in the way the work of one individual is related to the work of others. In a professional bureaucracy the work of teachers is loosely coupled, which means that there is a low level of interdependency. What a sixth grade teacher does has little bearing on what an eighth grade teacher does. The work of an English teacher is not related to what a science teacher does. A social studies teacher functions quite separately from a math teacher. Professionals in the work place can each carry out their fundamental duties independently of other specialists. However, in an adhocracy the work of teachers is reciprocally coupled through collaboration. The complex, uncertain work of the organization demands that professionals work together to exchange information and develop original responses to the learning needs that they encounter.

Within the framework of team interaction, information exchanges result from five types of mentoring that occur (Powell and Mills 1994, 1995). First, collaborative mentoring occurs when teachers willingly learn from each other. This type of mentoring is especially valuable for first-year teachers who have much to learn about everything from classroom management to curriculum. My own personal story is dramatic testimony to the power of collaborative mentoring. Without it, I would very likely not have written this chapter because I would have dropped out of middle grades education long, long ago.

A second type of mentoring is clerical mentoring. That occurs when teachers help each other learn administrative procedures and carry out functions necessary to operating the school. Team members help each other to prepare progress reports, eligibility reports, and so forth. The third type of mentoring is professional teacher mentoring which occurs as teachers encourage and challenge each other to grow professionally, which often involves working together to solve a professional problem, such as challenging high performing students on a team. For example, Yvonne and I once created more challenging tasks for two students whose maturity level was considerably higher than most of the rest of this one class. Other times, we created adaptations to lessons for students with reading problems—all without the benefit of IEPs or special educators to assist us. Fourth, when teachers held conversations about subject areas, unit planning, instructional strategies, and student activities, they engaged in interdisciplinary content mentoring. I (Erb 1997) have described three or four ways this type of mentoring occurred between Yvonne and me. It resulted in our planning and teaching several integrated thematic units on such topics as "Cities," "Futures," "Civil Rights," and "Exploration." Finally, teachers engage in social informal mentoring that fosters personal development and the growth of self-knowledge. Due to my lack of experience with children and even adults for that matter at the age of 22, this type of mentoring from Yvonne helped me grow as a person, not just as an educator.

These types of mentoring result not just from having common planning time scheduled regularly, nor even from following agendas to guide efficient discussions during team meetings. The mentoring that Powell and Mills have documented—especially the third, fourth, and fifth types—is fostered by what Kain (1995) has described as "adding dialogue to a team's agenda." These types of mentoring occur when the team moves beyond focusing on the immediate business of the team to engage in transformative conversations. He has concluded:

> If we want to create a new version of collaboration in schools and new connections for our students, team dialogues can provide the means for meeting of the minds, a meeting of different ways of thinking.
>
> But a team cannot simply sit down and say, "let's dialogue." The preliminaries—getting to know one another, commitment to dialogue, skills of inquiry and advocacy, and a sense of playfulness—must be developed over time. Throwing out the agenda won't guarantee dialogue, though rethinking the role agendas play in our teams and examining what kinds of issues appear on our agendas may help. As teams develop understanding of what dialogue involves and its rich potential, they can create . . . a sea of talk that supports professional growth and learning. (p. 6)

The interdependency of teachers results in more flexible thinking which supports problem solving. Again Powell and Mills (1994) have described this phenomena:

> Teachers who were less isolated and who shared the ordeal of teaching moved away from singular views of teaching. They also moved away from singular approaches to solving classroom problems as they shared ideas and suggestions. (p. 30)

When teachers interact on teams to discuss a wide range of issues, students, topics, and concerns, the work that they do is transformed from being centered around isolated classroom performances loosely connected to all else that is going on in the school, to becoming mutual adaptations born of discourse and collaboration that make the work of teachers really interdependent.

Transformative organizations are focused on problem solving

The professional bureaucracy can function (though not very well) on the backs of isolated professionals because the organization is performance oriented. The professionals are called upon to deliver the standardized performances that they are trained for and assigned to do. This explains the plethora of specialized "programs" in a bureaucratic school: honors science, remedial reading, sixth grade regular social studies, Chapter I math, learning disabled, gifted humanities, behavior disordered, and "at-risk" study skills just to name a few. There is a predetermined program available to meet whatever needs the school can determine that a student has. Skrtic has argued that a bureaucratic school's response to discovering a new need is to create another specialized, decoupled program to deal with it. That way the rest of the bureaucracy can continue to function as usual. Skrtic claimed that bureaucracies are threatened by heterogeneity. Students either fit into the school's repertoire of standardized programs or get pushed out of the system— being expelled, becoming dropouts, or being shipped off to "alternative" schools. Separate "programs" for "at risk" youth would be seen from this perspective to be just the latest in a string of bureaucracy's attempts to create a new specialization so that the rest of the organization could continue as usual to deliver its other standard programs.

On the contrary, "Student diversity is not a liability in a problem-solving organization; it is an asset, an enduring uncertainty, and thus the driving force behind innovation, growth of knowledge, and progress" (Skrtic 1991b, p. 177). Adhocracies are organizations designed to solve problems. Teaching would be seen not as delivering programs but as solving learning problems. If different students are having problems learning, teachers collaborate to create a solution (see Bohrer 1995). In fact, the students come to be viewed as part of the solution to problem solving. Mills and Ohlhausen (1992) described the process this way:

> As students continued to recognize themselves as partners in the learning process, interesting negotiations occurred, and teachers continued to see students as resources for problem solving. (p. 110)

The outcomes of schooling are unique, not standard products

These two different organizational types lead to different kinds of institutional outcomes. Professional bureaucracies deliver standard products, services, or programs. Adhocracies, however, create innovative solutions or novel products and services. Hart, Pate, Mizelle, and Reeves (1992) have shown this working on interdisciplinary teams:

Their planning emphasized decision making about flexible scheduling and grouping. They also emphasized planning about novel curriculum and instruction. (p. 93)

Though the purposes of middle grades schooling may be similar from school to school or team to team, in transformative adhocracies, the solutions to teaching and learning problems are unique—because the students are unique.

Transformative organizations are made for dynamic environments

A professional bureaucracy is designed to operate in a stable environment where standardized outcomes can be relied upon. Adhocracies are designed to function in dynamic environments that are constantly changing. The rate with which the "eWorld" is changing the way we do everything from communicating with each other, to shopping, to managing finances, to arranging travel plans, or even to simply enjoying entertainment is dramatic testimony to the dynamic society in which we live. Contemplate the rate with which 33 1/3 rpm records have given way to eight track tapes, have given way to CDs, are giving way to DVDs. Or the rate with which bank tellers have given way to drive through windows, are giving way to ATMs, are giving way to electronic banking via PCs. In our own profession carbon paper and purple dittos have given way to xeroxing, have given way to transparencies, are giving way to powerpoint presentations and interactive video. Retailing has moved from shops on Main Street to large department stores, to discount chains, to huge malls, to e-commerce. Companies to stay alive have transformed themselves—to wit: S.S. Kresge begat K-Mart which begat Big-K, which is moving to on-line sales. Is it not clear that an adhocracy, an organizational structure which assumes a rapidly changing external environment, is a far better arrangement to educate diverse learners than is a professional bureaucracy? Skrtic (1991a) summarized his description of an adhocracy:

> The adhocracy is premised on the principle of *innovation* rather than standardization; as such, it is a *problem-solving* organization configured to *invent new programs.* It is the organizational form that configures itself around work that is so ambiguous and uncertain that neither the programs *nor* the knowledge and skills for doing it are known. . . . [T]he adhocracy "engages in creative effort to find a novel solution; the professional bureaucracy pigeonholes it into a known contingency to which it can apply a standard program. One engages in divergent thinking aimed at innovation; the other in convergent thinking aimed at perfection." (Mintzberg 1979, p. 436). . . . Finally, under the organizational contingencies of collaboration, mutual adjustment, and discursive coupling,

accountability in the adhocracy is achieved through a presumed community of interests—a sense among workers of a shared interest in a common goal, in the well being of the organization with respect to progress
toward its mission. (pp. 182–184) (emphasis in the original)

Recent research has confirmed the inverse relationship between bureaucracy
and implementation of middle school practices. As schools transform themselves into true middle schools by implementing higher levels of the practices
recommended by *Turning Points* (Carnegie Council on Adolescent Development 1989), they do reveal lower levels of bureaucratization on such measures
as hierarchy of authority, division of labor/task specification, clearly defined
system of rules, and impersonality of interpersonal relations (Hosman 1999).
In more highly implemented, less bureaucratized middle schools, teachers engage in more collaboration and are less constrained by rigid master schedules
and departmental teaching assignments. These less bureaucratized organizational structures lead to several positive outcomes for students: fewer reten-
tions, fewer expulsions, a stronger sense of belonging to school, and greater
achievement on norm referenced tests. For teachers the results are equally encouraging: more collaboration with colleagues, more active involvement in
solving school problems, and more freedom to act on their ideas to determine
new directions (Hosman 1999). How can this perspective on organizations be
useful in understanding the functioning of teams in middle schools?

Making changes transformational

To the extent that the characteristics of professional bureaucracies persist,
teams become dysfunctional or, at the very least, plateau short of reaching their
full potential. These characteristics can take the form of either perceptions or
practices. As long as teachers see themselves as individually responsible for
teaching a prespecified area of the curriculum, they will self-limit their ability
to function on a team. As long as administrators persist in the belief that they
are ultimately responsible for what goes on in their schools so that they must
make schoolwide decisions and hand them down for teachers to follow, teacher
autonomy will be stymied. As long as a bell schedule dictates a prespecified
sameness for the duration of learning experiences, instructional planning will
be constrained. The same can be said for the practice of assigning students to
"classes" that they must remain in for the full semester or year. This last practice
becomes even more debilitating for teaming when students are assigned during
team time to special pull-out programs taught by people who are not on the
team. When teachers assigned to whatever subject area or program see themselves primarily as guardians of their area of the curriculum, combining expertise to meet students needs is unlikely except as a hit-and-miss occurrence.

Structural changes such as creating team meeting time, team space, and block schedules along with sharing students are not sufficient to define a transformative organizational change. This point has been verified by the work of the Project on High Performance Learning Communities (Felner, Kasak, Mulhall, and Flowers 1997), which has identified five features that go into defining the effective implementation of an organizational change. In studying the impact of implementing the recommendations made in the Carnegie Corporation's *Turning Points* report (Council on Adolescent Development 1989), researchers have identified four features in addition to the basic structural changes that are necessary to ensure that an organizational change has been implemented. These five features, identified by the Project on High Performance Learning Communities, and the questions that educators have to answer in the affirmative are the following (reported in Stevenson and Erb 1998):

1. Structural features: "Do I have the opportunity to do it?" Are the basic structural features, such as common planning time, shared students, block schedule, and team space, in place?

2. Normative/attitudinal features: "Do I believe in it?" "Do I want to do it?" Do teachers believe that they will be more effective in meeting the learning needs of diverse learners if they plan lessons together, discuss students taught in common, and coordinate expectations for students, and attempt to integrate the curriculum?

3. Skill and professional preparation features: "Do I know how to do it?" To make organizational changes transformative, teachers must have the skills and knowledge to liberate themselves from the constrictions of the past. To make teams work, teachers must not only have problem-solving skills, team-building skills, interpersonal communication skills, and intrapersonal skills, but they must also understand the concept of teaming, how to set team goals, and how to manage the work of a small work team. Number 1 and 2 without number 3 will not bode success.

4. Climate and interactive processes: "Do I have an environment that enables me and supports me in doing it? Once the structural features are in place, teachers believe in the innovation, and they have developed skill in teaming, transformative change can still be stymied. If the team members do not consistently control their team meeting time because the principal or the counselor or some other outside agent repeatedly usurps the agenda, or students are assigned to more than one core team so that no one team controls that student's instructional schedule, or a plethora of pull-out programs continually take students off the team so that the team cannot flexibly schedule the block, or competition

among teams leads to professional jealousies, then the larger school environment will fight rather than support teaming.

5. Instructional/practice features: "Do I do it?" If outside observers came into your school to observe team meetings, would they see students' academic and behavior problems being addressed? Would they see lesson plans being shared? Would they see attempts to coordinate lessons, topics, and units across subjects? Would they see a written list of team goals for the semester? Would they observe attempts to assess the progress on the team in reaching its goals? In other words with the first four features in place—i.e., all the barriers to teaming removed— would a neutral observer actually see teams working together?

Elements in each category are necessary for transformative structures to exist. Although the structural elements are *necessary* to create an interdisciplinary team, they are not *sufficient* to define it. Not only must the opportunity be provided, but teachers have to believe in it and want to do it. They must have the skills and professional development to make it happen. The climate of the school must be supportive of teaming, and teachers must actually engage in teaming practices.

Reform efforts hit a snag in the very beginning when all five elements of putting an innovation into practice are not present. Steffes and Valentine (1996) found that 80% of the teachers in their nationwide study of 99 schools indicated that they received only moderate amounts or no inservice for serving on teams. Trimble and Miller (1998) concluded that teachers needed to have more institutional support for carrying out their new roles on teams. Traditional hierarchical decision-making systems that did not foster close communication between administrators and teachers were a hindrance to implementing effective teaming. Just adding on more responsibilities to teacher roles will not lead to effective change; teachers' roles must be redefined. Without adequate support the purported reforms will not take hold in the first place.

On the other hand, as long as educators understand the nature of adhocracies, they will grow and continue to evolve into fully developed teams. When the complexity of teaching is acknowledged so that teachers come to believe that their effective functioning is dependent on reciprocal relationships with teammates, then teachers will work together to create unique pedagogical solutions for the learning problems that their students present them. Teachers will view teaching as a "problem-solving" enterprise where learning activities are designed to meet the needs of specific learners—for example, teachers, not bells, determine the duration of learning activities. Curricular and pedagogical adaptations, grouping and regrouping of students, and using a wide variety of learning strategies will become a natural part of teaching. When the permanent members of a team consult with those outside the team, their decisions regarding students, curriculum, and instruction will be better informed. When these practices are supported by interaction with teammates, block schedules, and flexible teaching spaces, they become a part of the reward system of teaching as opposed to being additional weights placed on already overburdened teachers. When teachers come to see that what they can contribute to the education of young adolescents can be multiplied by combining their talent and expertise with that of others, teams will flourish.

Finally, is "the classroom" still thought of as the place where teaching takes place? The classroom symbolizes the noninterdependent, specialized professional delivering a standardized program. In Lortie's (1975) words, it is the separate "cell," a collection of which makes up the "egg crate school" (p. 14). However, in a teamed middle school operating as an adhocracy, the "house" has replaced the classroom as the basic building block (Sullivan 1996). A house, staffed by a team, is a collection of flexible spaces designed to support a wide variety of learning activities.

Even in conventionally constructed middle schools, the separate classrooms conception of schools can be rethought, as we had to do in Wilmette. With three adjacent classrooms, the three of us often planned for our students to be regrouped to work in project teams. For example, when we would teach a unit on "Cities" or "Civil Rights," our students might work in any of the three classrooms, the connecting hallways, or even the library. During our third year of teaming, a commons area was built adjacent to our classrooms so that each of the three eighth grade teams had a flexible large-group area—that could be divided into four smaller units with folding walls—that we could schedule to carry out our instructional objectives. Teams have spaces, larger than conventional classrooms, within which to teach their students.

The nature of transformative organizational structures in middle schools

It is crucial to understand how organizing a school around interdisciplinary teams can profoundly change the nature of that school. Interdisciplinary teams form the basis of a whole new way of engaging in teaching and learning, if those who implement them, administrators and teachers alike, really understand the organizational concept of adhocracy. Otherwise, if the practices that were created to make bureaucratic schools work (e.g., tracking, bell schedules, separate classrooms, specialized programs) are still being implemented by educators who view interdisciplinary teams as just another programmatic add-on, then teaming will fail and the educators will fail to create an adaptive, problem-solving, innovative organizational structure.

A caveat is in order. Changes in thinking and practice take time. Teachers in most schools will find themselves at some point in a transition period where a mix of organizational paradigms is working at cross-purposes. However, if educators understand the adhocratic nature of teamed organizations, they can plan to take the incremental steps that will move them ever closer to effective teaming. Effective teams do not spring full blown like Phoenix from the ashes. They are each created by educators who, armed with knowledge and foresight, dare to be better. Understanding that effective teams themselves change at the same time they are modifying how schools function is also important in interpreting the current discussion about the relationship between interdisciplinary curriculum and interdisciplinary teams in middle schools. Erb (in press) has described the seven-year journey of one middle school faculty to shed the shackles of bureaucracy to create a transformed middle school. Such a journey is neither smooth nor linear. School reform proceeds "more like a tacking sailboat than a speeding bullet" (Erb 2000, p. 2).

Not only does implementing an innovation proceed in a nonlinear fashion, but observing positive outcomes suffers from the same phenomenon. When the outcomes of educational reform are measured over time, the results often define what is called a "J-curve" (Erb and Stevenson 1999c). When a transformational innovation such as interdisciplinary teaming is initiated, student achievement will be at some preexisting level. The desired result is that student achievement will be improved by making the organizational change. Indeed, nationwide studies are beginning to show just such results (Backes, Ralston, and Ingwalson 1999; Felner, Jackson, Kasak, Mulhall, Brand, and Flowers 1997; Flowers, Mertens, and Mulhall 1999; Lee and Smith 1993). However, the road to improved outcomes is seldom a straight line. Instead, the initial measurement of outcomes usually results in a *reduction* in scores! If educators persist in their attempts to get the innovation right, this initial reduction in outcome measures is followed by an increase in performance. But how often have half-convinced educators, or their critics in the general public, looked at the *initial* outcome results and brayed, "I told you it wouldn't work!" The promising innovation is then chucked in favor of the next innovation-of-the-month. Educators must understand that implementing transformational organizational changes will take understanding, determination, and persistence. Organizational change is not for the faint-hearted. However, making transformational organizational changes has a very high potential to pay off handsomely both for teachers and their students.

Common planning time is a nonnegotiable for transformation

The power in transformative organizations comes from the results of teacher dialogue and joint decision making. In every middle school organization that has transformed itself, team meeting time is scheduled into the teachers' workdays on a regular basis. And it is used. Warren and Muth (1995) investigated the differential impact of three types of structures: "teaming" without common planning time, departmentalization, and teaming with common planning time. Their findings were dramatic; and they confirm the view that without common planning time so-called teaming has very little effect. Their two-state, twelve-school, and nearly 500-student study showed that teams with common planning time were superior to departmentalized classrooms and "teams" without common planning time on every measure of student self-concept and student perception of school climate. Not only did students on teams where common planning time was being used perform higher on measures of self-concept, they scored higher on satisfaction with school, commitment to classwork, reactions to teachers, and overall perceptions of school climate. In addition, teachers on teams with common planning time had more positive perceptions of their working environment. Educators who claim that they are "teaming" but do not make use of common planning time in addition to individual planning time are making a big mistake to think that they will have much impact on school climate or student outcomes.

Other effects of common planning time for teacher teams have been documented by the Project on High Performance Learning Communities. This nationwide study involving thousands of schools, tens of thousands of teachers, and hundreds of thousands of students has shown common planning time of 180 to 225 minutes per week—in addition to individual planning time—increases each of the following practices: (1) contact with other building resource staff, (2) coordination of student assignments, assessment, and feedback, (3) quality of teaming as perceived by teachers, (4) parent contact and involvement, and (5) curriculum coordination (Erb and Stevenson 1999a). Related research being undertaken at the Center for Prevention Research and Development at the University of Illinois has found that common planning time—again in addition to individual planning time and not as a substitute for it—is associated with more positive work climates for teachers who feel a stronger affiliation and support network through their fellow team members. Teachers also report higher levels of job satisfaction, which increases the longer schools engage in teaming with common planning time. Teaming with common planning time also results in more frequent contact with parents not only about student problems and performance, but also about homework to do with students, information and activities to increase parent involvement, and information about referrals for health or social service needs (Flowers, Mertens and Mulhall 1999).

What happens during common planning time

What is it about the dynamics of common planning time that leads to school transformations? A number of qualitative and ethnographic studies in the 1990s have documented what happens on effective teams. These recent studies have documented the types of experiences that Yvonne and I and our science teammates had thirty years ago. Three studies examined more specifically what things are discussed in team meetings. Studying a four-person, 100-student team for a year, Hart, Pate, Mizelle, and Reeves (1992) found that this team used fifteen different communication strategies in their team meetings. The six most used strategies accounting for 70% of the total communication on the team were these: (1) considering alternatives, (2) describing, (3) sharing information, (4) creating, (5) telling stories, and (6) finalizing decisions. The researchers identified twenty-four topics that were discussed. Seventy-two percent of team meeting time was spent focusing on these seven topics: (1) scheduling of students into learning experiences, (2) teaming processes and collaboration, (3) grouping of students for instruction, (4) integrated curriculum and instruction, (5) other aspects of curriculum and instruction, (6) student behavior, and (7) student motivation. This particular team was dedicated to developing fully over a three-year period into an effective interdisciplinary team.

Typically, new teams without quite as much vision and sense of mission as the team that Hart and associates described show different patterns in the early stages of teaming. McQuaide (1994) divided teacher talk in team meetings into five categories: students, policy, pedagogy, subject matter, and evaluation. The first two categories occupied teams 80% to 90% of the time during the first year. As the year advanced the balance between students and policy shifted from roughly 40%/40% to 60%/30% in favor of students. As the year progressed, teachers spent more time discussing individual student academic and behavioral issues and less time discussing school and team policy and administrative matters. In another study, Shaw (1993) examined how the use of team planning time evolved from the first year of teaming to subsequent years by analyzing teacher talk into six categories. While both new and experienced teams spent more time discussing individual students than they did in discussing any of the other categories, there were interesting differences that distinguished new and experienced teams. The experienced teams spent nearly 15% more time discussing students and 50% more time discussing instruction than did new teams. On the other hand, new teams dealing with getting organized as teams and learning how to work together spent about a third more time discussing logistics and housekeeping than did the experienced teams.

Recent findings of the Project on High Performance Learning Communities have confirmed the significance of keeping team membership intact over several years. Teams that have been together five or more years engage in more team activities than teams in their first or second year. Teams together for three or four years fall into the middle (Flowers, Mertens, and Mulhall 2000). Based on another data set analyzed by Robert Felner, it was found that keeping teams together for at least three years was associated with more positive student outcomes (reported in Erb and Stevenson 1999a). The more complicated demands of teaming, such as creating integrated curriculum, are likely to emerge only after less complex operations are mastered. If teams do not stay together more than one year, they are not likely to develop to the point where the impact of their performance will result in a transformative experience.

Transformational structures create growth-inducing environments for students and teachers

Well implemented teaming practices transform middle schools in three ways that have been described by the Project on High Performance Learning Communities (Felner, Kasak, Mulhall, and Flowers 1997; also reported in Erb and Stevenson 1999b).

Teacher job satisfaction

Common planning time supports a more interactive worklife for teachers in transformed middle schools. When teaming is practiced well, it has an impact on teachers' perceptions of their jobs. In a study of 769 middle school teachers on 99 teams, Steffes and Valentine (1996) found several teaming practices to be related to positive teacher outcomes. These teaming practices were (1) input into team member selection, (2) flexible scheduling, (3) adjacent classrooms, (4) autonomy and decision-making opportunities, (5) inservice related to teaming, and (6) common planning time. When these practices were taking place, teachers perceived these five differences in their worklives: (1) greater teacher innovation and creativity, (2) greater empowerment and greater leadership opportunities, (3) more opportunities to capitalize on individual teacher strengths, (4) expansion of teaching repertoires, and (5) increased teacher collaboration. In their twelve school study, Warren and Muth (1995) also found that teachers on teams with common planning time had more positive perceptions of their working environment.

Two other early 1990s studies of teachers on teams have added to our understanding of how teachers view their work as members of teams. Teamed teachers have more positive professional images and feel less stress than do other teachers (Gatewood, Cline, Green, and Harris 1992). In addition, teamed teachers feel less isolated in their classrooms (Mills, Powell, and Pollak 1992), although their changed worklives can cause some teachers to feel isolated from staff other than teammates. We can better see how transformational structures change the worklife of teachers for the better, but what of the learning climate in a school?

School and classroom climate

Felner has identified a number of factors that change in the climate of a school implementing a high level of *Turning Points* reforms. Among these are that students are not stressed out by extraneous things. The "work of getting to work" is reduced for students. In addition, the teamed environment creates the sense of smallness and that all students are known and needed. Teachers tend to hold high expectations for students and students know it. These high expectations are associated with more positive, healthy, and academically engaged behavior on the part of students. These teams also create a pro-social focus characterized by helping students to make good choices, to develop democratic values, and explore career goals as part of the regular curriculum (Erb and Stevenson 1999b).

In transformative middle schools where *teachers* used common planning time, *students* had more positive perceptions of school climate than did students in departmentalized schools and students in those schools with flawed or incomplete reform efforts (e.g., implementing pseudo-teams without common planning time). Students in transforming schools expressed a greater satisfaction with school. They had a higher commitment to classwork and more positive reactions to teachers (Warren and Muth 1995). This last finding confirms earlier studies that showed that students in teamed schools bonded with their teachers and their schools more completely than did students in nonteamed settings (Arhar 1990, 1992, 1994). Furthermore, this effect was stronger for students in low-income communities that often do not provide the level of social and economic support found in more affluent communities (Arhar and Kromrey 1995).

Given what we know about the differences between at-risk students who succeed and those who do not, these findings are very important. Resilient at-risk students developed important relationships with at least one adult that provided them with support and direction during difficult times (Reed, McMillan, and McBee 1995). These findings are important in promoting the *Turning Points* recommendation "to ensure success for all students" in schools that represent "their last best chance to avoid a diminished future" (Carnegie Council on Adolescent Development 1989, p. 8). Perhaps there are no more important outcomes of implementing transformational structures in middle schools than these regarding the bonding of students at-risk with the adults in school.

Enhanced student support with less stress

If implementing middle school reforms improves teacher job satisfaction and school climate exemplified by more positive teacher-student relationships, does this mean that students actually receive more support in their quests to gain academically and to grow in other ways? The answer again appears to be affirmative. In reporting Felner's findings, Erb and Stevenson (1999b) listed seven results in the area of student support. First, students with different needs are treated differently. This differential treatment is intentional, and not random. Students, who are better known by teachers who spend 40% to 60% of their team meeting time talking about individual students, get better support in reformed middle schools than do students in departmentalized settings. In addition, health and fitness needs of students are recognized and addressed more frequently in reformed middle schools. Teams are more than just a succession of subject matter classes, they are small groups that stand for something as illustrated by rules, rituals, and boundaries. This small group of students is taught as part of a peer group for the better part of the school day. Finally, afterschool opportunities for positive activities are available as an alternative to unsupervised hanging out. All of this support results from a coordinated effort and are not just "ad-ons" to the "real" program. The empirical findings of the Project on High Performance Learning Communities are confirming the theoretical work done by Skrtic on adhocracies. The most salient conclusion is, that when implemented in middle schools, adhocracies work!

Team size is a very relevant issue to achieving these changes in school climate and support. Earlier in this chapter, we reported Felner's findings regarding the relationship between amount of common planning time and five teacher worklife, school climate, and student support outcomes. In the case of common planning time, the more teams had, up to about 200 minutes per week, the more positive the outcomes. With team size, it is just the opposite. As teams grow beyond 100 to 120 students, the climate and support outcomes diminish (Erb and Stevenson 1999a). Size counts, and bigger is not better. Flowers, Mertens, and Mulhall (2000) even suggested that teams with less that 90 students engage in more teaming activities such as curriculum coordination and coordination of student assignments. Team size also affects team contacts with parents and with other resource personnel in a building. Teams that consist of three or fewer teachers and 90 or fewer students offer real promise. Bishop and Stevenson (2000) enthusiastically sum up their experience with these smaller "partner teams" this way:

> Teachers who have invested themselves in creating partner teams enthusiastically have reported to us that their professional lives are considerably enhanced when they are able to work closely with colleagues of likeminds and enjoy the support of administrators and colleagues in developing and implementing a partner team plan (Bishop, 1997). The opportunity to pursue a shared professional vision in collaboration with others appears to be rare, and experienced teachers tell us that they cannot imagine returning to a more conventional format. They and their students grow and mature in ways that are closely tied to their teaming arrangements. This partner team design constitutes the next rendition of team organization. (p. 17)

The power of transformative structures is increased when these structures allow for more intimate and more personable collaborative arrangements.

When teaming is well implemented, both teacher professional involvement and student involvement in school affairs are increased. Teachers see their schools as more participatory in relationship to goal commitment, to decision-making processes, and to team cooperation. Teachers see themselves as more supportive of students and more receptive to student ideas. Teachers also see their schools as more supportive of students and students more receptive to ideas, more open with teachers, and higher in motivation (Walsh and Shay 1993).

Students, too, report less stress and more positive attitudes toward school in reformed settings (Warren and Muth 1995). They are less bored (Lee and Smith 1993), express less fear and worry (Felner, Jackson, Kasak, Mulhall, Brand, and Flowers 1997), and report more positive self-concepts (Warren and Muth 1995) and self-esteem (Felner, Jackson, Kasak, Mulhall, Brand, and Flowers 1997).

Not all middle schools are transformed structures

Failure to understand the transformative power of adhocracies in practice (i.e., team organization in middle schools) has condemned half the young adolescents in this nation and their teachers to outmoded and increasingly dysfunctional school organizations. As diversity and complexity increase, bureaucratic organizations lose their power to produce results. While many educators labor in ignorance of ways to transform their schools into growth-inducing learning communities for both students and teachers, thousands of others are bogged down in arrested development because they do not understand the nature of the organizational structures they are trying to implement.

Part of the real tragedy for so many American youths lies in the fact that society is losing faith in public education because it sees the dysfunctional nature of so many nontransformed, yet misnamed, middle schools. From Seattle on the Pacific (Bellevue Confronts 1998) to Howard County, Maryland, near the Atlantic (Bradley 1998), to the pages of the Yearbook of the Association for Supervision and Curriculum Development (Tucker and Codding 1999) "middle schools" have come under attack for failing in their fundamental academic missions. Yet when one looks at the results produced by transformed middle schools, those that do a more thorough job of implementing the *Turning Points* recommendations, one sees a consistent pattern of success in promoting positive student achievement.

Transformed middle schools increase student achievement

High levels of implementation of the *Turning Points* recommendations do have an impact on how teachers perform their duties, on how they feel about their own effectiveness (see especially Ashton and Webb 1986), on the climate and interpersonal relationships in that school, and on the system of support delivered to students. But does all of this activity have an impact on student achievement? The results from several large-scale studies in the 1990s are very encouraging. With the exception of Lee and Smith (1993) who used data from nearly 9,000 students in the National Educational Longitudinal Study, the other large-scale studies of the student achievement outcomes of middle school reform have been associated in one way or another with the multistate effort to assess the impact of the *Turning Points* recommendations. Most of these studies used whatever assessments of achievement that were being used in the various states where these studies were taking place.

There is now evidence that highly implemented middle schools show positive results across the core curriculum. Higher mathematics scores were reported by Lee and Smith (1993), Felner, Jackson, Kasak, Mulhall, Brand, and Flowers (1997), and Flowers, Mertens, and Mulhall (1999). These same three studies, involving data from thousands of students in several states, also reported higher achievement in reading. In addition, language arts scores were higher for students in reformed middle schools (Backes, Ralston, and Ingwalson 1999; Felner, Jackson, Kasak, Mulhall, Brand, and Flowers 1997). Finally, Backes and associates (1999) reported higher performance for students in science and social studies. Lee and Smith (1993) found that reorganized middle schools tended to distribute these benefits across social class lines better than did conventional departmentalized schools.

Middle schools that have undergone organizational transformations have been shown to improve not only the worklife for teachers, but also the organizational climate and support for students. These intermediate results have also been shown to lead to improved academic performances for students—of all types of backgrounds. With transformed organizations, middle schools raise the tide that lifts all ships. Unless one were only concerned about the academic success of one type of learner, one would want to figure out how to implement the interdisciplinary team organization that has moved beyond the "we *feel* it works" and the "we *think* it works" stage to "we *know* it works."

Transformed middle schools evoke sad enthusiasm

When I relive the positive experiences that kept me from fleeing middle grades education and come to thrive in it, I am very enthusiastic about what we know and are able to do to make schools pleasant, productive places for all participants. Over the years this enthusiasm has been reinforced by the opportunity I have had to interview hundreds of middle grades teachers organized into teams. While the path to getting teaming to work had not always been smooth, the overwhelming majority of teachers professed to having a more satisfying worklife—so much so that no one I talked to would dream of returning to the bureaucratic departmentalized structures from which they had emerged. The opening lines of Erb and Doda (1989) quote two such teachers:

> A year ago I was fighting this thing tooth and nail. The "Bright Boys" [central office administrators] were trying to force something else down our throats. But, you know, teaming is the best thing that ever happened to my teaching.
> —Math teacher, Missouri

> If they do away with teaming, I'll quit teaching.
> —English teacher, Kansas (p. 7)

The positive experiences that I had learning to teach in the late 60s and early 70s were continually being reinforced in the testimony of teachers in the 80s and 90s. However, I do not want to appear pollyannaish here. These teachers also told me of the trials and tribulations that they experienced trying to make teaming work. I have chronicled the seven year transformation of one such middle school faculty in "Transitioning to Middle School: A Whole Faculty Case" (Erb in press). However, what emerges from the struggle is an environment that invites both teachers and students to learn.

At the same time I am so enthusiastic about the accomplishments of so many middle schools that have successfully transformed themselves, I am sad for those that have not yet succeeded—or perhaps not even tried. When I look at the resigned acceptance of failure in the PDS junior high to which I am liaison—a school where teachers are not organized to effectively do their jobs, where they are not significantly involved in deciding how the school is being run, where frustrated talk about kids who are not doing well dominates faculty talk—my melancholy grows. When I observe what is happening—or more to the point, not happening—in this school, I am reminded that school change is indeed a phenomena that occurs one school at a time. While some schools made the transition thirty years ago and thousands more have followed suit in the last third of the twentieth century, there are just as many schools in America that have not transformed themselves. Some have tried and so far failed; others are not even aware of the possibilities.

The struggle to improve the learning conditions for the approximately twenty million young adolescents in the United States continues. Fortunately, we are learning more and more about how to effect transformations and more and more about what results we can expect when we go to the trouble to transform our middle schools into learning communities. Whether the middle school glass is half full or half empty depends on our will to act on the knowledge we have about transforming organizational structures for young adolescent and adult learning.

References

Arhar, J.M. (1990). The effects of interdisciplinary teaming on social bonding of middle level students. *Research in Middle Level Education, 14*(1), 1–10.

Arhar, J.M. (1992). Interdisciplinary teaming and the social bonding of middle level students. In J.L. Irvin (Ed.), *Transforming middle level education: Perspectives and possibilities* (pp. 139–161). Boston: Allyn & Bacon.

Arhar, J.M. (1994). Personalizing the social organization of middle-level schools: Does interdisciplinary teaming make a difference? In K.B. Borman and N.P. Greenman (Eds.), *Changing American education: Recapturing the past or inventing the future* (pp. 325–350). Albany, NY: State University of New York Press.

Arhar, J.M., and Kromrey, J. (1995). Interdisciplinary teaming and demographics of membership: A comparison of student belonging in high SES and low SES middle-level schools. *Research in Middle Level Education, 18*(2), 71–88.

Ashton, P.T., and Webb, R.B. (1986). *Making a difference: Teachers' sense of efficacy and student achievement.* New York: Longman.

Backes, J., Ralston, A., and Ingwalson, G. (1999). Middle level reform: The impact on student achievement. *Research in Middle Level Education Quarterly, 22*(3), 43–57.

Bellevue confronts its middle-school muddle. (1998, August 23). *Eastside Journal,* p. 1.

Bishop, P. (1997). *Portraits of partnership: The relational work of effective middle level partner teachers.* Unpublished doctoral dissertation, University of Vermont, Burlington.

Bishop, P., and Stevenson, C. (2000). When smaller is greater: Two or three person partner teams. *Middle School Journal, 31*(3),12–17.

Bohrer, K. (1995). Diverse learning styles: A classroom's greatest asset. *Middle School Journal, 27*(1), 50–55.

Bradley, A. (1998, April 15). Muddle in the middle. *Education Week, 17*(31), 38–42.

Carnegie Council on Adolescent Development. (1989). *Turning points: Preparing American youth for the 21st century.* New York: Carnegie Corporation.

Eisner, E.W. (1994). *The educational imagination: On the design and evaluation of school programs* (3rd ed.). New York: Macmillan College Publishing.

Erb, T.O. (1997). Thirty years of attempting to fathom teaming: Battling potholes and hairpin curves along the way. In T.S. Dickinson and T.O. Erb (Eds.), *We gain more than we give: Teaming in middle schools* (pp. 19–59). Columbus, OH: National Middle School Association.

Erb, T. (2000). Middle schools: Requiem or renewal? *Middle School Journal, 31*(3), 2.

Erb, T.O. (in press). Transitioning to a middle school: A whole faculty case. In T.S. Dickinson and C.K. McEwin (Eds.), *Cases and commentary: A middle school case book.* Westerville, OH: National Middle School Association.

Erb, T.O., and Doda, N.M. (1989). *Team organization: Promise—practices and possibilities.* Washington, DC: National Education Association.

Erb, T.O., and Stevenson, C. (1999a). What difference does teaming make? *Middle School Journal, 30*(3), 47–50.

Erb, T.O., and Stevenson, C. (1999b). Fostering growth inducing environments for student success. *Middle School Journal, 30*(4), 63–67.

Erb, T.O., and Stevenson, C. (1999c). Middle school reforms throw a "J-curve": Don't strike out. *Middle School Journal, 30*(5), 45–47.

Felner, R.D., Jackson, A., Kasak, D., Mulhall, P., Brand, S., and Flowers, N. (1997). The impact of school reform for the middle years: A longitudinal study of a network engaged in *Turning Points*-based comprehensive school transformation. *Phi Delta Kappan, 79*, 528–532, 541–550.

Felner, R.D., Kasak, D., Mulhall, P., and Flowers, N. (1997). The project on high performance learning communities: Applying the Land-Grant model to school reform. *Phi Delta Kappan, 79*, 520–527.

Flowers, N., Mertens, S. B., and Mulhall, P.F. (1999). The impact of teaming. *Middle School Journal, 31*(2), 57–60.

Flowers, N., Mertens, S.B., and Mulhall, P.F. (2000). Planning time, team size, and longevity all influence teaming activities and teacher interactions. *Middle School Journal, 31*(4), 50–54.

Gatewood, T.E., Cline, G., Green, G., and Harris, S.E. (1992). Middle school interdisciplinary team organization and its relationship to teacher stress. *Research in Middle Level Education, 15*(2), 27–40.

Hart, L.E., Pate, P.E., Mizelle, N.B., and Reeves, J.L. (1992). Interdisciplinary team development in the middle school: A study of the Delta Project. *Research in Middle Level Education, 16*(1), 79–98.

Hosman, A. (1999). *An analysis of exemplary middle schools as democratic alternatives to bureaucratic school oganization.* Unpublished doctoral dissertation, Arkansas State University, Jonesboro.

Kain, D.L. (1995). Adding dialogue to a team's agenda. *Middle School Journal, 26*(4), 3–6.

Lee, V.E., and Smith, J.B. (1993). Effects of school restructuring on the achievement and engagement of middle-grade students. *Sociology of Education, 66*, 164–187.

Lortie, D.C. (1975). *Schoolteacher: A sociological study.* Chicago: University of Chicago Press.

McEwin, C.K., Dickinson, T.S., and Jenkins, D.M. (1996). *America's middle schools: Practices and progress—A 25 year perspective.* Columbus, OH: National Middle School Association.

McQuaide, J. (1994). Implementation of team planning time. *Research in Middle Level Education, 17*(2), 27–45.

Mills, R.F., and Ohlhausen, M.M. (1992). Negotiating a workshop in middle school language arts: A case study of two team teachers. *Research in Middle Level Education, 16*(1), 99–114.

Mills, R.F., Powell, R.R., and Pollak, J.P. (1992). The influence of middle level interdisciplinary teaming on teacher isolation: A case study. *Research in Middle Level Education, 15*(2), 9–25.

Mintzberg, H. (1979). *The structuring of organizations.* Englewood Cliffs, NJ: Prentice-Hall.

Polite, M.M. (1994). Team negotiating and decision-making: Linking leadership to curricular and instructional innovation. *Research in Middle Level Education, 18*(1), 65–81.

Powell, R.R., and Mills, R. (1994). Five types of mentoring build knowledge on interdisciplinary teams. *Middle School Journal, 26*(2), 24–30.

Powell, R.R., and Mills, R. (1995). Professional knowledge sharing among interdisciplinary team teachers: A study of intra-team mentoring. *Research in Middle Level Education, 18*(3), 27–40.

Reed, D.F., McMillan, J.H., and McBee, R.H. (1995). Defying the odds: Middle schoolers in high risk circumstances who succeed. *Middle School Journal, 27*(1), 3–10.

Shaw, C.C. (1993). A content analysis of teacher talk during middle school team meetings. *Research in Middle Level Education, 17*(1), 27–45.

Skrtic, T M. (1991a). *Behind special education: A critical analysis of professional culture and school organization.* Denver: Love Publishing Company.

Skrtic, T M. (1991b). The special education paradox: Equity as the way to excellence. *Harvard Educational Review, 61*(2), 148–206.

Steffes, B., and Valentine, J. (1996). The relationship between organizational characteristics and expected benefits in interdisciplinary teams. *Research in Middle Level Education Quarterly, 19*(4), 83–102.

Stevenson, C., and Erb, T.O. (1998). How implementing *Turning Points* improves student outcomes. *Middle School Journal, 30*(1), 49–52.

Sullivan, K. (1996). Middle school program and participatory planning drive school design. *Middle School Journal, 27*(4), 3–7.

Toffler, A. (1970). *Future shock.* New York: Bantam Books.

Trimble, S.B., and Miller, J.W. (1998). Principals' and teachers' perceptions of the work of teaming teachers in restructured middle schools. *Research in Middle Level Education Quarterly, 21*(3), 1–13.

Tucker, M.S., and Codding, J.B. (1999). Education and the demands of democracy in the next millennium. In D. D. Marsh (Ed.), *Preparing our schools for the 21st century* (1999 Yearbook) (pp. 25–44). Alexandria, VA: Association for Supervision and Curriculum Development.

Walsh, K.J., and Shay, M.J. (1993). In support of interdisciplinary teaming: The climate factor. *Middle School Journal, 24*(4), 56–60.

Warren, L.L., and Muth, K.D. (1995). Common planning time in middle grades schools and its impact on students and teachers. *Research in Middle Level Education, 18*(3), 41–58.

Our Turn?
Teaming and the Professional Development of Teachers

DANIEL L. KAIN
Northern Arizona University

[Y]ou teach and you teach and you teach with no time for research, no time for contemplation, no time for participation in outside affairs. Just teach and teach and teach until your mind grows dull and your creativity vanishes and you become an automaton saying the same dull things over and over to endless waves of innocent students who cannot understand why you are so dull, lose respect and fan this disrespect out into the community.
—*Zen and the Art of Motorcycle Maintenance*
(Pirsig 1974, p. 140)

Team teaching makes better teachers, whatever else you say about it.
—*The Drama of History* (Fines and Verrier 1974, p. 108)

In their account of joining together to teach history and drama, Fines and Verrier (1974) explain how they developed into better teachers because of their work in a two-person team. They don't ignore the difficulties of teaming, and they are realistic in pointing out that the educational system in which they work may not be able to sustain their experiment in teaming. But in the end, they make the case that teaming helped them to develop as professionals. They saw their own weaknesses and strengths; their coming together helped to shift their focus away from the teacher's attention to "more and more dead information" and onto the "relevance, usefulness, and interest" that learning can hold for students (p. 83). Two good teachers became better because of their collaboration. They write that even if they were never to have a similar opportunity to work with and learn from another colleague, their "whole attitude to our work, our skills and techniques would remain radically altered for the better" (p. 108).

In contrast, Robert Pirsig's novel describes a vision of teaching—at the university level, but with implications for all levels—that is all too familiar to us. Teaching can be an endless grind of too much to do and no time to reflect or change. Teaching brings the stifling isolation of spending every day in a crowd, but with no meaningful connections to a peer. Teachers can come to rely on routines to make the job doable, but watch their own enthusiasm and creativity smother under this concession to the conditions of schooling.

Does the promise of teaming offer relief from the drudgery described by Pirsig?

Much has been said about teacher teams at the middle school level and the potential benefits to students from this practice. What about the teachers? Is team membership good for teachers? If there is to be a "reinventing" of the middle school, should teaming have a prominent position?

This chapter addresses the role of teaming in the professional development of teachers. I begin with a brief examination of teams in the world of business, with particular attention to how teaming might improve the lives of workers. Following this brief review, I recount the place of teaming in my own professional development. I then return to the role of teaming in the professional development of teachers more generally. Finally, I present some suggestions for enhancing professional development through teams.

Hopping on the bandwagon? Teams and the business world

Educators ought to vent their nervousness when anyone draws on business models to inform school practices. Businesses generally have a unidimensional measure of success, a bottom line of profits that can be calculated unequivocally and reported confidently, though there are exceptions (Collins and Porras 1994). Schools have no such "bottom line," and the closest thing to it—standardized test scores—represents a measurable temptation for bureaucrats that teachers should oppose vigorously.

Nevertheless, there are two reasons to give some consideration to business models. First, the history of education in this century has strong connections to business and management theory from the outset (Kliebard 1975). What we take to be normal in the world of schools, a world that still looks remarkably like a factory model even in an age where the factory model is diminishing in importance to business, is partially the result of management theories applied to education. In other words, applying a business lens to education is not a new idea—though one could argue that its history hasn't exactly benefited children or teachers.

A second reason to consider business models is that businesses do have the advantage of being able to respond quickly to changes in the environment, while schools tend to change like glaciers. Unless businesses adjust to changing social patterns and new information, they fail; schools can fail and still do business. If we can learn from the business experience, while maintaining a sense of what is important for children and the people who work with them, why not?

A promising trend in the business world is the reorganization of work structures to reflect a less hierarchical and functionally based organization (Ostroff 1999). Instead of breaking down production so that every person handles only a fragment of a total process whose goal is outside his or her purview, businesses are increasingly using a "horizontal organization." Ostroff identifies twelve principles of such organizations, but two key notions in relation to middle school structures are *process owners*—people who take responsibility for whole processes rather than just fragments of them—and the *use of teams* rather than individuals as the "cornerstone of organizational design and performance" (p. 10).

Let's start with the idea of process owners. This perspective says that workers will be more invested in their work if they understand the reasons behind what they do and take pride in the product they create. In contrast, the factory model (a paradigm for current schooling practices) argued that workers needed to know only a small part of the process. Workers were to refine their skills in a very narrow area of the assembly line, leaving someone else to put it all together. Ostroff (1999) contrasts the assembly line model, where workers continually make inefficient "hand-offs" with the horizontal model, where workers join together purposefully to accomplish a task. Fisher and Fisher (1998) describe the typical problem of "disconnects" and "handoffs" in an organization in this way: "Engineering does what is right from its perspective, but this may cause unforeseen manufacturing costs. Sales may locate customers with expectations that can't be satisfied with workable technology. Purchasing may make deals on supplies that are cost-effective but nonfunctional" (p. 87).

Consider how schools have placed teachers in the role of assembly-line workers. Generally beginning at the middle level, teachers develop narrow skills, apply these to the students passing through, and hand off their work to another worker after about forty-five minutes. The sense of process ownership—someone who is carefully attending to the "product" as a whole—is absent. The focus of each teacher's work is necessarily on what he or she does during the time the student is in that particular class, rather than on the whole "product," that is, what the individual student learns and becomes as a result of schooling. We face our own disconnects and handoffs: While an English teacher might be desperately trying to help students value writing, a PE teacher might undercut those efforts by assigning writing as punishment; what the social studies teacher targets for students to learn about democratic relationships may be turned into a farce by the autocratic practices in science or reading. Our fragmented structure, like that in many businesses, may work against our ultimate goals.

Ostroff (1999) also calls for a change to the team as the fundamental unit of an organization. Other writers have identified tremendous benefits to the organization and to workers when companies institute cross-functional teams in place of isolated employees or narrowly defined functional work roles. Benefits have included increased productivity per employee, greater creativity in idea generation, decreased production errors, faster time getting products to market, lower costs, and improved employee morale, empowerment, and well being (Donnellon 1996; Fisher 1993; Fisher and Fisher 1998; Hackman 1990; Ostroff 1999; Wellins, Byham, and Dixon 1994; Wellins, Byham, and Wilson 1991). It's quite a list of reasons to consider teaming, and many of the reasons involve greater growth and satisfaction on the part of workers, not merely profits for the companies.

One reason so many businesses have shifted to team structures as opposed to departmental or functional structures is the change in the nature of work. Increasingly, workers do "knowledge work" as opposed to "physical labor" (Fisher and Fisher 1998). Of course, good teachers have been engaged in knowledge work all along, and it is sadly ironic that the structure of schools has been built primarily around the metaphor of factory/physical labor.

With all the potential benefits, there are still voices in the business community cautioning that instituting teams is difficult and should be undertaken only when the work justifies the use of teams (Hackman and Oldham 1980). Indeed, if the organizational environment does not support teaming, a business ought to resist using teams. Wellins, Byham, and Wilson (1991) argue that "Teams work, however, only when an organization's culture is ready for them. This readiness can be determined by looking at how the organization treats its people. Are employees trusted and asked for their opinions? Are individuals allowed to try new things?" (p. 94). Donnellon's (1996) research into teams uncovered the tensions that exist between teams and organizations that are built to sustain, evaluate, and reward individuals, though she also noted that teams both affect and are affected by the organization.

The use of teams in business has not been a reaction to a trend or a position paper, but a deliberate decision to be more effective and to adjust to changes in the nature of work. As Ostroff (1999) puts it, "structure is derived from strategy to deliver success" (p. 18). Cross-functional teams have helped workers to do their jobs better and to find their work more fulfilling. What about teachers? Does a "strategy to deliver success" suggest a change in school structure?

Teaming in middle schools—Current practice

We know that about half of America's middle schools are currently using a team structure (Erb 1997). It is less clear *how* these schools are using teams. Indeed, the fact that teams are present, by itself, does not necessarily indicate any change in the way schools work. Teaming may be more of a surface change. As John Lounsbury put it, teams may be simply a portion of the middle school concept that has been more "organizational wizardry than educational wisdom" (in Kain 1999, p. 5). Although her research was with business teams, Ann Donnellon's assessment of the state of teaming could just as easily apply to the stalled work at the middle level:

> Team work, despite its overuse and fading cachet, remains the most effective way to accomplish the organizational tasks that require integration of diverse expertise and experience. Yet many companies have stalled in the development of teams, and many people who manage and work in teams have hit a plateau of frustration and skepticism. There is a pervasive sense of disappointment with what teams have produced and great uncertainty about the causes of, and solutions for, this problem. (p. 255)

That "pervasive sense of disappointment" is certainly apparent in the middle school literature. Teams simply haven't delivered as much as we had hoped. Although many middle schools use teaming, perhaps as few as ten percent of these schools offer teachers serious planning time to do their work (Strahan, Bowles, Richardson, and Hanawald 1997). Reviews of studies of teaming document benefits to students and teachers (Arhar 1997; Felner, Jackson, Kasak, Mulhall, Brand, and Flowers 1997; Flowers, Mertens, and Mulhall 1999; Kain 1998; Strahan et al. 1997; Trimble 1999), although some have argued that the widespread advocacy of teacher teaming is not supported by research on the effectiveness of this practice (Wraga 1997). Without repeating the reviews of research here, I would like to address the question of how teaming can help to reinvent the middle school experience for teachers. I acknowledge from the start that teaming brings costs as well as benefits, and this chapter will probe into those costs as well.

Reinvented by teaming?

Like many teachers of sixth, seventh, and eighth graders, I began my work at this level as a sort of foot-in-the-door move. I wanted to teach in a particular district, and I was a hirable candidate to them as long as I would coach at the high school and teach at the junior high school. Apparently, I wanted this district enough to do what they asked.

My initial years at the school were predictably difficult. I brought the mentality of a high school teacher to the reality of a junior high. I wanted to dazzle the children with my fascinating lectures (rehashed from college lecture notes), have the kids sit quietly, a little in awe, while producing brilliant work. Instead, I faced bored kids who wanted to do something else, kids who reflected G. K.

Chesterton's complaint that formal education was "the period during which I was being instructed by somebody I did not know, about something I did not want to know" (Marlin, Rabatin, and Swan 1987, p. 100). Where I was expecting students to engage in careful analysis, I got questions like this one from Greg as he began his English test: "Mr. Kain, do we have to put in the extras for this test?" "Extras?" I asked, "what extras?" "You know," Greg answered, "periods, commas, capitals—the extras!"

I dragged myself through the trenches of lunch duty, fearful that I couldn't contain the bursts of energy in the clanging hallways. I moved from classroom to classroom every period. I had to monitor a study hall, a task in which a powerless teacher tries to hide this condition from the students for a whole year. I wanted to quit by Christmas, but I also didn't want to lose face. And I liked this district.

For two spotty years I tried to do my best with the kids. I learned a lot about this age group of children, whether we house them in middle schools or junior high schools—and I was still waiting for a transfer to the high school. In my third year, a new principal came to our junior high. He immediately began to move us in the direction of becoming a middle school instead of a junior high. One of the key elements of this move was to restructure the faculty from a departmental organization into teams. More than all the articles we read about middle schools, more than all the inspirational speakers we heard about middle schools, more even than the continual admonitions from our principal, this move to teaming helped to reinvent who I was as a teacher.

I should clarify that I have never been a good candidate for teaming. I like to find my particular piece of work, focus on it, and get done. I like to work through my lunch hour instead of visiting with colleagues. My disposition is perfect for the autonomous, isolated teacher. Yet I found that teaming was a powerful means to change my teaching, and though I still work alone through lunch hours, I continue to work on a team of teachers—even at the university level! Why?

I found that nothing so challenged me to grow as working with my colleagues in a teamed situation. For all its drawbacks—and there are plenty—teaming moves teachers forward. Teaming can nurture a conversation of what it means to serve middle school children; teaming can challenge the easy slide into mediocrity and compromise. And, if we're not careful, teaming can also form a barrier to professional development (Kruse and Louis 1995).

My first year on a teaching team put me in the awkward position of being a relatively new teacher who had to resist a veteran's misconceptions of team work. Let me explain. I was the English teacher on the team, and as I indicated, a relative newcomer. Though I had been at the school for three years, the isolated conditions of teaching made me still an unknown. The social studies teacher on my team was a true veteran, with more than twenty-five years of experience. As our team began to talk about doing something to change our instruction, she approached me with a suggestion for interdisciplinary teaming.

"I've got an idea," she said to me one day. "Why don't we do an integrated unit? I'll assign a paper, and you can grade it."

Even new teachers know something. I was no more thrilled about grading her papers than I would have been if the neighbor had invited me to wash his dishes. "That's interesting," I wisely replied, and did nothing.

Some time later, she came back to me with a new suggestion. "How about we assign a paper in social studies, and I grade the content while you grade the mechanics? That way we will integrate," she said.

"That's interesting," I replied, even less excited about grading for mechanics only. As one might expect, we did little joint work that year. I don't think there was much I was ready to learn from this colleague, although on reflection, I admire her willingness even to consider doing something different after so many years and so many lesson plans. She had no basis from which to build interdisciplinary learning experiences, and she did the best she could.

However, I also worked with another veteran, a math teacher from whom I could learn a great deal. I talked to him often about his teaching; I watched him set up his class, work with kids, and advocate a different perspective on learning in our team meetings. I learned that math—and schooling in general—did not have to be merely a following of a text, but it could be an ongoing inquiry, a new way of thinking. In short, my math colleague, someone with whom I would never have come into contact in our former departmentalized structure, helped me learn to teach middle school students.

My math colleague showed me both an approach to teaching that connected with the middle school students and a willingness to step out and try new approaches to instruction—and this from a teacher with many years of experience. I watched how he started his classes, sparking curiosity in the children, hooking them with puzzling ideas, and plunging them into challenging work. He showed me how he built a community in his classroom, with students working together to meet goals even though he remained far from chummy, drawing clear lines in his relating to the children. He showed me that it is better to trust kids and risk being taken advantage of than to doubt them and trap them and triumph over them. In my formative years as a teacher, he showed me a great deal, and I would have missed it all if I had not been teamed with him.

At the same time, I was teamed with the social studies teacher I mentioned earlier and a veteran science teacher. The lessons they offered me grew out of long careers of frustration, characterized by adversarial relationships with young adolescents. They typified the teacher who is ever ready to express disbelief at "those kids." At each team meeting, it seemed, they had stories about our difficult children, stories that reinforced the notion that kids were getting worse every year. They grumbled about the work of teaching, which I never saw them take out of the school door. They grumbled about the administration, especially if the principal called on them to change. After all, they often reminded us, they had been at this business a lot longer than the principal. They seemed to have taken on an attitude that they had paid their dues, and the kids ought to show them the respect they deserved. The lines were clear: students are there to learn, and teachers should not have to coddle them. Far from reinventing these teachers, teaming merely facilitated their venting.

The teammates I had in my first experience (and they could characterize me, too!) help to underline the double-edged nature of the team relationship. I was put in daily contact with professionals who could help to form my professional identity. For good or for ill, the team has the power and the opportunity to mark the development of teachers, especially teachers early in their careers. Fortunately, the positive example of my math colleague won me over. Perhaps he learned a little as he taught me much. My other team members came to realize that the restructuring of our junior high to a middle school did not match their expectations of what teaching should be, and both soon opted for retirement.

Perhaps this, too, shows an advantage of teaming. The "fit" between these two teachers and working with young adolescents was not good. These teachers may have belonged elsewhere in the education system, but the middle school students suffered in their classes. Under the independent, isolated conditions of the junior high, these teachers could continue to battle the students in toxic environments. Teaming, in many respects, drove these teachers away from the school, making space for teachers whose professional vision matched the middle school environment better, and making my subsequent team experiences far more positive.

Some years later I found myself on a new team, this time in a position to assert some more positive leadership. Together, the teamed teachers at our school pulled off some amazing events for our students, ranging from short interdisciplinary experiences to full-scale, flashy units that caught the eyes of local journalists. Such events, however were generally exceptions to our day-to-day teaching. The teams were entrenched, but not trenchant. Teaming had become institutionalized in our school; teaming no longer seemed a disturbance of the status quo, but the normal way of life. Indeed, in its normality, teaming had become routine. As so often happens, the acceptance of this innovation took the edge off its power to change.

Wellins, Byham, and Wilson (1991), like other group researchers, write that teams develop in certain predictable stages, and one of these is "going in circles." Teams, they indicate, get *stuck*. Team members become apathetic or frustrated, and all the novelty of the team structure disappears. Our school's teams experienced this state of being stuck. We continued to meet, though with a minimal commitment, and our work together fell into routines. For the most part, we talked about students at our team meetings, and while we carried on a few of the team projects we had developed, we were not seeking new ideas.

Katzenbach and Smith (1993) also address the notion of teams becoming stuck in their development. In order for teams to get unstuck, Katzenbach and Smith (pp. 160–162) offer these suggestions:

1. "Revisit the basics." (The basics, they argue, involve the team's purpose, approach and performance goals.)
2. "Go for small wins." (They remind us that nothing will move a team forward as effectively as performance. We can set the team on a promising path by building in victories.)
3. "Inject new information and approaches." (Change perspectives for the team; try something different.)
4. "Take advantage of facilitators or training." (Often someone from outside the team can help it refocus.)
5. "Change the team's membership, including the leader."

Perhaps the key step is the first, to revisit the basics. In our school, we had instituted teaming because it was a central feature of the "middle school concept." However, we ignored virtually all the basics of teaming. In particular, we never articulated a clear purpose for our teams, either at the school level or at the team level. We wandered vaguely from (in)activity to (in)activity, certain that we should be doing something but never certain why. The tremendous possibilities for professional growth were squandered in a complacent routine.

I have, in subsequent years, visited and spoken to a host of middle school teams. I see the full range of commitments, from those who endure teaming because they can no longer resist administrative pressures to those who embrace teaming as a way to rejuvenate their careers. I do not see teaming as a magic bullet that will reform schools or revitalize burnt-out teachers by itself. I recognize that some teachers, perhaps excellent teachers, will never fit in a team—and they should not be forced to do so. I believe that teams should be widely and wisely used in middle schools, but I completely support teachers who argue that teaming is ineffective if teachers are not taught how to use teams and given time to make teaming work.

Can teaming help to reinvent the middle school teacher? Without question, I argue, it can. But teaming is not a mantra for administrators to chant wishfully without building a team environment and without helping teachers learn how to use teams. Teaming is hard work that requires understanding and time and reflection on the part of its practitioners. Teaming, when it becomes one more thing for teachers to do, is a yawn at best and a disaster at worst. Teaming offers a means of reinventing the middle school only when we allow teaming to reinvent how we think about teaching.

Reinventing teaching?

As I indicated earlier, I came to teach at a junior high school with a decidedly inappropriate notion of what it means to teach children at that level. What I had admired in my university professors' performances did not work well with my young adolescent students. My initial response to my failures with the children was to want to leave—to move to a different level of schooling. I suspect I would have moved in frustration if I hadn't been helped along by my colleagues and my principal. Stepping away from the isolated classroom into the team context helped me broaden my notion of what good teaching is.

Many of the practices of schooling have remained unchanged for generations. There is—still—a dominance of passive learning models, just as Goodlad's (1984) extensive study of the place called school showed us. There is—still—too much reliance on textbooks as the curriculum. There is—still—unhealthy competition when there might be cooperation and some healthy competition. Students still face too many worksheets and questions at the end of the chapter and general mindlessness (Sizer 1992). Still, the world of school seems artificial.

Teaming places teachers in a position where they have the opportunity to confront the practices that dominate schools. In the team environment, teachers are invited to seek ways to make learning more invitational, interactive, and relevant. Clearly, many teachers do this apart from teams. However, given the regularity of meeting with colleagues to examine our work, we are far less likely to continue the deadening practices that can so easily predominate when we work in isolation. Teaming is an invitation to reinvent teaching because our conversations lead us to see that there are other possibilities (Wasley 1994). The team conversation gives us perspective, helping us separate those ideas that are good from those that are "yet another burst of trigonometry in drag" (Fines and Verrier 1974, p. 38).

Reinventing teaching, though, assumes that teams are productive and positive. We know that is not always the case. Sometimes teams can interfere with the total school development, especially as teachers try to preserve important friendships on the team (Kruse and Louis 1995). Sometimes teams can squelch dissension and narrow the scope of what is acceptable in a professional conversation (Johnston 1995). Sometimes teams create their own isolation (Kain 1997; Wasley 1994). Therefore, it is important that we see how we might reinvent teaming in order for teaming to become an avenue for professional development rather than a venue for professional stagnation.

Reinventing teaming

In their discussion of how to make knowledge workers more effective, Fisher and Fisher (1998) caution their readers that too often organizations invert means and ends. Teams, they write, are a great way to improve the organization. But when teams become the end, when "the team concept somehow takes precedence over business effectiveness" (p. 49), teams can actually damage the organization. So, too, middle school teaching teams must be seen as the means to better teaching and ultimately better learning, not as ends in themselves. The indicator of a team's success is not holding regular meetings, but changing the learning experience for students.

What do we do to make teaming an avenue for professional growth? There are important perspectives for both school leaders and team members that deserve consideration.

School leaders

If teaming is to have an impact on the development of middle level teachers (and hence the learning of middle level children), school leaders must play a key role. Such leaders can help to reinvent teaming in several ways. First, school leaders **must be advocates** for teaming and the environment that can sustain teaming. It does little good to call for teaming in a school culture that will recognize only individual accomplishments. If teachers find their entire evaluation revolves around a classroom performance that fits the old factory model, they will not risk taking the sorts of actions that put them in new models of collaborative teaching. Consider how time is allotted. If teachers are given team assignments, but no time to work together, the environment will actually work against team success. Second, school leaders **must set up the initial conditions for team success**—or revisit these areas if teams are already functioning. Specifically, this means providing education and training for team members. It is unrealistic to expect that teachers will walk into their jobs with collaborative skills. Virtually nothing in the professional education of teachers prepares them to be effective team members. The models teachers experienced when they were students did not show them how to be team members. Given this lack of knowledge and experience, is it fair to expect team members to stumble into successful practices? No. When businesses make a transition into a team structure, they generally provide workers with hundreds of hours of training initially, and often include on-going training that takes 10–20 percent of a worker's time (Fisher and Fisher 1998). Schools often give an afternoon's inservice session. The school leader is in a unique position to rectify this problem.

Finally, school leaders **must set the tone for the entire school** to refocus its efforts. To carry out the notion of "process ownership," teachers must stop thinking of their work as providing a narrow set of skills and facts for inter-changeable students and start thinking of their work as producing graduates of whom the whole school can be proud. The school leader must help to make this shift. As Sizer (1996) put it, "leadership . . . is not merely being forceful or gung-ho or simply operating where no higher authority tells one what to do. It is first and foremost being persuasive and determined about matters that count—that is about learning and teaching and caring about kids and each other" (p. 96).

Team members

What do team members do to reinvent teaming? Probably the most important change teachers can make is to view teaming as a long-term means to become better teachers for the sake of the students. The team experience cannot be relegated to another educational trend; the team experience cannot be seen as complying with yet another administrative directive. When the team experience fits in the larger scheme of making a community of learners, teaming helps students (Felner et al. 1997) and teaming helps teachers.

Specifically, team members can work for the following goals in order to turn the team experience into professional development:

Use team time to talk about teaching, not just troubles with kids. There is a fundamental rule at play here: you will never exhaust the topic of the students with whom you work. The children are amazing and interesting and frustrating. Double your team time and you still won't have enough time to talk about them. But the prospects for your own growth are very limited in this discussion. Instead, turn the conversation away from individual students and toward teaching practices. What is each team member doing that is working—or not working? As the team members articulate teaching practices, each professional is given an opportunity to learn. I saw a terrific example of this in observing one team in British Columbia (Kain 1992). The science teacher described how he used student "watchdogs" to monitor participation in class discussions. Soon after, I saw the English teacher using the same technique. Then, I used it, too. We all grew because of the discussion of teaching practices. This does not mean teams quit talking about kids, but that teams set reasonable limits on that topic to open other opportunities.

Broaden the conversation to include core areas of your work. In addition to the conversations about particular teaching techniques, use the team as a means to examine the other facets of the occupation. Consider assessment, for example. When teachers talk about quality work—what it looks like, how we encourage it, how we judge it—they get at the center of the school experience. Yet teachers are reluctant to discuss assessment. It is an area that remains mysterious, both to the students and the teachers. The team context provides a place where such conversations can be nurtured. Beyond assessment, there are many aspects of the teacher's job that team members can learn about from each other: use of technology, managing transitions, organizing volunteers, taking attendance, and so on.

Create curriculum together. Much has been said about interdisciplinary and integrated curriculum at the middle level. Certainly, connecting the curriculum is a worthwhile goal and team activity. However, a team can get stalled if it puts expectations that are too high on its work. Start smaller. Start simply with the notion that you are working together to create learning experiences for your students. Pool ideas, resources, techniques, and if interdisciplinary experiences follow, great. If, on the other hand, one team member simply receives help in designing a unit for her course, that's fine. The important issue is that you work together to design learning experiences. Odds are that the communication will help all team members understand better the larger experience of the students.

Jacobs' (1997) system of curriculum mapping is a good example of how team members might organize their discussion of curriculum. Through the mapping process, team members gain a clear picture of what the overall experience for the children is like, providing the means to improve that experience.

Make your team a source of professional development. There is not a lot of evidence that teachers read professional literature in the same way that other professionals do. Through the simple activity of reading and discussing a journal article each month, the team can become a powerful force for each teacher's capacity to stay current in the field. The format and opportunity are there for the team. In my current work as a team teacher at the university level, my team members and I regularly share new ideas from our professional reading. Sometimes we all read the same thing; other times, one team member brings an idea drawn from personal reading to discuss with the rest of us. In either way, we create a learning perspective together that helps us to develop as teachers. We *expect* to grow professionally because we work together. Too often middle school teams don't expect that kind of result.

Limits to professional development through teaming

If teaming is to be reinvented for the sake of creating a learning organization, we need to consider what limitations are placed on this process. As I have indicated, we need a collective rethinking of how the process of learning is managed in our schools. As inheritors of a factory model of schooling, most middle school teachers have long worked in circumstances where they were encouraged to add their individual contribution to the "product" coming down the assembly line. This is clearly counterproductive, both in terms of student learning and in the satisfaction of teachers in accomplishing a meaningful task.

Yet, the model persists. As Erb (1997) points out, "As long as teachers see themselves as individually responsible for teaching a pre-specified area of the curriculum, they will self-limit their ability to function on a team" (p. 36). Team functioning is affected by this vision of learning, and teams have the opportunity to challenge this limitation.

Consider also how teams fit into the larger school structure. If teachers limit their vision of teaming to another layer of bureaucracy, they will grudgingly comply. We can break this limitation by reconceiving the role of teams. Not agents of bureaucratic control, teams are think tanks where new ideas are generated. Who would realistically expect a think tank to produce creative, energizing ideas without time and space to get together?

Another limit is the reluctant team member. Certainly some teachers have found themselves in a team assignment when they clearly wanted to work alone. This becomes an issue of school leadership. School leaders must make wise decisions in assigning people to teams, and leaders must be ready to intervene where team members don't take the assignment seriously. While other team members can do much to draw in their colleagues, a school leader should not allow a team to flounder due to the discontent of one member.

WIIFMs and teaming

Too often, leaders present the move to a teamed structure as a necessary, altruistic act on the part of teachers. It is time to recast our presentation of teaming. Teachers, like any workers, ought to ask realistically what teaming will do for them. Wellins, Byham and Wilson (1991) use the acronym WIIFM—what's in it for me?—to denote the potential benefits of moving to a team structure for workers. At the middle school level, we ought to articulate the WIIFMs teachers can experience. What is in it for me? I can learn new ways to reach my students. I can develop new techniques of instruction. I can create a community of learners. I can find support for my work and development in my dealings with colleagues. Teaming is sometimes presented to teachers with a list of WIIFSEs—what's in it for somebody else—and that sets up a different kind of expectation for the busy teacher who may not be certain how much to invest in the innovation.

What's in it for me? Changing our view of schooling from the factory model to the cooperative efforts of knowledge workers might do much to make the occupation richer. In the early part of this century, when Franklin Bobbitt presented his ideas for an efficient school-factory, it was Charles W. Eliot, architect of the Committee of Ten, who said that efficiency might be increased, but "the inevitable result was the destruction of the interest of the workman in his work" (in Kliebard 1975, p. 59). Perhaps the greatest promise of teaming for the development of teachers is that in changing our view of teaching, we might revive that interest in the profession.

Conclusion

Archimedes is reputed to have said that if he had a lever long enough, he could move the world. As educators, we are in need of a long lever to move schools. Teaming offers some hope, but only as we rethink the way teaming has become institutionalized in middle schools.

The question raised in the title of this chapter is deliberately vague. Our turn? we ask. In part, there is an element of reaching out for what might be seen as the teachers' due. Of course schools are there to serve children—there's no arguing with that. But the people who walk in and out of the doors day after day, year after year, need consideration, too. When teachers face that school-hallway smell in August, they should not have a reaction of dread or discouragement. We don't want teachers who are made dull and lifeless by the ruts and routines of teaching. The promise of teaming is to reduce the isolation that so readily infects the occupation, but not merely through social contacts that ignore the actual work of teaching. Teaming, as a rich environment for development, can and does lead to renewed energy and diversified skills. Teachers deserve a turn at learning and growth.

Still, "our turn" means more than grabbing at a deserved opportunity. The phrase also is a rallying cry and a mandate. The middle school concept has been far more "organizational wizardry" than "educational wisdom," as John Lounsbury put it (Kain 1999). There comes a time when we teachers must make a turn in the direction we are headed. There comes a time when teachers must change. Reinventing the middle school must start with a turning in a new direction—pulling away from worn traditions of passive learning, and encouraging students to inquire and become lifelong learners. No such change can occur without the teachers, and nothing promises more hope for teachers to make that change than their combined commitment and development through teaming. If there is a reinventing of middle schools, it will come when teams of teachers embrace the charge to make it "our turn."

References

Arhar, J.M. (1997). The effects of interdisciplinary teaming on teachers and students. In J.L. Irvin (Eds.), *What current research says to the middle level practitioner* (pp. 49–56). Columbus, OH: National Middle School Association.

Collins, J.C., and Porras, J.I. (1994). *Built to last: Successful habits of visionary companies.* New York: Harper Business.

Donnellon, A. (1996). *Team talk: The power of language in team dynamics.* Boston: Harvard Business School.

Erb, T.O. (1997). Thirty years of attempting to fathom teaming: Battling potholes and hairpin curves along the way. In T.S. Dickinson and T.O. Erb (Eds.), *We gain more than we give: Teaming in middle schools* (pp. 19–59). Columbus, OH: National Middle School Association.

Felner, R.D., Jackson, A.W., Kasak, D., Mulhall, P., Brand, S., and Flowers, N. (1997). The impact of school reform for the middle years: Longitudinal study of a network engaged in *Turning Points*-based comprehensive school transformation. *Phi Delta Kappan, 78*(7), 528–532, 541–550.

Fines, J., and Verrier, R. (1974). *The drama of history: An experiment in co-operative teaching.* London: New University Education.

Fisher, K. (1993). *Leading self-directed work teams: A guide to developing new team leadership skills.* New York: McGraw-Hill.

Fisher, K., and Fisher, M.D. (1998). *The distributed mind: Achieving high performance through the collective intelligence of knowledge work teams.* New York: AMACOM.

Flowers, N., Mertens, S.B., and Mulhall, P.F. (1999). The impact of teaming: Five research-based outcomes. *Middle School Journal, 31*(2), 57–60.

Goodlad, J.I. (1984). *A place called school.* New York: McGraw-Hill.

Hackman, J.R. (Ed.). (1990). *Groups that work (and those that don't): Creating conditions for effective teamwork.* San Francisco: Jossey-Bass.

Hackman, J.R., and Oldham, G.R. (1980). *Work redesign.* Reading, MA: Addison-Wesley.

Jacobs, H.H. (1997). *Mapping the big picture: Integrating curriculum & assessment K–12.* Alexandria, VA: Association for Supervision and Curriculum Development.

Johnston, S. (1995). Curriculum decision making at the school level: Is it just a case of teachers learning to act like administrators? *Journal of Curriculum and Supervision, 10*(2), 136–154.

Kain, D.L. (1992). *Collaborative planning of interdisciplinary experiences: A case study at the middle school level.* Unpublished doctoral dissertation. The University of British Columbia, Vancouver.

Kain, D.L. (1997). Teacher collaboration on interdisciplinary teams. *Research in Middle Level Education Quarterly, 21*(1), 1–29.

Kain, D. L. (1998). Teaming in the middle school: A review of recent literature. In P.S. Hlebowitsh and W.G. Wraga (Eds.), *Annual review of research for school leaders 1998* (pp. 51–75). New York: Simon & Schuster Macmillan.

Kain, D.L. (1999). Organizational wizardry or educational wisdom? John Lounsbury reflects on the middle school movement. *Focus on Middle School, 12*(1), 1–2, 4–6.

Katzenbach, J.R., and Smith, D.K. (1993). *The wisdom of teams: Creating the high-performance organization.* Boston: Harvard Business School.

Kliebard, H. (1975). Bureaucracy and curriculum theorizing. In W. Pinar (Ed.), *Curriculum theorizing* (pp. 51–69). Berkeley, CA: McCutchan.

Kruse, S., and Louis, K.S. (1995). Teacher teaming—Opportunities and dilemmas. *Brief to Principals (11).* Madison, WI: Center on Organization and Restructuring of Schools.

Marlin, G.J., Rabatin, R.P., and Swan, J.L. (Eds.). (1987). *The quotable Chesterton: A topical compilation of the wit, wisdom and satire of G. K. Chesterton.* Garden City, NY: Image Books.

Ostroff, F. (1999). *The horizontal organization: What the organization of the future looks like and how it delivers value to customers.* New York: Oxford University.

Pirsig, R.M. (1974). *Zen and the art of motorcycle maintenance.* New York: Bantam.

Sizer, T.R. (1992). *Horace's school: Redesigning the American high school.* Boston: Houghton Mifflin.

Sizer, T.R. (1996). *Horace's hope: What works for the American high school.* Boston: Houghton Mifflin.

Strahan, D., Bowles, N., Richardson, V., and Hanawald, S. (1997). Research on teaming: Insights from selected studies. In T.S. Dickinson and T.O. Erb (Eds.), *We gain more than we give: Teaming in middle schools* (pp. 359–384). Columbus, OH: National Middle School Association.

Trimble, S.B. (1999, October). *Moving beyond the process of teaming to student outcomes.* Paper presented at the meeting of the National Middle School Association Annual Conference, Orlando, FL.

Wasley, P.A. (1994). *Stirring the chalkdust: Tales of teachers changing classroom practice.* New York: Teachers College Press.

Wellins, R.S., Byham, W.C., and Dixon, G.R. (1994). *Inside teams: How 20 world-class organizations are winning through teamwork.* San Francisco: Jossey-Bass.

Wellins, R.S., Byham, W.C., and Wilson, J.M. (1991). *Empowered teams: Creating self-directed work groups that improve quality, productivity, and participation.* San Francisco: Jossey-Bass.

Wraga, W.G. (1997). Interdisciplinary team teaching: Sampling the literature. In T.S. Dickinson & T.O. Erb (Eds.), *We gain more than we give: Teaming in middle schools* (pp. 325–343). Columbus, OH: National Middle School Association.

The Role of Technology for Learning in the Reinvented Middle School

SUSAN M. POWERS
Indiana State University

CATHLEEN D. RAFFERTY
Humboldt State University

B.J. EIB
Educational Consultant

As we enter a new century, the notion of middle schools is nearly five decades old. In human terms, this would make middle schools "middle-aged," but like some middle-aged folks who experience a second childhood (or maybe have never grown up to begin with), too many middle schools have experienced "arrested development." This means that a middle school label does not guarantee a fully functioning or exemplary middle school (Alexander and George 1981; George and Alexander 1993). Further, "middle schools" may not have responded to either of the Carnegie Council on Adolescent Development reports suggesting ways to transform the education of young adolescents (1989) or to prepare adolescents for a new century (1996). Even more troubling is the phenomenon that too many "middle schools" may have suffered from no development at all, at least in terms of what the position paper *This We Believe* outlines regarding developmentally appropriate practices such as challenging, integrating, and exploratory curriculum; varied teaching, learning, and assessment practices; or flexible organizational structures and comprehensive support services (NMSA 1992, 1995).

As one of sixteen chapters in this volume, we will address the role of technology for learning in the reinvented middle school by (1) focusing on various middle school concepts and beliefs that undergird the use of technology and exploration as teaching and learning tools; (2) emphasizing the importance of an exploratory curriculum, illustrating how various technologies can enhance exploration, and linking such experiences to young adolescents' growth and development in moral, ethical, and democratic practices and processes; (3) introducing a conceptual model for successful technology integration to support young adolescent development and recently developed foundational standards for technology; (4) providing examples of schools that have successfully integrated multiple uses of technology for communication, productivity, and management as well as for constructing and presenting knowledge; and (5) describing a vision for technology in a reinvented middle school that focuses upon the pinnacle of the conceptual model with technologies that are all currently available.

Technology, exploration, and related middle school concepts

Given the pervasiveness of a variety of technologies, it could be argued that technology, especially explorations using technology, would enhance or support all facets of the middle school concept. For purposes of this chapter we will make connections to the most salient middle school characteristics as initially envisioned in the 1960s and further refined by leaders previously cited herein. The underlying theme, however, will be the nurturing of young adolescents as individuals, as learners, and as productive members of society through developmentally appropriate uses of technology. Figure 1 depicts the major connections to be addressed in this chapter. Note how all related components in the figure are embedded within a larger circle that represents the overall structure/organization of the middle school itself. Without vision, leadership, and a team structure, many of the ideas proposed herein would not be possible. A later section in this chapter will address how various technologies can enhance not only communication, productivity, and management capabilities but also the construction or creation and presentation of new knowledge by both teachers and students.

In addition to wrestling with various social, moral, ethical, emotional, and physical changes, young adolescents are often struggling to become independent learners. It is in the domain of curriculum and instruction that technology, exploration, and/or exploration through technology can be particularly productive for both teachers and middle grades students, as will be discussed in subsequent sections.

Curriculum and technology

Donald Eichhorn proposed three major goals or domains for middle grades curricula—Learning Processes, Personal Development, and Content Knowledge (1972, p. 41). Although each can certainly be enhanced through use of technology, in today's digital world at least two also demand concurrent instruction in critical thinking. Let's examine each component in turn.

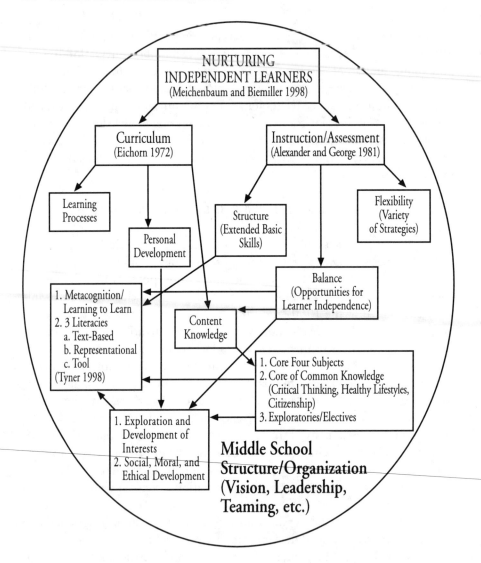

Figure 1: Technology, exploration, and related middle school concepts.

Learning processes

Learning to learn and monitoring one's level of understanding (metacognition) are essential elements to becoming an independent learner. If we expect middle grades students to be able to locate information, take notes, study, and know how to prepare for a variety of learning opportunities in various classes, then we must prepare them to do so. Students entering the middle grades are in transition from concrete to abstract abilities. As such, they initially need direct instruction, modeling, practice, and feedback—also known as instructional scaffolding—regarding their use of various learning skills. Often instruction and practice with learning to learn strategies can be combined with specific literacy instruction. Unfortunately, in too many middle schools, a formal and developmental focus on reading/literacy are missing. However, in the digital age wherein information availability and access are increasing exponentially, it is more important than ever that students continue to develop these literacy skills. It is almost as though literacy itself must be reinvented to meet the demands of a variety of new "texts" or formats wrought by new technologies. The very nature of reading and learning is in transition.

Recently, Tyner suggested three broad categories of literacy, two of which have specific connections to technology. A brief explanation of the three—(1) traditional text-based or alphabetic literacy, (2) representational literacy, and (3) tool literacy (Tyner 1998)—will provide a clearer picture of what middle grades students need and what teachers might do to help.

The first, *text based* or *alphabetic literacy* contains two well-known types of reading/literacy, namely interaction with narrative and expository text. Narrative in particular is emphasized in the elementary grades, while expository or informational text is too often overlooked. Perhaps a common assumption is that once students "learn to read" narrative text that they will automatically be able to read expository text as they "read to learn." The final text-based literacy, document literacy, is even less commonly known and developed. It can be described as "reading to do" and entails interpretation and application of information for a specific purpose such as following complicated sets of procedural diagrams and directions to assemble a computer hutch or interpreting pie charts, bar graphs, or other statistical representations to follow business trends or sports. (For additional discussion and examples of ways to support document literacy see Rafferty 2000.)

Tyner's second category, *representational literacy*, includes information, visual, and media literacies, all of which are relevant to the uses of technology in school because they underscore the importance of analyzing and evaluating information in order to understand how meaning is created. Nowhere is this more important than in determining the value of information found on the Internet where misinformation and disinformation are not readily discernible from fact. As we know, middle schoolers have not yet fully developed critical reading/thinking abilities. Therefore, educators can benefit much from using and/or adapting guidelines from sources such as the American Library Association (ALA 1991, 1998) or those developed by media educators to help students become critical consumers of messages portrayed via mass media or the Internet. For example, Thoman recently identified five questions that can be asked about such messages as teachers work with young adolescents to help them analyze and understand the power of a variety of images and technologies that convey information and ideas.

1. Who created this message and why?
2. What techniques are being used to attract my attention?
3. What lifestyles, values, and points of view are represented?
4. How might different people understand this message differently?
5. What is omitted from this message? (Thoman 1999 p. 52)

The third category, *tool literacy,* will continue to become increasingly important as more and more information, images, graphics, video, and audio are ac-
cessible using new software, hardware, and Internet connections. Of course, the
ability to interpret and use the information is related to the literacies described
in the previous two paragraphs. However, knowing that computers, networks,
and other technologies have immense potential as teaching and learning tools is
only the beginning. It is now critical that both young adolescents and their
teachers know how to use an array of new technology tools to enhance the learning process. For example, middle schoolers can now engage in a ThinkQuest
Internet Challenge (www.thinkquest.org) which emphasizes team collaboration, educational value, and active learning among student team members who
develop web sites to be used as learning tools by other students. There is even a
parallel challenge (ThinkQuest for Tomorrow's Teachers) to engage preservice
and inservice teachers and teacher educators in developing web-based curricula.
More specifics on the whats, hows, and particularly the whens/wheres/whys of
tool literacy will be the focus in a later part of this chapter.

Personal development

Eichhorn's second domain or goal for middle grades curricula is personal
development. In this realm the focus is on student opportunities to discover
and/or develop personal interests and to continue their social, moral, and ethical development. At no other time during a human's development are there so
many changes and transitions occurring. As stated in one NMSA publication,

> In their search for identity and a personality, learners seek to understand
> the meaning and the enigmas of life from many aspects. They are con-
> cerned with intellectual, philosophical, biological, sociological, moral, and
> ethical issues. They have an increased ability to see through situations and
> seek to find casual and correlative relationships (NMSA 1992, p. 12).

All of these transitions present a huge challenge for middle level educators,
especially if tackled in isolation. Fortunately, much that is represented in this
domain can be connected to and interwoven with other curricular considerations. For example, in Figure 1, note the arrows from "Social, Moral, and Ethical Development" to the box containing Learning Process examples such as
"Metacognition/Learning to Learn" and the "3 Literacies." According to Don

Tapscott, President of New Paradigm Learning Corporation, not only are today's digitally-literate students learning critical social skills for effective interaction in the digital economy, but they are also more actively engaged in their learning because use of new technologies has shifted the focus from teacher-centered to student-centered classrooms (Tapscott 1999).

Returning to the previous ThinkQuest Internet Challenge example, young adolescents who are actively engaged in creating learning activities for others are also reinforcing their own understanding. Further, via the Internet, these students can interact with peers worldwide, thereby gaining first-hand knowledge and insights about similarities, differences, and challenges faced by their counterparts around the globe. Such experiences can contribute to powerful growth experiences regarding their own social, moral, and ethical development, especially if the types of critical thinking questions suggested earlier are regularly used to determine whether messages and information received from and about different races and cultures provide fair and accurate representations thereof. By doing this, not only would the connection go from "Social, Moral, and Ethical Development" to various "Learning Processes" but it would also be linked to the "Core of Common Knowledge" under the next curriculum consideration, which is "Content Knowledge."

Content knowledge

Content knowledge represents Eichhorn's final goal or domain for curriculum, but it is critical to reiterate that the middle school, as originally conceived, is a place wherein young adolescents are nurtured socially, emotionally, physically, and cognitively. In order for this to occur there must be multiple opportunities and means for students to actively explore multiple subject areas in multiple ways. That is, the entire curriculum at the middle grades level should be exploratory in nature with much more than the traditional emphasis on the "Core Four" of English/Language Arts, Mathematics, Science, and Social Studies. As we all know, that somewhat restrictive focus looms in the not too distant future in many high schools.

Beyond the core, students must have opportunities to gain knowledge and experience with thinking critically not only about the social, moral, and ethical dilemmas mentioned in the previous section, but also regarding their own healthy lifestyle choices and their own growth and contributions to the larger society. A full exploratory program, as defined by NMSA, recognizes that

> The rapid physical, social, and intellectual development which occurs during these years requires the inclusion of brief but intense interest-based activities. A short attention span, difficulty in concentration, and the restlessness which accompanies changing physical bodies preclude learning modules which extend much beyond 15–20 minutes. There-

fore, students should be involved in some units of study which meet for considerably less that an hour, less than a semester, and are tied to changing interests. Mini-courses, exploratory courses, service clubs, special interest activities, and independent study projects are among the means of providing such activities. The need for exploratory activities and an exploratory attitude, however, can and should be met within the regular course work as well. (1992, p. 18)

There are numerous ways to incorporate instructional technology as a teaching and learning tool, whether it is with the Core Four, a Core of Common Knowledge, or within Exploratories/Electives, as will be examined later in this chapter. But before that, let us briefly explore some instructional considerations posed by Alexander and George in the early 1980s.

Instruction/assessment and technology

In 1981 Alexander and George stated that "in exemplary middle schools effective instruction is the primary goal" (p. 217) and that "the instructional strategies of the middle school are . . . a combination of structure, balance, and flexibility" (p. 219). Although student assessment and evaluation were not addressed by Alexander and George in the same chapter as was instruction in either of their editions, given more recent work by instruction and assessment experts (e.g., Wiggins 1998), we will address both simultaneously as is noted on the right-hand side of Figure 1. Further, as stated in *This We Believe,* "because cognitive growth occurs gradually, most middle level students require ongoing concrete, experiential learning in order to develop intellectually" (NMSA 1995, p. 6), it also makes sense that instruction and assessment be linked as a reminder that both the classroom activities and related formative and summative assessments need to actively engage the students. There are also additional instructional and assessment considerations such as structure, balance, and flexibility that will be addressed in the following subsections.

Structure

According to Alexander and George, a certain amount of structure or teacher-directedness is essential, especially regarding ongoing development of basic skills. For the purposes of this chapter, we define basic skills as "learning processes" or metacognition/learning to learn and being literate. Our earlier section with the same title gave specific definitions and descriptions of what is meant by each of these terms and underscored the need for specific formal and developmental instruction in all facets of literacy and learning to learn. The tacit assumption that seems to permeate too many middle schools is that "everyone is responsible for literacy development." Unfortunately, in the end no one seems to be responsible and it's the young adolescents and their skills (or lack thereof) that suffer. The following example will elaborate on one type of literacy (document literacy) and briefly illustrate how instruction, assessment, and technology can interact.

Young adolescents could be engaged in a unit designed to help them learn more about reading and understanding various types of documents such as charts, graphs, and figures. To make the unit developmentally appropriate, teachers could engage the students in an activity in which they would (1) develop and administer a survey to classmates regarding their favorite music artists, (2) collect and analyze the data, and (3) display and present their results using various type of charts, graphs, or figures. All of these steps would involve both instruction and assessment and could easily involve technologies such as word processing, spreadsheets or databases, and presentation software. See Rafferty (2000) for additional ideas regarding this type of document literacy activity.

The amount of structure or teacher-directedness necessary would depend on the students. In this case, how much prior knowledge they have about various types of documents, how much they know about "survey research," their mathematical backgrounds and level of understanding, their experiences with the types of technology that could be used, etc. would determine the amount of instruction required. When the teacher begins to explore these types of considerations, he or she has moved into the realm of balance, the next focal point.

Balance

Instruction/assessment provides balance when it offers "opportunities which will teach students the skills necessary for learning on their own and the attitudes that support such learning" (Alexander and George 1981, p. 219). This description seems inexorably connected with a firm foundation in "basic skills" as described in the previous section and also linked to students' personal development and their content knowledge. Recently, two developmental psychologists proposed a "three-dimensional model of mastery learning" (Meichenbaum and Biemiller 1998) which asserts that in order for students to fully develop as independent learners they must have opportunities and experiences to teach others. Their model conceptualizes learning and understanding along the three lines depicted in Figure 2.

Along the line pointing to the right (A) resides skill acquisition, which begins with simple concepts and becomes more difficult or complex as students have multiple experiences and acquire the accompanying vocabulary to support more complex levels of understanding. The line pointing up (B) includes metacognitive components such as planning, implementing, and monitoring one's performance. In early stages of skill acquisition students' self-directedness is likely to be limited to whether understanding is occurring or not. More sophisticated aspects listed previously become scaffolded considerations when

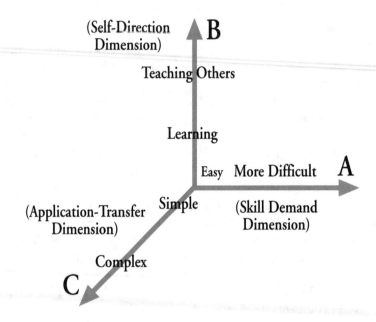

Figure 2: Nurturing independent learners.
(Adapted from Meichenbaum and Biemiller 1998.)

helping others learn. The final line (C) also calls for some metacognition, but in a different way. Once skills are learned, a crucial learning component is knowing when and how to apply the learning to new situations. As any teacher can attest, this seems to be a particularly difficult element for students to master. Once again, the ThinkQuest Internet Challenge provides a salient example of how all three dimensions of Meichenbaum's and Biemiller's model can be addressed, in this case through instructional technology.

The ThinkQuest Internet Challenge could easily support the model's dimensions primarily because of its broad appeal to the needs of young adolescents: students work in teams, use technologies such as computers and the Internet, and compete for prizes. More important, however, is its hands-on, project-oriented structure. Rather than being constrained to textbooks and/or worksheets, students can explore information and ideas related to any of five categories (Arts and Literature, Science and Mathematics, Social Sciences, Sports and Health, or Interdisciplinary) as they prepare their web sites to promote others' learning. It is this element—constructing a web site that has educational value, accuracy, and clear communication, and that encourages active participation by others in a learning community atmosphere—that holds much potential to move young adolescents along all three of the lines in Figure 2. That is, in order to construct a site that helps others learn, the student teams will need to be self-directed as they apply difficult concepts in more complex situations. Of course, teachers will need to help support the process, but it could be a wonderful learning opportunity for all involved, and one that would also reinforce the next concept, flexibility.

Flexibility

As noted by Alexander and George (1981) and *This We Believe,*

> The distinctive developmental and learning characteristics of young adolescents provide the foundation for selecting teaching strategies, just as they do for designing curriculum. Teaching techniques should enhance and accommodate the diverse skills, abilities, and knowledge of young adolescents, cultivate multiple intelligences, and capitalize on students' individual learning styles. (NMSA 1995, p. 24)

Flexibility is essential. Middle schoolers learn best through active engagement and hands-on experiences that directly involve them in their learning. As noted previously, though, especially in the realm of "basic skills," they still need direct instruction or teacher-directed focus. There is no one way to teach young adolescents. There must be structure, balance, and flexibility within a reinvented middle school program, all of which can be assisted through various types of technology.

Now the question remains as to how technology can be more than just a tool inserted here or there to support a middle school program. In other words, is there an overriding philosophy or principle that can help guide middle schools as they work to enhance the instructional technology experiences offered to their middle school students and staff? We now turn our attention to the introduction of a model for technology integration to support student development and the foundational standards that can also serve to guide the process. In addition, we will provide case studies of middle schools that are using technologies in a number of ways that are illustrative of the standards and model. Our chapter concludes with our vision for technology in the reinvented middle school.

Technology as a core component in the reinvented middle school

One thing that should be apparent from the discussion above and Figure 1 is the interconnectedness of the components and the degree to which each element depends on other elements for completeness. No one piece of the puzzle completes an effective middle school experience without the other elements nestled in beside it. To paint a more functional picture, eliminating one of the supporting, interlinked concepts from Figure 1 would bring the concept of the independent learner crashing down.

Therefore, it stands to reason that educational technologies can also stand as a support in this framework for the continued and enhanced development of the learners. However, the technology is more than just another component or box that undergirds an independent learner, it is a component that instead strengthens the elements of Curriculum and Instruction/Assessment in order to make the whole student better able to develop personally and intellectually. As we will see in subsequent examples, for the technology integration to be successful and wholly complete, it must also be a strengthening member of the school vision and administration. That technology encompasses all the other elements of the successful middle school, as discussed previously in the chapter and as will be shown in examples, is essential to the overall successful integration. However, before we consider the model and standards, we need to first arrive at a mutual definition of what we mean by technology.

Defining instructional technology

A recent study commissioned by the Milken Exchange on Education Technology and performed by the International Society for Technology in Education (ISTE), provides the following definition for technology in schools:

> Information Technology includes computer hardware and software, the networks that tie the computers together, and a host of devices that convert information (text, images, sounds, motion) into common digital formats. However, information technology is not just hardware, wires and binary code, but also the effective use of digital information to extend human capabilities. (1999, p. 5)

While that definition does cover a great deal of what we might think about when we consider technology, and also adds the important component of "effective use," it does not cover all technologies that we might see in a school.

The Association for Educational Communications and Technology (AECT) offers a broader definition of instructional technology:

> Instructional Technology is a complex, integrated process involving people, procedures, ideas, devices, and organization for analyzing problems, and devising, implementing, evaluating and managing solutions to those problems, in situations in which learning is purposive and controlled. (AECT 1996, p. 4)

This definition again brings to the forefront the importance of the use of the devices, and also highlights the role of the people, procedures, and the organization to instructional technology. Although a little more difficult to visualize, this second definition better represents the discussion of technology in this chapter. While reading the remainder of the chapter, it is important to conceive of technology as being more than computer hardware, software, or other technical devise. The ways in which those inanimate objects are used are what make it an instructional technology.

Conceptualizing a technology model

We are accustomed to seeing technology used in bits and pieces in our schools. A teacher may have an interesting software title that supports a curriculum unit, so the computer is used at that time. Another likely scenario might be that a class is scheduled to be able to use a computer lab at a specific time, therefore, Internet resources, such as the ThinkQuest described earlier, are incorporated (although it should be noted that this is not the intention of *how* ThinkQuest is utilized). Also, without the overarching vision of technology by school leaders, the use of instructional technologies is limited to those teachers with the knowledge and initiative.

Pellegrino and Altman (1997) struggled with the concept of how to make instructional technologies a functioning part of teacher education. In their research and experience, they developed a conceptual model whereby teacher education faculty could transform their courses with technology, while at the same time transforming their thinking and the thinking and experiences of their teacher education students. The model provides an excellent conceptual framework for those in teacher education. In turn, a revision of this model (presented in Figure 3) provides a conceptual model for how the use of instructional technology in the reinvented middle school can support the overall development of a middle school student.

This model provides a three-axis construct for how a middle school can view its technology integration and use. On the left-hand side (the y-axis) is the continuum that transforms a student from a consumer of information and knowledge to one who can create his or her own knowledge and development from information provided. This process is the actualization of creating an independent learner. As discussed previously, technology can facilitate this role admirably when tools like ThinkQuest are used in a more integrative manner.

The x-axis is how the school itself wholly incorporates technology. At the left-hand extreme of the continuum, software is used in isolated incidents, whether at the lower level of drill and practice, or the higher end for cognitive and social development with knowledge-producing technology tools. When a school begins to use technology to enhance its ability to communicate internally, with external constituents (parents, businesses, other schools, etc.), to allow students to communicate with other students across the country and world, and to allow students and teachers to consult with experts around the world, the school has begun to find ways to envelop technology into a central concept within the school. Making technology central to the concept of the

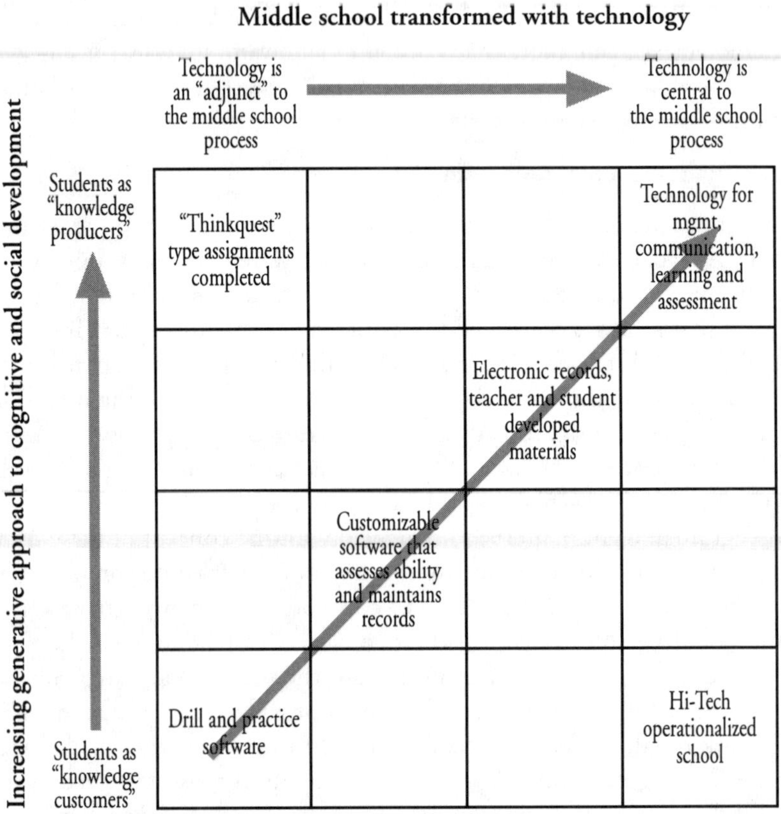

Middle school transformed with technology

Technology is an "adjunct" to the middle school process → Technology is central to the middle school process

Increasing generative approach to cognitive and social development

Students as "knowledge producers"

"Thinkquest" type assignments completed			Technology for mgmt, communication, learning and assessment
		Electronic records, teacher and student developed materials	
	Customizable software that assesses ability and maintains records		
Drill and practice software			Hi-Tech operationalized school

Students as "knowledge customers"

Figure 3: Model for transforming technology integration.
(Adapted from Pellegrino and Altman 1997)

school goes beyond electronic communications. It also includes assessment, reports, monitoring, and other administrative functions. It is important to note that a school can become highly operationalized with technology, but when the technology is only in that outer core of Figure 1, and not affecting the elements that nurture independent thinking in the students, the school still has work to complete.

That type of work is evidenced in the third dimension of Figure 3—the diagonal arrow that cuts from the lower left-hand corner to the upper right-hand corner. At this corner point in the upper right-hand corner, the school is embracing technology as an element that provides the structure and support discussed previously. When a school has reached this point, technology is central to the vision and the support of the school, and is also a function that encourages cognitive and social development for everyone within the middle school.

A diagram such as the one in Figure 3 can be nice to help visualize a concept, to better understand a theory; but it is not necessarily effective at providing a roadmap for how an individual school that desires to reach that corner block can do so. Frankly, while there are middle schools in this country that are doing admirable work with technology, there are probably very few that have fully reached this transformation point. However, a number of organizations are working to develop documents that can guide schools through the process. One such project is described in the next section, The National Educational Technology Standards (NETS) Project (International Society for Technology in Education 1998).

Technology standards for middle schools

The International Society for Technology in Education (ISTE), in conjunction with the Milken Exchange on Education Technology, NASA, Apple Computer, Inc., and the U.S. Department of Education, along with many other organizations,[1] have joined together on an ambitious project to develop technology foundation standards for students, standards for the use of technology in learning and teaching, educational technology support standards, and standards for the assessment and evaluation of technology use. To date, the first document has been completed, which was to describe what students at different educational levels should know about technology and be able to do with technology.

Table 1: National Educational Technology Standards for Students

1. **Basic operations and concepts**
   - Students demonstrate a sound understanding of the nature and operation of technology systems.
   - Students are proficient in the use of technology.
2. **Social, ethical, and human issues**
   - Students understand the ethical, cultural, and societal issues related to technology.
   - Students practice responsible use of technology systems, information, and software.
   - Students develop positive attitudes toward technology uses that support lifelong learning, collaboration, personal pursuits, and productivity.
3. **Technology productivity tools**
   - Students use technology tools to enhance learning, increase productivity, and promote creativity.
   - Students use productivity tools to collaborate in constructing technology-enhanced models, preparing publications, and producing other creative works.
4. **Technology communications tools**
   - Students use telecommunications to collaborate, publish, and interact with peers, experts, and other audiences.

continued next page

Table 1 continued

- Students use a variety of media and formats to communicate information and ideas effectively to multiple audiences.
5. **Technology research tools**
   - Students use technology to locate, evaluate, and collect information from a variety of sources.
   - Students use technology tools to process data and report results.
   - Students evaluate and select new information resources and technological innovations based on the appropriateness to specific tasks.
6. **Technology problem-solving and decision-making tools**
   - Students use technology resources for solving problems and making informed decisions.
   - Students employ technology in the development of strategies for solving problems in the real world. (ISTE 1998, p. 5–6)

As a core, there are six basic foundational standards for all students (see Table 1 for the standards and explanative statements). These foundational standards are then exemplified into a technology profile for developmental levels of students. For students in grades 6–8, the performance indicators can be found in Table 2. The numbers following each item indicate which foundational standard(s) is being supported by the performance.

Table 2: Technology Performance Indicators—Grades 6–8

Prior to the completion of Grade 8 students will
1. Apply strategies for identifying and solving routine hardware and software problems that occur during everyday use. (1)
2. Demonstrate knowledge of current changes in information technologies and the effect those changes have on the workplace and society. (2)
3. Exhibit legal and ethical behaviors when using information and technology, and discuss consequences of misuse. (2)
4. Use content-specific tools, software, and simulations (e.g., environmental probes, graphing calculators, exploratory environments, Web tools) to support learning and research. (3, 5)
5. Apply productivity/multimedia tools and peripherals to support personal productivity, group collaboration, and learning throughout the curriculum. (3, 6)
6. Design, develop, publish, and present products (e.g., Web pages, video tapes) using technology resources that demonstrate and communicate curriculum concepts to audiences inside and outside the classroom. (4, 5, 6)

continued next page

Table 2 continued

7. Collaborate with peers, experts, and others using telecommunications and collaborative tools to investigate curriculum-related problems, issues, and information, and to develop solutions or products for audiences inside and outside the classroom. (4, 5)

8. Select and use appropriate tools and technology resources to accomplish a variety of tasks and solve problems. (5, 6)

9. Demonstrate an understanding of concepts underlying hardware, software, and connectivity, and practical applications to learning and problem solving. (1, 6)

10. Research and evaluate the accuracy, relevance, appropriateness, comprehensiveness, and bias of electronic information sources concerning real-world problems. (2, 5, 6) (ISTE 1998, p. 13)

These performance indicators provide a framework for conceptualizing how the model in Figure 3 can be operationalized. Each performance indicator represents a variety of stages in the model, which, when put together, can place a student high on the "knowledge producer" scale, which in turn assists the student in becoming a learner who grows into an independent learner through the dimensions of Meichenbaum and Biemiller (see Figure 2) and can assist a school in making technology more central to the middle school process (the standards that are yet to be developed and distributed by the NETS project will probably do more for helping a school envision how technology can become central to its entire function).

Linking the NETS performance indicators to the model

Again, the performance indicators and the foundational standards of the NETS Project (see Table 2) can provide some guidance for technology integration in the middle school that the model alone may not be able to do. However, perhaps integrating the two can provide even a better vision for how a school must develop its vision and create its technology support systems. Additionally, several of these performance indicators will be examined further with examples of activities in which a variety of middle schools are involved that exemplify the standards. Refer to Figure 4 when reading about the application of the following performance indicators, and for our perception of placement of the other indicators of the standards not discussed in this text.

Performance Indicator 4—Simulations. Performance indicator 4 can move students higher on the realm of generative development as students are actually performing a variety of problem-solving activities and coming close to producing their own knowledge representations. There is also a certain level of assumption that the school as a whole is moving toward a holistic embrace of

Middle school transformed with technology

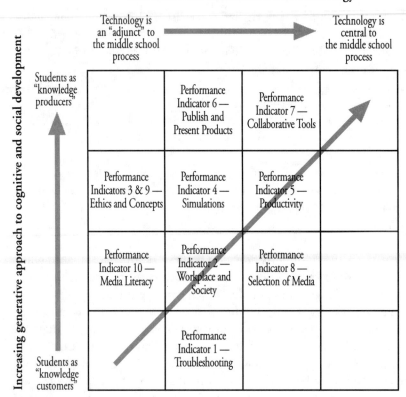

Figure 4: Conceptual model and technology performance indicators.
(Adapted from Pellegrino and Altman 1997)

technology since increased technology and teacher support must be available to make the technology tools available and have readily trained staff and faculty.

One such example of this type of tool to support learning and research may be familiar to a number of people. Denise Lockman at Scarborough Middle School in Portland, Maine began using computerized babies in a pilot program with eighth graders (Powers, personal communication, May 17, 1999). These are real-size infants that carry a computer chip and can be programmed to cry at intervals that range from the colicky baby to a more normal waking, sleeping, and eating pattern. Eighth grade students and their parents sign a consent form to take the baby home overnight, or in some instances for the weekend. To stop the baby from crying, the student must insert a special key in the back of the baby and hold it for a specific amount of time. The computer chip within the doll records how much time the baby has spent crying and how quick the response time was of the student. The record will be maintained until the battery runs out, which could occur in those instances when the baby is locked out in the garage and allowed to cry until the batteries run out! Through this simulation, the students gain a better sense of what they might expect if they were to have a baby of their own.

In another example, faculty from Southern Illinois University at Edwardsville and a teacher from North Middle School used a modeling and simulation software package called STELLA to help math students develop a deeper understanding of ratios (Andris, Crooks, and Hawkins 1999). The simulation demonstrated to students the application of a therapeutic medicine to a sick animal and how the amount of medicine had different effects (ranging from no effect to toxicity). These amounts, of course, changed as the type and size of animal changed. The students practiced with the simulation to determine the optimal ratio of drips to seconds that needed to be administered to keep the animal from dying. Such a simulation provides students with real-life application of the math concepts they are learning, with no danger to real animals!

Performance Indicator 6—Publish and Present Products. Performance indicator 6 can be considered to be at a higher level of generative knowledge as students are in the process of creating products of knowledge representation through the use of technology. However, because these types of activities can take place in isolated environments in the classrooms of motivated teachers, it is not necessarily reflective of a school that integrates technology into all aspects of the middle school. It should, however, be noted that when students are working at a higher level of knowledge production with technology, they are also moving outward on all three axes of Figure 2.

Linda Baab at Whittier Middle School (Baab 1999) took advantage of a grant that purchased equipment and Internet access to enhance her elective journalism course. Electronic communication tools allowed students to share information and ideas with each other and with the teacher as they worked toward the finished project of a published school newspaper. Plans are in place to extend the collaboration to other middle schools in the area.

Performance Indicator 7—Collaborative Tools. This performance indicator can be assumed to take students to a higher level on the generative approach as indicator 4, in that they are applying the productivity tools to their work, and working and collaborating with others to create new information from the resources they access. Additionally, the degree to which the school is centrally involved with the technology increases because to facilitate these activities throughout a curriculum, multiple teachers and resources must be actively involved (see Figure 4). The Baltimore Learning Community Project is an example of performance indicator 7 (Enomoto, Nolet, and Marchionini 1999).

As part of a technology challenge grant, researchers at the University of

Maryland developed an expansive inventory of social studies and science resources that could be used by teachers when developing their lessons. The resources are comprised of still images, text, web sites, and video all accessed through the Internet with all resources available upon demand. Additional software is made available to allow students and teachers to collaborate with each other as they use these materials, and to develop a learning community that spreads beyond just the one school.

Performance Indicator 10—Media Literacy. This indicator provides the basis for the definition of media literacy. While students may not be working at as high a level of knowledge production as they are with other indicators, they are incorporating and learning the skills of media literacy, which means to evaluate, research information, determine appropriateness, bias, etc. (Bowen 1992) and build a foundation that will enable them to grow. In terms of transformation of the middle school with technology, although this type of activity could take place in the isolated classroom, the time and effort needed to achieve this type of work assumes to a certain degree that the school has embraced information technology, provides ready access for teachers and students, and considers it to be an important learning tool.

A real-life example of this performance indicator can be found again at Scarborough Middle School in Portland, Maine (Powers, personal communication, May 17, 1999). Two teachers, Marty Wilmer and Cathy Stevens, received a grant to create a webquest for their class. A webquest is an activity of considerable length where students interact with information technology resources to solve a problem and present a solution (Dodge 1997). Teachers guide the students through the resources and help them with their inquiry. Wilmer and Stevens created a project for their students on Global Warming (Wilmer 1999). The students were placed into groups that represent different viewpoints regarding the Kyoto Protocol—an international agreement to reduce emissions. This project had students use a variety of Internet, CD, and library resources; they developed materials to defend their positions for a presentation, including the use of presentation software; and students and teachers alike called upon the resources of librarians and instructional technologists in the middle school for assistance.

The examples of the performance indicators presented above are just a handful of the myriad examples that exist in middle schools around the country. However, they serve to illustrate how the foundational technology standards can be implemented, and how those standards in a variety of ways support the movement toward a middle school that considers technology to support all aspects of its administration, vision, curriculum, instruction, and assessment. The case studies presented below will provide further examples of how real schools are working with technology in their schools to optimize the goal of nurturing independent learners.

Case study examples of middle schools and technology

Angola Middle School

Angola Middle School is located in northeast Indiana. The school serves 670 students with a staff of 45, a principal, and assistant principal. The district incorporates a large farming area, the small communities of various lakes, and the city of Angola. Most parents are employed at various industries and businesses located within the city of Angola and receive wages of median income. The school is organized into teams of teachers: Unified Arts team, eighth grade team, seventh grade team, and two sixth grade teams. The sixth grade teams are comprised of five persons (science, reading, math, social studies, and a resource teacher who adapts lessons for students with special needs) with approximately 120 students, the seventh and eighth grades function as two large teams that also work with a resource person. Daily, each teacher has a personal planning period and a team planning period. The school is recognized for its commitment to an inclusion model for special education students and a site-based leadership structure.

In 1990–91 the administration made a commitment to purchase computers and hardware to network the office for administrative tasks. A building level technology committee came into existence. A new central office position of technology coordinator was established and staffed. Beginning in 1992 a commitment was made by the building principal to put a computer on the desk of each teacher. Over the course of the next two years computers were purchased from a wide variety of funds to put on teacher's desks. Several Zenith laptops were also purchased for staff to take home. Teachers and students experimented with software such as First Choice, Print Shop, Pops Menu, Linkway, Express Publisher, and CD-ROM programs like Mammals and Encyclopedia Britannica.

In 1996 plans to renovate and add on to the building also included a vision to make AMS as technology rich as possible. The renovation was recently completed and was recognized in American School & University (ASU) as an award-winning outstanding school project. The following objectives were met with the renovation:

- A phone was put in each classroom.
- A building-wide video retrieval system was placed in the media center.
- Two modern computer labs were planned and equipped.
- A new teaching position was added to staff one of the labs all day.
- An electronic music lab was designed and added to the building.
- Three computers were purchased for each classroom.
- Each room had Internet accessibility.
- All computers were networked and had printing capabilities.

Overall, the technology integration effort has great support from administration, particularly at the building level, as well as from the community. Teachers readily acknowledge the energy and empowerment they feel from this support.

Table 3: Student Learning and Teaching Objectives of Angola Middle School

Student Learning Objectives:

- Access and apply technological tools and resources for demonstrating proficiencies in problem-solving, inquiry, and critical thinking through the completion of integrated projects in the library media center and computer labs.
- Think critically, problem solve, apply inquiry, and research skills using technology at home.
- Use online and network services for information gathering, virtual field trips, video conferencing, electronic process writing, and communicating with other students in other schools, states, and countries.
- Access online services for virtual appearances by community leaders, authors, scientists, etc., and participate in electronic mentoring.
- Participate in flexible learning environments that use technology to make learning proactive and interactive for each student.
- Learn content that is personalized and individualized for each individual whether it be remediation or acceleration.
- Produce reports and presentations using a variety of media that teachers judge to be of a high quality.
- Utilize students capable of mentoring both other students and adults.

Teaching Objectives:

- Produce technology portfolios showcasing the technology used by students in their classes.
- Use resources available on Internet for accessing resources for lessons, research, and collaboration.
- Collaborate and learn from other teachers through on-line access in their classrooms.
- Use and apply selected software relevant to subject areas for remediation and acceleration.
- Expand thematic and integrated curriculum lessons with colleagues through multimedia presentations.
- Extend problem solving, inquiry, and research methods with software and online resources in all curriculum areas.
- Develop and share curriculum units and electronic resources with interdisciplinary teams and the community at large by use of the district web site.

continued next page

Table 3 continued

- Track technology progress through electronic logs that include reflection on one's own practice and present skills, thus allowing for self-evaluation, perception of needs, and goal-setting.

To further amplify the importance that has been placed upon technology at Angola Middle School, the school has adopted a number of student learning and teaching objectives (see Table 3). These objectives help to support activities such as a team-implemented inquiry-based research project on the Middle Ages. The thematic unit focused on key concepts of change, power, conflict, culture, patterns, and region. Each teacher linked his or her subject to the concepts rather than the broad topic of the Middle Ages. For example: Reading/Language/Spelling—King Arthur, Song of Roland, Castle in the Attic; Math and Science—alchemy, battle techniques, castles, siege weapons, etc.; Music and Art—Gregorian chant, troubadours, heraldry, stained glass, etc.; and Social Studies—feudalism, guilds, architecture, historical figures, etc.

Additionally, a media retrieval system is heavily used—increasingly doing more with it than showing movies:

- An eighth grader needing a good dose of self-esteem built a Power-Point presentation to play through the system for the entire school. His grades and behavior have improved dramatically since then.
- For an all-school theme event, a seventh grade classroom developed multimedia presentations about the shootings at Kent State using a large screen video projector playing film footage downloaded from the Internet; listening stations with recorded voices from interactive computer conferences with people who were there; a looped still video floppy slide show created from digital camera pictures taken on campus; PowerPoints including downloaded sound recordings of news reports, and songs about the shootings. Visual displays were generated when the class used one of the two computer labs.
- One eighth grade class hosted a parents' evening where multiple televisions showed students' personal PowerPoint scrapbooks filled with family photos. In the Media Center, twelve networked computers were available for students to demonstrate how they made their presentations. In an amphitheater-like setting, video-edited student poetry readings played.

What should be most convincing about this case study is not how the technology is being used to enhance knowledge construction and the ability of these students to mature into independent learners, but the extent to which this effort is holistic, involving all aspects of the middle school and that the technology is a part of the school vision and plan which guides all aspects of learner development. Although from this case study, we don't know the degree to which technology is being used in school administration, the focus on the relevance of technology to the preparation of these children is apparent. (See http://www.msdsteuben.k12.in.us/AMS/MS.HTML for more information.)

Ligon Middle School

Ligon Middle School, located in Raleigh, North Carolina, is a magnet school for students from all over the Wake County area who are state identified as academically gifted and those who are artistically gifted. A rich assortment of electives is available. Students choose three of the courses they take each day from a variety of offerings in the areas of academics, technology, visual and performing arts, foreign language, vocational, and physical education. Thus, Ligon students take courses in their areas of interest and explore many new opportunities.

In the early 1990s, the principal decided that technology needed to be implemented in the school. A grant funded the very first technology resources. One of the first technology elective teachers, Caroline McCullen, was *Technology & Learning's* 1996 Teacher of the Year. She brought web design, Internet Safari (introductory Internet), and the first experimentation with 3D Design to the school. Ann Thompson followed McCullen's tenure and added the 3D Design course, a Black History technology course, and the GIS course (with Rita Hagevik). Skip Thibault followed adding desktop publishing and Corel Draw. This is a school where teachers can experiment with new courses and tread the bleeding edge.

Every classroom at Ligon has one networked (T1) computer. About ten computers are available in the media center for research. Two computer labs of nineteen computers are used for technology electives—electronic publishing, desktop publishing, multimedia, Internet Safari, Corel Draw, Satellites, Computers & Mapping (GIS), and 3D Design; one vocational lab of twenty-eight computers is used for Business Computer Technology—keyboarding, databases, spreadsheets; one vocational lab has stations that teach units on robotics, CAD, multimedia, etc.

Ligon teachers who integrate technology frequently are not left alone in the process. They often begin their projects by working closely with the technology elective teachers; the media specialists are also instrumental in assisting teachers. Additional personnel resources are available to the teachers as well, including a Curriculum Integration Coordinator.

Students at Ligon Middle School in Internet classes develop a broader view of the world and build relationships as they communicate with other students worldwide. Students may receive e-mail from California, Utah, Italy, Germany,

Sweden, Japan, and China, all in the same class! An exchange of virtual artifacts with students in New York gave students new insights into their own world and that of their peers. Keypals from Japan sent pictures, videos, snacks, and postcards. Students feel "connected" when they discover how much they have in common with students halfway around the world. There are no walls in these classes. Students use the Internet and traditional media to explore the world. They write articles and create original artwork or use graphics from the Internet, pictures they take with digital cameras, and scanned graphics to illustrate their work. Students are also changing their view of school assignments. They no longer do tasks just to get a grade; instead they seek information and eagerly communicate their ideas because they know people value their opinions.

The students are also using electronic communication tools to communicate with experts and expand their learning environment. Sci-BLAST is a collaborative project initiated by Dr. Jay Levine, a professor at the School of Veterinary Medicine, North Carolina State University. In a workshop at the School of Veterinary Medicine, Stuart Levenworth, science editor of the *News and Observer,* trained students from three middle schools in interview techniques. Graphic artists at the vet school gave them tips to improve their photography. The students also spent some time exploring the Internet analyzing effective web pages. The middle school students interviewed scientists about their research and how they became interested in their science career. They took pictures and wrote articles about the scientists that documented their work. Graduate students at the School of Veterinary Medicine edited their work and the scientists approved it for publication. The articles were published on the Internet. These students have learned a lot about the topics researched by the scientists they interviewed, project organization, and implementation.

In another successful collaboration, Hagevik and Thompson created an elective called Satellites, Computers, and Mapping. In this elective, students use spatial modeling to explore the environment using geographic information systems. GIS is a computer-based tool that links maps to corresponding databases. This software allows students to create maps to which they can add data layers such as population, elevation, precipitation, highways, etc. A simple click of a mouse allows students to access an interactive atlas and almanac. They use the data to analyze and solve problem questions. For example, using layers such as population density, education levels, natural resources, railroads, roads, major cities, etc., students predict why the GNP in African countries varies. Students also make interactive maps from data they collect. They can connect data about their school to a map of the school or collect water quality data and link it to a map of a local stream. Using this technology, students develop life skills that may form the foundation for a future career.

In a 3D Design elective class students use Virtus 3D Website Builder software. Imaginations soar as students create virtual worlds. They make Egyptian,

Roman, farm, and space scenes. They design their dream house and model an actual room in the school complete with furnishings. Students create aquariums for which they make textures in a paint program and import them. They also create models related to school subjects. The most impressive model showed a slave's perspective as he escaped the South by the Underground Railroad.

In all of these examples use of technology resources empowers students. They apply a wide variety of skills traditionally isolated in content instruction with new skills they develop in using technology. Students read, write, and do research. They think critically. They create. They publish their work and communicate their ideas. They explore the world and interact with a variety of people from their desktop. Through such experiences they gain a wider perspective of the world and their place of importance in it. Students and teachers in all examples have benefited from collaboration. Partnerships and resources are not limited to those available at Ligon GT Magnet Middle School. Collaborating with other students and teachers and using university, community, and Internet resources, they experience a dynamic educational environment.

Ligon Middle School provides another example of a school where teachers are employed in innovative activities with their students and technology. The teachers who are using these technologies are following a middle school concept that provides for the development and education of the whole student. Again, although it is difficult to determine the degree to which the vision of the entire school and the administration focus is present, the initiatives that are present today are a result of an administrative vision that technology was important. Key personnel have facilitated the realization of that vision. (For more information, see http://www2.ncsu.edu/ligon/)

This chapter has tried to provide a sense of how instructional technologies can be melded into a middle school in such a way that the concept of the middle school, as proposed by Alexander and George, and the Carnegie Council, is not only supported, but also strengthened. A conceptual model and standards have been presented, as well as a variety of real examples of the work some middle schools have been doing with instructional technology. This chapter concludes with one last exercise: to examine what a middle school might look like where technology is central to the middle school process, and students are functioning as knowledge producers and independent learners.

A vision of technology in the reinvented middle school

It is just another Tuesday afternoon at Wayville Middle School. It is time for the weekly team meeting for this seventh grade team. Everything is as usual in that there are people missing from the meeting room, interruptions will take place, and there is more to get done than there is time to meet! Ms. Snider could not be physically present today, as she is attending the National Middle

School Association Conference. She is videoconferencing into the meeting from her laptop in between sessions. Mr. Watkins is also not physically present, as he had to stay home with his youngest daughter who has the chicken pox. He is participating over an audio conference. Once everyone is settled in, Ms. Ranger calls the team meeting to order.

As a first order of business, Ms. Snider asks about the student presentations that were made earlier during the day. In particular, she is interested in the presentation that Wendy made. Wendy struggled with her topic and was nervous to have her multimedia presentation shown during assembly. The team assured Ms. Snider that it went extremely well and that Wendy was pleased with the reactions from her peers. With a few mouse clicks, Ms. Ranger accessed the presentation from the school server and transmitted it to Ms. Snider so she could view it later.

Mr. Fife suggested that the team next spend some time on the parental questions and responses from the team's web site. He brings up the items on the video projection board, and faxes them to Mr. Watkins as well. Parents have submitted eight different questions in the last week. The team discusses their collective responses. Ms. Snider takes notes and volunteers to send the team responses this week, both via e-mail directly to the parent(s), and to post more public responses to the web site on the team's FAQ (Frequently Asked Questions) section.

Ms. Parnell asks if the group can finalize plans for the next integrated curriculum unit on the stock market. Part of the plan was to hold a virtual field trip to Wayville's sister school in Tokyo and visit the stock exchange there. Ms. Parnell says that she heard from Mr. Yamamoto at the school and he indicated he would make himself available today to finalize those preparations. Ms. Parnell asks permission to excuse herself from the meeting to go to the next room to videoconference with Mr. Yamamoto. The team agrees. She is able to make contact with the teacher in Japan, and together they view web sites they would like to use for the unit, visit the stock exchange on the web camera, and Mr. Yamamoto contacts the stockbroker who has agreed to be a tour guide for the students. The two teachers and the stockbroker finalize the timing of the virtual field trip for the next week, and download to each other all the necessary documents. Ms. Parnell drags the video clips they have viewed and the web sites to her desktop and saves them to the server. These items join the multimedia pool of information that the students will access while working on this project.

Mr. Watkins reluctantly brings up the topic of Richard. He has been a topic of concern for the last several weeks in team meetings, but the last few days have been particularly bad for him, and they feel that he needs to talk to someone immediately. Ms. Ranger goes to the online calendar for the school counselor and compares her schedule to the student's electronic schedule. She sees that play rehearsal has been cancelled for Richard today, and that the counselor has some open time. Ms. Ranger requests an appointment time with the counselor and once it has been electronically confirmed Mr. Fife uses the school's electronic paging system to privately page the student to come to the team room. Mr. Fife will then take a few minutes to talk privately with the student and walk him to the counselor.

Ms. Parnell came back from her meeting and told the team that they still needed to schedule the video titles for next week about Japan and the stock market. While the onsite teachers are taking care of Richard, Ms. Snider logs into the state library system and schedules some videos to be shown at the date and time already decided upon by the team. She requests that one of the videos be shown with local control so that Mr. Fife can periodically stop the video to allow students to do a variety of exercises on their graphing calculators. Ms. Snider also remembers that she must remind the library media specialist to load the novel about Japan she is using onto the digital book readers to which the students will have access this next week.

The team is preparing to wrap up when they receive a flash notice from the principal that she has reviewed their team and individual schedules, and the schedules of an eighth grade team, and is requesting a meeting for both teams to sit down and discuss the recent set of standardized scores. The team confirms the meeting time and then downloads the scores from the school's central computer, the state scores from the state system, and the scores for their students for the last several years. They place these into their graphing program to view trends. Mr. Fife accepts responsibility to place these graphs into the team-shared folder on the network. Before she signs off, Ms. Snider tells her team members about an interesting session she attended yesterday on standardized scores and sends the video clip to the team room SmartBoard for everyone to view. Ms. Parnell saves several pieces of the presentation to forward on to the principal.

Ms. Ranger now glances at the clock and sees that they have 3 minutes before the bell. She sends a reminder over the pager system to all of their classes to remind them that the next period they will be meeting in the presentation amphitheater for the live download from the Mars Explorer. As the team moves to disband from the meeting, they bid best wishes to their remote colleagues, and turn off the light in the meeting room—it's a typical Tuesday, and time for fifth period.

References

Alexander, W.M., and George, P. (1981). *The exemplary middle school.* New York: Harcourt, Brace Jovanovich.

American Library Association. (1991). *American library association handbook of organi-*

zation and membership directory. Chicago: Author.

American Library Association. (1998). *Information power: Building partnerships for learning.* Chicago: Author.

Andris, J.F., Crooks, S.M., and Hawkins, G.C. (1999). *Disseminating engaged learning strategies in the middle school through technology.* Paper presented at the annual meeting of the Society for Information Technology in Teacher Education (SITE), March 1–4, 1999, San Antonio, Texas.

Assocation for Educational Communications and Technology (AECT) (1996). The definition of educational technology: A summary. In D.P. Ely and T. Plomp (Eds.), *Classic writings on instructional technology* (pp. 3–14). Englewood, CO: Libraries Unlimited, Inc.

Baab, L. (1999). Middle school computer literacy. *The ClearingHouse, 72*(4), 197–198.

Bowen, W. (1992). Defining media literacy: Summary of Harvard institute on media education. [Online] Available: http://interact.uoregon.edu/MediaLit/FA/MLArticleFolder/defharvard.html.

Carnegie Council on Adolescent Development. (1989). *Turning points: Preparing American youth for the twenty-first century.* Washington, DC: Carnegie Corporation.

Carnegie Council on Adolescent Development. (1996). *Great transitions: Preparing adolescents for a new century.* Washington, DC: Carnegie Corporation.

Dodge, B. (1997). Some thoughts about webquests. [Online] Available: http://edweb.sdsu.edu/courses/edtec596/about_webquests.html. Accessed January 25, 2000.

Eichhorn, D. (1972). The emerging adolescent school of the future-now. In J. Galen Saylor (Ed.), *The school of the future—now* (pp. 35–52). Reston, VA: Association for Supervision and Curriculum Development.

Enomoto, E., Nolet, V., and Marchionini, G. (1999). The Baltimore learning community project: Creating a networked learning community across middle schools. *Journal of Educational Multimedia and Hypermedia, 8*(1), 99–115.

George, P.S., and Alexander, W.M. (1993). *The exemplary middle school* (2nd ed.). New York: Harcourt, Brace Jovanovich.

International Society for Technology in Education (1998). *National educational technology standards for students.* Eugene, OR: Author.

International Society for Technology in Education (1999). *Will new teachers be prepared to teach in a digital age?.* Santa Monica, CA: Milken Family Foundation.

Meichenbaum, D., and Biemiller, A. (1998). *Nurturing independent learners: Helping students take charge of their learning.* Cambridge, MA: Brookline Books.

National Middle School Association. (1992). *This we believe.* Columbus, OH: Author.

National Middle School Association. (1995). *This we believe: Developmentally responsive middle schools.* Columbus, OH: Author.

Pellegrino, J.W., and Altman, J.E. (1997). Information technology and teacher preparation: Some critical and illustrative solutions. *Peabody Journal of Education, 72*(1), 89–121.

Powers, S.M. (1999). Personal interviews at Scarborough Middle School.

Rafferty, C.D. (1999). Reconceptualizing literacy for learning in the information age. *Educational Leadership, 57*(2), 22–25.

Rafferty, C.D. (2000). Preparing intermediate and middle grades students to be document literate. In K.D. Wood and T.S. Dickinson (Eds.), *Promoting literacy in the 21st century: A handbook for administrators and teachers in grades 4–8.* Boston: Allyn & Bacon.

Tapscott, D. (1999). Educating the net generation. *Educational Leadership, 56*(5), 6–11.

Thoman, E. (1999). Skills and strategies for media education. *Educational Leadership, 56*(5), 50–54.

Tyner, K. (1998). *Literacy in a digital world: Teaching and learning in the age of information.* Mahwah, NJ: Lawrence Erlbaum Associates.

Wiggins, G. (1998). *Educative assessment: Designing assessments to inform and improve student performance.* San Francisco: Jossey-Bass.

Wilmer, M. (1999). Global warming: A heated debate. [Online] Available: http://www.scarborough.k12.me.us/middle/quest/studentp.html. Accessed January 25, 2000.

Note

1. Other partner, participating organizations include the American Federation of Teachers (AFT), the American Association of School Libraries (AASL), the Association for Supervision and Curriculum Development (ASCD), the Council of Chief State School Officers (CCSSO), the Council for Exceptional Children (CEC), the National Association of Elementary School Principals (NAESP), the National Association for Secondary School Principals, (NASSP), the National Education Association (NEA), the National School Boards Association (NSBA) Institute for the Transfer of Technology to Education, the National Foundation for the Improvement of Education (NFIE), and the Software Publishers Association (SPA).

Unresolved Issues

Transformation and Context in Middle Grades Reform

GAYLE A. DAVIS
University of Maryland

Introduction

We pushed the tables together for our last group discussion so we could all see each other as we talked. It was Saturday afternoon on the final day of the final project directors meeting for the Middle Grade School State Policy Initiative (MGSSPI). Our setting, a hotel room in a western city, lacked windows and featured the neutral wallpaper, wildly patterned carpet, and "cocktail" lighting I had grown to expect in hotels. We'd met in so many hotels, in so many cities, over the ten-year life of the project that we didn't even think to comment on the room itself. Only about twenty meeting participants were left from the original group of thirty, our ranks thinned by departures for points east and south as people left for home. We were all tired, partly from jet lag and the rigors of an intense two-day meeting, but more to the point, tired as the result of a decade's work and the realization that it was all coming to an end.

We all settled into our seats, and the audiotape started rolling. We began, hesitantly at first, to explore our thoughts about what we had and had not accomplished in this Carnegie-funded initiative to implement the *Turning Points* recommendations in middle grades schools. Some of the talk was like exploring the gaping hole left when a baby tooth falls out—alarming but promising nonetheless. We had not done everything we had hoped to, thus the holes, but our efforts seemed to have set the stage for what would come. Other parts of the discussion felt almost triumphant, as we waved our respective flags of success and recognized what we had achieved together. We also tried to examine the flaws in our work, the places where we wished we had taken a different path to avoid entanglement in the creeping vines of things like bureaucracy and politics, without the machete of clear vision and leadership we needed to hack our way back out.

Where had it all gone right? And, where had it all gone wrong? In looking back at my own eight-year tenure with Carnegie Corporation of New York's Middle Grade School State Policy Initiative to answer those two questions, I have tried to analyze the effects of contextual issues on our efforts to improve schooling for young adolescents. I referred to Seymour Sarason's (1990 p. 122) definition of the "social-institutional contexts" within which all changes must take place:

> That context has structure, implicit and explicit rules, traditions, power relationships, and purposes variously defined by its members. It is dynamic in that it is characterized by continuous activity and interchanges both within its boundaries and between it and its community surround. . . . It has covert as well as overt features.

In this chapter, I will examine several aspects of context relevant to middle grades reform, using examples drawn from the MGSSPI, other national middle grades improvement efforts, and my dissertation research on influences affecting the middle school movement. Specifically, I will discuss the following contextual themes:

- Ideology
- Power
- Commitment
- Knowledge and skills
- Resources

Although I will describe the above contextual aspects separately, each of them interacts with all the others. To use a quick agricultural analogy, imagine that the effort to improve middle grades schools is a new tomato plant, about to be embedded in the soil. Many factors will affect the successful growth, flowering, and production of that plant—the nature of the soil itself, its location relative to sun and shade, the weather, the knowledge and skill of the farmer, the timing of the harvest, etc. If the soil does not provide the nutrients necessary to tomato plants, the plant will die, regardless of every other factor. If the farmer doesn't know when to harvest, then the tomatoes will rot on the vine. In like fashion, resources affect commitment, ideology affects the acquisition of knowledge and skills, and power seems to affect everything. If only it were as simple as raising a good tomato.

Personal context

Before delving into the various aspects of context, I will provide a little background on my involvement in middle grades reform and the MGSSPI itself.

Back in 1989, early in my tenure as a project coordinator for the Center for Early Adolescence in North Carolina, I designed a T-shirt. The T-shirts with my design would be party favors of a sort for the participants in a conference on urban middle school reform to be held in Raleigh, North Carolina, in December of that year. The Center was organizing the meeting, but the Edna McConnell Clark Foundation in New York funded the conference and the project the conference was a part of, the Urban Youth Initiative.

This small conference for fifty people was the first I'd ever organized, and I felt like a nervous wedding director, making sure everything was aligned with the color scheme. The scheme for the project revolved around the three "highs" that Clark program officer M. Hayes Mizell used to describe the project's goals: high content, high support, and high expectations. My T-shirt design featured the three highs, one each emblazoned across a school bus, a billboard, and a building, all in the foreground set against an urban skyline backdrop, a la the New York Mets' logo. A spotlight in the middle, like those associated with Hollywood premieres, sent a shaft of light skyward, highlighting the letters "EMC" in a manner meant to be reminiscent of the caped crusader's infamous "bat light." I'd always thrilled to Batman's victories over the villains of Gotham. It seemed natural to present the foundation as the avenging hero for urban schools.

At that point, I was new enough to this reform business to think that the Clark Foundation, with help from the Center, would save the day for the project's five urban school districts and twelve middle schools, bringing in resources, wisdom, energy, and hope. It turns out I was very naive, especially about the capacity of any organization to swoop in and "save" urban middle schools. In the eleven years since the conference participants donned those T-shirts and set about trying to wrestle their middle schools from the grips of inertia and defeat, I've learned quite a bit about the effects of context, the nature of change, and the saving graces of hope.

I have been involved in middle grades education for sixteen years now, stretching back to my years as a middle grades teacher, through several major reform efforts and a lengthy stint in graduate school, made lengthier by the financial necessity of keeping a full-time job while I completed my doctorate. The job at the Center as a project coordinator was the first full-time position I'd held since leaving the public school classroom to go to graduate school. In joining the world of education reform, I had to master quickly the proliferation of confusing acronyms for projects and organizations with excruciatingly long names. My first day at the Center I received a dictionary of sorts for all the acronyms that seemed to fly around the place like, well, bats. My new professional context had its own lexicon, and I needed to become fluent quickly.

I worked at the Center for Early Adolescence for three years, then moved with my husband and one large dog to Washington, D.C. I'd been hired by the

Council of Chief State School Officers (CCSSO) to join their technical assistance team for Carnegie Corporation of New York's Middle Grade School State Policy Initiative (MGSSPI).

Begun in 1990, a year after the release of Carnegie's landmark report, *Turning Points: Preparing American Youth for the 21st Century* (1989), the MGSSPI was a program of grants to states designed to stimulate statewide changes in the policy and practice of middle grades education. The Carnegie initiative had two main goals:

1. To promote widespread implementation of the *Turning Points* reform principles through changes in state policies that encourage local schools to adopt promising practices.
2. To stimulate the development of schools serving those most in need—youth from low-income families—to produce high-achieving, healthy young adolescents.

The Corporation focused its support for the MGSSPI, in a series of two-year grants, on fifteen states: Arkansas, California, Colorado, Connecticut, Delaware, Illinois, Maryland, Massachusetts, New Mexico, New York, North Dakota, Rhode Island, South Carolina, Texas, and Vermont. Carnegie also funded MGSSPI projects in Boston, Los Angeles, New York City, and Puerto Rico. Each of the projects supported a network of schools, totaling approximately 225 middle grades schools across the national initiative. About fifty percent of the students in the MGSSPI schools receive free or reduced-price lunch (Jackson and Davis 2000, pp. 17–18).

The MGSSPI ended in September of 1999, bringing to a close almost ten years of intensive support from a foundation for middle grades reform, a long stretch by most any measure. I was involved in the MGSSPI for nearly eight of those years, first as a project associate, then senior associate, and finally as national director. I helped in producing reams of documents, dozens of meetings and conferences, and our fair share of doodads and giveaways, from MGSSPI bags and, yes, T-shirts, to clocks and calculators. I'm too close to the Initiative, both in time and personal relationships, to say what it all meant, assuming it's ever possible to boil such a complicated effort down to a few bromides. I will, in subsequent sections, discuss a little of what I learned about the impact of context from the MGSSPI and the other middle grades reform efforts to which I've been party, either directly or indirectly.

Contextual issues for middle grades reform

Too often, Sarason argues, a reformer has woven (or patched) together a conceptual framework for his or her ideas but is "unaware of how inadequately he knows the context. He or she assumes a degree of understanding the limits of which only become clear when implementation fails" (1990, pp. 122–123). My limited understanding of context's potential impact is evident in the T-shirt design—I focused on the foundation as all-powerful crusader, highlighting the bat light in the foreground while ignoring the shadows cast by the city skyline in the background.

I guess I can take some measure of comfort in knowing I'm certainly not the first or the only reform advocate to ignore the background for improvement efforts. The battlegrounds of school reform are littered with the casualties of failed reforms, each mortally wounded by the barrage of contextual issues that the battle plans never considered. Indeed, an educational fad may be defined by its inattention to context, and the resulting kick off the bandwagon as the next fad jumps on in its place.

In their book, *Tinkering Toward Utopia* (1995), David Tyack and Larry Cuban examine 100 years of public school reform. One theme of their book, "hybridization," is particularly relevant to this discussion of context, and provides a lens through which to view how middle grades reform is taking on different shapes as reformers find themselves coping with the realities of context. In describing efforts to raise academic achievement, Tyack and Cuban commented on why educators turned to hybridization.

> In the decade from 1983 to 1993 . . . reformers adopted various strategies to increase the academic achievement of students. When one approach to reform did not appear to work, innovators quickly turned to alternatives but generally left the original reform laws and layers of rules and regulations in place. As a result, exhortations for change and mandated practices often worked at cross-purposes. "We are asked to reinvent schools, to break the mold," complained a central office administrator, "and they put a moat of mandates around us. It's like putting on handcuffs and leg irons and saying climb Mt. Everest." Confronted with contrary reform demands, practitioners sought refuge through strategies of accommodation, resistance, and hybridization. In the process, schools changed reforms quite as much as reforms changed schools. (p. 78)

In this example, the layers of reforms and mandates, like sediment building up in a river basin, represent the context within which educators try to keep "schooling" flowing. The following sections describe other forms of context that affect the river's flow and educators' attempts to keep their schools afloat.

Ideology

George Noblit (1987), an experienced educational sociologist, outlines how it can be said that the middle school movement has an ideology:

The middle school movement . . . has a middle school ideology in that the beliefs are (a) widely shared by the proponents; (b) systematically interconnected; (c) central to what the movement is about, and; (d) have influence on behavior. (p. 204)

The middle school ideology is the ultimate context for all our efforts to improve middle schools; it overarches everything we do. So, what is the ideology of the middle school movement? During my dissertation research (Davis 1996), I asked participants in my study to describe the mission and goals of the middle school, and how the mission related to the middle school's functions (i.e., practices). Though all the respondents basically agreed that the ideology centers on a belief in the unique nature of early adolescence and a response to the developmental needs of young adolescents, most did not make the leap from their innate acceptance of middle school theory to its implications for practice.

In my dissertation, I described many of my respondents as missionaries, spreading the good word of middle schools to all who would listen. One of the respondents for my research even described her teaching career as a "moral calling," a notion quite in keeping with the idea of middle school advocates as missionaries (Davis 1996, p. 119). In like fashion, Noblit (1987) argues that the main task of an ideological movement's members is to "create converts and expand the ranks of believers" (p. 204).

The missionaries for the middle school, though, face a couple of real problems in expanding the ranks of believers. The first relates to their inability to articulate specifically how their ideology should look in practice. I wrote:

> Middle school missionaries may be devoted to the concept, devout even, but perhaps they also accept the great mysteries of their chosen cause on faith, sort of like Catholic mysticism. . . . Like many of them, I believed middle school theory and practices were good for kids in my former-teacher gut, and did not actively seek out evidence to support or contradict my belief. However, we [advocates] are in a weak position in any toe-to-toe confrontation. Without reviewing and understanding the existing research on the veracity of all those middle school [ideas], we are like advertisers selling detergent, relying on flash and bright ketchup stains—in our case anecdotal evidence—to distract the audience from the lack of evidence that our detergent is better than anyone else's. (Davis 1996, p. 116)

The middle school missionaries' other problem is a potentially conflicting ideology that has gained attention and strength over the past ten years. The standards-based reform movement—with its emphasis on knowledge and skills, assessment, and high-stakes accountability for both schools and students—

threatens to drown out the voices of missionaries focused on developmental responsiveness. The middle school ideology has centered essentially on children, not curriculum. It potentially puts us at a disadvantage as the tide of standards and testing gains ground among the public and the politicians. One of the MGSSPI project directors described the problem during the directors' final meeting in August 1999:

> We have learned how important this [middle school reform] is and we probably know that better and deeper than most people in the country. We have also learned its limitations. . . . It's not enough. You can have the most developmentally appropriate environment in which to learn, and absent rigorous instruction, it ain't enough. (MGSSPI 1999, pp. 27–28)

Another project director agreed, pointing out that most schools had not made the link between the child-centered, developmentally appropriate practices they had been using and the real need to improve students' achievement (MGSSPI 1999, p. 29). One director summed it up:

> I think we are looking at a real serious backlash in this country that is inadvertently being driven by the content standards movement. . . . There is a mentality in this country that, if you want higher test results, you get back and you tighten up on the [subject-matter] disciplines. You get rid of common planning time. You just don't need that. They [teachers] need to teach content, because content is going to drive the test scores. My fear is it is going to erode a lot of the personalization and developmental responsiveness that we have been able to crank into schedules and staff development time. I can see all of that going in a heart beat. (MGSSPI 1999, pp. 30–31)

However, the standards movement also poses an opportunity for middle school missionaries to expand their message and draw more converts. If research provides evidence that developmentally responsive practices, with an accompanying focus on rich curriculum and differentiated instruction, improves student outcomes across the board, including achievement, then we can preach our more comprehensive gospel without fear of the infidels.

Early results from research on Michigan middle schools provides hope we can expand our message about middle school's effectiveness to include academic excellence. The W.K. Kellogg Foundation's Middle Start Initiative provides grant funds to twenty schools for middle grades improvement efforts. The Center for Prevention Research and Development (CPRD) at the University of Illinois, using the School Improvement Self-Study,[1] is collecting data on these twenty schools and 125 other Michigan middle grades schools not receiving support to pursue comprehensive improvements. In comparison to the 125 schools not receiving funds, the twenty grant schools "showed dramatic gains in seventh grade reading scores (+ ten percent) and substantial gains in seventh grade math scores (+ six percent) from 1994/95 to 1996/97 on state achievement tests. Non-grant schools improved by four percent in both reading and mathematics over the two year period" (Jackson and Davis 2000, p. 5; Mertens, Flowers, and Mulhall 1998).

Power

In her case study of how a large-scale innovation was implemented in Charlotte, North Carolina, Betty Lou Whitford (1987) described the influence of power on the implementation:

> The way the innovation was embedded in the power and authority structure of the school system significantly affected the operation of the program. The failure of the program to become integrated into the line structure caused numerous problems. . . . These observations suggest the conclusion that change is affected by the degree to which planners and initiators are integrated into the line authority structure of the organization. Not only does the degree of integration seem to affect the daily operation of the change effort itself, the same condition seems to affect the likelihood that an innovation will eventually be institutionalized. (p. 115)

Power seems to come down to "voice," that is the capacity to be heard by those whose attention is needed to make a difference. In a contextual sense, change efforts have to be situated with those people and institutions that have enough power to "make it happen." Without that context of substantive power, innovations will likely fail.

In an attempt to infuse their MGSSPI state projects into their state power structures, while simultaneously building awareness of the middle school ideology, virtually every state project began their MGSSPI effort by convening a task force (CCSSO 1992, pp. 24–30). The task forces diverged widely in the constituencies represented, though most included some high-ranking state officials and some practitioners. Their charge was to analyze the status of middle grades education in their individual states and make policy recommendations for improving middle schools.

Almost all the task forces produced a policy statement or report intended to draw attention to middle schools and provide a call to action. With catchy titles like "The Middle Matters" (Vermont), "From the Margins to the Middle" (Rhode Island), and "Right in the Middle" (Illinois and Connecticut), the policy statements did indeed seem to generate interest and support for improving middle schools (CCSSO 1992, pp. 85–96). In fact, in preparing to write this chapter, I looked back at the status of middle grades education in the MGSSPI states back in 1990. It was pretty dismal, by all accounts, though obviously some states were further along than others. All fifteen states that continued their involvement in the Initiative from the beginning have seen real gains in such things as awareness of young adolescents' developmental needs and the middle school ideology, infrastructure development (e.g., a middle grades department in the state education agency), and middle grades teacher licensure.

However, back in 1993, in reviewing progress across the MGSSPI states after most of the task force reports were published, the MGSSPI national leaders agreed that the reports had not done enough. The locus of the power that brought attention to the middle grades had been in the people on those task forces; their voices lent credibility and energy to the calls to action. Once these groups disbanded, state-level attention to the projects necessarily diminished, despite the continued role of an MGSSPI project director typically based in the state education agency (SEA) within each state.

The state project directors varied widely in the amount and kind of power they held within their state education agencies. It seems, in retrospect, that the more power a director had in the agency, the less time they had to attend to the MGSSPI. A few directors, especially in the early years, were contributing only 5–10 percent of their time to the project, not nearly enough to manage the state's project activities, much less serve as a voice for middle grades reform in the agency more generally. Their power within the agencies meant multiple, pressing responsibilities, many of which carried more weight in how they were viewed in the agency than did their efforts for the MGSSPI.

On the flip side, a lack of status in the SEA could effectively cripple efforts to make change. In one state, a dedicated state director was continually stymied by lack of access. When groups met within the agency to make decisions that would affect education state wide, this director was never invited, thus effectively silencing the voice of middle grades in the state.

As a group, the state project directors gradually took on increasing power within the national Initiative's management structure. Initially, they were essentially passive recipients of technical assistance and Carnegie mandates. As Carnegie put more pressure on the states to improve middle schools, the directors began to take control over decisions that affected the support they received for making the expected changes. This move toward an active leadership role for the MGSSPI project directors became tangible in 1995–1996 when the directors drafted and voted to accept their own strategic plan for the Initiative. The strategic plan, which became the guiding document for their local networks and for the Initiative as a whole, had three primary goals:

Goal 1: Each state will develop and sustain a substantial cadre of highly implemented, high-performance systemic change schools serving economically disadvantaged students.

Goal 2: Each state will develop and sustain a system that addresses and promotes comprehensive middle grades school reform.

Goal 3: A national middle grade resource exchange network will be developed and sustained to support and expand systemic change efforts in middle grades schools.

In addition, the directors identified objectives and strategies for implementing those objectives under each goal. All three goals shared objectives centered on networking, resources, accountability, and communications. The directors eventually formed work groups—for professional development, local networks' capacity, and research and development—that guided the work of the national Initiative.

What does all that say about power as context? The MGSSPI started out with the assumption that grantees would, as grantees typically do, participate in technical assistance activities, not lead them, and accept proclamations about the overall direction of the project, not guide decisions about that direction. In such a context of limited power, the directors seemed to disengage, in effect, from the national level of the Initiative. Oh, they attended meetings and went out to dinner together, but they did not become earnestly engaged in figuring out how to make it all work. Once Carnegie and the national MGSSPI leadership ceded significant decision-making power to the directors, they owned the sucker, so to speak, for good or ill.

In like manner, obviously, school-level practitioners have been traditionally expected to passively accept district and state-level mandates. The calls for school-based decision making and local control seem to arise from the recognition that passive recipients are just that, passive, and have no personal investment in success or failure. Site-based decision making seems to be a powerful strategy in a democratic system, providing a supportive context for change efforts as decisions are made close to those most affected by them. However, Hayes Mizell raised important cautions about the alleged power of local control in a recent speech on the lessons he'd learned since the Clark Foundation's middle grades project began in the late 1980s:

This is not to argue that school systems should discourage site-based management, but rather that it is not as powerful a tool for reform as its proponents claim. In fact, in many school systems it means that neither schools nor the central office play a leadership role that develops and advances reforms to increase student achievement. Instead, some school boards and superintendents seem to use site-based management as an excuse for why they cannot provide more forceful leadership reform. They say they cannot act because under site-based management key decisions are reserved to the schools. Schools say they cannot act because, in fact, the central office exercises more authority than it claims. The result is a leadership stalemate that stifles rather than stimulates reform. (December 6, 1999)

One final note related to a context of power: the ultimate power in today's educational system, as alluded to in the previous section on ideology, seems to be high-stakes accountability. State accountability systems—which too often depend on the results of a single, norm-referenced test—affect everyone in the educational system, from students who are not promoted to the next grade to district superintendents pushed out the door before they've had a chance to settle into their offices. The drive toward the subject disciplines that one of the MGSSPI directors mentioned grows ever stronger as school report cards proliferate, and jobs are on the line. Common planning time for teams seems to be a frequent and early casualty of efforts to increase rigor in the core disciplines. Without power, and the capacity to show clear connections between middle school ideology and strong curriculum and instruction, we will see many more of the structural elements we have all fought for discarded in the drive to raise test scores.

Commitment

In the executive summary of Johns Hopkins University's extensive study of school improvement efforts, Sam Stringfield points out that "Full and active district, school administration, and faculty commitment to the final choice of reforms was not always sought. Yet there was always a price paid when the commitment of one of the three groups was not achieved. We found an initial and sustaining lift for the program when multi-level commitments were obtained" (United States Department of Education 1997, p. xvii).

Commitment seems to be at the heart of successful reforms: in a context of commitment, reforms bloom; without it, they wither on the vine. In his case studies of successful middle schools, Noblit found a common thread: "The cases presented here indicate that the essential element of a successful middle school is the honest belief by the participants that what they are doing is well worthwhile. . . ." (1987, p. 217). Michael Fullan argues that in "moving" schools, those that are making progress in their efforts to improve, the educators share a "common quest for continuous improvement. Having their colleagues show support and communicating more with them about what they did led these teachers to have more confidence, more certainty about what they are trying to achieve and how well they are achieving it" (1993, p. 85).

Early on in the MGSSPI, commitment levels served quickly to, in a sense, weed out those states that could not or would not commit energy and activity to improving middle grades schools. The Initiative began with twenty-seven states in 1990, then made a planned reduction to fifteen states in 1991. One criteria for deciding which states would continue was the evidence of commitment, as demonstrated in staff time to be contributed to the project, concrete and realistic plans for establishing a supportive infrastructure for change in the state, etc.

As for the MGSSPI schools, state project leaders decided which schools to include in the project and could use whatever process they wanted to make the decisions. Some states actually put out requests for proposals; others simply made the choices based on the input of a few people. Carnegie's criteria for school selection, ironically, did not require any evidence of commitment on the part of the school faculties or administrators.

Carnegie did insist that the majority of the schools have large populations of students from disadvantaged communities, usually identified by the percentage of children in a school on free or reduced-price lunch. For some states, this criteria immediately eliminated some of their most successful, and committed, middle grades schools, which tended to be located in more affluent suburban communities. In attempting to meet the criteria for disadvantaged student populations, states sometimes just designated which schools would be involved, with little or no consultation with the school communities. Finding a school with a large free and reduced-price lunch population that also was committed to middle grades reform had proven to be very difficult. For a few state directors, that meant many years of coping with recalcitrant school administrators and teachers who lacked the commitment to *Turning Points*-based reforms that success would require. Some of the schools of "nonbelievers" gradually embraced the reforms. Others, unfortunately, seemed to continually be in the "building awareness" stage, always trying to convince members of the school community that the reforms were worthwhile, while never actually making much progress in putting changes in place. In contrast, however, most schools in the Initiative demonstrated what California project director Thaddeus Dumas called "uncommon commitment," the willingness to take on new ideas and practices without any expectation of reward.

In 1998 and 1999, as the project directors and national MGSSPI leaders began talking about a post-MGSSPI network of schools, they agreed that any schools in the new network would have to somehow demonstrate that at least 80 percent of the faculty was committed to *Turning Points*-based reform. The context of commitment, or its lack, had made a significant impression on all of us over the course of the Initiative. By this point, we also knew that most New American School design models (e.g., Success for All in elementary schools and the new Turning Points Design) also require an 80 percent faculty commitment before agreeing to work in a school, a commitment they consider vital to any potential for success.

As an Initiative, we basically ignored one level of the educational system, the district or central office. We, especially our schools, paid a price for not doing more to reach out to the district to ensure their commitment and support for our efforts. One of the project directors lamented this significant gap in our efforts to build commitment to and support for the Initiative from the district: "I don't think that in our state we did enough with the central office folks. . . . You know, the annual breakfast, bringing them on board and celebrating them and so forth was nice, but not enough" (MGSSPI 1999, p. 12).

Stringfield notes that in their research on school improvement designs, "Strategies that were not consistently supported by school principals and central office personnel were marginalized or eliminated" (USDOE 1997, p. xix). Although only a half dozen or so schools officially were dropped from the Initiative by their states, many others suffered from the lack of oxygen—space and resources—they needed from their districts to try, fail, and try again.

Knowledge and skills

Ignorance is not bliss, contrary to the old saying, and this is particularly true when trying to implement substantial changes in middle grades schools. In my dissertation research, the interview respondents defined ignorance as "the lack of knowledge, not stupidity" (Davis 1996, p. 120). In contexts in which educators lack the real knowledge and skills they need to successfully improve middle grades schools, reform efforts face an uphill climb.

In *Turning Points 2000* (2000), Anthony Jackson and I argue that middle grades teachers need much more substantial, and much more targeted preservice preparation before entering middle grades classrooms. I will not go into detail here about the potential nature of an improved middle grades teacher preparation program (see Allen and McEwin, this volume), except to say that such programs are vital to any hope of continuing and enriching our efforts to improve middle grades schools for young adolescents. A lack of knowledge and skills among educators can lead to "reform avoidance" and misapplication of reform strategies. The only way to remedy a context of ignorance among *practicing* educators is to provide intensive, job-embedded, ongoing professional development, a complicated task with potentially vast rewards for middle grades advocates.

One of the project directors commented on the irony of the focus on academic excellence for students in a situation where the adults tend to avoid intellectual challenges:

One of the things I continually struggled with is that people who were faced with an intellectual struggle didn't want to face it. It was easy for them [the adults] to say the student had to face that, but not very often did I find a principal or a teacher who wanted to say, "I'll take on an

intellectual struggle and I'll look beyond what I already think and know."
(MGSSPI 1999, p. 17)

In a similar vein, Hayes Mizell discussed the realities of reform acceptance
and avoidance:

Reform means difficult professional and perhaps personal change. For
these reasons it is understandable that educators welcome reforms that
require more of others than of themselves. Reductions in class size, more
teachers, equitable school financing, full service schools, and new school
buildings and safer schools are all essential, but they will not cause students to develop the knowledge and skills necessary to perform at standard. That will only occur as a result of more effective leadership at the
school and classroom levels, and better teaching. (December 6, 1999)

The lack of knowledge and skills in middle grades contexts can also lead to
misapplication or misdirection of middle grades strategies. The never-ending
search for the perfect advisory, for example, wasted a lot of good people's time,
without ever bringing them closer to creating the kinds of relationships with
students they meant to develop. In perhaps misunderstanding the purpose of
advisory, and in lacking the knowledge and skills to achieve that purpose, they
spun their wheels but made no progress. The abuses of common team planning
time are legion, unfortunately, and I attribute that, at least partially, to a lack of
knowledge and skill in how to effectively use that time to integrate curriculum
and strengthen instruction. Scheduling decisions meant to free up teaching and
learning practices can instead constrict them, as administrators juggle compet-
ing priorities for schedules, without the skills they need to develop a truly flexible schedule.

The scheduling example brings up a pet peeve of mine, the lack of high-
quality preparation and professional development for principals. Virtually ignored by most higher education institutions, middle grades administrators sink
or swim of their own volition, with nary a life jacket in sight. In the MGSSPI,
the national network meetings brought together principals from around the
country, giving them the chance to commiserate, but more importantly to realize they shared similar struggles and could learn from each other's solutions and
problem-solving skills. Our conference evaluations for the national meetings
always included requests for still more time to network. Despite the dissimilar-
ities of their contexts, the principals provided professional development for
each other.

Successfully improving middle grades schools requires intensive professional
development. In the MGSSPI, initially our conferences were a parade of "talk-

ing heads," keynote speakers, and panel presentations featuring all the hot luminaries of the day. These sessions provided some valuable information, true enough, but also used the "sit and get" strategy that the National Staff Development Council decries as ineffective. As we grew more sophisticated about professional development, and as the state project directors took on more of a planning role for all meetings and conferences, we moved away from speakers and panels, and toward practitioner-run, hands-on workshops.

Although we got much better at trying to strengthen the context of knowledge and skills within which we hoped our reforms would take hold in schools, we at the national level still did not, admittedly, ever really provide the kind of professional development follow-up the practitioners needed. Many of the states picked up the slack, serving their schools intensively as coaches through state-level workshops and conferences and various and sundry other means of reinforcing and expanding what we did at the national level.

Resources

Last but not least in this exploration of context is the notion of resources. Stringfield and his colleagues (USDOE 1997, pp. 10-2–10-3) describe resources as a potentially stabilizing or destabilizing force in implementing comprehensive reforms. When resources are stable (i.e., continuing and certain from year to year) a reform effort obviously has a much better chance for sustainability. When the stability is lacking, however, as is often the case for school reform of any kind, commitment and the resulting investment in improving knowledge and skills are likely to suffer.

For example, perennial struggles to continue funding, as seen in seeking continuation grants or engaging in annual budget battles with the school board and superintendent, can take a toll on even the most dedicated reform advocates, leading to "energy-draining cynicism" (USDOE 1997, p. 10-3). In describing a teacher who fought a "ghost battle" year after year to continue a successful program that benefited students and provided her salary, Stringfield and his colleagues describe the toll of resource instability:

> Mrs. Autry knew that every year she grappled with leaving the position and taking a more secure one. She knew that this grappling and battling each year took time and energy—time and energy that could have been better spent in strengthening the program for the students at her school. She knew that her own level of commitment to the program waned each time she went to battle. She knew that neither the teachers nor the administration at her school had quite the same fervor about and commitment to the program as they had at the outset of its implementation because at any time, it could be lost. (p. 10-2)

In the MGSSPI, the states had to apply for continuation grants every two years. The whole proposal process seemed stressful for almost everybody involved, even for those states that had little reason to fear a loss of funding. Human nature and soft money being what they are, competition among the states for Carnegie's approval led to some jockeying for position among the state directors, and a reluctance to reveal any perceived weaknesses or mistakes to each other. Though the positive spins we heard at meetings were not harmful in and of themselves, they did hide what could have been useful information about mistakes not to be repeated and obstacles overcome. Though the directors learned a tremendous amount from each other over the course of the Initiative, it seemed they had the potential to gain so much more.

The resource context goes beyond funding, of course. Human resources, physical plants, the availability of technology, geographic location, and demographics can each be considered part of the resource context. For example, Carnegie and the state projects severely underestimated the human resources required to accomplish the goals they set for themselves in the first round of grants back in 1990. In their first project reports to the foundation, almost every state commented that the activities had taken longer and required more staff than they had anticipated. As the states and the funder got a better handle on the human resources required, goals were necessarily scaled back, while attention to providing adequate staffing to accomplish the goals increased.

As one tangible proof of the human resources required to run the state-level projects, almost every MGSSPI project had co-directors by the time the Initiative ended in 1999. Back in 1990, all but one state had only one director. The co-directors could divide and conquer, drawing on their different positions (e.g., one in the SEA and one in a university), and their different roles and strengths within the state (e.g., one who focused on policy and the other who focused on direct support to schools). Our national directors' meetings grew in size, as co-directors were joined by Carnegie state project coordinators, school coaches, and assorted individuals with other backgrounds and responsibilities.

Physical plants and the availability of technology like computers and Internet access have fairly obvious connotations with regard to context. Schools designed as middle schools (e.g., with classrooms clustered to facilitate interdisciplinary teams and small meeting rooms for teachers) seemed much better able to provide the structure to support middle school practices. Schools without those kinds of features, and most MGSSPI schools would fit into this category, had to adapt and accommodate. Sometimes they were successful, as with the middle grades school I visited that was housed in an elementary school building that used the playground for meetings of whole student teams and the primary color paint as backdrop for student work. Other times the schools weren't so successful in adapting ideology to environment. A small library went unused, despite its potential as a gathering place for learning as well as materials.

Stairwells in a former high school contained chain link, floor-to-ceiling barriers and metal guards obscured hallway clocks, like facemasks for football players. Everything in that school seemed to scream "We don't trust you," symbolically (at least) undermining the efforts of teachers to become closer to their students.

Perhaps the saddest waste of a resource I saw in a school was a large darkened computer lab, with rows of new equipment under dust protectors. The school had managed to muster the resources to purchase the computers, but they all stood idle for the lack of a human resource—someone to oversee the lab, train teachers and students in how to use the equipment, and keep all that valuable technology up and running.

Geography and demographics both factored in as resources for MGSSPI states and schools. Some states enjoyed the intimacy of smallness—e.g., Delaware, Rhode Island, and Vermont—making their state directors' efforts to provide assistance and keep in touch with schools much easier. Contrast their situations, geographically at least, with states like Texas, New Mexico, or California, where the directors had to not only drive several hours, but even climb aboard planes to visit many of their schools.

On the other hand, geographic intimacy could be a disadvantage, like living in a very small town where everybody knows everybody a little too well, and distance could be an advantage. Schools in states like Texas and California gained strength from the regional networks they formed in the absence of frequent visits from the state project leaders.

Demographically, the MGSSPI states could scarcely have been more different. Vermont, for example, has a very small, primarily Caucasian, English-speaking population. North Dakota and New Mexico, though their overall populations are small, each has distinct minority populations (Native American in the former and both Native American and Hispanic in the latter). Texas, California, and New York have incredibly large, ethnically diverse populations, with a growing number of regions within each that are becoming majority minority and an incredible variety of languages spoken by the students the schools serve.

The geographic and demographic diversity across the MGSSPI states led the directors and national leaders to try a few different configurations to bring together states with similar concerns and issues. We divided the states by region, by geographic size, and by population, depending on the topic of discussion. We also did our version of heterogeneous grouping, intentionally composing discussion groups to include representatives of states with dissimilar geographic and demographic resources. The variety was unending, and ve' useful in sharing ideas and advice within and across the MGSSPI landscapᵉ

Human resources appear again in this list of resources, because thᵉ without doubt, the most important element of the resource contex' which the MGSSPI, or any reform effort, operates. The knowle⌐

personal characteristics, and idiosyncrasies of all the people who tried to put *Turning Points* into practice had significant impact on the success of their efforts. Most of the directors and many of the practitioners entered the Initiative knowing the basics of middle grades ideology and committed to the *Turning Points* principles. They positioned themselves to make the best use of available power, often by using their interpersonal skills to build key relationships within and across organizations and leveraging those relationships to make their voices heard. They also were incredibly creative in making silk purses out of sow's ears, crafting ingenious uses of often limited funding, staff, and technology to make real progress.

Conclusion

In a recent editorial for *Education Week*, Jeannie Oakes and her colleagues (2000) outlined what they had learned about civic virtue and reform in their research on five of the MGSSPI states and sixteen middle grades schools. They described local heroes, crusaders without superpowers, capes, or bat lights who

> . . . sought to create caring, socially just, and democratic learning communities for their students and themselves. With civic virtue at the fore, they acted in idiosyncratic, opportunistic, and contextually appropriate ways that were often truer to the spirit of the reform than policymakers could have anticipated. (February, p. 43 and p. 68)

The contexts of ideology, power, commitment, knowledge and skills, and resources necessarily impact, and often alter, efforts to improve middle grades schools. Each contextual factor acts in relationship to all the others, like currents in a river working in concert or in opposition to carve out contours and canyons. Sometimes the schools that used to be on the riverbank with easy access to water are left high and dry by a change in the river's direction. Powerful contextual issues that overwhelm their efforts to dam the flood can also inundate schools on the river. Some schools manage to direct the river's flow, using what they can to power their "reform mills" (Oakes et al. 2000) and building bridges over the rest.

Andy Hargreaves and Michael Fullan define the nature of hope in their book, *What's Worth Fighting for Out There*:

> Hope is definitely not the same as optimism. It is not the conviction that something will turn out well, but the certainty that something makes sense, regardless of how it turns out. It is hope, above all, that gives us strength to live and to continually try new things, even in conditions that seem hopeless. (1998, p. 68)

My hope for improving and reinventing middle grades schools is vested primarily in the people who often have to swim against the current to make progress. To perhaps help those folks in their mission, I have developed what I can only call an emerging, and I hasten to add, untested theory of "differentiated reform," in which change agents target their assistance to schools in line with the contexts within which those schools operate. I envision differentiated reform as akin to Carol Ann Tomlinson's model of differentiated instruction, in which teachers become "students of their students" (1999, p. 2). In a differentiated classroom, teachers "prescribe the best possible instruction for their students" based on the students' diverse levels of readiness, interests, and learning profiles.

In my theory of differentiated reform, every reform effort would be differentiated to mesh with the contexts of school communities, so that reform efforts meet schools where they are and assist them in making progress in variable currents, while remaining true to the ideology propelling the reform itself. Leaders of the effort would make decisions about the content of the reform—what participants at all levels will need to know and be able to do—based on the existing context of knowledge and skills. They would determine instructional methods—how to provide effective professional development and bring new believers into the fold—based on the context of ideology, commitment, and resources. Reform leaders would decide on entry and leverage points for advancing the reform—who should shepherd it, what relationships should be developed, how it should be presented—based on the power context.

I've been playing with this theory of differentiated reform while working on this chapter, turning and twisting it in my head like a Rubik's cube to consider its implications, downsides, and prospects. I don't know if it yet shows promise, but I know it gives me hope.

References

Carnegie Council on Adolescent Development. (1989). *Turning points: Preparing American youth for the 21st century.* Washington, DC: Author.

Council of Chief State School Officers (1992). *Turning Points: States in action.* Washington, DC: Author.

Davis, G.A. (1996). *Is everything old new again?: Influences on the evolution of the junior high school and the middle school.* Unpublished doctoral dissertation. University of North Carolina at Chapel Hill.

Fullan, M. (1993). *Change forces: Probing the depths of educational reform.* London: The Falmer Press.

Hargreaves, A., and Fullan, M. (1998). *What's worth fighting for out there?* New York: Teachers College Press.

Jackson, A.W., and Davis, G. A. (2000). *Turning points 2000: Educating adolescents in the 21st century.* New York: Teachers College Press.

Mertens, S.B., Flowers, N., and Mulhall, P. F. (1998 August). *The Middle Start Initiative, Phase I: A Longitudinal Analysis of Michigan Middle-Level Schools.* Champaign, IL: Center for Prevention Research and Development, University of Illinois.

Middle Grade School State Policy Initiative. (1999 August). [Transcript of discussion during MGSSPI directors' meeting.] Unpublished raw data.

Mizell, M.H. (1999, December 6). *What key reformers have learned about reform.* Remarks at the annual conference of the National Staff Development Council, Dallas, Texas.

Noblit, G.W. (1987). Ideological purity and variety in effective middle schools. In G.W. Noblit and W.T. Pink (Eds.), *Schooling in social context: Qualitative studies* (pp. 203–217). Norwood, NJ: Ablex.

Oakes, J., Quartz, K. H., Ryan, S., and Lipton, M. (2000). Civic virtue and the reform mill: The struggle for schools that are as good as they are efficient. *Education Week, 19*(24), 68–43.

Sarason, S. (1990). *The predictable failure of educational reform: Can we change course before it's too late?* San Francisco: Jossey Bass.

Tomlinson, C.A. (1999). *The differentiated classroom: Responding to the needs of all learners.* Alexandria, VA: Association for Supervision and Curriculum Development.

Tyack, D., and Cuban, L. (1995). *Tinkering toward utopia: A century of public school reform.* Cambridge, MA: Harvard University Press.

U.S. Department of Education. (1997). *Special strategies for educating disadvantaged children: Final report.* (Contract #LC90010001). Cambridge, MA: Abt Associates, Inc.

Whitford, B.L. (1987). Effects of organizational context on program implementation. In. G.W. Noblit and W.T. Pink (Eds.), *Schooling in social context: Qualitative studies* (pp. 93–118). Norwood, NJ: Ablex.

Note

1. The School Improvement Self-Study is a data collection system consisting of a set of surveys completed by teachers, principals, students, and parents in a school. The results of the surveys are reported to the school for use in planning and monitoring school improvement efforts.

13

Coming Together to Raise Our Children: Community and the Reinvented Middle School

KIM K. RUEBEL
Georgia Southern University

An old African saying states, "It takes the whole village to educate a child," a message that should be embraced by all middle level educators. It is necessary for schools, families, and communities to become more collaborative in sharing the role of educating young adolescents. (Clark and Clark 1994; Davies 1991; Bembry 1998)

Without a doubt, most of us would agree with the old African proverb; it is a phrase we often hear and repeat today. So often, in fact, people have begun to simply mention, "it takes a village," and leave it at that. Many leaders, politicians especially, have created a cliché, throwing out a seemingly simple message to our country; some of us are left asking if the message here is really that simple. It appears that many have not anticipated the bumpy ride ahead. As with much we see and hear in education, a top-down directive is dropped our way and we are left to figure out the details. We can, as has happened with many school/family/community partnerships, decide to use this metaphor for life in name only. This approach wouldn't be any different from the one many junior highs took in the transition toward a middle school. Digging up one sign and replacing it with another doesn't mean much in the long or short of it, but after a decade and a half of hard-hitting research and observation in the schools, common perceptions and ways of thinking are beginning to emerge concerning partnerships. The purpose of this chapter is fourfold: to discuss the impact of national, state, and local imperatives on family/school/community partnerships; to define the major aspects of these partnerships; to review many of the questions asked and answered through partnership research; and to share practices and programs that have worked well for schools. Much has been done to build the foundation for positive relationships among schools, parents, and community members and it is time to go beyond the boundaries that have been established.

Federal, state, and local imperatives for partnerships

> At the core of educative communities are schools. Why schools? Quite simply, because they are where the children are. (Bembry 1998, p. 18)

The research on school/family/community partnerships has strengthened by supporting and responding to a number of federal, state, and local reform initiatives and recommendations. *Goals 2000* recommends forming partnerships as a voluntary goal for all schools. *Turning Points, This We Believe,* and other highly-regarded research studies have also called for collaboration and communication between school and community (Epstein 1995). What became clear a few years ago (Epstein 1996a), and remains so as we enter the twenty-first century, is that school administrators, teachers, parents, students, and others in communities are increasingly working together to meet various mandates and guidelines which call for the development of partnerships and individualized programs and policies. It is important to review the language and nature of some of these imperatives.

Turning Points

Turning Points (Carnegie Council on Adolescent Development 1989) released a series of recommendations for middle level schools that have been a source for initial and continuing support of many reform efforts. One of the *Turning Points* recommendations, reengaging families in the education of young adolescents, calls for families and middle grade schools to join together through trust and respect if young adolescents are to succeed in school. This early initiative also reports some of the gloomy realities that we sometimes still face as students move out of elementary schools and into the secondary schools.

> Despite clearly documented benefits of parental involvement for students' achievement and attitudes toward school, parental involvement declines progressively during the elementary school years. . . . Many parents believe they should increasingly disengage from their young adolescents. Yet, while young adolescents need greater autonomy, they neither need nor desire a complete break with their parents and families. (p. 22)

Many middle schools do not encourage, and some actively discourage, parental involvement at school. Especially in low-income and minority neighborhoods, school personnel often consider parents to be part of the problem of educating young adolescents, rather than an important educational resource. (p. 22)

This We Believe

NMSA's position paper (*This We Believe* 1995) calls attention to the essentials of philosophy and practice, providing a list of characteristics of developmentally responsive schools. One of the overarching characteristics describing responsive middle level schools is the establishment of family and community partnerships. NMSA recognizes that families and community members are vital stakeholders in developmentally responsive middle level schools.

> Schools recognize and support families and community members as participants in school programs by encouraging their roles in supporting learning and honoring them as essential volunteers. Parents, families, and community members can enrich the curriculum and facilitate learning. The school takes the initiative in providing a wide variety of opportunities for parent and community involvement. (p. 17)

> . . . since school achievement is directly related to the degree of family support and involvement in the child's education, systematic, two-way communication with parents and families becomes especially critical. (p. 18)

> Schools should expect families and the community to take advantage of opportunities provided for involvement in support of education. Further, families should spend time sharing and engaging in their children's learning and modeling behaviors and skills essential for school success. (p. 18)

A Vision of Excellence

In *A Vision of Excellence* (McEwin, Dickinson, Erb, and Scales 1995), six areas of competence are described for the wise and experienced middle grades teacher. One of these areas of competence is families and community relations. This competency includes:

- the ability to build ever-expanding community involvement in the education of young adolescents;
- the ability to engage diverse community resources to further student academic and social learning;
- a thorough understanding of the role of family in a students' development;
- the ability to assist and support families in their young adolescent's education; and

- the ability to work with a range of community health providers, youth organizations, and social service agencies that deal with young adolescents and their families. (pp. 18–19)

The authors of this text further elaborated on the expectations of the middle level teacher:

Community and neighborhood organizations, social clubs, athletic teams, libraries, museums are all engaged in aspects of educating youth. Wise and experienced middle grades teachers are knowledgeable about their community and its educational opportunities and are able to build strong alliances and connections with community groups. With such connections to the community, they are able to draw on diverse community resources to support service learning and community service projects and otherwise enhance the curriculum for young adolescents. (p. 18)

The Eight-Year Study Revisited: Lessons from the Past for the Present

In 1998, a group of researchers (Lipka, Lounsbury, Toepfer, Vars, Alessi, and Kridel) revisited the Eight-Year Study to look at lessons learned and the pertinence of this long-term study for our continued learning. From 1934 to 1943, the Eight-Year Study was conducted in various school settings. Prior to the study, in 1930, the Commission on the Relation of School and College found that "our secondary schools did not prepare adequately for the responsibilities of community life" and that "traditional subjects of the curriculum had lost much of their vitality and significance" (p. 96).

As the Eight-Year Study progressed, the schools involved became closer with their communities and "more time was devoted to exploring the physical and human resources of the localities in which students lived" (Lipka et al. 1998, p. 106). Communities today are full of resources, allowing youth to do useful things in the adult world: participate in community projects, study community problems, or lend a helping hand to others outside of the school setting. The authors of this text remind us that service learning initiatives are now rediscovering the importance of building positive relationships between the school and community as well as teaching students to be active community members.

Federal Initiatives: Goals 2000 (1994), Partnerships for Family Involvement in Education (1998), and America Goes Back to School (1999)

On August 1, 1999, the U.S. Secretary of Education, Richard Riley, wrote a letter addressing school leaders (e.g., see web sites: http://www.pfie.ed.gov, http://www.ed.gov/G2K/community/99-08-sp.html). This letter encouraged schools "reach to families, communities, cultural and religious organizations, and businesses and colleges in your area to get involved in children's educa-tion." Riley further asked schools to invite these people and agencies to join in the school's partnership or create a new one to improve schools and connect more students with caring adults.

The Secretary of Education remarked, "research has found that children have better attendance records, complete more homework, achieve higher grades and test scores, and exhibit more positive attitudes and better behavior when their families are active in their education." Riley may have been a little overzealous in his understanding of the research, but positive correlations be-tween these areas and active family involvement have certainly been established by research on several occasions (Epstein 1995).

Riley goes on to review the Partnership for Family Involvement in Educa-tion (U.S. Department of Education 1998), which grew out of the *GOALS 2000* (U.S. Department of Education 1994) initiative. PFIE has helped to or-ganize thousands of events for schools and communities. *America Goes Back to School* (U.S. Department of Education 1999), however, is the most recent fed-eral initiative which focuses on helping students prepare for the future. Plan-ning back-to-school events, a major aspect of this initiative, is encouraged. Examples include:

- a breakfast discussion for families, community organizations, and stu-dents;
- teaming with local businesses for job-shadowing;
- organizing a family fair, with information booths for students and par-ents;
- joining with colleges to arrange a "Looking Ahead" night for parents and middle school and high school students;
- sponsoring a Dad's Club to involve fathers in schools through chaper-oning, maintenance, guest lectures, and tutoring;
- creating a parent resource room for support groups, meetings, materi-als, and research; and
- connecting with college alumni, civic clubs, or retired community members to develop a Saturday tutoring program.

Further reflections on imperatives for partnership development

David Seeley, the author of *Education Through Partnership* (1981), re-marked that reform depends on working on relationships with the home, com-munity groups, politicians, and business. Almost two decades later, Jones and Brader-Araje (1999, p. 42) echoed his sentiment: "realigning the focus of edu-cation to foster a community of learners can be a difficult task if traditional ed-ucational and philosophical foundations are not revisited and reinterpreted." The diversity and interworkings within systems make identifying and meeting the specific needs of each school a daunting task. However, initiating reform and building partnerships should occur simultaneously because both must be based on the context of the school, students, parents, and teachers themselves, as well as the particular community involved. Other successful programs may serve as a guiding example, but ultimately, every effort at school reform and partnerships should be distinct—designed to respond to the voices of that school community.

A number of documents and publications have been mentioned which focused recent attention on the connections among parents, communities, and the schools. These imperatives have grown out of public concerns. One concern is with the make-up and life of families. A second is the quality and quantity of preparation prior to entering school for children and parents who are not proficient speakers of English. Yet another concern is the recognition that schools and communities must join forces to provide resources for educational efforts. Furthermore, a new commitment to parent and community involvement in education and the strengthening of home learning for all parents is becoming evident in legislation and other imperatives (Rutherford 1995). Rutherford further describes these concerns:

> The diversity within families, communities, cultures, and economies, however, make uniform conceptualization of a school/parent/community partnership difficult. With no "typical" family structure, no "typical" family culture and values, and no "typical" economic status, it is difficult for schools or districts to define realistic expectations for home learning, parent and community support, or even constellations of activities that will meet the needs and fall within the abilities of both partners. (p. 26)

To make matters even more frustrating is the existence of differing perceptions on the part of each group regarding the definition of appropriate roles and relationships. While teachers and parents do agree that more involvement is important, they do not agree on the role of parents in governance or on the degree to which parents are interested and even willing to help their children at home (Rutherford 1995). Factors within the school setting itself may also limit involvement and skew perceptions. Departmentalized or very large schools, schools in perceivably unsafe areas, or even schools that have a confusing layout may prevent parents from coming on-site (Rutherford 1995).

Students themselves can influence family/school/community partnerships. During the early adolescent years, children change physically, mentally, and socially. They tend to seek more independence from their families while at the same time needing guidance as new and difficult challenges arise (NMSA 1995; George and Alexander 1993; Rutherford 1995). During these years, a sense of belonging to a community larger than school, family, and peer group emerges

(Manning 1993). Community service is a developmentally appropriate activity for young adolescents as they are already experiencing feelings of "altruism and idealism" (Manning 1993). During the initial stages of partnership development, this knowledge about students and school contexts should be considered.

These initial stages of development may elicit frustration because of the all-too-familiar notion that active involvement of parents as caretakers on a sustained basis in middle level schools is the exception, not the rule (Van Hoose and Legrand 2000). Involvement for most families decreases as their children progress from elementary to middle school despite studies illustrating the importance of parental involvement for adolescents' school success (Epstein 1992). Middle schools can help reverse this decline by developing comprehensive, permanent school, family, and community partnership programs (Sanders 1999). To accomplish this goal, staff must make a conscious effort to develop ongoing conversations, support, and services to adults with the goal of better serving the children and young adolescents in that community (Van Hoose and Legrand 2000). It is important to remember that establishing a relationship with all adults in the community, not just parents, is critical to being more effective with students. As Sanders (1999) puts it,

> The families and the community people are the ones who drive the image of the school. They're your spokespersons. The way people talk about the school outside is the impression that people will get forever. (p. 36)

Defining school/family/community partnerships

> The way schools care about children is reflected in the way schools care about children's families. (Epstein 1995, p. 1)

School/family/community partnerships

> Although more schools are recognizing the importance of such involvement, their numbers are still small. If further progress is to be made, there must be more widespread, meaningful change in the attitudes and practices of teachers and principals. Parents who do participate in the school feel useful, develop confidence in their relations with school staff, and are more likely to attend school activities, which signal to young adolescents the importance of education. (Carnegie Council on Adolescent Development 1996, p. 22)

When parents, teachers, students, and community members view each other as partners in education, a caring community develops around students (Epstein 1995). As probably the most notable researcher on this subject,

Epstein believes that in a partnership, teachers and administrators create a more family-like school, which "recognizes each child's individuality and makes each child feel special and included" (p. 2). The opposite is true of partnerships and parents, which create a more school-like family, which "recognizes that each child is also a student" (p. 2). Families can reinforce the importance of school and communities can create school-like opportunities that reinforce, recognize, and reward students. "The concept of a community school is reemerging. It refers to a place where programs and services for students, parents, and others are offered before, during, and after the regular school day" (p. 1).

Epstein has been a leading advocate for the development of family/school/community partnerships. Her work has helped to lay the groundwork for long lasting connections between schools and communities. Epstein (1995) devised a framework outlining six types of involvement:

- Parenting—refers to child-rearing skills, understanding of development, and supportive home conditions.
- Communicating—means school-to-home and home-to-school communications about school programs and students' progress.
- Volunteering—enables families and communities to give their time and talents to support schools, teachers, and children.
- Learning at home—refers to how families can help their children with learning at home.
- Decision making—allows families to participate in school decisions that affect their own or other children (e.g., representatives on action teams, PTAs, councils, committees, and other organizations).
- Collaborating with the community—facilitates cooperation and collaboration among schools, families, community groups, agencies, and individuals.

The six types of involvement can guide the development of a balanced, comprehensive program of partnership, including opportunities for family involvement at school and at home, with potentially important results for students, parents, and teachers. Epstein (1995) has also stated that the results for students, parents, and teachers will depend on the particular types of involvement that are implemented, as well as on the quality of implementation.

Developing a partnership: Forming committees and action teams

There are several important steps to take in the development of a partnership with programs of support. One of the first steps is to create an action team which can take responsibility for "assessing present practices, organizing options for new partnerships, implementing selected activities, evaluating next steps, and continuing to improve and coordinate practices for all six types of involvement" (Epstein, 1995, p. 6). Action teams should consist of teachers, administrators, students, parents, and community members and be further assisted by representatives of each group as well. The action team will have to ask a series of important questions addressing many concerns with regard to present strengths, needed changes, expectations of a partnership, knowledge or awareness of community, and links to future goals. These questions and answers should be used to form a long-term plan with an outline of steps, roles and responsibilities, costs, and evaluation.

The Action Team guides the development and implementation of a comprehensive program of partnership in each school. This team also "monitors all school, family, and community connections to identify and describe the school's program of partnership and to note progress in reaching all families" (Epstein 1996a, p. 6). Epstein (1996a) provides many reasons to develop good school, family, and community connections:

- to improve school programs and school climate;
- to provide family services and support;
- to increase parents' skills and leadership in school matters;
- to connect families with others in the school and in the community;
- to help teachers with their work; and
- to increase ownership and commitment to the school by the community (p. 1).

The foremost reason for better communications and exchanges among schools, families, and community groups is to assist students at all grade levels to succeed in school and in life. As noted earlier, different purposes require distinct practices in comprehensive programs (Epstein 1996a).

These first steps, creating forums for discussion and planning, are vital. Epstein (1996a), among others, has found that the most effective families, schools, and communities had shared goals and missions concerning children's learning and development. Communication between teachers and families increases understanding and cooperation between the school and the home and shows students that their teachers and parents are working together on shared goals to help them succeed in school (Sanders 1999).

Youth programs

Youth programs allow students to become aware of life opportunities that are available to them (Sanders 1999). These programs can take on many forms, including in-school and out-of-school experiences. Later in this chapter, many different examples of youth programs and service learning opportunities are reviewed. The key to establishing worthwhile programs is to involve students in the planning process. Dundon (1999/2000) tells us that students should know that we are there to find out more about them and to hear who they are and what they care about. The simple act of asking students has power and the conversation itself increases enthusiasm (Dundon 1999/2000).

The most relevant and appropriate youth service programs, like partnerships, are developed at the local school setting, based on needs and resources. "Service strengthens the school program when activities reflect the school curriculum" (Manning 1993, p. 72). Young people left on their own or only with peers have a significantly greater chance of becoming involved in high-risk behaviors than their counterparts involved in activities under responsible adult guidance (Carnegie Council on Adolescent Development 1996, p. 36). Youth programs are effective when they are safe, open to all students, and supported by parents and community members (Carnegie Council on Adolescent Development 1996). Early intervention from trained and committed individuals is necessary to help prevent destructive behaviors because once they reach high school these youths are often beyond effective intervention (Bembry 1998, p. 20).

Service learning

> For most young adolescents, the feeling of belonging to a community that offers mutual aid and a sense of common purpose, whether it is found in their families, schools, neighborhoods, houses of worship, or youth organizations, has been compromised. Young people from all economic strata often find themselves alone in communities where there are few adults to turn to and hardly a safe place to go. (Carnegie Council on Adolescent Development 1996, p. 36)

Learning out in the community, particularly through providing service to others, offers unique experiences for middle level students to extend learning that occurs in the school setting (Clark and Clark 1994). Service learning is a powerful tool that helps students gain and refine academic and social skills and knowledge as they engage in service to meet real community needs. Service learning encompasses more than community service projects alone. "It combines carefully structured educational components with real world service experience" (Fertman, White, and White 1996, p. 50). Through self-discovery and service to others, students learn who they are, while developing empathy, compassion, and democratic values. Later in this chapter, many types and examples of service learning are reviewed.

Establishing roles

Although partnerships may look different, there are critical roles that parents and community members should take in the education of their children. According to Rutherford (1995), there are three major roles. First and foremost, the parent is and should remain the primary resource for the child. Second, parents and community members can support and become advocates for school restructuring. Third, parents and community members are participants in the education of all children. This final role is played out in action teams and other communication forums and invitations for dialogue and service.

Through these three major roles, parent and community involvement in middle grades school restructuring is likely. Additional actions are necessary (Rutherford 1995, pp. 38–39) to support involvement such as a clear, welcoming parent involvement policy, and a school commitment to advisory programs in which every child has at least one adult who knows him or her well. In addition, the school office should be open and friendly, parent-to-parent events should be sponsored, and a full-time parent contact person needs to be in charge of bringing parents and school together. Rutherford (1995) also suggests that a parent room should be established somewhere in the school building.

With a clearly defined partnership in hand, established roles, and additional support materials and training available, parents can

- become primary educational resources for their children;
- become supporters and/or advocates for children through site-based school restructuring efforts; and
- participate in the development and implementation of district programs that support partnerships (p. 49).

Parent communication forums work well to get parents involved in the life of the school. Lipsitz (1984) found that an action team or other teacher/parent/community member advisory committee can become a successful entity that "scotches rumors, advocates for the school at board meetings and for parents at school meetings, and advises the administration about issues of current concern in the school" (Clark and Clark 1994, p. 155). Hargreaves and Fullan (1998) caution, however, that "professional collaboration is no longer sufficient. Teachers who work with other teachers are sometimes less inclined to work with anyone else. Collaboration can include the school professional but exclude the wider community. And when families, communities and workplaces are changing as rapidly and dramatically as they are today, this flaw can be fatal" (p. 4).

Home learning

Home learning is the activity, or set of activities, that parents and family members may engage in to help their children succeed academically (Rutherford 1995). Middle school teachers and administrators must look beyond the school and actively engage parents and the community in the education of young adolescents (Clark and Clark 1994). In order to improve home learning practices, Rutherford addresses several important factors. First, well-developed local practices for home learning must be established. Information regarding the appropriate home learning environment should be provided to parents. Beyond being informative, teachers must be willing to build on parent strengths. Ongoing recruitment of parent involvement may be necessary during the time in which schools develop effective strategies for promoting home learning which can be provided to parents through workshops or newsletters.

Benefits of family/school/community partnerships

> With frequent interactions between schools, families, and communities, more students are likely to receive common messages from various people about the importance of school, of working hard, of thinking creatively, of helping one another, and of staying in school. (Epstein 1995, p. 2)

Programs that involve parents and community members provide many benefits to students and teachers (Clarke and Clarke 1994, pp. 158–159). Students gain long-term support from parents and other adults while teachers have a partner to support learning at school. Teachers can share common goals with parents regarding education; becoming partners can make a teacher's job become easier and sometimes more successful. When students receive help at home, they often become more skilled and knowledgeable, developing a more positive attitude in general. Teachers can further enjoy these improvements with added help from trained tutors and volunteers. Students receive a better education when schools, parents, and communities share the responsibility for education. This type of involvement reduces teacher burdens, isolation, and stress.

What happens now

The traditionally identified needs of adolescents such as self-exploration, self-definition, positive interaction with peers and adults, and physical activity (George and Alexander 1993; Jones and Brader-Araje 1999) lay a foundation upon which a school's educational philosophy should be created. "Maintaining a focus on the community keeps the child as central, respect as a given and voice as vital" (Jones and Brader-Araje 1999, p. 43). There are many further ideas and suggestions for involvement of parents and community members.

Van Hoose and Legrand (2000) suggest afternoon tutoring, fund-raising activities to provide materials and resources, and an increased cultural awareness for all. Some schools have considered implementing narrative forms of assessment or a nongraded system altogether in place of traditional grading systems to help make expectations, learning outcomes, and performances clear. An increase in student self-confidence and awareness of achievement can lead to self-evaluation. This skill, the ability to assess one's own performance and see the bigger picture, can help students become more viable members of the community.

There are several reasons why schools need to connect more effectively with the wider world beyond them (Hargreaves and Fullan 1998). "Schools cannot shut their gates and leave the outside world on the doorstep" (Hargreaves and Fullan 1998, p. 7). Schools must go beyond the boundaries of the classroom; we can no longer pretend that the walls will keep the outside world in check. In 1997, Elkind said that schools have become porous and permeable institutions. What's out there, beyond the classroom, for teachers, "stares back at them through the eyes of the students they teach" (Hargreaves et al. 1998, p. 7). The question left to answer is not whether teachers connect; it's how effectively they do just that.

Another reason to connect with the wider world is that "more diversity demands greater flexibility" (Hargreaves et al. 1998, p. 7). Making a few adjustments here and there for culture and language differences is not enough to serve a diverse student population. Every child has a life, a story, which often causes disengagement from learning. Teachers have the difficult job of trying to enter the student's world. The need for flexibility in teaching is overwhelming.

Ranking right up there with a growing diversity in our schools is the influx of technology. "The technology juggernaut is breaking down the walls of schooling." Hargreaves and Fullan (1998, p. 8) report that forty percent of people in America have access to a personal computer at home. With the still successful economy, Americans are spending more now than ever, and we know that number is growing. The use of TV, video, and music CDs is especially ubiquitous among adolescents. New, and not so new, technologies can allow students to connect with peers, adults, and actually, other worlds. Computers and other forms of multimedia will ultimately do more good than harm. With guidance and training of students and parents, learning and networking at home have limitless possibilities. We now know technology is and will be a part of our world; the most important consideration is how we will respond.

Many adults outside of schools believe that "schools are one of our last hopes for rescuing and reinventing community" (Hargreaves et al. 1998, p. 9). Modernization of the world is replacing traditional norms and values. Science and technology offer spic and span solutions for disease, travel, home life, and even learning. Community gatherings and organizations have seemed to decline in attendance while suburbs are bursting at the seams. Our inner cities still exist, left behind, in a fast-moving superhighway of growth and advances. "The neighborhood school is the most obvious focus for community building efforts" (Hargreaves et al. 1998, p. 10). "Teachers can do with more help; and so can parents and communities" (Hargreaves and Fullan 1998, p. 10). This point has been made a number of times already in this chapter. A reciprocal relationship should be established between the school and community. We have the shared responsibility of educating our children.

Building communities within schools is essential because "education is essential for democracy. Family is not always the best metaphor for community" (Hargreaves and Fullan 1998, p. 13). Schools should build democratic communities which value participation, equality, inclusiveness, and social justice, in addition to loyalty and service among all members. "These communities should start in the classroom where students share responsibility for their own learning and for regulating each other's behavior. Involving students and parents in . . . teaching and learning decisions, parent conferences and assessment of achievement extend these democratic principles" (p. 13).

"Schools can no longer be indifferent to what kinds of living and working await their students when they move into the adult world. When students leave school or even university, there is no immediate work for many of them anymore, or the work is very different than it used to be. Restructuring and downsizing are pervasive" (p. 17). If we want "closer connections between school and work, we should advocate partnerships with industry, corporate investment in education, business involvement in curriculum, more student placements on work experience, put more emphasis on the skills that business requires, and restructure management and organization of schooling among similar lines to the restructuring that has taken place elsewhere" (p. 18).

Creating good practice

Criteria for successful involvement programs include a variety of key players and resources. The key players include teachers, students, parents, administrators and other school leaders, support staff, and business and community leaders. Key resources include, but are not limited to, time, funding, personnel, training, communication, and coordination. In general, Epstein (1995) notes that successful middle grades school/family partnerships are supported through well-developed policies at the school, district, state, and federal levels. Trends and factors specific to middle grades should be given priority in the design, plan, and implementation of these programs. Parents, families, and community members should be used in appropriate roles through home learning, school restructuring activities, and district-wide involvement programs. Schools must employ frequent, varied, two-way communication and value the roles of key players, such as parents, teachers, school personnel, and community members. Furthermore, schools must provide sufficient physical, human, and fiscal resources and training, as well as attempt to measure student, parent, teacher, school, and district outcomes through both formative and summative evaluation methods (Epstein 1995).

Characteristics of successful programs include gradual, yet consistent and continual progress, a clear connection to curriculum and instruction, and a reconsideration of staff and professional development (Epstein 1995). Fertman, White, and White (1996) provide sample service activities including peer tutors, peer mentoring, conflict mediation, drug and alcohol awareness, senior companions, hunger awareness programs, creek reclamation, and animal adoption to name a few. The outcomes of these activities include personal efficacy, a sense of responsibility, exploration of new roles, moral development, healthy risk-taking, critical thinking, concern for others, civic participation, and basic communication skills.

Straight from the schools: Examples of partnerships in action

This final section puts all of the initiatives, definitions, and criteria into action. What follows is a collection of school/family/community partnerships in action. These are good examples of service learning, dialogue, and parent and community involvement. However, these schools are merely examples. They provide a springboard for schools, families, and communities to design their own distinct programs and partnerships.

Sanders (1999) described a positive student response to using parents as attendance monitors. "When the kids found out that their parents were coming to school volunteering, there was a big turnaround. And, it wasn't just fear, some of the students were proud that their parents were a part of the school" (parent quote, p. 38). This same type of belongingness was found by Jones and Brader-Araje (1999) when they visited the Carolina Friends School. This school has joined together an understanding of adolescent development with Quaker beliefs to create a "community that values the contributions of young people as well as various ideals including cooperation, responsibility, and conversation" (p. 42).

Each day at the Carolina Friends School begins with a coming together of the school community for a ten-minute quiet time. As unusual as that may sound, it works for these folks and students rarely disrupt the peaceful start of each new day. At the Friends School,

> Parents have an open invitation to voice their concerns, suggestions, and support. Students also have a variety of opportunities in which their voices can be heard. Business meetings are often held in which students can participate in conversation with school faculty . . . students can 'speak into the silence' if there is a personal or community concern a child would like to voice, and even the structuring of the school day is decided in conjunction with student input. (p. 43)

Less philosophical and more basic restructuring was found by Rutherford (1995) in the parent involvement programs in McAllen, Texas. These programs originally centered around Chapter 1, bilingual education, and migrant funding. Now that parent involvement is a district-wide goal, community efforts have increased greatly. Each school has its own school/family/community partnership program, while many of the services provided to parents are funded at the district level. Practices in the McAllen schools include two planning periods a day for middle school teachers during which they may communicate with parents or go on home visits. Administrators volunteer to teach classes in support of these practices. There is also a weekly radio program, *Discusiones Escolares,* encouraging parent involvement.

Indianapolis, Indiana, has also developed a parent involvement program that focuses on two-way communication allowing parents to stay in touch with the school and become partners with it in the education of their children (Rutherford 1995). Parents in Touch centers around conferences, folders, student/teacher/parent (STP) contracts, and weekly calendars. Conference hours have been adjusted to accommodate working parents and offer materials on parenting, one of Epstein's six frameworks for partnerships.

At the well-known Shoreham-Wading River Middle School (Fertman et al. 1996; Lipsitz 1984), one student says it all: "They absolutely know me here" (Lipsitz 1984, p. 129). Every student at this middle school (e.g., the name has now changed) is involved in at least one service-learning unit. Students are bussed to sites for career exploration, work with mentally challenged students or the elderly, or even work at local libraries or Head Start Programs. There are many varieties of these six to ten week units. In 1984, Lipsitz commented that "in its commitment to service, Shoreham-Wading River Middle School is responding to what they and many social observers have concluded about the role of youth in American society" (p. 136). Just as Epstein has been a leader of substantial research on school/family/community partnerships, this middle school has been a shining example of service learning in the schools.

Davies (1991) describes Schools Reaching Out, a national project which includes three practices developed within the project's demonstration schools. Parent centers, home visitors, and action research teams have been successfully implemented at these schools and include paid coordinators, breakfast meetings, school stores, pamphlets, action plans, and face-to-face communication to name a few.

Manning (1993) cited several successful programs. Whittier Middle School in Sioux Falls, South Dakota, is "known for its community service and volunteerism, the school collected 14,000 pounds of food for the local food pantries, raised $15,000 for charity and $25,000 for March of Dimes through Walk-American programs" (p. 73). Manning also mentioned the Magic Me program in Maryland that pairs middle school students with nursing home residents, and the Lutheran Brotherhood's social studies program, Speak for Yourself, which encourages seventh and eighth graders to reflect on current issues and share opinions with government leaders.

Bembry (1998) described Project SUCCESS, which "has demonstrated for more than six years that institutions can overcome the formidable obstacles of historical antagonisms, organizational pluralism, and differing values and goals" (p. 22). This partnership has also provided service opportunities for middle schools in local nursing homes. Students must first participate in intensive training sessions where they are put in situations in which they can experience some of the debilitating situations the elderly live with every day. The students then commit to weekly visits for anywhere from one to three years.

Finally, Cale (1990) put together ideas and materials for teachers, parents, and administrators for use for parent involvement planning. This handbook includes benefits, how to involve parents, ways parents would like to be involved, as well as information on families today. Included are questionnaires, checklists, ideas, and references.

Conclusion

One of the overarching characteristics describing responsive middle level schools is the establishment of family and community partnerships. Each and every effort at school reform and partnerships should be distinct—designed to respond to the voices of that school community. It is important to remember that involvement for most families decreases as their children progress from elementary to middle school despite studies illustrating the importance of parental involvement for adolescents' school success (Epstein 1992). Middle schools can help reverse this decline by developing comprehensive, permanent school, family, and community partnership programs (Sanders 1999).

To accomplish this goal, staff must make a conscious effort to develop ongoing dialogue, support, and services to adults with the goal of better serving the children and young adolescents in that community (Van Hoose and Legrand 2000). It is also important to remember that establishing a relationship with all adults in the community, not just parents, is critical to being more effective with students. When parents, teachers, students, and community members view each other as partners in education, a caring community develops around students (Epstein 1995). Many studies have found that the most effective families, schools, and communities have shared goals and missions concerning children's learning and development.

Communication between teachers and families increases understanding and cooperation between the school and the home and shows students that their teachers and parents are working together on shared goals to help them succeed in school (Sanders 1999). Successful middle grades school/family partnerships are supported through well-developed policies at the school, district, state, and federal levels (Eptsein 1995). Trends and factors specific to middle grades should be given priority in the design, plan, and implementation of these programs. Parents, families, and community members should be used in appropriate roles through home learning, school restructuring activities, and district-wide involvement programs. Schools must employ frequent, varied, two-way communication and value the roles of key players, such as students, parents, teachers, school personnel, and community members.

References

Bembry, J.X. (1998). Forming an educative community in the village. *Middle School Journal, 30*(1), 18–24.

Cale, L. (1990). *Planning for parent involvement: A handbook for administrators, teachers, and parents.* Phoenix, AZ: Author.

Carnegie Council on Adolescent Development. (1989). *Turning points: Preparing American youth for the 21st century.* New York: Carnegie Corporation.

Carnegie Council on Adolescent Development. (1996). *Great transitions: Preparing adolescents for a new century.* New York: Carnegie Corporation.

Clark, S.N., and Clark, D.C. (1994). *Restructuring the middle level school: Implications for school leaders.* Albany, NY: State University of New York Press.

Davies, D. (1991). Schools reaching out: Family, school and community partnerships for students' success. *Phi Delta Kappan, 72*, 376–382.

Dundon, B.L. (1999/2000). My voice: An advocacy approach to service learning. *Educational Leadership, 57*(4), 34–37.

Elkind, D. (1997). Schooling in the postmodern world. In A. Hargreaves (Ed.), *Rethinking educational change with heart and mind* (pp. 27–42). Alexandra, VA: Association for Supervisions and Curriculum Development.

Epstein, J.L. (1988). How do we improve programs for parent involvement? *Educational Horizon, 66*(2), 58–59.

Epstein, J.L. (1992). School and family partnerships. In M. Alkin (Ed.), *Encyclopedia of educational research* (6th ed., pp. 1139–1151). New York: Macmillan.

Epstein, J.L. (1995). School/family/community partnerships. *Phi Delta Kappan, 7*(9), 701–712.

Epstein, J.L. (1996a). Advances in family, community, and school partnerships. *New Schools, New Communities, 12*(3), 5–13.

Fertman, C.I., White, G.P., and White, L.J. (1996). *Service learning in the middle school: Building a culture of service.* Columbus, OH: National Middle School Association.

George, P.S., and Alexander, W.M. (1993). *The exemplary middle school,* (2nd ed.) Fort Worth, TX: Harcourt Brace College Publishers.

Hargreaves, A., and Fullan, M. (1998). *What's worth fighting for out there?* New York: Teachers College Press.

Jones, M.G., and Brader-Araje, L. (1999). Middle schools are communities of many voices. *Middle School Journal, 31*(2), 42–48.

Lipka, R.P., Lounsbury, J.H., Toepfer, C.F., Vars, G.F., Alessi, S.P., and Kridel, G.

(1998). *The eight-year study revisited: Lessons from the past for the present.* Columbus, OH: National Middle School Association.

Lipsitz, J. (1984). *Successful schools for young adolescents.* New Brunswick, NJ: Transaction Books.

Manning, M.L. (1993). *Developmentally appropriate middle level schools.* Wheaton, MD: Childhood Educational International.

McEwin, C.K., Dickinson, T.S., Erb, T.O., and Scales, P.C. (1995). *A vision of excellence: Organizing principles for middle grades teacher preparation.* Chapel Hill, NC: Center for Early Adolescence and Columbus, OH: National Middle School Association.

National Middle School Association (1995). *This we believe.* Columbus, OH: NMSA.

Rutherford, B. (Ed.). (1995). *Creating family/school partnerships.* Columbus, OH: National Middle School Association.

Sanders, M.G. (1999). Improving school, family, and community partnerships in urban middle schools. *Middle School Journal, 31*(2), 35–41.

Seeley, D.S. (1981). *Educating through partnerships: Mediating structures and education.* Cambridge, MA: Ballinger.

U.S. Department of Education. (1998). *Partnership for family involvement in education.* URL address: http://pfie.ed.gov/. U.S. Department of Education.

U.S. Department of Education. (1999). *Community update.* URL address: http://www.ed.gov/G2K/community/99-08-sp.html. U.S. Department of Education.

Van Hoose, J., and Legrand, P. (2000). It takes parents, the whole village, and school to raise the children. *Middle School Journal, 31*(3), 32–37.

14

Engineering Success through Purposeful Articulation

JEANNEINE P. JONES
University of North Carolina at Charlotte

Tony and Ben haunted me for years because they were classic examples of children who'd gotten the short end of life. Both came from homes where alcohol was more important than kids and where if you stepped in the way of a good time, well, you just might get the whipping of your life. Both had younger siblings they were determined to protect, even if that meant lying their rear ends off. Both came to school every day exhausted, Tony mean and Ben silently begging for a hug. Both had simply seen a little too much of the ugly side of life.

Those boys were in my eighth grade classroom during the same year, and what a year that was. A person can make the decision to quit school in North Carolina at age sixteen, and they were counting the days until their spring birthdays. The decision to drop out of formal education made sense to them because they were sure of only one thing: real life didn't include school.

Those boys taught me one of my most valuable lessons about teaching, that all the good intentions in the world can't make a world of difference. Instead, it takes purposeful work among all the school's adults to even begin to undo what a lifetime of hurt has done, and those adults don't include just the grade levels represented by the middle school, either. They include every teacher, every counselor, every administrator, every school person who has ever touched the lives of the children involved, from kindergarten to grade twelve and beyond to the university. That's called articulation, and like the word implies, it has to be clear and strong and precise.

Both Tony and Ben were repeaters, those kids who've been in eighth grade for a year already, so it was no wonder that my partner was dismayed when I told her that I'd volunteered our two-person team as the site for their second try. *She* haunted me for the next ten months and with good reason; we failed those boys miserably for the better part of that year and that failure took just about all of our energy.

Our team—and our school—worked and worked well, so my intentions were good, just not well informed and certainly not well supported. Our district really did nothing to smooth the transition between eighth grade and that first year in high school, so we knew deep down that we could work with those kids until our hearts fell out but once they left eighth grade, well, that was basically it. They left. Period.

My team partner and I kept those two boys in school until the end of the year, and we were frankly proud of that fact; it was an accomplishment. After they left, we spent a lot of long hours discussing the "what ifs" of the situation: What if the high school had . . . What if we had also . . . What if their parents . . . What if Tony and Ben . . . What if our school . . . What if the district . . . What if we had simply known more and been better prepared for them? All that's to say that we spent a lot of time pushed to the emotional edge on their account, and to this day we've never quite gotten over them.

Those two boys opened up holes in my own preparation that were as big as craters and I've been determined to fill them in ever since. I've found a strong research base that translates into successful transitions for the Bens and the Tonys and the thousands of other kids who aren't quite so obvious in their academic, social, and emotional needs. This chapter is a small attempt to share with you some of the many things that I've learned on their behalf.

The need for purposeful articulation

From the initial experiences of elementary school

As became clear to me, there is no argument about the importance of a smooth and purposeful transition from elementary into middle school and from middle into high school. Educational scholars emphasize that schools must acknowledge the potential stress, and benefits, of transitioning from one level of schooling to the next if they are to be successful places for students.

In terms of elementary school, for instance, Schoffner and Williamson (2000) remind us that moving into middle school is not only a rite of passage into early adolescence, but that it is also a new stage of schooling. Gone are the five or six years of comfortable relationships and routines enjoyed in elementary school, and introduced instead are varying levels of academic rigor, larger teams of both students and teachers, and unexpected relationships with unknown peers who merge from the surrounding feeder schools. These very changes often lead students to the impression that they are academically and socially less able than they once were; therefore, they give up on themselves and their schooling more readily because they think there's no adult in the building who really knows them well. This in turn initiates a downward spiral in overall achievement that must be specifically counteracted by the middle school they are entering (Midgley and Urdan 1992; Mac Iver 1990).

Others clarify these thoughts with students' voices. In one example, Odegaard and Heath (1992) surveyed 225 elementary students about the things that made the students most anxious concerning their upcoming transition to middle school. They responded with issues like getting lost or being late to class, being in contact with older and possibly rougher students, and facing heavier homework assignments. Brighton (in McAdoo 1999) echoes this, noting that many students entering middle school actually worry as much over academics as they do over peer relationships, contrary to what many middle school teachers assume. Weldy (1991) adds more specifics from a three-year demonstration project with Indiana students. He found that they also worry about different grading standards, less help from teachers, more stressful examinations, adjusting to new rules, having less time to spend with friends and family, and more complex schedules.

Parents of elementary students share these same concerns (Kaiser 1995) and fear that among other things, their children will be swallowed by the sheer size of the building and the volume of people moving through it. Yet others (Weldy 1991; Midgley and Urdan 1992) add that parents also worry about unreasonably high expectations and standards, the teachers' unwillingness to extend extra help, punitive policies on class attendance, inflexibility from the school's adults, the complexity of the work taught and assigned, and the increasing influence of peer pressure on academic achievement.

On the other hand, students also volunteer many things that provide sources of excitement and great anticipation for them, including personal lockers, different teachers across the day, changing classes, eating in the cafeteria, a comprehensive athletic program, and making new friends (Odegaard and Heath 1992).

When we consider this information, two things become clear in terms of the transition from elementary to middle school:

First, students like Tony, Ben, and all of their peers come into the middle grades without having made a major adjustment to the concept of formal schooling since kindergarten. However, unlike then, this particular adjustment occurs during a life-changing period of enormous physical and emotional development with which they must also grapple. Unlike then as well, there is often less adult guidance from parents and teachers, as both push students toward more responsible and independent scholarly attitudes, and as the young teens themselves become less available because of time spent outside the home with friends. Unfortunately, as with Tony and Ben, some students also realize the negative impact that their parents can have on them, and they suddenly discount those adults, a decision that leaves them more alone than others.

Exacerbating the entire problem is a lack of coping skills that many young adolescents have yet to cultivate because of fewer life experiences.

All told, the result can be an incoming group of middle school students who actually begin those years excited, yes, but also insecure, misinformed, and even frightened to varying degrees. Without a purposeful articulation plan that addresses this dilemma, these children may well go through their entire middle school careers with the problem hidden rather than addressed. This can, in turn, ensure declining academic achievement throughout the remainder of their educational careers.

Second, a smooth transition into the middle grades from elementary school can serve as a precursor to a successful high school transition. In schools with purposeful plans, students will have made the initial adjustment once and maintained the flow throughout their middle grades years. They are therefore better prepared to extend the experience into the next four years of their educational careers. Healthy high schools recognize this extended experience as both an opportunity and a necessity, and they articulate fluently with the middle schools that provide their ninth grade populations.

Into the adult world of high school

Just as children abandon comfortable elementary buildings for the unknown world of middle school, they later leave the now secure environment of those same middle schools and again enter the unknown: high school. Purposeful articulation between the educators in both buildings is once again critical for student success, and as we've learned through our experiences with Tony and Ben, perhaps even more so now because of the immediate potential to quit school all together.

Ninth grade is a particularly challenging year for young adolescents for a variety of reasons. Most are either through those initial developmental changes or close to closure, and they now face new horizons which invite them to respond to their new interests; for example: increased mobility, exciting new peer circles, less parent restrictions, and more campus social opportunities. Juxtaposed to this is an unprecedented year of academic seriousness, one that demands success with difficult coursework required for high school graduation four years later. Without specific guidance, most students are simply too immature to integrate their new social freedom and interests with these heavy academic requirements.

Researchers focusing on the ninth grade year agree with both the difficulty of this grade and the serious attention that it must receive, particularly in light of potential school dropouts. For example, studies suggest that several things happen during this year that can be irreversible if some measure of programmatic attention is not devoted to the situations.

First, there is clearly a link between a difficult transition during ninth grade and the likelihood that a student will quit school (Hertzog, Morgan, Diamond, and Walker 1996; George 1995; Kadel 1994; Jett, Pulling, and Ross 1994; Marshall 1992). Specifically, the following have been suggested as accurate predictors of potential dropouts: the number of school absences during the eighth grade year, and poor performance during both the eighth and ninth grades; obvious difficulties in the adjustment to ninth grade; and low incidences of participation in school activities (Hertzog, Morgan, Diamond, and Walker 1996).

Further, administrators from the Austin, Texas Independent School District (as reported by Kadel 1994), in an effort to understand declining ninth grade achievement scores, found the following true of their ninth graders:

- More students were retained in this grade than any other.
- More ninth graders were absent on any given school day than any other grade.
- More disciplinary action was required of these students than any others.
- Half of all ninth graders in their district took home at least one failing grade every marking period.
- More students dropped out during this grade level than any other.

Encouraging educators to be proactive, George (1995) echoes these as on-going indicators of students in potential trouble:

- Poor attendance
- Increased discipline problems
- Failing grades
- The inability to match the expectations of the new level of schooling
- Complaints from parents and/or students
- A lack of articulated curriculum between grade levels
- A lack of communication across levels

Finally, young adolescents entering grade nine are doing so after a full year of being the equivalent of seniors in their middle schools. Suddenly, a brief summer break has plunged them from the top of the order to the bottom. This abrupt change is understandably traumatic for many students and can, in fact, result in their having negative feelings about their physical bodies, their readiness to accept responsibility through part-time employment, their appeal to the opposite sex, their behavior patterns, and even how much they like themselves in general (Hertzog, Morgan, Diamond, and Walker 1996).

Though the need for some type of transitional intervention is obvious, there is generally less focus on this type of program in the move from middle to high school than there is from elementary. Perhaps the assumption is once again that students are more mature by then and can self-initiate some of the concentrated focus that they need for a healthy adjustment. Maybe parents and teachers in the high school believe that the middle school is handling the transition, and vice versa. Perhaps an outward appearance of social poise on the part of some students is simply mistaken for sophistication and happiness. Maybe good academic records in eighth grade precede ninth graders and their high school teachers don't pay a lot of attention to the "what ifs" because they expect that flow of scholarly productivity to continue.

No matter what the desire and the wish list, the results are simply not there in those schools and districts without purposeful transition programs. Instead, as I learned through poor planning and bad experience, Tony and Ben and even their more academically inclined friends often drift through grade nine, setting themselves on a course from which they may never recover academically, socially, or emotionally. This too often causes them to give up and get out, a result that America simply can't afford.

An illustration

So how do we address this dilemma? Charlotte Mecklenburg Schools (CMS) provide a solid initial response to that question; they would certainly have been better prepared than my system for Ben and Tony and the millions like them enrolled in schools across the country. The teachers within this huge district work tenaciously to ensure an effective transition for all children who need guidance beyond that provided within a regular classroom setting, and their efforts are working.

CMS is the twenty-third largest system in the United States, hosting approximately ninety elementary schools, twenty-eight middle schools, fourteen high schools, and seven middle and high alternative schools. Further, 7,000 employees work daily with about 101,000 students, all of which increases the difficulty of consistently implementing anything new. Articulation programs are in place and working, however, with special target audiences of about 9,000 fifth graders who transition into the middle schools and about 8,000 to 10,000 eighth graders who move into the high schools during the school year.

One illustration of a successful transition program employed in the district is AVID, or Advancement Via Individual Determination. Part of a national network, AVID is a college preparatory program designed to specifically prepare average middle and high school students for the possibility of college. Like other systems, however, CMS uses the opportunities presented by AVID to target not only average achievers, but those who lack motivation or who could simply use the extra support prior to leaving middle and entering high school.

For example, many of the middle schools have AVID classes in sixth, seventh, and eighth grades to prepare students for the heavier content requirements of high school. These same AVID students then move into ninth grade with continued support, though this is gradually replaced with more student responsibilities as the ninth graders ease out into more demanding classes in later grades. Topics for exploration and application within the class period include such things as study skills, note taking, self-discipline, goal setting, personal development, writing, and organization. In addition, students enjoy guest speakers who discuss topics like best sellers from popular booklists, career options, high school registration, and high school life.

Many of these same AVID topics and objectives are found in the district's Freshman Focus, a semester-long course that all high schoolers must take during their ninth grade year. This program deals specifically with eighth graders' transition to the next grade, and stresses such things as study skills, reading skills, and character education.

A third illustration from CMS is vertical teaming, a program that has only recently been implemented within the district. Vertical teaming is a collaborative effort between teachers to provide a continuum of skills building from one grade to the next. As such, it involves teachers from grades six through twelve meeting regularly to discuss issues pertaining to their common content. For example, seven CMS English teachers representing those grade levels meet to discuss topics such as the state's Standard Course of Study, developmental characteristics of students within those age levels, enriching literacy proficiency, and tailoring instructional strategies to meet increased levels of curriculum complexity.

Among other things, vertical teaming improves students' critical and analytical thinking skills, two areas that are generally weak spots for Charlotte's middle school students who are entering the area's high schools. As a result of the content team's common focus, vertical teaming also leads to rigorous standards, an increase in student expectations, and an enhanced quality of instruction per grade level. In addition, there is an emphasis across content areas on such things as vocabulary, reading comprehension, and the writing process.

In an effort to stress quality and understanding, educators in CMS decided to institute the concept with grades 6–12 mathematics and English only the first year, pilot social studies the second, add science after that, and then other subjects and grades as needed. The projected results of their efforts are quickly becoming reality, and teachers report that they are "busy and happy" with their work. Among the student benefits that Charlotte educators anticipate are:

- A higher level of learning for all students
- More stimulating, challenging, coordinated, and relevant curricula
- A forum for on-going professional development
- Improved teacher communication
- More efficient use of time

- Student acquisition of critical thinking skills
- Student and teacher acquisition of a common vision
- Greater opportunities for all students to acquire the skills and knowledge necessary for success on Advanced Placement (AP) exams and in college

Although CMS originally instituted the concept of vertical teaming to enhance its Advanced Placement courses, educators there quickly realized that, like AVID, the program would benefit many other students who are probably not interested in attending college. Therefore, teachers also consider it a transitional program for in-coming ninth graders, who can benefit from the increased emphasis on thinking and analytical skills.

Two other priorities that are used when possible involve the geographic location of students within the school or even clusters of whole schools. For example, high schools with space are able to group their ninth graders away from the rest of the school's population while the students get acquainted with each other and their teachers, and while they become acclimated to the social and academic atmosphere of high school. Once this is accomplished, students are gradually mainstreamed into the remainder of the school's students, where they feel better prepared to make independent decisions about course work and social activities.

On a grander scale, the district has actually clustered at least one set of new school buildings in such close proximity that students and teachers can freely walk between the elementary, middle, and high schools. Known as the Governor's Village, these schools work regularly to support an open-door policy that allows for exchange activities and relationships. The result is a group of students K–12 who feel comfortable with one another and who accept transitions between the buildings as a natural occurrence.

A final example from among many in the district is Freshman Academy, a summer program that targets ninth graders who were not successful their freshman year in reading and writing. The district is now working toward a technology component for the Academy. On a similar yet more limited note, CMS also offers a summer enrichment course after grade eight and before grade nine for those students who are considered low literacy achievers, particularly in the area of writing.

When considered in sum, Charlotte Mecklenburg Schools would have had much more to offer Tony and Ben than my district did. My team partner and I would have had access to members of the Vertical Team in both English and mathematics, where we could have talked about content applications relevant to the lives of these two young men. The AVID program with its individualized perspectives and small class sizes would have given them targeted attention, which could have continued across their early high school years.

Likewise, Freshman Focus would have introduced appropriate high school behaviors to Tony and Ben and would have offered them the opportunity to interact immediately with both adults and students. Because each had strong abilities but low scores, they would have qualified for the summer enrichment course after eighth grade and, if the necessity continued, could have picked up the Freshman Academy after their ninth grade year. With AVID still in place as needed, they would have had continued guidance after that summer and into tenth grade and perhaps beyond, with a renewed interest in school and meaningful experiences possible.

Other districts contribute to the possibilities for success

When you spend a great deal of time with kids like Tony and Ben, it becomes apparent that they don't always have the capacity to cope with changes as eventful as the shift from one level of schooling to the next; this is particularly true if they are part of a district that is not as focused on their transitional needs as Charlotte Mecklenburg might have been. That lack of coping skills has, therefore, become the focal point for a great deal of the transition work employed in successful districts.

By definition in our sense, coping means learning to handle or adjust to new and often difficult situations, like those encountered when students leave the security of one school building and move into the next, whether that be elementary, middle, high school, or a university. As students move closer to college age, they can of course provide many of their own coping mechanisms, as they've had several opportunities to meet and adjust to changes in their lives. That is, of course, much more difficult for younger students. Therefore, having a structured program by which to teach those skills while simultaneously applying them is critical to successful school transitions.

Like Charlotte Mecklenburg, many districts across the country have refined their approaches to student transitions over the past few years, with equal efforts focused on the moves to middle and later high school settings. One logical and seamless way to cluster these transitional strategies is to think of them in terms of spring semester before the transition, then summer activities, and finally the period of time following the actual move to the new school.

The following represents a compilation of proven suggestions that have been employed by successful schools and districts. A word to the wise belongs here, however: these transitional events should be more than segregated activities. Instead, they must be encased in a well articulated program which is informed by the developmental needs of the young adolescent, whether that child be eleven or fifteen. In other words, one should pick from these or other activities based on the developmental and cultural needs of the school populations involved, and likewise, one must select carefully and frugally, with long-range goals clearly established.

Spring semester before the transition to middle or high school

Because transitioning is made easier through familiar and trustworthy relationships, it is important to establish clear links with all members of the school community who will receive the new students. Illustrations of this type of relationship building abound; for example:

- One of the most successful strategies is to establish a buddy, or mentoring, program between students in elementary and middle school or middle and high school. These new friends can exchange letters, information, photographs, visits, and the younger students can even shadow the older ones for a partial or entire day. Topics for letter writing, e-mails, and personal dialogue can focus on concerns like those that students noted earlier: homework, being fearful of older students, harder content, and large numbers of students and teachers. A survey would, of course, confirm issues that were specific to students and parents in your local area. An additional possibility might be to establish single relationships between entire classes if interactions between individuals aren't possible.
- Students will also enjoy receiving a letter that has been designed by the teachers who will be members of their team during the coming year. Including specific questions will uncover a bit of biographical information about the students, which can be accompanied by exchange information about the teachers and perhaps a photo of them. Compiling the data will give the teachers an opportunity to learn specifics about their upcoming students while continuing to detail further transitional concerns that can be immediately addressed by the team.
- Middle or high school counselors, administrators, and a panel of students may also choose to visit the feeder school during spring semester. This provides an opportunity to talk about such things as classes and events, to give an overview of a typical school day, to share summer opportunities, and to answer questions.
- If held in the evenings, this type of meeting could be expanded to include parents who, as you'll recall, bring their own set of concerns about the next level of schooling. Setting up concurrent sessions would give small groups an opportunity to move through topics such as helping your child with advanced content, what to expect during the earlier/later adolescent years, or understanding the school's organization and traditions. If current students were involved, they could simultaneously host sessions for their incoming peers on such topics as demonstration content lessons, extracurricular opportunities, or making new friends.
- Continue the invitation by making copies of the school's yearbook,

newspapers, and other publications available in the feeder school's library for checkout.

- Invite parents of incoming students to a PTA meeting or other activity at the new school. Invite their children to attend a sporting event free of charge.
- Hold a year-end ceremony at your school to celebrate the students' rite of passage to the next level. This will demonstrate to students that they are celebrated and will be missed, and it will give them a healthy opportunity to express their feelings about leaving. Invite representatives from the next grade level to attend so that they can then close the event by welcoming the students to the new environment.
- Above all, make certain that the elementary, middle, and high school teachers are all part of vertical teams that address issues like curriculum and relationships on a regular basis. This single loop of continuous information is invaluable to a smooth and successful articulation program.

Summer activities

Although the bulk of a good transition program will be initiated in the spring semester before the move occurs, there are specific continuation pieces that can be set aside for the summer months. For example:

- Consider mailing updates to families during mid-summer. Packet contents could include anything from a copy of the last school newspaper to upcoming athletic events. Of course specifics like individual schedules are always appropriate if finalized in time for bulk mailings.
- Contact your local cable station about the possibility of hosting a small segment about your school. Sedgwick Middle School (Kaiser 1995) actually did a thirty-minute show featuring the principal, sixth grade team leaders, and three students who had just completed the year. The students discussed the past term, shared individual stories, and offered suggestions. The teachers discussed the transition to middle school and emphasized September activities. Everyone then welcomed the newcomers. The entire flavor was informational and informal. On a less individualized note, some associations like the North Carolina Middle School Association have professionally prepared videos on middle schools within their states. Airing such tapes can be a good substitute and can also provide general information on both middle school philosophy and early adolescent development.
- Summer is also an excellent time to host professional development sessions for ninth grade teachers on early adolescent development and what to expect from their new students. This will help eliminate the

possibility of teachers expecting ninth grade students to squelch their natural energy levels in order to conform to an organizational structure that actually targets 16, 17, and 18 year olds (Jett, Pulling, and Ross 1994).

- Host a floating summer session in the school's library or cafeteria for interested students and parents. Keep the mood informal and light, yet make available those adults who can answer the most difficult of questions. Ask members of the existing student body to host campus tours on request.

Fall semester following the move and beyond

As is obvious, a well articulated transition program doesn't simply include spring and summer months and then end about mid-October with the arrival and acclimation of students. Rather, as Charlotte Mecklenburg has stressed, it continues throughout the Freshman year and beyond as necessary. No student is left to chance, and no opportunity to provide a service is unanswered. Examples of fall semester activities include such things as:

- Address logistics like lockers and schedules immediately. This can be a two-fold effort between the grade-level teachers and the buddies or mentors established in the spring. Make certain, as well, that high school students understand such things as diploma options and appropriate sequences of study, course offerings and levels of courses, the implications of a permanent record, the consequences of repeated absences, high school rules and regulations, the activities and atmosphere associated with student life, and the layout of the school and its facilities (Kadel 1994).
- Make certain that each new student feels comfortable with the school's guidance counselors and that they know the counselors' schedules and how to contact them during the school day. Consider initiating a teacher-based program like Advisor-Advisee in the ninth grade.
- Continue the mentor or buddy program.
- As in Charlotte, try to cluster ninth graders either physically or instructionally so they'll have an opportunity to act like, and be with, fourteen year olds. If teams aren't physically grouped in the middle school, do so.
- Consider an exciting introductory topic of study for an interdisciplinary unit, an approach that will also function as a team ice breaker. Focus on the new school, expectations, developmental issues, social situations, and the like. There is a wealth of adolescent literature available for study that can provide characters and situations similar to the ones described here.

- Carefully select speakers for the opening PTA meetings who can address relevant issues. Craft an air of celebration and welcome.
- Establish courses like CMS's Freshman Focus, Freshmen Academy, and AVID.

Conclusion

As became clear to me through my own experiences, there is no argument about the importance of a smooth and purposeful transition from elementary into middle school and from middle into high school. The water becomes cloudy, however, when you try to actually articulate what schools are systematically doing and the ways in which these activities and programs address specific developmental needs as defined by middle school philosophy and early adolescent development. The need for affective and effective structures never diminishes, and can, in fact, make the difference between a successful transition out into life, or future failure. Although no one model provides the perfect response, an overview of many suggestions can lead a district to personalize the possibilities, thus ensuring their success. Tony and Ben deserved that, as do all of those who have followed them and those who are yet to come.

References

George, P. (1995). Strengthening school transitions: Research and action. *The High School Magazine, 3*(1), 4–7.

Hertzog, C.J., Morgan, P.L., Diamond, P.A., and Walker, M.J. (1996). Transition to high school: A look at student perceptions. *Becoming, 7*(2), 6–8.

Jett, D.L., Pulling, D.N., and Ross, J. (1994). Preparing high schools for eighth grade students. *NASSP Bulletin, 78,* 85–91.

Kadel, S. (1994). Improving the transition from middle school to high school. *Reengineering high schools for student success: Hot topics: Useable research.* (ERIC Document Reproduction Service No. 366 076)

Kaiser, J.S. (1995). Eight months of activities: Unity through purpose. *Schools in the Middle, 4*(3), 15–18.

Mac Iver, D.J. (1990). Meeting the needs of young adolescents: Advisory groups, interdisciplinary teaching teams, and school transition programs. *Phi Delta Kappan, 71,* 458–464.

Marshall, D. (1992). Making a smooth move to high school. *Middle School Journal, 24*(2), 26–29.

McAdoo, M. (1999). Studies in transition: How to help adolescents navigate the path to and from middle school. Middle *Ground, 2*(3), 21–23.

Midgley, C., and Urdan, T. (1992). Transition to middle level schools: Making it a good experience for all students. *Middle School Journal, 24*(2), 5–14.

Odegaard, S.L., and Heath, J. (1992). Assisting the elementary school student in the transition to a middle level school. *Middle School Journal, 24*(2), 21–25.

Schoffner, M.F., and Williamson, R. (2000). Facilitating student transitions into middle school. *Middle School Journal, 31*(4), 47–52.

Weldy, G. (1991). *Stronger school transitions improve student achievement: A final report on a three-year demonstration project "Strengthening school transitions for students K–13."* New York: William and Mary Greve Foundation.

15

Reinventing Middle Level Teacher Preparation via Professional Development Schools

LAURA VAN ZANDT ALLEN
Trinity University

C. KENNETH McEWIN
Appalachian State University

Despite significant gains in middle grades education in the past decade, many have, in effect, hit a glass ceiling with regard to continuing the initial wave of reform. As a result, realizing the full benefits of comprehensive middle level reform also remains elusive, given the time required for systemic change and the compounding effect of recommended practices (Felner, Jackson, Kasak, Mulhall, Brand, and Flowers 1997; McEwin, Dickinson, and Jenkins 1996; Van Zandt and Totten 1995). Although numerous reasons exist for this lack of continued progress, a major barrier to the further development of excellent middle schools continues to be insufficient numbers of middle level teachers who have the specialized professional preparation needed to successfully understand and teach young adolescents (McEwin and Dickinson 1995, 1997).

One demonstrated means of moving middle schools from the "arrested development" stage to one of full development is through the establishment of professional development schools (PDS). These schools offer opportunities for university and school-based educators to simultaneously reform middle level education and middle level teacher preparation, while functioning in myriad cultural, institutional, and political settings. The knowledge base regarding the nature and importance of the PDS model has been presented extensively in the literature and will not be discussed here (i.e., Carnegie Forum on Education and the Economy 1986; Holmes Group 1986, 1990). Instead, the following narrative addresses reasons supporting the use of a collaborative partnership model at the middle level. Next, we tackle some of the practical considerations necessary for the creation of collaborative environments by describing two different PDS programs, incorporating true examples from our own experiences as guideposts. Throughout, the chapter illustrates that this model is an essential key to strengthening existing middle level teacher preparation programs and helping create new programs whether or not middle level licensure is available.

Why the professional development school?

Simultaneous renewal

"Putting seventh graders in groups is simply asking for trouble."

I had heard Mary Beth utter these words repeatedly and knew without a doubt she meant every one. Despite and sometimes because of her outstanding success as a language arts and reading teacher, Mary Beth embraced change only after she had seen its effectiveness firsthand. Her acceptance of teaming was the result of two full years of interdisciplinary teamwork which focused on a writing across the curriculum unit and establishing team-wide rules and procedures. Both professionally and personally, skepticism was her motto.

I also knew that Mary Beth had had student teachers in the past, prior to the school's establishment as a PDS. Her supervisory style had closely followed the cooperating teacher paradigm as opposed to the two-way mentorship model the PDS now espoused. Armed with the new design of the PDS, I approached Mary Beth about mentoring an intern the following year for two reasons; first, she was undoubtedly one of the best middle school teachers I had observed at the school, and second, she herself needed a specific reason to reexamine her perspective toward cooperative learning.

One of the requirements of the middle level teacher education program is that interns must try out various practices in their classrooms. Appointment as a mentor teacher requires a number of commitments, one of which is providing the opportunity and support for interns to implement new instructional models. This requires that mentors familiarize themselves with these practices as well, usually through readings, attending site-based workshops, or helping teach a class on the topic.

October of the following year rolled around, and it was now time for Mary Beth's intern, Holly, to begin using cooperative learning models in the classroom, beginning with simple warm-ups and advancing to a full lesson implementation. I remember clearly the Friday afternoon that Holly rearranged the desks into groups in preparation for Monday's class.

"I think she's really upset about me moving the desks around," Holly relayed to me. "She didn't say anything when I told her what I needed to do, but I could just tell it made her really uncomfortable."

Good, I thought to myself. While there is a fine line between constructing meaningful learning experiences and overstepping one's welcome in the classroom, most of us need a little motivation to change established patterns, especially those that have served us well in the past.

Thankfully, my risk-taking paid off. Through the correct implementation of cooperative models, which I oversaw behind the scenes, classroom energy rose, and student grades began to improve.

After complimenting the two on an excellent class I had seen one afternoon, Mary Beth spoke up and said, "You know, the kids have so much fun I don't think they realize they're learning."

The year ended with Mary Beth and Holly's presentation at the state middle school conference on the benefits of cooperative learning in the language arts classroom.

As Goodlad (1994, 1999) and others have pointed out, one of the critical lessons learned from the reform efforts of the 1980s was the need for connectedness among levels of education. In other words, there is no chicken and egg dilemma when it comes to improving schools and teacher education. One cannot precede the other; they must occur concurrently for they are each dependent upon one another for success. Levine (1997) states that in the PDS model, we no longer think about staff development, student learning, and teacher education separately. Instead, these endeavors are one. Mary Beth and Holly's experience provides a good example of how these three areas interact in an authentic context. For teachers, embracing the role of teacher educator in the middle level PDS opens up new avenues for learning which often result in fundamental changes in teacher perspective and practice (Grossman and McDaniel 1990; Grossman 1992). For interns, learning to teach in a middle level PDS results in increased knowledge about young adolescents and a higher level of support when compared with beginning teachers in traditional programs (Grossman 1994; Yerian and Grossman 1993).

Due to such interaction, PDSs carry out a key role in enabling other reform strategies to take hold (Darling-Hammond 1994; Grossman 1994; Levine 1997; Ruscoe and Whitford 1991). The success or failure of middle level reforms depends heavily on the supply of teachers who buy into middle level ideals and have the knowledge and experience necessary to implement these strategies in the classroom. Thus, issues such as teacher resistance and faculty turnover may dramatically affect the level of implementation of recommended practices. Conversely, the preparation to work in middle grade schools must occur for beginning teachers in contexts that not only ascribe to middle level philosophy but also model these behaviors. To learn about teaming, one must be part of a team; to learn about advisory, one must plan, teach, and assess a program. In PDSs, teachers and interns work on these skills together, realizing that learning never ceases.

As a result, PDSs engender a spirit of renewal, a climate of continuous learning and experimentation bolstered by care and support. In such environments, individuals are more likely to break out of traditional patterns, engage in self-inquiry, view education as a life-long process, accept failure as one of the best teachers, and begin to develop mutually caring and respectful relationships with others (Sirotnik 1999).

Parallel designs

In many ways, the fundamental concepts underlying the middle school and the professional development school run parallel. By design, they each strive to create supportive, reflective, educative environments during stages of life recognized as complex and defining (e.g., Carnegie Council on Adolescent Development 1989; Carnegie Forum on Education and the Economy 1986; Holmes Group 1986; Kagan 1992). Consider the similarities between a sixth graders first week at middle school and that of the teaching intern. As excitement and anticipation intertwine with fear and doubt, neither sleeps well the night before school begins. Once there, they each find themselves thrown into a context full of unknowns, from "How will I find all of my classes?" to "What do all of these acronyms stand for?" Switching roles from oldest to youngest and student to teacher requires continual redefinition of self. The rules have changed, and confidence gained in the past quickly wanes. Accordingly, teachers asked to embark on reform agendas that include new organizational, curricular, or instructional mandates typically experience similar dissonance issues. It should be no surprise, then, that programs addressing the related needs of these three groups complement one another.

Goodlad (1994) contends that "programs for the education of educators must be characterized in all respects by the conditions for learning that future teachers are to establish in their own schools and classroom" (p. 84). This goes beyond the aspects of simultaneous renewal discussed previously and into the realm of how teacher education programs function on a day-to-day basis. In short, programs for teachers should, as much as possible, parallel programs for students. He further argues that such programs should intentionally disclose their own structures, conditions, processes, curriculum, and outcomes so that these are clearly modeled for prospective teachers. This forces individuals to form connections between their own experiences and those of their students.

While the messages of educational reform movements today often sound akin, the PDS and the middle school display uncommonly congruent goals and structures.

	Middle School	*Professional Development School*
Organization	Interdisciplinary teams of teachers and students	Cohorts of interns and university faculty assigned to each PDS
Logistics	Teams located together on campus	Each cohort located at one PDS; more than one intern

		per team; field experiences and classes provided on-site
Support	Advisory programs; team structure; transition programs	University faculty and coordinators work at PDS daily; mentors function as coaches rather than supervisors; teams and cohorts support members
Time	Flexible scheduling; possible looping of teachers and students throughout grade transitions	Extended, in-depth and focused; long-term work with school; flexible to address PDS initiatives
Instruction	Active, hands-on activities geared toward developmental needs; cooperative groups common	University and school-based faculty team teach classes by modeling best practice; experiential and collective in nature; informal as important as formal
Curriculum	Interdisciplinary with focus on broad rather than specific knowledge	Taught by interdisciplinary teams of faculty; meshing of theory with practice
Evaluation	Performance-based, process-oriented; interested in finding out student strengths	Authentic, performance-based assessment; process-oriented; interested in helping interns and teachers set and achieve goals

Practicing what we preach, regardless of age or experience, sends a powerful message to learners about the importance of curriculum. In many respects, middle level PDSs are well positioned to utilize this relationship to improve teaching and learning for all involved.

Contextually independent

For too long, most middle level teacher education programs have existed in states requiring special licensures or endorsements for teaching young adolescents. In a survey of middle level teacher preparation programs, McEwin (1992) found that eighty-two percent of such programs were located in states where middle level licensing or endorsements were available and that fifty-seven percent of these programs were located in the five states requiring middle level licensure. While the number of states mandating some form of middle level teacher preparation has remained relatively unchanged in recent years, the development of middle level professional development schools opens up an ancillary route toward the same end. Simply put, PDSs are contextually independent; they can be established almost anywhere since PDS programs often exceed state teacher preparation requirements. Middle level PDSs, therefore, are in a prime position to recruit and prepare teachers of young adolescents, especially in states without strong middle grades licensure requirements.

Two middle level professional development school models

The two PDS models presented in this chapter were selected because they have both successfully helped reinvent their schools and universities, albeit in quite dissimilar contexts. Ken teaches in a middle level teacher preparation program that was established in 1975 and in a state that now has mandatory middle level licensure requirements. The teacher preparation program at Appalachian State University, Boone, North Carolina, is relatively large, with about 500 graduates each academic year. The middle grades program, which averages about eighty majors, has been revised several times over the years but recently moved to the professional development school, performance-based model. Laura, on the other hand, teaches at Trinity University, San Antonio, Texas, a relatively small, private liberal arts university in a state where authentic middle level licensure has been elusive and controversial until recently.[1] At Trinity, teacher preparation is designed around a five-year, MAT program that has been located exclusively in PDS settings since the late 1980s. While our backgrounds and situations differ dramatically in some aspects, there is solid agreement that (a) high functioning middle schools cannot exist without well-prepared middle school teachers; and (b) collaborative teacher preparation models have the power to simultaneously reinvent both middle schools and teacher preparation programs.

The Trinity University model

In 1987, Trinity University along with two school districts in San Antonio, Texas (San Antonio Independent School District and Northeast Independent School District), established a partnership known as the Alliance for Better Schools. These collaborative partnerships, set up with two elementary, one middle, and one high school, created environments designed to support the reform efforts of each partner. For example, the middle school embraced the challenge of becoming a developmentally responsive middle school by implementing recommendations first from *This We Believe* (National Middle School

Association 1982) and later from *Turning Points* (Carnegie Council on Adolescent Development 1989). In so doing, university faculty assigned to the PDS provided on-going training related to middle level philosophy as well as grants to help teachers begin the shift from departmental to interdisciplinary team organizations. In turn, the school provided guaranteed placements for undergraduates and graduate interns in an environment implementing the latest research on young adolescent developmental needs. Aside from the novelty of the PDS itself at this time, most notable was that Texas required no special preparation for teaching at the middle level, allowing anyone, licensed elementary or secondary, to teach grades 6–8. Establishment of the PDS ensured that half of newly certified secondary graduates would be well prepared to teach young adolescents, while providing similar in-depth training for experienced teachers.

With partnerships in place, teachers, administrators, preservice teachers, and university faculty from academic departments as well as education met regularly during the 1987–88 school year to develop the Master of Arts in Teaching (MAT) degree, a five-year program for the preparation of beginning teachers that gradually replaced the traditional four-year program. Significant changes included:

- requirement of a bachelor's degree in humanities for elementary majors (a new degree program created specifically for elementary teachers) or one or more disciplines for secondary majors;
- 10–12 hours of undergraduate education coursework including a minimum of 135 contact hours in PDS practica settings beginning the first year;
- a year-long internship in one PDS during the fifth year (five days a week, August to April);
- all PDSs located in urban areas with high populations of at-risk students;
- graduate coursework paralleling the internship experience and emphasizing individual school reforms as well as the connection between theory and practice;
- graduation portfolio and presentation to cohort, mentors, and university faculty;
- creation of cohort groups for progression through the fifth year;
- movement of four university faculty members from traditional to clinical, tenure-track positions to provide liaisons with each PDS. One university faculty member was assigned to each PDS, spending time on-site at the school four or more days each week;
- appointment of coordinators at each PDS who teach practica courses and work with other collaborative efforts (these are full-time teachers; the university pays coordinators a stipend for additional duties);

- development of cohorts of mentor teachers at each PDS appointed as clinical faculty of the university who collaborate with university faculty on all aspects of the PDS from continual program development to specific school reform needs;
- securing outside funds for the support of partnership schools and graduate internships.

Undergraduates concentrate primarily on completion of the bachelor's degree (minimum of 36 hours in major with an optional 24-hour minor) while taking 10–12 hours of education classes. Cohort groups and intense coursework toward certification begin the summer of the graduate year.

The Master of Arts in Teaching Degree Plan (30 credit hours)

	Fall	Spring
Fifth Year	EDUC 5671 Clinical Practice; EDUC 5670 Pedagogics (3 hours of 5670 is devoted to middle level specific pedagogy for the middle level cohort)	EDUC 5973 Advanced Clinical Practice (includes middle level specific curriculum and experiences for middle school cohort); EDUC 5352 School Leadership, Supervision, and Evaluation
Summer	EDUC 5352 Teaching Inquiry and Practice	
	EDUC 5350 Curriculum Inquiry and Practice	
Senior	EDUC 3321 Schooling in America	EDUC 3124 Practicum: The Student
Junior	EDUC 3320 Growing Up in America	EDUC 3123 Practicum: The Master Teacher
Sophomore	EDUC 2107 Practicum: The School	EDUC 2108 Seminar: The Child in Society
First Year	EDUC 1105* Seminar: Current Issues in Education	EDUC 1106* Seminar: School and Community

Note: All courses except EDUC 3320 involve students in work at PDS sites.
*These courses are recommended not required.

The Forum, as the group of stakeholders is now known, continues to meet several times each year to continually refine and revisit program objectives and needs. Concurrently, formal program evaluations have led to a number of insights regarding creating and maintaining healthy school-university partnerships (e.g., Van Zandt 1998). Specific lessons learned from the middle level PDS partnership follow:

University faculty assigned to the PDS must be committed to the middle school concept as well as the PDS model. Reinvention requires leadership from both partners concerning setting and implementing collaborative program goals and objectives. The university is no exception. Too often, however, faculty are assigned collaborative roles in schools where they have little knowledge about or interest in the reform agendas. In our experience, finding good matches between university faculty and the PDS is critical to initial or continued renewal at both levels. Some essentials include:

- a solid background at the middle level that includes 5–8 teaching and advanced study;
- good interpersonal skills, including the ability to be "down to earth";
- a background or capacity for counseling and problem-solving with groups and individuals;
- a desire to work as both practitioner and researcher in school and university contexts; and
- a "heart" for improving middle schools and middle level teacher preparation.

Professional development activities must be ongoing. Institutions, while seemingly constant, are always in the midst of change. A turnover in administration or even a few key mentor teachers can threaten continued growth of school and university reform efforts. For such reasons, professional development activities at the PDS must run continuously and not only be front loaded during initial planning stages. Means for doing so at Trinity have included:

- Co-teaching classes for undergraduates and graduate interns (PDS mentors/teachers and university faculty);
- Annual meetings of the Forum;
- Annual presentations by administrators, mentors, interns, and university faculty at local, state, and national conferences (e.g., presenting and attending the Texas Middle School Association conference with their mentors and university faculty is a requirement for all middle school interns during the spring semester);
- Annual weekend retreats for mentors and interns (e.g., all mentors, interns, and the university professor attend a fall retreat in the Texas Hill Country. Activities include guest speakers, mentor meetings, relationship building, horseback riding, ropes courses, and curriculum planning);

- Collaborative action research (i.e., interns must complete a research project and paper similar to a thesis during the fall semester. Mentors are encouraged to work as co-researchers, trying out new ideas in the classroom. Afterward, results are shared through conference presentations and publications);
- Providing additional time for teams as well as mentors/interns to plan together during the summer and the school year;
- University guest lecturers knowledgeable about PDS reform issues;
- Implementation of middle level practices by graduate interns (e.g., interns are required to construct and teach lessons that include the use of cooperative learning, multiple intelligences, etc. In so doing, mentors as well as other teachers are exposed to new instructional techniques through grade-level content area meetings); and
- Fiscal support for sending mentors and interns to discipline-specific conferences throughout the year.

Place interns with highly knowledgeable and dedicated mentor teachers on healthy, high-functioning teams. Given that one objective of the PDS model is to promote educational renewal at the school, finding sufficient numbers of outstanding teams and mentors for intern placements at low-functioning middle schools may appear to be putting the cart before the horse. In our experience, however, careful placement of interns is critical for the development of beginning and experienced faculty. When adequate time and care have not been taken in assigning placements, two problems occur. First, interns experience one thing in the classroom while learning the converse in university classes. Often dissonance levels become too great, especially as interns debrief with cohort members who are immersed in developmentally appropriate classrooms. Thus, trying out middle level practices without a mentor knowledgeable about the whys and hows can cause the intern and mentor frustration and end in both rejecting middle level philosophy. The second problem revolves around the team structure. Ideally, team members other than the mentor teacher serve as surrogate mentors for interns throughout the year. At Trinity, we refer to them as "aunts and uncles." However, placing interns on teams where the majority has rejected the teaming concept further alienates interns from middle level ideals. In fact, the negativity surrounding such teams can easily drive beginning teachers out of the profession as a whole.

To prevent these problems, we have found the following necessary:

- Place beginning interns with mentors who consciously or unconsciously understand adolescent needs and are open to new learning strategies. To do so, university faculty and school administration must be familiar with teaching practices and philosophies of the faculty;

- Utilize inventories designed to (1) identify interns with traits necessary for teaching at the middle level and (2) match mentors and interns with similar but not identical teaching philosophies and organizational styles (see, e.g., Van Zandt and Denny 1998);
- Place two interns on a team. The effect of a low-functioning team can be diminished through the support and reflection of another intern;
- Construct teams as you would cooperative learning groups: two mentors and their interns; one teacher or more adaptable to middle level ideals, and one who has not yet bought into the philosophy. This sets up conditions necessary for growth; and
- Offer and encourage professional development activities for all team members, not only those with interns.

The Appalachian State University model

When middle level teacher preparation programs were created at Appalachian State University in 1975, successful candidates received degrees in Elementary Education with a specialization in Middle/Junior High School Education and licensure in grades 4–9. In the early 1980s, the middle grades license was changed to grades 6–9 and made subject specific (e.g., middle grades mathematics) and mandatory for middle grades teaching. The University of North Carolina system also created options for separate degrees in Middle Grades Education during the 1980s. These circumstances make possible full preparation programs which focus exclusively on middle level education. Prospective teachers who successfully complete the preservice program receive a Bachelor of Science in Middle Grades Education with two teaching fields (concentration areas) chosen from language arts, mathematics, science, and social studies.

The decision to move to the professional development school, performance-based teacher preparation model was made in 1996. To accomplish this goal, the Middle Grades Advisory Board was established. This board included middle grades teachers, middle school principals, district administrators and curriculum coordinators, professors from the Colleges of Arts and Sciences and Education, recent graduates, and other stakeholders. Members used state and national curricular guidelines, the middle level knowledge base, the expertise of accomplished middle level educators, and other resources to guide the program revision process. Teacher preparation standards from professional associations (e.g., National Middle School Association; National Council of Teachers of Mathematics) were used as major resources during the revision. All curricular revisions were made collaboratively. For example, all existing methods courses were redesigned by teams which included middle grades university faculty members from the Colleges of Education and Arts and Sciences, highly accomplished middle grades teachers, and other middle level educators.

Performance-based program standards were also written by the Middle Grades Advisory Board to guide the program. These standards were written in performance-based language, with each standard followed by examples of knowledge, dispositions, and performances that are descriptive of that standard. Below an example is provided:

Standard 2: Middle Grades Philosophy and School Organization

Middle grades teachers understand the major concepts, principles, theories, and research underlying the philosophical foundations of developmentally responsive middle level programs and schools, and work successfully within the organizational components of these programs and schools.

Knowledge Middle grades teachers:	Dispositions Middle grades teachers:	Performances Middle grades teachers:
• Understand the philosophical foundations of developmentally responsive middle level programs and schools	• Are committed to the philosophical foundations that support developmentally responsive programs and schools that maximize student learning	• Use their knowledge of the philosophical foundations of middle level education when making decisions about curriculum and instruction
• Are knowledgeable about historical and contemporary models of schooling for young adolescents and the advantages and disadvantages of these models	• Are committed to the application of middle grades philosophical foundations in their practice	• Embrace developmentally responsive organizational components and work successfully within them to maximize student learning
• Understand the underpinning rationale and characteristic components of developmentally responsive middle grades schools	• Are supportive of organizational components that reflect developmental responsiveness and support student learning	• Apply their knowledge of the philosophical foundations of middle level education in their classrooms, schools, and communities
• Know best practices for the schooling of young adolescents in a variety of school organizational settings (e.g., K–8, 5–8, 7–12 organizational plans)	• Are committed to developmentally responsive teaching, learning, and schooling in a variety of organizational settings	• Implement developmentally responsive programs, practices, and organizational components that reflect the philosophical foundations of middle level education

These standards are used to help ensure the curriculum is appropriate and as a basis for continuing assessment. To complete the program, candidates must pass through several gateways and successfully present their portfolios before graduation. Table 1 includes a brief description of the sequence of the program.

Table 1: Program Sequence		
Freshman and Sophomore	General Studies Courses Teaching Field Content Courses Teachers, School, and Learners (first field experience)	
Junior	Teaching Field Content Courses Educational Psychology Foundations of American Education Literacy, Technology, and Instruction	Middle Grades Internship Middle Level Education Teaching Young Adolescents Teaching Field Content Courses
Senior	Two Content-Specific Methods Courses Interdisciplinary Internship Reading in the Content Areas Integrating Media and Technology into Teaching	Student Teaching Portfolio/Exhibition

The last three semesters are the cohort terms. During the first cohort term, prospective teachers take courses on campus three days a week and spend the remaining two days in the professional development school internship. During the second cohort term, an increasing amount of time is spent in the schools with most classes being taught at the PDS sites. The student teaching experience is full time with special seminars being held at the school sites.

Some additional features of the program are:

- Field experiences are supervised by both practitioners and professors;
- A middle school practitioner-in-residence works closely with all aspects of the program;
- All teachers who work with interns hold the position of master teacher;
- Each professional development school has a teacher who is the school site coordinator;
- Prospective middle level teachers are placed in schools with diverse student populations for at least one semester;

- All prospective middle level teachers have concentrations in two teaching fields for which they will be licensed (e.g., mathematics and science); courses included in the two concentration areas are selected based on national standards of professional associations (e.g., National Science Teachers Association), state curriculum standards, the content of assessments, educator expertise, and other important sources;
- Teaching field concentrations range from 19 to 27 semester hours each;
- Total number of semester hours in the degree is 128;
- A three-semester cohort model is used;
- Selected middle level courses/seminars are co-taught by professors and middle level clinical teachers;
- Some classes are taught on the university campus and some in the professional development middle schools;
- Prospective middle grades teachers have content-specific methods courses as well as interdisciplinary learning experiences;
- A distinguished middle level teacher in residence plays a major role in the preparation program (e.g., supervision, co-teaching, assessment, curriculum development); and
- A graduation portfolio/exhibition is required.

The promise of the professional development middle school model

At the school level, many problems surrounding the implementation of middle level practices can be traced back to the culture of reform itself. Quartz (1996) found that when implementing middle level reform efforts, too often schools rely on "enduring and stable norms" when enacting change such as providing disjointed staff development, utilizing experts rather than encouraging teacher inquiry, mandating converse reform agendas, and failing to adequately address problems as they arise (e.g., teaming dividing rather than unifying faculties). Goodlad (1999) identifies this as an emphasis on reform rather than renewal, where the former connotes top-down corrective action as opposed to the latter's process-approach to collaborative rejuvenation and growth.

By design, collaborative partnerships embrace a social constructivist paradigm. Darling-Hammond (1994) notes that "knowledge that is constructed by experienced teachers, novices, and teacher educators in conjunction with the children they serve, informs both research and practice in ways that create new possibilities for each" (p. 16). Constructivist-oriented approaches that frame learning opportunities around teachers' beliefs and experiences through discourse, reflection, and inquiry are more likely than conventional approaches to result in desirable teacher change. The praxis of learning together within the

PDS promotes an environment conducive to change where ownership of middle level reforms may be challenged and formed by individuals within the school community.

References

Carnegie Council on Adolescent Development. (1989). *Turning points: Preparing American youth for the 21st century.* New York: Author.

Carnegie Forum on Education and the Economy. (1986). *A nation prepared: Teachers for the 21st century.* New York: Author.

Darling-Hammond, L. (1994). *Professional development schools: Schools for developing a profession* . New York: Teachers College Press.

Felner, R.D., Jackson, A.W., Kasak, D., Mulhall, P., Brand, S., and Flowers, N. (1997). The impact of school reform for the middle years: Longitudinal study of a network engaged in *Turning Points*-based comprehensive school transformation. *Phi Delta Kappan, 78*(7), 528–550.

Goodlad, J. I. (1994). *Educational renewal: Better teachers, better schools.* San Francisco, CA: Jossey-Bass Publishers.

Goodlad, J.I. (1999). Flow, eros, and ethos in educational renewal. *Phi Delta Kappan, 80*(8), 571–578.

Grossman, P.L. (1992). Teaching to learn. In A Lieberman (Ed.), *The changing contexts of teaching: 91st NSSE yearbook* (pp. 179–196). Chicago: University of Chicago.

Grossman, P.L. (1994). In pursuit of a dual agenda: Creating a middle level professional development school. In L. Darling-Hammond (Ed.), *Professional development schools: Schools for developing a profession* (pp. 50–73). New York: Teachers College Press.

Grossman, P.L., and McDaniel, J. E. (1990). *Breaking boundaries: Restructuring preservice teacher education as a collaborative school/university venture.* Paper presented at the annual meeting of the American Educational Research Association, Boston, MA.

Holmes Group. (1986). *Tomorrow's teachers: A report of the Holmes Group.* East Lansing, MI: Author.

Holmes Group. (1990). *Tomorrow's schools: A report of the Holmes Group.* East Lansing, MI: Author.

Kagan, D. (1992). Professional growth among preservice and beginning teachers. *Review of Educational Research, 62*, 129–169.

Levine, M. (1997). Introduction. In M. Levine & R. Trachtman (Eds.), *Making professional development schools work: Politics, practice, and policy* (pp. 1–11). New York: Teachers College Press.

McEwin, C.K. (1992). Middle level teacher preparation and certification. In J.L. Irvin (Ed.), *Transforming middle level education: Perspectives and possibilities* (pp. 369–380). Boston: Allyn & Bacon.

McEwin, C.K., and Dickinson, T.S.(1995). *The professional preparation of middle level teachers: Profiles of successful programs.* Columbus, OH: National Middle School Association.

McEwin, C.K., and Dickinson, T.S. (1997). Educators committed to young adolescents. *Middle School Journal, 28*(5), 50–53.

McEwin, C.K., Dickinson, T.S., and Jenkins, D.M. (1996). *America's middle schools: Practices and progress—A 25 year perspective.* Columbus, OH: National Middle School Association.

National Middle School Association. (1982/1992). *This we believe.* Columbus, OH: Author.

Quartz, K.H. (1996). Becoming better: The struggle to create a new culture of school reform. *Research in Middle Level Education Quarterly, 20*(1), 1–25.

Ruscoe, G.C., and Whitford, B.L. (1991). *Quantitative and qualitative perspectives on teacher attitudes: The third year.* Paper presented at the annual meeting of the American Educational Research Association, Chicago, IL.

Sirotnik, K.A. (1999). Making sense of educational renewal. *Phi Delta Kappan, 80*(8), 606–610.

Van Zandt, L.M. (1998). Assessing the effects of reform in teacher education: An evaluation of the 5-year MAT program at Trinity University. *Journal of Teacher Education, 49*(2), 120–131.

Van Zandt, L.M., and Denny, G.S. (1998). Predicting teacher effectiveness with students at risk: Instrument development and validation. *Current Issues in Middle Level Education, 7*(1), 40–64.

Van Zandt, L.M., and Totten, S. (1995). The current status of middle level education research: A critical review. *Research in Middle Level Education, 18*(3), 1–25.

Yerian, S., and Grossman, P.L. (1993). *Emerging themes on the effectiveness of teacher preparation through professional development schools.* Paper presented at the annual meeting of the American Educational Research Association, Atlanta, GA.

Note

1. A complete review of licensure structures in Texas has resulted in a grades 4–8 license (overlapping with other license levels only in grades 4 and 8). Initial licensure may be obtained at one or two licensure levels. Scheduled implementation is fall 2003.

Closing

16

On a Good Day Everyone Grows:
Reflections on the Reinvention of a School

THOMAS S. DICKINSON
Indiana State University

DEBORAH A. BUTLER
Wabash College

One of the premises of this book is that the middle school concept is not in need of reinvention, but instead, that the school is. All the chapters in this text say as much. They are ripe with numerical, quantitative data—recent research that makes this point, but equally, the chapters burst with stories of success and portraits of powerful teachers. The personal perspectives of these researchers are clear, and their voices calling for reinvention of the school carry a strong message, a different kind of call for action than that of the middle school reinvention in the middle of the twentieth century. It is a call grounded more firmly in foundational elements of the middle school concept, supported by data, but also in a deeply felt need to create the school anew which permeates each writer's text.

But to the major matter of the book. Yes, we agree that the middle school concept is not in need of reinvention. Deborah Pitton (this volume, p. 21–22) quoted the 1997 Felner study (Felner, Jackson, Kasak, Mulhall, Brand, and Flowers 1997) that looked at the level of implementation of middle level reforms, then suggested that positive things for students, including achievement gains, are associated with higher levels of implementation of the concept. Others quote this and other data which point to the same truth. So why are we not okay?

We think it is our *conceptual understandings* of the middle school concept as contemporary educators that are in need of reinvention. We believe that a reinvention of the concept in broader, deeper, more current terms, while still keeping true to the heart of the concept, is necessary. This reinvention of *our thinking and understanding* is fundamental to moving forward on any of the suggestions for reinvention that appear in this book.

Surely, we must remain aware of our historical roots and foundational premises as we look forward to the twenty-first century. Such important items as these must be part of our collective historical memories:

- the six defining characteristics of the middle level school—articulation, integration, exploration, differentiation, guidance, and socialization (Gruhn and Douglas 1947) (although we need to be sure that functions like guidance and socialization are defined to maximize equity, not to classify and stratify our students into a class system as James Beane reminded us that the earlier junior high school set out to do; Beane, this volume, p. xiii–xv);
- Alexander's classical definition of middle schools and his "essential characteristics of exemplary middle schools" (Alexander and George 1981, pp. 3, 18–19);
- the historical development of teams and team organization over time (Erb and Dickinson 1997);
- the search for appropriate curriculum and instruction, from separate disciplines to multidisciplinary experiments to fully integrated content (Beane 1993);
- and most important, the understanding that the middle school exists to support the holistic needs and development of young adolescent learners, who themselves bear continued observation through the lenses of development related to gender, language and culture difference, race, ethnicity, and propensity for learning differently in a digital world (Butler and Manning 1998; Feldman and Elliott 1990; Finders 1997; Manning 1993; Powell, Zehm and Garcia 1996; Powers, Rafferty and Eib, this volume). We must remain aware of how the world our students will live in is and will change and the challenges they will need to be prepared to confront. As Deborah Pitton noted (this volume, p. 32–34), we have to take this particular old platitude of the middle school movement seriously now, by implementing what it really means, which is, as adults, by listening to students, helping them explore their questions about their world. We have to, in essence, share control and learn to help students meet their goals, not ours.

We must be aware of our history's dark side as Beane described it, and its purer aims for young adolescent learners (Beane, this volume, p. xiii–xix). It is these aims that we must push for far more than we have.

The critical underpinning of change

However, educators need to reinvent and deepen their understandings of the concept in three fundamental ways. First, our *disposition matters*. We all need an *awareness* that the middle school concept is suffering from an arrested development stage. We must acknowledge this. That is, although there are some good aspects to most middle schools, and many are better because they have implemented part of the concept, we must not be complacent, thinking that all is said and done. Statistics of learners, how they fare in schools, in families, and in society tell us differently. The *acceptance* of this, and developing the *disposition toward continued change* and an openness to change, even more than we already have done, is paramount to a continuing healthy development of the concept as an educational effort. On top of this, we must allow ourselves to let go of our own fear of change, and allow those critical shifts in our development as educators to occur. To accept change will be an aspect of the future—because stasis *is* arrested development.

Second, movement toward developing and implementing the concept further requires the awareness and understanding of the middle school concept as an *ecology* of highly complex elements working simultaneously together. Across all of these chapters is the notion that implementing all elements is absolutely fundamental. This notion of *ecology* applies to all the components of the middle school concept as a schooling concept, but this is not all. As a corollary to this, treating arrested development requires an understanding that the middle level concept is part of the larger concept of education and schooling in several ways:

- *as a K–16 continuum.* Jeanneine Jones (this volume, p. 289–293) noted that the middle level school plays a central position in articulation. We have no choice but to help young adolescents adjust to their first major transition since kindergarten while setting up a solid preparation for high school transition and success;
- *as an important societal institution in this country.* Janet McDaniel and her colleagues (this volume, p. 58) remind us that this level of schooling holds the promise of "social justice in the schooling of early adolescents";
- *as a part of the larger picture of current educational reform movements.* Although this larger picture of reform gives us mixed messages on some fronts (standardized testing as the main measure of success, for example, vs. the clear constructivist message that collaboration and integration of people and subjects promise authentic and deep learning that cannot be measured by paper and pencil tests alone), the time is right for reinvention. Elizabeth Pate (this volume, p. 79–82) addressed this while describing a peaceful co-existence of the middle level concept and standards. With carefully detailed pictures of existing classrooms and their stories of student achievement and success, she offered us the hope for persistence in the face of off-putting politically

motivated reforms. Doug Mac Iver and his co-researchers (this volume, p. 167–170) outlined, too, how middle level concept implementation happens right now in urban situations—which, far from being sad counterparts of exemplary middle schools, are the blueprints for the concept! If it can happen in those schools, it can be done. But, if as James Beane said (this volume, p. xix–xxi), the conservative political forces working against the concept remain too great, then at least we can do as he suggests—hunker down and do some thinking. The important point is to persist, do the right things, and get our stories out there for everyone to hear.

Third, in recent years, the middle school concept, especially through the promise of a relevant and integrated curriculum component, has been reconceived as the best hope for realizing a truly Deweyian progressive education philosophy. Janet McDaniel and her colleagues (this volume, p. 62) noted this critical feature of the middle school concept when they described Apple's and Beane's democratic school (Apple and Beane 1995), its curriculum, structures, and processes, and they are not alone in thinking this. As a reformed notion of schooling, the middle school concept is perceived by many as having the potential to go beyond the rhetoric of schooling for a democracy and an intelligent democratic citizenry, to become through the realization of its proposed structures and content, an environment that supports those ideals.

Reinvention and deep themes of change

And so we come to the main point. The school itself is in need of reinvention then, based on the understandings and reinvention of the concept as noted above. Can we create a school where everyone grows? Can we make them good places for all? For the individual, the society, and mutual futures? The answer is yes, based on the above points, and based on paying attention to the basic themes resonating deeply in these chapters in this text that are the keys to reinventing the middle school as an entity. We see these as the deep themes arising from these chapters.

Educating educators and others

Decreasing the disconnect between what we know and what we do by educating the educators, including principals, teachers, and guidance personnel, as well as other personnel in the school, *but also including education of the central office administrators, higher educators preparing them, and school boards, government, the media, business people, and ordinary citizens.*

The italicized group's education will take efforts by the current cadre of researchers, theorists, and middle school leaders, including the Lillys, Carnegies, Kellogs, and the McConnell-Clarkes, to press for the realization that the middle school concept works (Lipsitz, Jackson and Austin 1997). This on-going education of the noneducator world is part of reinvention and deeply fundamental to continued successes of the middle level movement.

Preservice education needs to be focused on significant content learning and middle level schooling concepts, but must also focus far more than it does now on the dispositions it takes to be a middle level educator: risk-taking attitude, lack of fear of responsive and responsible change, and a grounding in moral perspectives of equity and diversity. We will do well to remember what both Janet McDaniel and David Strahan and their colleagues said on this issue. McDaniel (this volume, p. 56) talked about teachers being "cathedral builders," those teachers who work "for something larger than they, not bound by time," while Strahan (this volume, p. 115) said we must simply recruit "teachers who care passionately about their students and their work."

Can it be said enough? **We must have separate and independent teacher education for this level of schooling.** We need to finally break away from the preparation of teachers for a marketplace to the preparation of teachers to teach particular students (McEwin and Dickinson 1996). Gayle Davis pointed out that she and Tony Jackson will argue again in *Turning Points 2000* (2000) that middle grades teachers need much more substantial education before entering middle grades classrooms. ". . . such programs are vital" (Davis, this volume, p. 261). It remains a critical concern that this rather remedial lesson must be taught for the third time in the history of middle level education in the twentieth century.

Likewise, the continued professional development of educators must become centered around better staff development models, which, in turn, make it a point to focus on the middle level concept in continuing education, such as PDS and team models promote. Laura Allen and Ken McEwin (this volume, p. 304) spoke well to the power of the well-run Professional Development School: "They engender a sense of renewal," and provide a "climate of continuous learning." Both Daniel Kain and Tom Erb convinced us, or reconvinced us, of the role of teaming in professional development. Remember that Erb (this volume, p. 196) found that the "overwhelming majority of teachers profess to having a more satisfying work-life" as team teachers, and Daniel Kain (this volume, p. 205–210) told his own powerful story of reinvention as a middle level teacher solely because of his contact with a teammate while learning to teach. But Mac Iver and his colleagues (this volume, p. 170–172) put close quotes around the issue of professional development saying that absolutely critical is the on-going nature of professional development of any kind;

it cannot be solely relegated to the first few years of a school's change or a teacher's education.

Finally, fundamental too, is the notion that on-going development for adult educators must encompass the education of their attitudes, cultivating openness, and acknowledging the emotional and spiritual growth of the educator. Recall that Mary Gallagher-Polite (this volume, p. 43–44), in describing her transformative model for arrested development at the middle level, clearly underscored this by noting that "personal growth cannot be separated from professional growth . . . we can't continue to give this aspect mere lip service."

Reinventing the learning environment as a learning community

Reinventing the middle level school environment as a "learning community" for adults and children. We have tried, through a variety of curricular and instructional reforms, moving toward integration and authenticity, to create positive learning environments for students, but we have failed on an ecological level because we have left out adults as learners. Again, Mary Gallagher-Polite got at some of the point: "middle school organization must model the components in its structure for adults" (this volume, p. 40). It is clearly more than that. Middle level education must now act on the concept of lifelong learning for students, giving them the knowledge, skills, and heart it takes; but also do the same for the adult educators, providing all educators with continued and appropriate professional development for a middle level educator, and an environment in which they can learn daily with other peer educators.

Reinventing further this "learning community" to be inclusive in the broadest sense, that is, of all children (*really*, as Janet McDaniel and Doug Mac Iver and their colleagues describe), and empowering these children by being willing, as Richard Powell shared, to give students a real voice in a school concept trying to reinvent itself as a democratic entity. Reinventing for inclusion also touches adult educators, as well as the community of partners who can learn with us and from whom adults and children can learn. We must reinvent now the boundaries of the school so that they are *permeable and fluid boundaries,* and so that the learning environment becomes the tangible community beyond the school walls. Kim Ruebel (this volume, p. 269–286) gave us many well-researched strategies for creating and sustaining family and community partnerships. These fluid boundaries must also capture and include the global community of which middle school learners are all a part thanks to the coming and existing technology that Powers and her colleagues (Powers, Rafferty, and Eib, this volume, p. 237–244) so aptly engaged us in considering.

Reinventing the learning environment so that the emotional and spiritual (not in a religious sense) components of all deep and lasting learning are freely cultivated and occur along with content and skills. This means cultivating relationships as learners together. The point is that educators are realizing more and more how important, to put it in Bloom's terms, the affective domain is in relation to the cognitive domain, or to put it in intelligence terms, how important cultivating emotional intelligence is for both student and adult learning. Not only must we, as Mary Gallagher-Polite said, reinvent ourselves as a "community of spirit and truth" (this volume, p. 45), but we must realize the impact of emotion and spirit on actual instruction. David Strahan (this volume, p. 104), Richard Powell (this volume, p. 147), and Deborah Pitton (this volume, p. 36–37) all suggest strongly that these are key to effective instruction at the middle level; in fact, Strahan and his colleagues (this volume, p. 97) linked these with high academic achievement, describing "the caring classroom's academic edge."

Close

Several overarching themes ripple through the book; we hope we've captured most of them in its conclusion—the constructivist and democratic underpinnings of the middle school concept, and the middle school concept's reliance on these exhortations to educators: expect, connect, respect, and reflect. Young adolescent learning, the many dimensions of it, is the bottom line for all of us, and learning occurs when educators expect a lot of learners and of themselves; when they connect subjects, people, and multiple communities; when they respect learners and themselves; and when they care enough to reflect on their own and their student's development.

References

Alexander, W.M., and George P.S. (1981). *The exemplary middle school*. New York: Holt, Rinehart & Winston.

Apple, M.W., and Beane, J.A. (Eds.). (1995). *Democratic schools*. Alexandria, VA: Association of Supervision and Curriculum Development.

Beane, J.A. (1993). *A middle school curriculum: From rhetoric to reality* (2nd ed.). Columbus, OH: National Middle School Association.

Butler, D.A., and Manning, M.L. (1998). *Addressing gender differences in young adolescents*. Olney, MD: Association of Childhood Education International.

Erb, T.O., and Dickinson, T.S. (1997). The future of teaming. In T.S. Dickinson and T.O. Erb (Eds.), *We gain more than we give: Teaming in middle schools* (pp. 525–540). Columbus, OH: National Middle School Association.

Feldman, S.S., and Eliott, G.R. (Eds.). (1990). *At the threshold: The developing adolescent*. Cambridge, MA: Harvard University Press.

Felner, R.D., Jackson, A.W., Kasak, D., Mulhall, P., Brand, S., and Flowers, N. (1997). The impact of school reform for the middle years. *Phi Delta Kappan, 78* (7), 528–532, 541–550.

Finders, M.J. (1997). *Just girls: Hidden literacies and life in junior high*. New York: Teachers College Press and Urbana, IL: National Council of Teachers of English.

Gruhn, W.T., and Douglass, H.R. (1947). *The modern junior high school*. New York: Ronald Press.

Jackson, A.W., and Davis, G.A. (2000). *Turning points 2000: Educating adolescents in the 21st century*. New York: Teachers College Press.

Lipsitz, J., Jackson, A.W., and Austin, L.M. (1997). What works in middle-grades school reform. *Phi Delta Kappan, 78* (7), 517–519.

Manning, M.L. (1993). *Developmentally appropriate middle level schools*. Wheaton, MD: Association for Childhood Education International.

McEwin, C.K., and Dickinson, T.S. (1996). *Forgotten youth, forgotten teachers: Transformation of the professional preparation of teachers of young adolescents*. Background paper prepared for the Middle Grade School State Policy Initiative (MGSSPI), Carnegie Corporation of New York.

Powell, R.R., Zehm, S., and Garcia, J. (1996). *Field experiences: Strategies for exploring diversity in schools*. Englewood Cliffs, NJ: Merrill.

AUTHOR BIOGRAPHIES

LAURA VAN ZANDT ALLEN is Associate Professor of Educaton at Trinity University in San Antonio, Texas. After teaching for several years at both the middle and high school levels, she completed her Ph.D. at the University of Arkansas. She has published a number of articles in journals such as *The Journal of Teacher Education, Research in Middle Level Education, the Middle School Journal,* and *Current Issues in Middle Level Education.* Her primary areas of interest include middle level teacher education and professional development schools. She lives in San Antonio with her husband Bruce and daughter Abby.

ROBERT BALFANZ is Associate Research Scientist at the Center for the Social Organization of Schools at Johns Hopkins University. His research focuses on urban secondary education, mathematics education, and the multiple layers of implementation support and technical assistance that teachers need to offer high quality learning opportunities. He is co-director of the Talent Development Middle Schools program.

JAMES A. BEANE is a Professor in the National College of Education at National-Louis University. He was previously a Professor of Education at St. Bonaventure University and has served as a Visiting Professor at several other colleges and universities. He has taught in junior high/middle and high schools and was a Project Director for new York State Regional Education Planning Centers. Professor Beane is author of *Curriculum Integration: Designing the Core of a Democratic Education, Affect in the Curriculum: Toward Democracy, Dignity ,and Diversity* and *A Middle School Curriculum: From Rhetoric to Reality;* co-author of *Self-Concept, Self-Esteem and the Curriculum, Curriculum Planning and Development, The Middle School and Beyond,* and *When the Kids Come First: Enhancing Self-Esteem at the Middle Level;* co-editor of *Democratic Schools;* and editor of the 1995 ASCD Yearbook, *Toward a Coherent Curriculum.* In addition he has written forewords and chapters for many books and articles for a variety of professional journals. He has spoken at numerous natiojnal, state, and local conferences, been a consultant for educational projects in the U.S. and elsewhere, and served in various capacities for several professional associations. In 1997 he received the John Lounsbury Award from the National Middle School Association.

DEBORAH A. BUTLER is Professor and Director of Teacher Education at Wabash College in Indiana. She received her Ed.D. from the University of Virginia in Curriculum and Instruction (English Education, English, and Supervision). Her fields of specialty include middle and secondary school teacher education and middle school language arts. Her publications about middle level education include *On-Site: Preparing Middle Level Teachers Through Field Experiences* (with Mary Davies and Tom Dickinson, NMSA, 1991), *Rooms to Grow: Natural Language Arts in the Middle School,* second edition (with Tom Liner, Carolina Academic Press, 1998), *Addressing Gender Issues for Young Adolescents* (with Lee Manning, ACEI, 1999), as well as other articles and chapters on middle level education. Her current research and scholarly interests include gender and young adolescence and women's literature, especially literature written by American women on the Vietnam War.

AMY COHEN is a teacher on special assignment to the Philadelphia Education Fund.

GAYLE A. DAVIS is Faculty Research Associate at the University of Maryland at College Park, where she manages projects within the Institute for the Study of Exceptional Children and Youth. She is currently chair of the National Middle School Association's Research Committee, serves on the National Forum to Accelerate Middle Grades Reform and the advisory board for the Success for All Middle School Project and recently coo-authored *Turning Points 2000: Educating adolescents in the 21st century* (with Anthony Jackson, Teachers College Press, 2000). Prior to joining the University of Maryland staff in 1999, she was on the technical assistance team for the Middle Grade School State Policy Initiative (MGSSPI) for nearly eight years, first as project associate, then senior associate, and finally as national director. A graduate of the University of North Carolina at Chapel Hill (B.A. and Ph.D.), Gayle has also been a middle grades teacher, a project coordinator for the Center for Early Adolescence, and a consultant for various middle grades reform efforts. She lives with her husband, Bryant, her son, Jackson, and two rather large dogs in Silver Spring, Maryland.

THOMAS S. DICKINSON is Professor of Curriculum, Instruction and Media Technology at Indiana State University, Terre Haute. Educated at Wake Forest University (B.A., History) and the University of Virginia (M.Ed. and Ed.D., Social Studies Education and Supervision of Instruction), he taught middle and high schools in his native Virginia before pursuing a college teaching career. A former editor of *Middle School Journal* for the National Middle School Association, he is the author and editor of a number of works dealing with a variety of middle school topics including most recently *Promoting Literacy in Grades 4–9: A Handbook for Teachers and Administrators* (with Karen Wood, Allyn & Bacon, 2000) and *We Gain More Than We Give: Teaming in Middle Schools* (with Tom Erb, National Middle School Association, 1997). He maintains a special interest in middle school teacher education, state and national middle school standards, and the professional development of middle school teachers. He lives with his wife and three cats in Greencastle, Indiana.

B.J. EIB provides support and advice to schools and other educational organizations on topics relating to technology, leadership, and change. B.J. earned a Bachelor's Degree from Knox College, Galesburg, Illinois and her Master's Degree from Indiana University. Her 21 years of teaching experience range from inner-city Chicago to suburban Indianapolis to the Havasupai Indian Reservation in Arizona to rural southern Indiana. She has taught elementary school, middle school, high school, and undergraduate education students. B.J. has served as a technology coordinator for a school system, as an instructional technology consultant for the Indiana Department of Education, and as Associate Director for the Center for Excellence in Education at Indiana University. Current and recent projects include working with the TEAMS project (Technology for Enhanced and Active Middle Schools), Leadership Training for Technology Coordinators, and Technology Professional Development Portfolio Pilot.

THOMAS O. ERB is Professor of Teaching and Leadership at the University of Kansas and Editor of the *Middle School Journal.* He holds an undergraduate degree from De-Pauw University and graduate degrees from Northwestern University and the University of Florida. Dr. Erb has been engaged in middle grades teacher education for the past 23 years. Prior to that, he taught social studies, language arts, math, art, and physical education for seven years in three different middle schools on two continents. His published work has been focused in three areas: interdisciplinary teaming, middle grades teacher education, and middle school curriculum. Most notable among his writing on teaming are two books: *We Gain More Than We Give: Teaming in Middle Schools* (with T.S. Dickinson) and *Team Organization: Promise—Practices and Possibilities* (with N.M. Doda). In the area of teacher education, he co-authored the monograph *A Vision of Excellence: Organizing Principles for Middle Grades Teacher Preparation* (with C.K. McEwin, T.S. Dickinson, and P.C. Scales) as well as the case "Transitioning to Middle School" in *Cases and Commentary: A Middle School Casebook* (T.S. Dickinson and C.K. McEwin, Eds., in press). His most recent curriculum work is *Dilemmas in Talent Development in the Middle Grades: Two Views* (with P. S. George, J. S. Renzulli, and S. M. Reis) and the forthcoming *This We Believe and Now We Must Act* for the National Middle School Association. He is the father of three sons, a daughter, a foster son, and grandfather of one grandson. He lives in Lawrence with Karen, his wife of twenty-nine years.

MARY M. GALLAGHER-POLITE is Dean of the School of Education and Professor of Educational Administration at Southern Illinois University Edwardsville. Educated at Augustana College and Illinois State University, she was principal and taught elementary and middle school before pursuing a career in higher education. A former editor for the Association of Illinois Middle-Level School's *AIMS Journal*, she is a co-author of a book, book chapters, and numerous articles on middle level education and leadership. Through initial funding from the Danforth Foundation, she developed an integrated teacher-administrator preparation program for the middle grades with university and school-based colleagues using the professional development school model.

MARIA GARRIOTT is a curriculum writer for the Talent Development Middle Schools program.

JEANNEINE P. JONES is Associate Professor of and Program Coordinator for Middle Grades Education at the University of North Carolina at Charlotte. Prior to graduation from the University of North Carolina at Greensboro (M.Ed. and Ed.D.), she taught fifteen years in a nationally acclaimed middle school within that state. The former author of the "Teacher to Teacher" column in *Middle School Journal,* she has published a variety of articles, columns, and textbook chapters on her teaching experiences and research. In addition, she has shared these same stories and lessons learned at conferences and meetings, and has worked with more than 150 schools and districts to facilitate their improved implementation of middle grades programs and concepts. She lives happily with her husband and two young children in Kannapolis, North Carolina.

DANIEL L. KAIN is Associate Professor of Instructional Leadership in the Center for Excellence in Education at Northern Arizona University, Flagstaff. He began his teaching career at a junior high school in Montana, where he participated in the transformation of that school from the junior high to the middle school model. His interest in teacher teaming led to a doctoral dissertation on the subject at the University of British Columbia, Vancouver, Canada. He continues to research teacher teaming, integrated/interdisciplinary studies, and problem-based learning. He is the author of *Camel-Makers: Building Effective Teacher Teams Together* (from NMSA) and numerous articles and chapters on teaming and integrated instruction. He is currently working on a book about problem-based learning in teacher education.

CHARLOTTE KRITZER represents the Oceanside Unified School District as a Distinguished Teacher in Residence at California State University San Marcos. Prior to this position she taught middle school language arts and English language development for five years at Martin Luther King Jr. Middle School in Oceanside, California. She also served as a literacy coach and as a site mentor assisting new and veteran teachers. She holds an M.A. in Literacy Education from CSU San Marcos. Her research interests are multicultural literature, democratic teaching, and middle level education. She is in the process of applying for a Ph.D. program in Language and Literacy.

DOUGLAS J. MAC IVER is Principal Research Scientist at the Center for Social Organization of Schools at the Johns Hopkins University. His research focuses on middle level education, motivation and achievement in early adolescence, and the social structuring of schools. He is the Director of the Talent Development Middle Schools program.

JANET E. MCDANIEL is Associate Professor of Education at California State University San Marcos. She serves as Coordinator of the Middle Level Teacher Education Program, which recently received the Multicultural Program Award of the National Association for Multicultural Education. She received her M.Ed. and Ph.D. from the University of Washington. Dr. McDaniel's research interests are middle school teaching and teacher education.

MIKE MCELRATH currently serves as the Coordinator of Guidance in his hometown, Jamestown, New York. He is a recent Graduate of the University of North Carolina at Greensboro with a Ph.D. in Curriculum and Teaching. His specialization areas include young adolescent development, middle school promotion and teacher preparation, and school change processes. He is actively involved in the National Middle School Association, advocating for an expanded role for middle school counselors, creative and responsive school transition programs, and students at-risk. He received his M.Ed. from Temple University in Philadelphia, and his B.A. from Gannon University, in Erie, PA. In his spare time, Mike enjoys golf, basketball, and outdoor activities.

C. KENNETH MCEWIN is Professor of Curriculum and Instruction at Appalachian State University, Boone, North Carolina. He is a researcher and consultant in middle school education and author of numerous professional publications. Dr. McEwin is active in the National Middle School Association and other professional associations. He is coauthor of several books including *The Professional Preparation of Middle Level Teachers: Profiles of Successful Programs* (1995), *Visions of Excellence: Organizing Principles for Middle Grades Teacher Preparation* (1995), *America's Middle Schools: Practices and Progress, A 25 Year Perspective* (1996), and *The Exemplary High School* (2000).

JUAN NECOCHEA is Associate Professor of Education at California State University San Marcos. He also served as an elementary and secondary school principal for the Lompoc Unified School District in California. Dr. Necochea, who received his Ph.D. from the University of California at Santa Barbara, has conducted research in the areas of school reform, policy implementation, leadership, labor relations, character education, bilingual education, and diversity, with a scholar practitioner perspective. With Zulmara Cline, he recently edited *Advances in Confluent Education: Multicultural Dynamics of Educational Change*.

P. ELIZABETH PATE is Associate Professor in the Middle School Program and a Faculty Associate/Research Scientist in the Learning and Performance Support Laboratory at The University of Georgia. She has twenty-two years of teaching experience at the elementary, middle, and college level. Dr. Pate received her Ph.D. in Curriculum and Instruction from Texas A & M University in 1989. Her co-authored book entitled *Making Curriculum Integration Work: Teachers, Students, and the Quest for Coherent Curriculum* tells the story of an eighth grade team in search for a curriculum intersection of excellence. She received the Richard B. Russell Undergraduate Teaching Award at The University of Georgia in 1999 and was a finalist for the Thomas Ehrlich Faculty Award for Service Learning in 2000. Her research and teaching interests revolve around curriculum and instruction, with particular interest in curriculum integration, service learning, and community building.

DEBRA ECKERMAN PITTON is Associate Professor of Education at Gustavus Adolphus College in St. Peter, Minnesota, where she teaches middle level philosophy and methods. Educated at Loras College in Dubuque, Iowa, she taught English, speech, and drama for several years in Iowa and Illinois before receiving her M.Ed. from Northeastern Illinois University. A move to Texas introduced her to middle schools, where she taught and completed her Ph.D. in Curriculum and Instruction from the University of

North Texas in Denton. Debra has taught at several higher education institutions and served as an Assistant Superintendent for Curriculum and Instruction in a Minneapolis area school district. She is the author of two books: *Stories of Student Teaching; A Case Approach to the Student Teaching Experience* and *Mentoring the Novice Teacher: Fostering a Dialogue Approach.* She maintains a strong interest in middle level education and the professional development of middle school teachers. She lives in Burnsville, MN with her husband and three children.

RICHARD POWELL is Associate Professor of Curriculum and Teacher Education, University of Colorado at Denver. Dr. Powell received his doctorate from Indiana University in Bloomington, and has taught courses in curriculum and research methods at the University of Nevada at Las Vegas and Texas Tech University. He is the author of a number of articles, book chapters, and books. His most recent book, *Classroom Management: Perspectives on the Social Curriculum,* was published by Merrill/Prentice Hall. Dr. Powell maintains a keen interest in middle level integrative curriculum reform. He has maintained a research agenda in this area for over six years, and has published empirical reports on integrative curriculum reform in selected middle schools. He presently lives in Denver, Colorado.

SUSAN M. POWERS is Associate Professor of Education in the Department of Curriculum, Instruction and Media Technology at Indiana State University in Terre Haute, Indiana. She works with teacher education students on computer technology skills, and teaches graduate courses in media technology. Dr. Powers earned her Ed.D. at the University of Virginia in Instructional Technology. She also holds an M.S. in Education in Higher Education and Student Affairs and a B.S. in Business in Marketing; both of these degrees were awarded by Indiana University in Bloomington. Her research interests include the instructional design of web-based instruction, community-building in distance education, writing for electronic media, and technology in teacher education. She lives in the Terre Haute area with her husband (also faculty at ISU), 2 daughters, son, and dog.

CATHLEEN D. RAFFERTY is Professor of Education and the new Director of a Center for Educational Renewal at Humboldt State University in Arcata, California. Educated at Southern Illinois University—Carbondale, she earned both a bachelor's and master's degree in education before teaching remedial reading in Illinois and developmental reading and social studies at a middle school in Gunnison, Colorado. While living in Colorado, Cathleen also received a Ph.D. in Curriculum and Instruction at the University of Colorado—Boulder. Since becoming a teacher educator, she has worked at Eastern Illinois University, Central Michigan University, and Indiana State University, where she was actively involved as a liaison to a middle level Professional Development School. Special interests include school-university collaboration, the impact of technology on literacy and learning, and performance-based teacher education.

FRANCISCO RÍOS is Associate Professor in the College of Education at the University of Wyoming. Formerly, he was an Associate Professor in the College of Education at California State University San Marcos. A graduate of the University of Wisconsin, he teaches courses in learning and instruction, educational foundations, and and multicultural/bilingual education. His research interests focus on teaching and learning in cultural contexts, multicultural education for preservice teachers, and the experiences of ethnic minority preservice teacher candidates. His scholarship has appeared in *Teacher Education Quarterly, Multicultural Education,* and *Excellence and Equity in Education.* He currently sits as Parliamentarian of the National Association for Multicultural Education Board of Directors.

KIM K. RUEBEL is Assistant Professor of Middle Grades at Georgia Southern University in Statesboro. Kim was educated at the University of Texas at Austin where she received a Bachelor's Degree in Applied Learning and Development with specializations in English and Spanish. Kim taught public school and English as Second Language students in Texas before moving to Indiana. Indiana provided further opportunity to teach ESL students as well as time to complete a Master's and doctorate from Indiana State University in Curriculum and Instruction with a specialization in English. Kim taught education courses at Indiana State and has now moved on to teach at Georgia Southern. Recent works include a chapter on technology in a monograph entitled *Integrating Technology in Education: Stories of Success from K–16* (Powers and Dutt-Doner, Eds., 1998), and a resource chapter in *Cases and Commentary: A Middle School Case Book* (Dickinson and McEwin, Eds., in press). Kim lives in Statesboro, Georgia, with her husband, two dogs, and a new daughter.

ALTA SHAW is Senior Instructional Facilitator in English/language arts for the Talent Development Middle Schools program.

TRACY SMITH is Assistant Professor of Curriculum and Instruction at Appalachian State University in Boone, North Carolina. A graduate of the University of North Carolina at Chapel Hill (A.B.), Appalachian State University (M.A.), and the University of North Carolina at Greensboro (Ph.D.), Tracy has taught adolescents at the middle and high school levels and has been a school district coordinator for gifted education and middle grades education. Her research interests include literacy development for young adolescents, student and teacher motivation and goal orientation, and dimensions of expertise in teaching.

LAURA P. STOWELL is Associate Professor of Education at California State University San Marcos, where her primary responsibilities are teaching language and literacy courses in the middle level and elementary education teacher credential programs, as well as children's literature. She earned her M.A. in Reading and Ph.D. from the Ohio State University. Her research interests are children's literature, writing, critical pedagogy, and middle level literacy and assessment.

DAVID STRAHAN has been a member of the faculty at the University of North Carolina at Greensboro since 1984. After graduating from Miami University of Ohio (B.S. and M.Ed.), he taught middle level Language Arts for six years and served as a Reading Specialist while completing his Ed.D. in Curriculum and Instruction at the University of Cincinnati. He is currently Professor of Curriculum and Instruction and Coordinator of Middle Grades Education at UNCG. His areas of specialization include young adolescent development, curriculum and instruction, teacher education, and school improvement. He has written more than 60 professional articles and directed several grant projects that have explored school improvement processes. His most recent book, entitled *Mindful Learning: Teaching Self-Discipline and Academic Achievement,* provides middle level teachers a framework for integrating academic and affective instruction. *Mindful Learning* was selected as one of *Choice* magazine's Outstanding Academic Books for 1998. Dr. Strahan is currently serving as director of two projects that focus on improving the quality of schooling for "disconnected" students and enhancing support for their teachers.

CECILIA TOOLE is a doctoral candidate at the University of North Carolina at Greensboro. She received a B.S. in Intermediate Education at the University of North Carolina at Greensboro and received an M.Ed. in Middle Grades Education at the University of North Carolina at Charlotte. She has six years experience as a middle grades classroom teacher and three years experience as an elementary school classroom teacher. Her research interests include classroom culture and motivation, heterogeneous grouping in middle grades mathematics, algebra curriculum in middle schools, and constructivist teaching strategies in mathematics. She is currently working on a dissertation that will measure formal reasoning ability in seventh grade students and predict their success on an end-of-grade assessment in mathematics.

ESTELLE YOUNG is a Ph.D. candidate in Sociology at the Johns Hopkins University. Her research focuses on the effects of major public policy reforms in education and welfare, as well as the effect of neighborhood conditions on social and economic mobility. She is data analyst for the Talent Development Middle Schools program.

INDEX

AUTHOR INDEX